Wiltshire Record Society

(formerly the Records Branch of the Wiltshire
Archaeological and Natural History Society)

VOLUME 67

Page from the Order Book recording Sessions held at Warminster 15 July 1652
*(see **789–791**)*

WILTSHIRE QUARTER SESSIONS ORDER BOOK
1642–1654

edited by

IVOR SLOCOMBE

CHIPPENHAM

2014

ISBN 978-0-901333-44-5

*The Wiltshire Record Society gratefully acknowledges the continued
financial support of Wiltshire Council.*

Typeset by John Chandler
Produced for the Society by
Salisbury Printing Company Ltd, Salisbury
Printed in Great Britain

CONTENTS

PREFACE

Work on transcribing the Quarter Sessions Order Book has been particularly enjoyable because of the number of surprising and sometimes amusing cases it records as well as the more important and significant ones. I am especially grateful to Steven Hobbs for his direction as General Editor, for writing the section of the Introduction which deals with the technical aspects of the Quarter Sessions and, above all, for his constant enthusiasm and encouragement. I would also like to thank Dr Alex Craven for his useful comments arising from his specialist knowledge of the 17th century. The staff of the Wiltshire and Swindon History Centre have responded positively to my many pleas for help. Finally, as always, Dr John Chandler has ensured that the published volume comes up to his exacting standards.

The society is grateful to Claire Skinner, Principal Archivist, Wiltshire and Swindon History Centre, for making the order book available for publication.

Ivor Slocombe

INTRODUCTION

IN THE 17th century Quarter Sessions, as well as having a judicial function, was the main administrative body for the county. Although it met only four times a year, its work was more continuous through the county-wide network of Justices of the Peace acting individually and in Petty Sessions. Individual cases were frequently referred to named justices who were expected to carry out a thorough examination of the matter in hand, and make a decision or report back to the next meeting of Quarter Sessions. The Justices of the Peace were supported by a whole raft of local officials, notably the constables of the hundreds and, within the parishes, the churchwardens, overseers of the poor and tithingmen or petty constables.

The particular interest of the Quarter Sessions Order Book for this period is how it illustrates the extent to which this administrative system was affected by the disruption caused by the Civil War and how the lives of local communities and individuals were also unsettled. At the same time, many aspects of the 'normal' business such as the inevitable disputes over Poor Law settlements continued.

THE RECORDS OF THE QUARTER SESSIONS

The two main series in the Quarter Sessions archives are the minute or entry books, containing all the criminal and administrative business of the court, and the Great Rolls or sessions bundles, comprising the original documents used at each particular sessions. Both series are impressively complete for Wiltshire, with the origins of the former extant in what has been described as 'A Notebook of the Clerk of the Peace' in 1574, but which by the end of the century had formalised into a full record of the sessions. It one of the earliest existing documents of its type in the country.[1] The great rolls survive from 1601 and are virtually complete down to 1973 with only a few gaps when the sessions were not held.[2]

The volume edited here marks a significant change in the record keeping of the Wiltshire Quarter Sessions. Full copies (in English written in a cursive hand) of routine administrative orders dealing with roads, bridges and prisons, and judicial orders on cases brought by appeal, mainly removal orders, bastardy cases, or rate assessments, were now recorded separately and elevated from their subsidiary position to the criminal business of the court in the entry books. The original orders, together with supporting documents, were filed on the Great Rolls, and both series should be used in conjunction with each other to pursue lines of research as thoroughly as possible: in fact the Order book works as a partial index to the Great Rolls. The Clerk of the Peace, George Frampton, was responsible for this administrative innovation, which arose undoubtedly from the difficulties faced in maintaining local government during the conflict of the English Civil War, and the importance of doing so during the hiatus in national government. The powerful and destructive forces thus unleashed swept over the county however, with the result that no Sessions were held in Wiltshire in the spring and summer of 1643 nor between the summers of 1644 and 1646. During the latter period Frampton was succeeded as clerk by William Coles, who remained in post throughout the rest of the years covered by this volume. The series of Order books continued until 1755.

Although primarily a record of the orders of the court, there are several notable exceptions. An order of Parliament of 1646 requiring an amnesty for anyone brought before the court who had acted in accordance with any of Parliament's ordinances (**266**), and two petitions to Parliament concerning the difficulties facing the cloth trade in general and weavers in particular in 1652 (**831**) illustrate direct links between central and local government. An agreement concerning parochial responsibilities for roads in Chippenham of 1654 (**854**) was enrolled presumably in order to enhance its authority to increase the likelihood of compliance by the parties.[3]

At the back of the book accounts of the treasurers of King's Bench, Marshalsea and Hospitals for the north part and of Maimed Soldiers for the south were written with the note that they were received at the Hilary sessions of 1644 from William Croome, described in (**88**) as deputy to the treasurers. Several other documents were similarly enrolled, the originals of which can be found in the appropriate Great Roll, or Minute book.

Two documents appear only to survive in the order book: a rate for the repair of Burdensball bridge, Wilton, as a result of an order made by Lord Chief Justice Finch at the summer assize of 1637, and list of hundreds, liberties and boroughs in Wiltshire with a breakdown of the sessions to which those jurisdictions subject to the Wiltshire Quarter sessions were to attend, based on their proximity to the sessions towns. None of the documents in this appendix are included in this volume.

In his edition of Wiltshire records Fowle suggested that the inclusion of such items indicated 'That the tendency for the clerks to regard their records as general personal notebooks seemed to have returned'.[4] This seems to be something of an exaggeration; for although some of the documents might have been considered as useful exemplars or even of semi current importance, they form a small part of the content of the order book which provides a full record of the business of the court. The reason behind the appendix may lie more in the the uncertainties and instability caused by the Civil War than a weakening of rigorous bureaucratic practice. At the Michaelmas sessions of 1642, the last to be held for twelve months, the justices' final instruction (**91**) was for the records of the court to be moved to the vestry of Warminster church: in all probability from the Bridewell in Devizes, their home since 1606.[5] The safety and relative security offered by the church would have seemed a more sensible option in those desperate times, because of the strategic importance of Devizes, the centre of county administration, to Royalists and Parliamentarians alike. Any disadvantage this presented to the clerk and his officials, in accessing the records was alleviated by the requirement that the Sessions rolls for the previous three years were to be kept to hand for easy referral, while the older ones were sent to Warminster. Notwithstanding this the pressures of the time may have encouraged the copying of material to hand which might be overlooked during the administrative hiatus.[6]

No attempt was made to arrange or classify the different types, and they were presumably recorded in the order that they were dealt with by the court. The heading for each sessions is the same as that in the corresponding entry book, stating the purpose being to hear and determine felonies, trespasses and other misdemeanours committed in the county. As happened in all record keeping during the period of the Commonwealth, English replaced Latin in the headings from 1651.[7]

JUSTICES OF THE PEACE AND ADMINISTRATION OF THE COUNTY[8]

During the period covered by this order book 68 justices are named as attending the court (see appendix 1), although it is difficult to be precise about the actual numbers of attendances as the lists of justices are frequently followed by the phrase 'and others'. It is quite clear that there was an almost complete change in the justices after 1643-4. In 1642 a number of Royalist supporters sat as justices, in particular Robert Hyde (Recorder of Salisbury), John Penruddock, James Long and Thomas Hall. It is significant that none of these justices (with one exception) appears again after 1646.

The one exception was Francis Swanton who attended throughout the period. He was an eminent lawyer and not only a justice in Wiltshire from 1641 but later a member of parliament. He was appointed Clerk of Assize for the Western Circuit in 1637. After the war, his estate was sequestered because he had acted in this capacity under Royalist auspices during the war. But he seems to have convinced the sequestrators that he had acted under force majeure and, as a result, not only had his estate returned but he was allowed to continue in his post.[9]

After 1646 a much wider list of justices appears, the majority at least being Parliamentary supporters with some also serving as MPs in the Long Parliament. It was said that at the breaking point with the King in 1642 21 of the 29 Wiltshire M.P.s supported Parliament. These included Edward Baynton, Robert Jenner, Edmund Ludlow and Robert Nicholas who all played leading roles as justices.[10] Added to this list between 1645 and 1648 were Alexander Thistlethwaite, Anthony Ashley Cooper, John Dove and William Eyre.[11] Baynton, Jenner and Thistlethwaite, together with Edward Tooker, also served on the Wiltshire committee to raise money for the Parliamentary army in 1643.[12] Thomas Eyre of Bromham, Nicholas Greene of Grittleton and Sir Anthony Ashley Cooper represented Wiltshire in the Barebone's Parliament of 1653.

There can be little doubt that the Civil War caused considerable disruption in this administrative system of the county. Quarter Sessions began to be affected in 1644 with only two justices in attendance in July and very little business done. They did not meet again until July 1646. There is then a distinct feeling of a return to more regular order with a large backlog of cases to deal with.

At the Michaelmas sessions of 1650 it was reported that in late years the courts had had a problem of forming juries of men sufficiently able to deal with the cases before them. This was partly due to the fact that the book containing the lists of freeholders was not being updated but also because it was possible to be excused from jury duty by bribing the corrupt court officials (**655**).

A recurring theme in the matters brought before Quarter Sessions was the failure, for a variety of reasons, to hold many local lawdays or court leets. This meant that the various local officials, who were elected at these meetings and who should have held office for one year only, were not being replaced. As the holding of such offices was an onerous duty, the only recourse was to go to Quarter Sessions to plead to be discharged and to get a replacement nominated. Some 68 entries (about 7% of the total) are on this particular matter. It is significant that such entries tail off after 1652, as the Commonwealth established itself and a degree of normality and calm returned to public life.

The difficulty in finding men to fill the various offices sometimes led to quite unsuitable persons being nominated or forced to take office and these had to be replaced by Quarter Sessions. Simon White was nominated as constable of the hundred of Chalk but he said he had an estate of only £10 a year and nine children to support (**117**). Thomas Hopkins in the hundred of Elstub and Everleigh was not only poor but could neither read nor write (**138**) while Giles Gantlet, constable of Alderbury, was both elderly and also could not read or write (**939**). The problem of nominating an inhabitant to serve was met at Sherston Pinkney by the decision to have a paid tithingman with the inhabitants meeting on the village green each year to decide who to appoint (**808**).

OFFICERS OF THE COURT

The two Clerks of the Peace during the period covered by the Order book, George Frampton and William Coles, are hardly mentioned by name, in fact Frampton not at all, but theirs were the guiding hands heading the county administration, advising the justices and implementing their orders. The responsibilities of the clerk beyond the administrative duties involved at each sessions increased during the 17th century, such that by January 1643 two deputies, William Coles and Francis Bennett, had been appointed (**91**). The protracted investigation to discover who was responsible to repair Harnham bridge was just one example of work behind the scenes.[13]

The court appointed the several treasurers of the county and supervised their work. The original role of the Treasurer of King's Bench and Marshalsea was to collect and administer money for poor prisoners in those prisons and those in local hospitals and almshouses, but this was expanded to cover repairs to the prisons (**611, 657, 668, 678, 946**) and, bridges, in cases where liability could not be established (**851**). The distribution of pensions to servicemen and their dependants was the responsibility of the Treasurer for Maimed Soldiers and Mariners.[14] For each function two treasurers were appointed, for the north and south parts of the county. In 1647 a potential difficulty was dealt with neatly by the appointment of John Hunt, the executor of the previous treasurer, John Hunt (**326**)

Difficulties arose over Leonard Ferris, who died in post in 1643. His executors were instructed to present his accounts, which they did (**92, 93, 108, 152**). In the same year William Biggs and Francis Topp were fined for not passing accounts according to statute;

Topp's fine was respited on his compliance with the order (**86, 87, 103, 121**).

In 1649, clearly as a result of the civil war, it was reported that there were considerable delays in the presenting of accounts by several treasurers for Maimed Soldiers and Mariners since 1642, due it was claimed to parishes and hundreds withholding payments. Two justices, assisted by William Croome, a former treasurer, were nominated to investigate (**529**). This problem had been recognised in the previous year affecting all the treasurers, whom the justices felt to have been negligent (**437, 448, 462**).

THE CIVIL WAR IN WILTSHIRE

Its Impact

Wiltshire experienced several changes of control, Royalist then Parliamentarian, during the course of the war. This particularly manifested itself in the sieges, capture and re-capture of the main towns, Marlborough, Devizes, Salisbury and Malmesbury. There was also the prolonged siege of Wardour Castle and the notorious execution of soldiers by the Royalist commander, Sir Francis Dodington, after the siege at Woodhouse at Longleat in Horningsham. Apart from these 'set pieces', Wiltshire was on the strategic route from London to Bristol and the south west. Consequently it saw the frequent movement of both armies through the county with the inevitable disruption this caused, especially the major battle at Roundway Down in 1643. Various entries in the Order Book make indirect references to many of these events, while the petitions of maimed soldiers often detail the soldier's service and the place where he was wounded or killed.

A number of these soldiers served under Colonel Edmund Ludlow and were wounded or killed within Wiltshire; at Wardour Castle (**570, 625**), at Salisbury (**406, 559**), at the siege of Devizes (**427**) and at Broad Chalke (**623**). Two Wiltshire soldiers, John Carroway (**622**) and Roger Younge (**528**), were amongst those executed at Woodhouse, near Longleat in Horningsham. Others saw action in different parts of the country: at Winchester (**123**), at Newbury (**243**), at Goodrich Castle (**443**), at Colchester (**631**), at Maidstone (**560**) and at the relief of Taunton (**572**). Others served much further afield with, in particular, at least five serving in Ireland (**567, 588, 673, 750, 807**).

Other petitions to the court provide evidence of the direct impact of the Civil War on the county. Joan Golding of Devizes (**339**) sought relief because her house had been burnt down when the

Parliamentary forces entered the town. There are several references to Malmesbury and the disruption caused by the town being garrisoned for much of the war, for example the impossibility of taking convicted prisoners to the county gaol at Fisherton Anger, and the necessity of keeping them under the care of the garrison commander (**177**). Reimbursement of the governor for this service took some time to authorise and came to the attention of the justices on several occasions (**210, 246, 272, 324**). In the north of the county two bridges, at Hannington (**203**) and Castle Eaton (**364**), were destroyed by the garrison commander at Cirencester in an endeavour to prevent the possible advance on the town by the Royalist troops then at Faringdon.

The supply needs of the Parliamentary and Royalist armies when passing through the county might be met by legitimate purchases or by more irregular pillaging. Two particular incidents were brought to the court with a request for compensation. Thomas Hanniball of Mere was ordered by the constables of the hundred to supply two hundred (weight) of cheeses at 16s a hundred and take them to the Royalist troops at Faringdon. The journey took him eight days with three horses but he had never been paid (**174**). The Parliamentary forces were no different. Thomas White, a tavern keeper at Potterne, was commanded by Sir William Waller to supply beer and sack to the value of £12 for his soldiers at Roundway Hill and, again, no payment had been received (**171**).

Travel through the county was disrupted and dangerous because of the bands of soldiers and wandering vagrants. In 1643 those who failed to make an appearance at Quarter Sessions were excused as 'the ways are now very dangerous to travel by reason of the interruptions of soldiers' (**101**). William Sadler, one of the justices, gave his apologies for non-attendance in 1649 as he had with him 'a troop of soldiers and those none of the civillest that I have seen'.[15] There are frequent references to the number of vagrants and wandering soldiers and the subsequent increase in the number of robberies and other crimes. The traditional watching and warding had been neglected and orders were issued in 1646 to all constables and tithingmen to ensure that watches were kept both day and night in all towns and villages at bridges and crossways to 'apprehend all wandering soldiers and mariners, rogues, vagabonds and suspicious persons' (**158**). In 1649 Edward Bull of Westbury was specially commissioned to apprehend all such vagrants and ensure they were taken before the magistrates (**545**). Perhaps inevitably in a time of war, soldiers passing through the county left behind a number of illegitimate children who had to be maintained by the parish (**155, 548**).

Maimed Soldiers: Pensions

The Elizabethan statute of 1593 'for the necessary relief of maimed soldiers and mariners' had placed the financial responsibility on each county through a weekly levy on each parish.[16] This was continued in the 17th century and was the basis for the help given to the soldiers who were injured during the Civil War or their families in the case of those who were killed. The number of claimants clearly increased because of the war and, as a result, the tax demand on the parishes became quite significant. All 56 named soldiers had, apparently, fought for Parliament, although these probably represent only a proportion of the total number who received pensions. All applications had to be supported by a certificate from the appropriate army commander. The court dealt with the cases sympathetically, usually with a one-off payment to meet immediate needs followed by an annual pension of up to £4. Higher pensions were awarded in special circumstances such as the £10 a year to Susan Coles who had to maintain four small children (**406**). Most of the applicants were ordinary troopers but the few officers were also likely to receive more, such as Captain Smyth also given £10 a year (**617**). Jane Jackman, whose surgeon husband had been killed in Ireland, had her annual pension increased from £4 to £10 through the direct intervention of Cromwell (**690**).

The cost of these pensions became increasingly onerous. In 1648 the rate was doubled to six pence a week for every parish (**408**). Mr Soper's account for 1641 showed that the cost of the pensions for soldiers for the south part of the county was £75 (**483**). The problem was not helped by the difficulty of collecting the tax specifically levied for this purpose. Other strategies were sometimes resorted to. In 1651, for example, Lieutenant Knowles had his annual pension of 20 marks (£13 6s. 8d.) cancelled but was given a one-off payment of £10 'now that there are so many pensions paid to maimed soldiers within the county by reason of the late wars that the rates of the county will not amount to pay all' (**680**).

NATURAL DISASTERS AND OTHER CRISES

Plague

Plague was endemic in the 17th century and Wiltshire did not escape. Some time before 1642 there had been serious outbreaks at Calne (**9**) and Malmesbury (**67**). In the early 1640s Devizes (**175**) and Bradford-on-Avon (**162**) had been visited by the 'pestilence'. There are also references in 1646 to the plague at Wilton, Fisherton Anger, Maiden Bradley and Horningsham, although by January 1647 it had ceased at

Fisherton and was decreasing at the other places (**232**). Potterne and
Marston were infected but not the neighbouring village of Worton
(**263**). Fuggleston and Quidhampton (**160**), Highworth and Wootton
Bassett (**239**) and Aldbourne (**386**) are also mentioned as having had
the plague. The general method adopted to try to prevent the spread
of the disease was to confine the inhabitants of the infected area. This
necessitated some form of relief especially for those tradesmen whose
living depended on selling in surrounding markets. A tax to provide
the necessary money might be levied on the whole county to help
the larger towns but usually the burden was put on the villages within
five miles of the infected community. Again it was difficult to collect
the full amount of the taxes and many local traders, who had supplied
goods to plague victims, were still trying to get payment some years
later (**162, 180, 513**).

Food Shortages
Severe shortages of grain were reported in 1647 and 1648 both within
the county and in the country at large, probably the result of poor
harvests. The reaction of Quarter Sessions was to restrict the use of
grain to produce malt and so reserve supplies for making bread, the
staple part of the diet for most people. In July 1647 maltsters were
forbidden to buy any barley to convert to malt until after Michaelmas
(**297**). It seems likely that this order was not fully followed for, later,
all maltsters were 'suppressed' and it was ordered that all corn had to
be sold on the open market and not 'within doors' or by sample (**321**).
There was still a problem after Michaelmas, when it was ordered that
for the first hour after the bell had been rung to start the market,
only the poor and those buying for their own use could purchase any
corn. The constables were also authorised to search lofts to discover
corn forestalled or bought out of the open market (**351**). Another
novel approach was to target those who made malt as a sideline but
who had other trades sufficient to maintain themselves (**375**). These
actions were prompted as much by the fear of insurrection and unrest
as by humanitarian concern.

    In 1648 more positive action was taken to protect the poor from
the high price of corn caused by the shortages. At the Hindon and
Warminster markets, all merchants had to agree to sell one bushel of
barley at 4s for every quarter they brought to the market. This barley
was then kept in a central store and made available to the poor and
other labourers, who were required to produce a certificate signed by
the minister and four or five of the 'chiefest inhabitants' where they
lived (**360**).

Fire

The threat of fire was a constant hazard especially as most houses were thatched. During this period Quarter Sessions received 23 petitions from people asking for some relief after their houses had been burnt down and this probably represents only a small proportion of all the fires which occurred. Usually they were given a grant of between £5 and £10.

The most serious fire was that at Mere in 1642 when 12 people said their houses had been burnt down within the space of three hours and all their goods lost. All the houses were thatched and the season was very dry (**332**). Devizes also experienced at least two fires. In 1644 a fire which started in one house at one o'clock in the morning quickly spread to six other houses (**149**). Several houses were destroyed by fire in St Mary's parish in 1648 (**381**). It was at this or an earlier fire that Thomas Leach's house was pulled down to form a firebreak (**453**). Villages were not immune and appeals for relief came from, for example, Preshute (**97**), Alderbury (**106**) and Keevil (**317**). Bromham had two fires: in 1651 when two houses were destroyed (**737**) and again in 1653 (**837**). Snap (Aldbourne) also witnessed a multiple fire in 1649 when three houses were burnt (**583**). In two cases the petition was not for financial compensation but for permission to build a replacement cottage on the waste, at Orcheston St George (**196**) and Coate (**338**). There is also reference to a little house destroyed by fire in Clarendon Park next to Winchester Gate (**927**).

LOCAL AND COUNTY RATES

A recurring issue for the justices concerned rates, both levying and collection. Undoubtedly the Civil War had seriously increased the burden of taxation until it became difficult to sustain. Throughout the 1640s and 1650s the Royalist and Parliamentarian regimes were remarkably efficient at raising large sums of money, a success in part explained by the use of soldiers to enforce collection. This must have put pressure on hard pressed tax payers to contribute to local rates. There was also the problem that, as well as the general taxes, there were other specific levies from time to time on different communities, for example to give relief to neighbouring towns or villages when they were affected by the plague, to repair the parish highways or bridges, to pay for taking prisoners to the gaol at Fisherton Anger and for watching and warding. Some cases, such as the taxes for the relief of the inhabitants of Calne, Devizes and Malmesbury when they had the plague, rumbled on for years and never seem to have been completely settled. In 1642 Malmesbury had been awarded £30 a week to be raised by the parishes within a five mile radius of the town but in 1646 they were still complaining that they had received for the first six weeks only £87 of the £180 due to them (**179**). It was the constables and tithingmen who bore the brunt of collecting these taxes and they frequently had to take recourse to Quarter Sessions to get warrants against those who had not paid. Often it was a local official who had to meet the initial cost of, for example, carrying prisoners to gaol, or having their goods distrained in payment of a fine levied on the community for neglecting the highways. There are 57 entries from such officials looking to Quarter Sessions to authorise the levying of a rate to repay them. In some cases these officers were not allowed to be relieved of their post until all the arrears had been accounted for.

Rates were normally assessed by the yardland and this, in itself, led to disputes. Burbage complained that it was unfair that the yardlands but not the bordlands were taxed (**355**).[17] At Urchfont the money to repair the highways was raised by a tax of 4s per yardland while others had either to work for so many days for no wage or pay 6d a day instead (**285**).[18] There does seem to have been in some parishes an attempt to modify the assessments so that the apparently more wealthy inhabitants, not least the clergy, paid more. At Swallowfield (now in Berkshire) Sir John Backhouse complained that his property was now rated at three yardlands instead of two as previously (**464**). At Dinton and Teffont the parsonage was raised from four to nine yardlands (**202**). The minister at Shorncote (now in Gloucestershire) complained that the parishioners had overrated the parsonage so that they could underrate themselves (**368**). The usual reaction of Quarter Sessions was to order a return to the original assessment until evidence could be produced to show why it should be changed. The gold standard was to set an 'indifferent (ie impartial) rate', something that was often most challenging.

Sometimes it was an individual who objected. At West Knoyle William Willoughby was said to have demesne lands worth £300, the parsonage and other land producing £120 a year plus income from old rents. He had always paid a third of the total rates of the parish but in 1646 he suddenly refused to be rated at all (**166**). Robert Hooker of Corsley had owned a yardland of 32 acres but had sold 23 acres yet was charged rates at half a yardland (**425**). John Barkesdale of Seend had sold half his messuage but could obtain no reduction in his rates (**492**).

There were also disputes between communities over what proportion of a particular rate each should pay. In 1649 the eastern part of the hundred of Amesbury objected to having to pay one eighth of the total for the hundred whereas previously they had paid only one fourteenth (**536**). There was a long running battle between the tithing of Charnhamstreet which lay in Wiltshire and the rest of the parish of Hungerford which was in Berkshire. It claimed that it should not have to pay the poor rate levied by Hungerford, a view supported by the justices (**480**). In the north of the county Blunsdon St Andrew had always made an annual contribution of £5 6s towards the poor in Purton because it was said there were no poor people in Blunsdon but in 1646 they tried to stop this (**182, 193**).

It was quite common for a parish or tithing which was experiencing a particularly heavy burden of the poor to look for help from a less pressed neighbouring community. In 1648 Potterne said it was very full of poor people and looked to Worton which was 'not charged with many poor and the inhabitants there for the most part are of very good worth' (**376**). Three years later Worton was again ordered to help Potterne (**689**). Chalfield was expected in the same year to help both South Wraxall (**519**) and Atworth (**543**). Similar cases involved Little Langford to assist Fisherton Anger (**415**), Chilmark and Knoyle (**581**), Castle Eaton and Highworth (**733**), Winterbourne and Lyneham (**735**), Heddington and Calne (**760**), Upton Scudamore and Warminster (**804**) and Baverstock and Barford (**929**).

ORDINARY BUSINESS

Houses of Correction and the County Gaol
In 1631 a county rate was levied to raise £1200 to repair the house of correction at Devizes and to build three new houses so that the county was adequately covered.[19] There was a problem, however, with the Marlborough house. In 1647 Quarter Sessions were made aware that it was owned by the county but Marlborough was 'an exempt corporation from the county and holding Sessions by themselves' and therefore did not have access to the house even though they had contributed £8 towards the cost and cleared some old cottages to provide a site (**327**). It was later agreed that Marlborough could use the house provided it paid its share towards the running costs (**398**). The need to repair the houses arose quite regularly. In 1650 grants were made to all three houses: Marlborough was allocated £22 (**611**), Fisherton Anger £10 (**657**) and Devizes £10 (although the repairs were estimated to cost £30) (**630**). The detailed accounts give some indication of the nature of the buildings and their features (see Appendix 2).

Quarter Sessions appointed the masters of the houses. In 1642 John Freeland became master at Fisherton Anger. He was to receive

£50 a year to run the house but, because of the amount of equipment
and goods under his care, he had to produce a bond of £100 with two
'sufficient securities' (**21**). This seems to have become the standard
form of contract for masters of the other houses. There was a fierce
contest for the vacant post at Devizes in 1643 between Abraham Hall
and Thomas Peirce. Two justices were nominated to interview both
and to make a recommendation. They reported that both were very
suitable and both had acceptable sureties but Hall was 'the better
spirited man to execute the office' and so he was appointed (**99,109**).
However. In 1653 Hall was dismissed for 'several misdemeanours' and
replaced by George Sloper, a worsted comber (**915**).

There was also the question of the county gaol and responsibility
for its repair. In 1642 the Assizes 'fined' the county £40 for not
keeping the gaol in repair. Quarter Sessions retaliated by appointing
counsel to try to prove it was not the county's responsibility (**38**)
although the outcome does not seem to have been recorded. But the
same issue arose again in 1649 when the gaol needed some serious
repair at an estimated cost of £183 10s. This time Quarter Sessions
maintained that the gaol had always been maintained by a grant from
the Exchequer to the Sheriff and they petitioned accordingly (**485**).
The outcome of this is not recorded in the Order book

Cottages on the Waste
An Elizabethan statute[20] had imposed restrictions on the building of
cottages including, for example, a requirement that each should have
four acres of land, and imposed fines for any breach of these regulations.
In the 17th century Quarter Sessions had a steady stream of petitions for
exemption from 'the forfeitures mentioned in the statute'. Invariably
these were from poor people who said they had no house for their
family and no other way of obtaining one. The petitioners produced a
licence from the lord of the manor giving them permission to erect a
cottage on some part of the waste and often they were supported by
some of the local inhabitants. A typical example is Henry Spackman
of Lydiard Millicent in 1647 who needed a house for himself, his
wife, five small children and his mother. He had a licence from Sir
Anthony Ashley Cooper, lord of the manor (**280**).

Sometimes more information is given about the actual building
of the cottage but, unfortunately, never any details about the cottage
itself, its structure, size and accommodation. At Westbury in 1647 the
cottage of Anne Greenhill, widow, was said to have been built for her
by her son-in-law John Lane and some other charitable people (**287**).

On two occasions Quarter Sessions ordered, or at least
recommended, the overseers of the poor to build a cottage for a

poor person as part of their relief. In 1648 the overseers of Urchfont were directed to erect a cottage for William Gardner and his wife at Estcourt (**362**). A similar recommendation was made in 1650 to the churchwardens and overseers of Winterbourne Bassett for William Verryer (**638**).

The petitions, such as the one from Henry Keeble of Great Durnford, often specifically mention the 'great scarcity of houses for labouring people' (**724**). It was also made quite clear that the cottages so erected were to be held for the lifetime of the petitioner and no longer, presumably then reverting to the lord of the manor: Roger Ward at Ashton Keynes (**941**) and Richard Gay at Kington St Michael (**942**) are two examples which illustrate this. Overall some 44 petitions for building a cottage on the waste were received and approved during this period.

Highways and Bridges
The supervision of highways and bridges had always been one of the most important administrative functions of Quarter Sessions. There are frequent references to parishes being fined for not keeping their roads in good repair. Disputes arose about whether a road or track had been put in sufficient good order such as that at Pouchers Ragge, a cartway between Purton and Cricklade (**68**). There were, also, frequent orders against those inhabitants who had not paid a specific highway rate. At Foxham in 1642 Quarter Sessions confirmed the arrangement agreed by the inhabitants for the repair of their highways. Certain named people were to provide each year a certain number of loads of stone, some 78 loads in all. This ranged from Edward Hungerford, who had to provide four loads for his holding in Foxham and four for Avon tithing, to Margery Hammons and others who were levied at only one load (**71**). But, increasingly, the provision of direct labour or materials was being replaced by the levy of a rate. At both Heddington (**870**) and Atworth (**940**) it was said that ordinary labourers could not repair the pitched causeways while Worton (**391**) did not have an available supply of stones within the parish and had to buy materials from elsewhere.

The position that each parish was responsible for its own roads could lead to inefficiencies and most complex situations where parish boundaries did not fit naturally with important through roads. This is particularly well illustrated in Chippenham where the peculiarities of its boundaries and those of Langley Burrell and Hardenhuish led to a quite impossible hotchpotch of responsibility for different sections of the roads. This was resolved by a lengthy agreement between the three parishes to rationalise their responsibilities (**854**).[21]

Bridges were perhaps seen as even more important than the highways especially those on major routes through the county. The Salisbury bridges, in particular, gave a lot of trouble. In 1642 Harnham bridge was said to be in such a bad state that the upper part was worn down to the ribs (**14**). Further repairs were needed in 1653 (**877**). St Thomas, Muttons and Milford bridges needed attention in 1643 (**89**), 1647 (**286**) and 1651 (**683**). There was a very contentious issue at Lacock in 1653 when it was agreed to knock down Raybridge and use the stone to repair and improve Foot bridge, a proposal that was hotly opposed by many inhabitants (**905**).²² Kellaways bridge on another important road in the north of the county, which carried Maud Heath's causeway over the river Avon, had still not been repaired in 1652 after its partial destruction during the war (**784**). There are also references to the bridges at Blackbridge, Calne (**65**), Potterne (**236**), Cow bridge, at Leigh in Ashton Keynes (**311**) and Heath bridge, East Grafton (**526**).

There was often a problem in discovering who was responsible for the repair of a bridge and although the county had to pay as a last resort, Quarter Sessions did everything possible to avoid this situation arising. At the Hilary sessions of 1642 it was agreed that Harnham bridge should be repaired at the expense of the county, with the proviso that this should not serve as a precedent (**14**). The question of responsibility appears have been unresolved. There was a suggestion that at some time some property had been left to help pay for its upkeep but several commissions, ordered by the Assize judges and extensive research by the Clerk of the Peace, reported at the Easter sessions of 1652, proved inconclusive (**706, 783**). ²³ At Castle Eaton the high cost of repairing the bridge over the River Isis led to a special enquiry by four justices who identified a number of parishes and tithings which should exceptionally be jointly responsible (**364**). Bremhill and Langley Burrell were in dispute over responsibility for repairing Kellaways bridge (**865**).

Often bridges linked two areas which were expected to share the cost of repairs. In 1647 Melksham hundred spent £5 on its share of the cost of repairing Monkton bridge; Bradford hundred was responsible for the other part (**252**). There was rather less agreement about responsibility for setting up a bridge between Colerne and Corsham (**400**).

The Regulation of Alehouses
The attempt to return to a greater semblance of law and order in 1646, probably also with the Puritan influence, included a purge on alehouses. They were thought to encourage idleness and dissolute

living among the serving and labouring classes with possible implications on the burdens of poor relief. Demand for malt used in brewing ale threatened supplies of corn for bread particularly in times of shortage (see section above on Food Shortages). Quarter Sessions referred to the abuses, inconveniences and mischief which had arisen because of the multiplicity of alehouses in the county. All alehouses were therefore to be suppressed, and new licences would be issued (**159**). Later in the year it was reported that the officers in Pewsey had not received notice of this order and seven people still kept alehouses without a licence. These were then also suppressed (**204**). But the limitation of such places of refreshment did have drawbacks and in 1647 Pewsey complained that they had only one inn which was not sufficient to meet the large number of travellers passing through the village. It was requested that Simon Lane, who already ran a common alehouse, might be licensed to meet this need (**273**). This is an example of the distinction between an inn, which should provide refreshment and accommodation and an alehouse, which was under no such obligation.

Other alehouses continued for a while without a licence, such as the three at Maiden Bradley in 1647, but when they were reported they were soon suppressed (**262**). At Tisbury in 1650, the alehouse run by William Cantloe was suppressed because of a range of disorders but, at the next Quarter Sessions, there was a petition for his licence to be restored which was supported surprisingly not only by the 'most sufficient inhabitants' but also by the vicar (**578, 607**). Keeping a disorderly house was considered a particularly serious offence, such as John Kember at Ham who was said also to keep two daughters of 'light and loose living' (**606**). At Great Bedwyn no fewer than four men were accused of selling ale illegally and to 'suffer menservants to lie there tippling at unseasonable times' (**455**). The punishments for illegal activities connected to alehouses could be severe. Thomas Jones of Broad Hinton was to pay a fine of twenty shillings or be whipped (**456**) while William Cottle of Box had been committed to the house of correction at Devizes (**906**).

THE POOR LAW

Settlement and Removal
The Elizabethan poor law, based on the principle that each person was the responsibility of an identified parish (the place of settlement), became extremely complicated and led to numerous cases before Quarter Sessions and, occasionally, the Assizes. It was perhaps only natural that, because of the burden of the poor rates,

parishes should try to shift responsibility for poor persons to some other parish.

The case of Roger Harding dragged on for over a year in 1649–50 with the family shuttled between Calne and Bremhill as new evidence was produced and previous decisions reversed. Eventually a compromise was reached with Roger, his wife and three of his children being settled at Bremhill while two daughters remained at Calne to be apprenticed there (**486, 556, 596, 627**). Often the process of settlement seemed particularly harsh especially when children were involved. Two cases stand out. In 1644 Elizabeth Hobbes with her three year-old son, John, was arrested as a vagrant at Coombe Bissett. It was decided she should be sent back to her place of birth, Piddletrenthide in Dorset, but they only got as far as Bowerchalke where Elizabeth died. John was sent on to Piddletrenthide but they refused to accept him and he then arrived back at Bowerchalke. Quarter Sessions ordered that he should first be taken to Coombe Bissett who would be responsible for sending him again to Piddletrenthide (**112, 114**). Mary Watts was only five when she was taken as a vagrant at Whiteparish in 1649 and was then sent from tithing to tithing to Bristol who refused her and she next appeared at Salisbury. It was ordered that she should be sent back to Whiteparish who would be responsible for her (**475**).

Another complication arose with Elizabeth Laggatt who was born at Latton but, on her marriage, went to join her husband at Inglesham. When he died she returned to her home parish of Latton but it was decided that she could not stay there and had to go again to Inglesham which was deemed to be her place of settlement (**549**). In 1652 Enford and Winterslow had a long battle which was referred to the Lord Chief Justice, concerning responsibility for Jane Carter and her illegitimate child fathered by a man from Sussex 'not to be heard of' (**755**).

Some cases were even more complex. Elianor Gest lived with her husband and child at Kemble but they fled when he was threatened with arrest because of debt. They went to Cradley in Worcestershire but Elianor and child were not accepted and were sent back to Kemble which, in turn, refused to accept them (**647**). The story of Elizabeth Somner perhaps illustrates an extreme case where identifying the correct parish for children was almost impossible. Elizabeth was a widow living at Seend who had one child and then another illegitimate one. She then moved to Langley Burrell as a covenant servant but almost immediately became pregnant again and went back to Seend. She then married John Brewer and moved to his house at St John's, Devizes but left her children at Seend. Quarter Sessions, on the appeal by Seend, ordered that the children be sent to Devizes but St John's parish then appealed against this decision. Where did these children really belong? (**592**, **800**, **823**) In some cases families could be left completely in limbo. This happened to a group of people living in cottages built on some waste land between Stockton and Codford St Mary. Neither parish claimed the land so two justices were sent to examine 'some ancient and discreet persons' and decide to which parish the families should belong (**669**).

Illegitimacy
There were some 30 cases concerning illegitimate children in almost all of which there was a dispute about which parish was responsible for maintaining the woman and child. The normal practice was to try to find the reputed father and make him responsible for the maintenance of the child. This was difficult in the several cases involving soldiers who had moved on to other areas and could not be found. Often the case involved master and servant. There was a standard punishment for the mother of a year in a house of correction, as in the case of Edith Browne of Horningsham (**1**).

There was a strange case in 1642 involving Elizabeth Ponting of Ramsbury who tried to get money fraudulently from John Prestwood. She claimed he was the father of her child but it was later discovered that she had only pretended to be pregnant (stuffing wool under her apron) and trying to borrow a child to exhibit when necessary (**4,13**). Not unusually an employer and servant were involved as in the case of Marie Brown and her master, William Fowle of All Cannings (**793, 832**).

Family Responsibilities
There was a strong sense of the extended family which should be responsible for its members who became poor or ill. This worked both ways – with parents and grandparents expected to maintain their offspring, and children to support their parents. In several cases, a grandparent was considered to have sufficient means to support their grandchildren, one or both of whose parents had died: Robert Ricketts of East Knoyle in 1648 (**377**), Bretiza Miller of Idmiston in 1649 (**516**), Elizabeth Villier of Highworth in 1650 (**645**), John Galloway of Corsham in 1651 (**739**) and Thomas Chandler of Stratton in 1653 (**908**). Edward Coombes of Kingston Deverill was already keeping one of his four orphaned grandchildren, the others being relieved by the parish. In 1654 he was considered wealthy enough to keep a second grandchild (**957**).

Robert Norrice of Brinkworth (**222**), and Richard Reynolds (**566**) were considered to have sufficient means to support their parents who had fallen on hard times and were ordered to do so. John Whatley was said to be worth eight or nine score pounds (£160-180) and was ordered to pay his parents two shillings a week. On his refusal to do so, he was brought back to the court and then apparently obeyed a further order (**738, 802, 819**)

Compassionate Cases and Distracted Persons
Quarter Sessions considered petitions from poor people who did not seem to have received proper relief from the local overseers of the poor and often ordered some higher rate of relief to be provided. John Rugge had been curate at West Knoyle for eleven years when he became too weak and old to continue work. The overseers were ordered to pay him a relatively high pension of 2s 6d a week (**563**). Richard Madderinge, blind and with an invalid wife, was to be provided for properly by the overseers of Chiseldon although the justices added rather impatiently 'that the court be no further troubled herewith' (**209**). John Allwood of Norton Bavant, near 100 and having lost his sight, had his relief stopped for no accountable reason (**299**). The overseers of the poor of Ashton Gifford were ordered to pay Edith Willis, a poor widow with four female children, 12d a week (**467**).

Perhaps surprisingly, Quarter Sessions dealt quite sympathetically with a number of 'distracted' or mentally ill people. In 1642 Richard Symons of Highworth came before the court charged with petty larceny but they decided he was an 'idiot' and ordered the overseers to treat him as one of the poor and to prevent him from wandering around (**15**). Susan Barter, a 'distracted' person of Warminster, walked up and down the town and was considered to be a danger to others. The overseers were to look after her until such time as it was hoped that she would be cured (**294**). At Ludgershall Richard Helton had been wandering about to the annoyance of people. The overseers were ordered to 'provide for him as his case requires' (**449**). Despite all their efforts, the local doctors had not been able to cure Susan Candy of the King's Evil. The justices took action to try to get her received by the master of St Thomas's Hospital at Southwark where it was hoped she might receive more effective treatment (**471**).

Apprentices
Indentures of apprenticeship were considered to be important legal contracts and could only be rescinded with the consent of Quarter Sessions. A number of such cases came before the court with apprentices asking to be released from their articles because of some failing or mistreatment by their masters.

In 1646 John Rogers was released because he had 'received divers abuses and hard usage' from his master, Thomas Harris of Warminster (**173**). At Westbury in 1647, Edward Hall, apprentice to Edward Weste, tailor, had been given only household jobs and very little at his trade (**270**). Sometimes a master was not able to fulfil his obligations to his apprentice. In 1647 Richard Clarke, shoemaker, with his family, simply went away from Malmesbury leaving his apprentice, Richard Hall, behind (**343**). At Mere, Thomas Longier, tailor, had been put in prison for debt and consequently his apprentice, Richard Smyth, had to be released (**508**).

On other occasions the master was released from the contract because the apprentice proved to be unsuitable. William Pontinge was not fit for husbandry being 'infirm and broke bellied' and was removed from his master, Thomas Snowswell (**815**). John Somers was also able to prove that his apprentice, William Naish, was not fitted to the trade of a shoemaker (**869**).

Apprenticeship also formed an essential part of the poor law system with poor children being apprenticed as soon as they reached seven years old, so that they could be taken off the responsibility of the parish. Local employers could be forced to take such apprentices and fined if they refused to do so. This arrangement seems to have become somewhat neglected for in 1649 there was a strict directive from Quarter Sessions to churchwardens and overseers ordering them to be more diligent in putting out poor children to apprenticeships. The justices were to meet in each division and review the local provisions with punishments to be handed out to any officer found at fault (**470**). Some landowners were still reluctant to take these 'poor law' apprentices and came to Quarter Sessions to plead to be excused. John Webb of Chiseldon successfully argued that he had already taken an apprentice while there were others in the parish who had not done so (**817**). The case of Sir John Glanville, who had refused to take an apprentice in respect of his lands at Ogbourne St Andrew, was referred to the Assizes for a decision (**551**).

PERSONAL DISPUTES

Quarter Sessions also considered a number of personal disputes or civil cases. The non-payment of wages was a particular issue. Perhaps Francis Baskerville was the greatest offender. He was accused of not paying the wages of some of his covenant servants and of several employees who had been employed on harvesting (**768, 901, 903, 904**). Eventually he was threatened with imprisonment if he did not pay (**926**). Sir William Button was similar, appearing twice for not paying for building work done and the salary of one of his servants (**593, 874**). It is noteworthy that the court was so supportive of these workers against their employers from the gentry. It may also be significant that Sir William Button had been a Royalist supporter and was one of those heavily fined at the end of the war.[24]

A panel of justices might be appointed to adjudicate in these cases. Examples include the dispute between Henry Younge and John Watkin (**30**), conflict over ownership of a tenement in Purton (**60**) and over the distribution of the property of Richard Hayward deceased (**895**). Justices were also requested to investigate a peculiar case in 1650 when Anne Hutchins complained that John Barnes of Laverstock had persuaded her husband to leave her to go and live with him (**574**).

In 1646 William Pound and his wife and Robert Rolfe were fined for pulling up a length of hedge at Lydiard Millicent belonging to Sir Anthony Ashley Cooper (**199**) although it is not clear whether this was simply stealing timber or a protest against enclosure. If they did not pay the fine, they were to be publicly whipped but, when it came to this, the tithingman Thomas Little refused to carry out the punishment and was himself imprisoned for this default (**284**).

Claims for personal injury could also arise as with Elizabeth Smyth who had been injured when falling through a cellar door that extended into the road at Ludgershall (**349**).

MISCELLANEOUS

Finally, the range of the work of Quarter Sessions during this period was very extensive, dealing with a number of one-off and unusual items, some important and others perhaps less so.

There is an early reference in 1643 to water meadows at Britford, near Salisbury when several men were accused of stopping up the newly-made water courses (**80**). Robert Lawes and Walter Keynton were each given a reward for apprehending two highwaymen (**579, 580**). The parish of Downton was fined for not keeping its stocks in good repair (**922**). Tobias Blisse and Richard Cater were on trial for setting fire to the cottage of Jane Cowles whom they claimed was a witch (**662**).

Perhaps of greater significance was the long petition to Parliament in 1652 about the decay of the cloth trade in Wiltshire which was seen as part of a more general decay in trade. Fewer than ten in a hundred looms were in use and there was concern that the resulting widespread poverty would lead to serious unrest in the county (**831**).

The regulation of weights and measures was given due attention. In 1647 the bakers and alehouse keepers of Warminster were accused of not giving full measure (**318**). Later, In 1654, Quarter Sessions were given the specific task of enforcing in Wiltshire the statute introducing standard weights and measures throughout the country. Responsibility was delegated to the churchwardens and overseers of the poor with the inducement that they could retain any fines for the use of the poor locally (**930**).

Matters that had previously come under the purview of the ecclesiastical authorities, which were abolished under the Commonwealth, now came to Quarter Sessions, especially concerning the repair of churches. At Chiseldon there was a dispute over repairs and alterations to the church, and Mr Calley was one of those who refused to pay the rate to cover the cost (**694**). Responsibility for repair of the chancel at Ebbesbourne was ascribed to John Boddenham and William Penny (**847**). Finally it was agreed in 1654 that the small parish of Westport (whose church had been demolished) could be united with Malmesbury (**938**).[25]

EDITORIAL NOTE

The manuscript has been transcribed in full, although with some gentle pruning of repetitive legal phrases and the headings for each sessions. Throughout the phrases 'Justices of the Peace for the county of Wiltshire' and 'Treasurer for the King's Bench and Marshalsea' have been abbreviated to justices and treasurer. Numbers **95, 126-136, 886-891** have been heavily calendared to avoid repetition of their preceding entries. Christian names have been omitted after the first mention of the individual in the entry.

The aim is to present the document in a way that makes it easily accessible while retaining the original phrasing, although modern spelling has been adopted to ease reading of the text. Where possible forenames have been standardised. In the manuscript each entry has a title in the margin in a different hand for easy reference. In cases of inconsistencies between these and the text, the latter has been assumed to be authoritative and the titles have been amended accordingly. Editorial additions to the text are given in square brackets. Editorial comments, usually cross references to related documents in the papers of each sessions known as the Great Rolls (A1/110), are given at the foot of the entry in a smaller font.

Dates have been converted to the modern 'new style' order taking account that the year began on 25 March until 1752. As its name suggests the Quarter Sessions were held four times a year

Hilary (January; although occasionally December, but not in the present volume); Easter (March or April; Trinity; June; Michaelmas, October).

Some of the original petitions, summarised in the Order Book, are filed with the Great Roll and contain useful additional information. Where appropriate, this material has been added in smaller print at the end of the entry.

GLOSSARY

Amerced; fined

Bastard getter: no definition necessary but it is a phrase worth drawing to the attention of the reader (**361**).

Bayed up: held up, dammed (water) (**228**).

Bordland: demesne land divided up and leased, as opposed to yardland, originally the holding of an unfree tenant, a house and *c* 30acres (**355**).

Distringas: a writ ordering the sheriff to seize the goods of a person to obtain satisfaction.

Freehold book; list of men between 21 and 70 qualified for jury service owning land worth £10 pa under Act 1696 yet mentioned in Order Book.

Implead: to raise an action against a person in court, to accuse.

Indifferent: impartial, fair here frequently applied to rates.

Leagure: a military camp engaged in a siege (**498**).

Plough: in the contexts here meaning a wagon and team of horses or beasts.

Traverse: the denial of something alleged by the other side in a legal case.

NOTES TO INTRODUCTION

1   Minute books survive for Cheshire and Devon from 1559: Jeremy Gibson, *Quarter Sessions Records for Family Historians* 4th edition (Federation of Family History Societies Publications Ltd 1995)

2   For a fuller description of these records see H C Johnson, *Minutes of Proceedings in Sessions, 1574-1592* (Wiltshire Record Society (WRS) vol 4, 1949), J P M Fowle, *Wiltshire Quarter Sessions and Assizes, 1736* (WRS vol 11 1955)

3   In this it was not particularly successful as the agreement was re-issued in 1699. WSA 811/53

4   Fowle p lv

5   See Maurice Rathbone, *Guide to the Records in the Custody of the Clerk of the Peace for Wiltshire*, (Wilshire County Council, 1959), p x, citing

records for Hilary and Easter sessions 1606.

6   This is an early practical example of the understanding of the distinction between records and archives.

7   The change from Latin to English was the result of a specific law passed on 22 November 1650: An Act for turning the Books of the Law, and all Process and Proceedings in Courts of Justice, into English., *Acts and Ordinances of the Interregnum, 1642-1660* (1911), pp. 455-456. British History Online

8   *Victoria County History of Wiltshire* vol 5 pp 80-109 *inter al.* includes a useful summary of the period, although it names the Clerk of the Peace John Frampton, not George, as in Fowle.

9   B D Henning, *History of Parliament: House of Commons 1660-1690*, (Secker and Warburg 1983), pp 517-18

10   *Victoria County History of Wiltshire* vol 6, p138.

11   F H Manley 'A List of the Representatives in Parliament from 1295-1832' *Wiltshire Archaeological Magazine* vol 47 (1935), pp 177-264

12   Tony Maclachan *The Civil War in Wiltshire* (Rowan books, 1997), p 78

13   See below p XX section on Roads and Bridges

14   The treasurers' duties were set out under two Acts for the relief of the Poor, 39 Eliz1 c3 (1597-8), 43 Eliz1 (1600-1601) c2, and An Act for the necessary Relief of Soldiers and Mariners, 43 Eliz1 c3 respectively. Guide by Rathbone *op cit*

15   WSA A1/110/1649E/103.

16   35 Eliz 1 c4. Continued by Act of the same title, 43 Eliz 1 c3 (1600-1601).

17   Yardland (or virgate) was originally a holding of the unfree tenant, nominally 30 acres. Bordland was demesne land that had been leased out at a later date.

18   The responsibility for maintenance of the main roads was placed on the parishes under the Statute for the mending of Highways, 2-3 Phil & Mary (1555-1556) c8. 'Statute labour' on the roads became obligatory – the parish inhabitants being required to work on the roads annually without payment, or pay 12d per day by default, for a stipulated period – and the appointment of unpaid Surveyors of the roads within the parishes was required.

19   Houses of correction were built at Fisherton Anger and Marlborough but the third one does not seem to have been built.

20   An Act against the erecting and maintaining of Cottages, 31Eliz (1589) c7, and An Act for the Relief of the Poor, 43 Eliz 1(1600-1601) c2

21   For plans showing arrangements before and after the agreement see WSA 118/53

22   Foot bridge was the main bridge in the parish which carried the London road over the river Avon, so named because of its position at the foot of the Bowden Hill, not that is was restricted to foot passengers.

23   The justices paid for repairs in 1661, once more without prejudice: see A1/160/2 Hilary 1661, cited in *Victoria County History of Wiltshire* vol 5, p 107

24   *Victoria County History of Wilshire* vol 6, p 144.

25 The Act 'Touching Marriages and the Registering thereof, and also Touching Births and Burials', 1653 also included a provision for uniting parishes and this provided the basis for this action.

1642

General Sessions of the Peace held at Salisbury Tuesday next after feast of Epiphany 11 January 17 Charles (1642). Robert Hyde, William Button, John Penruddock, Francis Swanton.

1. *Horningsham inhabitants and Edith Browne.*
The court is informed by John Draper and Richard Farr overseers of the poor of Horningsham that Edith Browne was lately delivered there of a bastard child whereof she accused one Edward Norbonne to be the reputed father which bastard is likely to be chargeable to the parish. Ordered that Edith shall be sent to the house of correction at Devizes there to remain for the space of one whole year according to the statute.

2. *Calne money in Malmesbury hundred.*
At the last Quarter Sessions it was ordered that the now constables of the hundred of Malmesbury should assist the old constables in levying and collecting the moneys arrear for the relief of the late infected and other distressed poor of the borough and parish of Calne according to former orders of the court the whole moneys arrear amounting to the sum of £13 5s and the old constables were by that order to have out of that money for themselves six pounds which they had formerly paid out of their purses for the relief before they received it and the residue being £7 5s was to be paid into the court at the next Quarter Sessions. The court is now informed by Mr Staples that they cannot gather the money in regard the persons rated do refuse to pay it. Ordered that if any person shall refuse to pay their rates in arrear to the constables then the old constables shall repair to the two next justices for their warrant to the new constables for the levying thereof upon the refusers goods according to the law and the justices are desired to grant their warrants accordingly.
(If any refuse to pay, to be bound over.)
(The plague seems to have started about 1637.)

3. *Inter Robert Keynton gent and Mathew Wallis solicitor for Countess of Marlborough.*
Ordered by consent of parties that William Whe(-ke-) gent, William

Clift the elder, Wiliam Clift the younger, John Lane, John Clift and Adam Watts shall all plead to the indictments depending now against them at the next Quarter Sessions and then try the same without any delay and that George Banston who has now appeared and pleaded shall also try the indictment against him at the same Sessions.

4. *Ramsbury inhabitants John Prestwood.* (See also **13**)
At the Quarter Sessions held at Salisbury the eleventh day of January 17 Charles it appeared to the court upon examination of the matter between the inhabitants of Ramsbury and John Prestwood (ordered at the last Quarter Sessions to be the reputed father of a bastard child born of the body of Elizabeth Pontinge) and that Elizabeth left a child at Ramsbury which is chargeable to the parish and that she before endeavoured to borrow a child of one Christian Potterne to lay it to Prestwood of purpose to get money from him unto which order Prestwood appealed at this Sessions and upon full hearing of the matter was discharged from the order and it also appeared that Elizabeth was of lewd life and conversation. These are to will and require you that you apprehend and take the body of Elizabeth and carry her to the house of correction at Marlborough there to remain and be set to work and there is to be defaulted weekly out of her labour six pence to be paid to the overseers of the poor of Ramsbury towards the keeping and breeding up of the child and Elizabeth is not to be delivered from thence until she shall put in sufficient security to discharge the parish from the child.

5. *Thomas Husse.*
It appears to the court by the certificate of divers of the inhabitants of the parish of Tisbury that Thomas Husse blacksmith is destitute of a habitation for himself and his family to live in. It also appears to the court by the special licence of the right honourable Thomas Lord Arundel Baron of Wardour lord of the manor of Tisbury under his hand and seal that he is well pleased that Thomas shall erect a cottage for his habitation upon some convenient place of the manor. Ordered that Thomas shall and may erect and build one cottage there which cottage shall remain for his habitation without incurring the penalties of the statute.

6. *Edward Gillo.*
It appears unto the court by the petition of Edward Gillo of the city of Salisbury tailor that in August 1639 he being in Ireland bestowed much money in cattle and other goods and shipped them for England which were all cast away on the sea by reason of a tempest happening

when the ship came to the bay of Douglas at the Isle of Man 22nd August to the loss of Edward £180 at the least to his utter undoing. Ordered that Mr Marshall late Treasurer shall pay unto Edward towards his losses the sum of five pounds forth of the moneys remaining in his hands. And that Edward shall not trouble the court at any time hereafter for any further relief for his loss.

(The petition adds that the ship was beset by a tempest for twelve hours. To save their lives, the crew ran the ship on to the sand where it broke up with the violence of the waves. A1/110/1642H/168)

7. *Milford inhabitants.*
The inhabitants of Milford were acquitted the last Assizes upon their trial for not repairing of Milford bridge. Ordered that if the inhabitants will repair the bridge for the present the same shall not be prejudicial to them in point of right in time to come.

8. *Hackleston* [Fittleton] *inhabitants John Hill.*
John Hill of Hackleston was committed to the house of correction at Fisherton for threatening to burn his house and to run away and to leave his wife upon the parish. Ordered that if John Hill and John Hill his father shall give bond to the churchwardens and overseers of Hackleston for the discharge of the parish from his wife that then he shall be forthwith delivered out of the house of correction.

9. *Calne money in hundred of Whorwellsdown Nicholas Flower.* (See also **33**)
The court is now informed by Mr York of counsel with Nicholas Flower one of the constables of the hundred of Whorwellsdown that Flower has demanded the moneys arrear within the hundred for the relief of the poor people of Calne lately infected with the plague of such parties who are behind in payment thereof according to an order made at the last Quarter Sessions and that divers of them refuse to pay the same. And that the weather has been of late so unseasonable that he could not travel about the same matter to prosecute the order and desired the last order may be renewed. Ordered that the order shall be ratified and renewed and the court desires the next justice to grant warrants to the now constables of the hundred to levy by distress the moneys arrear on the parties refusing to pay the same.

10. *Calne money in hundred of Cawden.* (See also **35**)
William Mills and Osmond Martyn constables of the hundred of Cawden and Cadworth were bound over to this sessions for not collecting the moneys arrear within the hundred for the relief of the poor people of Calne. The court is now informed that divers persons

refuse to pay their rates in arrear. Ordered that the constables shall repair to the justices within or near the hundred for their warrants to the now constables to distrain the parties refusing to pay and the justices are desired to grant their warrants accordingly that the moneys may be levied and paid in at the next Quarter Sessions.

11.   *William Selfe, James Blatch.*
At the last Quarter Sessions a writ of the good behaviour was awarded by the court against William Selfe and James Blatch constables of the hundred of Westbury upon a contempt for neglecting the execution of the process of court against Mr William Whetaker and other persons indicted. Now upon the full hearing of the matter the constables are discharged of the good behaviour for the contempt.

12.   *Mr Dewarth.*
Ordered that the plea of Mr Dewarth shall be received de bene esse [i.e. conditionally] and because it is a case of difficulty the court orders that the Judges of Assize shall be attended with the plea at the next Assizes whether the plea may be received or not.

13.   *John Prestwood, Elizabeth Pontinge, order upon the appeal.* (See also **4**)
At the last Sessions John Prestwood was charged to be the reputed father of a bastard child supposed to be born on the body of Elizabeth Pontinge and upon some examination and proof produced by the inhabitants of Ramsbury where the child was chargeable that John Prestwood had offered some money to Elizabeth to free himself from the bastard child by reason of which testimony John was declared to be the reputed father of the child and was thereupon the last Sessions ordered to pay to the overseers of the poor of Ramsbury the sum of 12d weekly for the space of seven years from the birth of the child and that John should give security to discharge the parishioners of Ramsbury from the child (with this that John might appeal from the order at this Sessions if he should see cause). Now John appeals from the order and has made appear to the court by divers witnesses upon oath that Elizabeth endeavoured to borrow a child of one Christian Potterne but afterward told her she had got a fitter child for her purpose about the time that her supposed bastard was born to the intent the father the same upon John Prestwood and it was also proved that she used to wear wool and other things under her apron to seem to be with child whereas in truth it could be proved by any testimony and better examination of the clause and in long debate of both sides that John is not the reputed father of the bastard child but frees, acquits and discharges him from the same and likewise the order and every clause therein contained.

14. *Harnham bridge.*
Harnham bridge near Salisbury is a bridge of great and public passage and travel from most of the western parts of this kingdom towards London and is now grown into great decay for want of reparation so that the upper part of the bridge is worn even to the ribs it not being yet known whether the same ought to be repaired by the county or any other particular person. Ordered for the present that Mr Arthur Poore shall forthwith provide flints and other materials for the speedy mending and repair of the upper parts of the bridge the charge thereof to be paid him again upon his bill of disbursements by the Clerk of the Peace. And the same to repaid again to the county when it shall be known by what particular person the same ought to be repaired but this is not done out of any opinion the court has that the county ought to repair the bridge nor is any advantage to be taken or use made of this order as any evidence against the county in time to come but the same is merely out of care that the bridge come not to further ruin until such time it may be known upon due trial and proof who ought to repair the same.

15. *Richard Symons.*
It appears to the court upon the trial of Richard Symons of Highworth being indicted and convicted of petty larceny at the present sessions that he is impotent and an idiot and not of discretion to get his maintenance. Ordered that the overseers of the poor of Highworth shall provide for him as a poor of that parish and shall keep him from roguering and wandering up and down the country that he not falling into the like offence again for want of relief.

16. *Calne money in the hundred of Amesbury.*
John Swaine gent and Stephen Kent late constables of the hundred of Amesbury were in arrear in payment of moneys due out of the hundred for the relief of the poor people of Calne lately infected with the plague the sum of £12 1s 7d which money John and Stephen paid into the court at the last Sessions notwithstanding they had not collected the same and the constables informed the court at this present sessions that divers persons refused to pay their rates in arrear. Ordered that the constables shall repair to the justices within or near the hundred for their warrants to the new constables to distrain the parties refusing to pay and the justices are desired to grant their warrants accordingly that the moneys may be levied and paid to Swaine and Kent before the next Quarter Sessions.

17. *Calne money in hundred of Branch and Dole, Richard Gilbert.*
Richard Gilbert late one of the constables of the hundred of Branch
and Dole is in arrear in payment of moneys due out of the hundred
for the relief of the poor people of Calne. The court is now informed
that divers persons refuse to pay their rates in arrear.
(Ordered as in **16.**)

18. *Thomas Compton.* (See also **39**)
Thomas Compton was bound over unto Easter Sessions last for coming
into the parish of Longbridge Deverill with his family and likely to be
chargeable to the parish. Upon hearing the matter in open court and
proof made that Compton was last settled at Brixton Deverill it was
then ordered that Compton should be sent to Brixton Deverill there
to remain until the inhabitants of Brixton Deverill should show good
cause to alter the same and that the order should not be prejudicial unto
them when cause could be shown to the contrary. At the Midsummer
Sessions last the court was informed by Mr Yorke of counsel with
the inhabitants of Longbridge Deverill that Compton refused to
obey the former order and kept himself in a cottage at Longbridge
Deverill as an inmate and that he and his family did then remain in
the cottage. It was then ordered that the constables of the Liberty of
Longbridge Deverill should remove Compton and his family out of
the possession of the cottage and send them to Brixton Deverill there
to remain. Also at the last Sessions the court was then again informed
by Mr Yorke that notwithstanding the former order Compton in an
obstinate manner then remained at Longbridge Deverill and that he
gave forth in speeches that he would cut off his own fingers and maim
himself or go a-begging whereby he might be a vagrant and become
chargeable to that parish which speeches were proved in court upon
the oath of William Longe one of the constables of the Liberty. It
was then ordered that if Compton should not conform himself to the
order of Midsummer Sessions then the constables of the Liberty of
Longbridge Deverill should forthwith take Compton and carry him
before the next justice who was desired to commit Compton to the
house of correction there to remain until he conform himself to the
order or show good cause to the contrary. Now upon hearing of Mr
Yorke (counsel for Longbridge Deverill) and Mr Hyde (counsel for
Brixton Deverill) it appears that Compton has not yet conformed
himself and that the constables carried Compton and delivered him
unto the overseers of the poor of Brixton Deverill and that presently
afterwards Compton returned again into the parish of Longbridge
Deverill and yet remains there. And upon the speeches proved in
court the court thought fit to commit Compton unto the house of

correction there to remain until he put in security for the discharge of the parish of Longbridge Deverill and not to run away nor maim himself. Upon the request of John Beach of Salisbury ironmonger and Henry Rice of Brixton Deverill yeoman who undertook in court to bring in Compton at the next Sessions and that in the meantime he should not become chargeable to Longbridge Deverill nor make himself impotent. Thereupon the court discharged Compton of his commitment. Ordered both parishes shall attend at the next Quarter Sessions and then the court will settle Compton according to law.

19. *Robert Watson for 53s 4d.*
Ordered that Mr Francis Bennett one of the clerks of the court shall pay unto Francis Swanton Clerk of the Assizes for the western circuit fifty three shillings and four pence out of the moneys paid into court upon Mr Marshall's account he being late Treasurer for the south towards the procuring of a pardon for one Robert Watson a poor prisoner now remaining in the gaol of Fisherton Anger reprieved after judgment.

20. *Wiltshire.*
The account of George Marshall Treasurer for the King's Bench and Marshalsea for the south part of this county chosen the 23rd day of April 1639 at the sessions held at Devizes for one whole year.

Imprimis received of the several hundreds (and liberties) as follows:

Underditch	0	8	8
Downton	0	8	8
Bishopston (Liberty)	0	4	4
Knoyles Hindon and Fonthill (Liberty)	0	8	8
Whorwellsdown	2	3	4
Warminster	1	9	4
Melksham	0	15	2
Bradford	0	17	4
Cawden and Cadworth	2	12	0
Branch and Dole	3	5	0
Chalke	1	8	8
Damerham south	0	19	6
Dunworth	2	7	8
Frustfield	0	8	8
Elstub and Everleigh	2	12	0
Alderbury	1	19	0
Amesbury	2	7	8
Mere	1	6	0

Heytesbsury	I	16	0
Trowbridge	0	6	0
	28	15	2
R. in stock of Mr Stockman	26	11	0
	55	11	0

The disbursements are:

John Shute of Milford	5	0	0
Devizes and Marlborough			
bridewells for their fees	6	13	4
Hospital of East Harnham	5	0	0
King's Bench and Marshalsea	I	0	0
For an acquittance	0	I	0
Repair of the bridewell at Devizes	8	0	0
Repair of bridewell at Fisherton Anger	11	0	0
	36	14	4
Rest	18	16	8

4 October 1641

The account passed before us the day and year abovesaid and we do allow thereof and order the sum of £18 16s 8d remaining in stock to be delivered over to William Feltham the succeeding treasurer.

Anthony Weekes   Francis Swanton

21. *John Freeland to be master of the house of correction at Fisherton Anger and for the allowance of £50 per annum to relieve the prisoners.*
Ordered that John Freeland now keeper of the gaol of Fisherton Anger shall be master of the house of correction there and that he shall correct all such prisoners as shall be thither sent and set them to work and that William Croome now collector of the relief of the poor prisoners which now are in gaol or shall be hereafter thither sent and committed shall pay unto Freeland fifty pounds per annum in full satisfaction of the relief of the prisoners and in consideration thereof Freeland accepts the same to relieve the prisoners. Further ordered that Freeland shall be bound in a bond of one hundred pounds to the Clerk of the Peace with two sufficient sureties as well for the due execution and discharge of his office of being master of the house of correction as for the answering redelivery and satisfaction as well of the county's stock committed in his charge as of all such goods and implements of the county's as are now remaining in the house of correction or which shall hereafter be delivered to his custody and Freeland is to continue

master of the house of correction until the court shall alter the same. (John Freeland had petitioned the Justices for the position of master, the previous holder John Pinchon having recently died. A1/110/1642H/171)

22. *For receipt of the Treasurers moneys and payment out of the same.* Ordered that all Treasurers of this county as well for the relief of the King's Bench and Marshalsea as for the relief of maimed soldiers and mariners within this county shall pay into this court all moneys remaining in their hands upon the surplussage of their accounts unto Mr Francis Bennett one of the clerks of this court who is authorised to receive the same and pay it out as this court shall order and appoint.

General Sessions of the Peace held at Devizes Tuesday after Easter 19 April 18 Charles (1642). William Button, Edward Hungerford, Theobald Gorges, Thomas Hall, John Penruddock, Robert Drew, Walter Norborne, Charles Gore, Robert Eyre.

23. *Mary Croker.*
Mary Croker of Upavon widow was indicted for selling ale without licence and thereupon was convicted in open court by her own confession and was adjudged to pay twenty shillings for her fine. The court desires the next justice unto Upavon to grant his warrant for the levying of the twenty shillings and in case she has no goods whereon to levy the same then to cause her to be whipped.

24. *Treasurers of the maimed soldiers not to pay money without the justices allowance.*
Ordered that from henceforth no Treasurers of the collection for the relief of maimed soldiers and mariners shall pay or give any moneys to any soldiers other than pensioners without the allowance of some one justice.

25. *Leigh and Woolley and Cumberwell tithings, highways rate.*
The court is informed by the inhabitants of the tithings of Leigh, Woolley and Cumberwell in the parish of Bradford that of late years much of the arable land in the three tithings or hamlets has been converted to meadow and pasture and is still so employed that there are not now in the three hamlets above the third part of the ploughs that in former times were kept there by means whereof the highways are grown much in decay and desired that a rate may be made among

the inhabitants for repairing of their highways rateable by the yardlands on such as have livings and on others according to their several abilities. The court desires Sir Thomas Hall and Robert Eyre justices to make an indifferent rate on the inhabitants for the repair of their highways.

26. *Warrant to be made against all constables which have not paid in Calne money.*
Ordered that the Clerk of the Peace shall grant warrants against all constables who have not collected and paid in their moneys arrear for the relief of the late infected place of Calne with the plague. The court appoints the Clerk of the Peace to make out the orders of this court to all constables of hundreds who shall desire the same for the levying and collecting of the arrears in such manner as is agreed on at this present Sessions he taking his due fees for the same.

27. *For watching and warding.*
Ordered that watching and warding shall be duly observed in all places within this county for the apprehending of all idle and suspicious wandering persons. The court desires all justices in their several divisions to cause the same to be done accordingly and to bind over to the next Sessions all such persons as shall neglect or wilfully refuse to do the same that justice may be done unto them.

28. *William Dick and Mr Northey.*
The court is now informed by Mr Northey of counsel with William Dick that the prosecution against Dick has not proceeded against him concerning the order of Michaelmas Sessions last and that Dick is and shall be ready to clear himself concerning the accusation laid against him by the prosecution when the justices appointed by the court to hear and examine the matter will be pleased to meet about it and the court is also informed that the credit and reputation of Dick hangs in suspense in the face of his country the matter complained against him being not heard and determined and prayed that some speedy course may be taken therein. The court now desires Mr Drew, Mr Ernle and Mr Bower justices to hear and examine the matter complained of and thereupon Mr Drew and Mr Ernle promised in open court that if Mr Northey the prosecutor and Dick would wait upon them at their convenience they would be pleased to appoint a time and place to hear and examine the same matters before the next Sessions and would then certify the court of their doings therein. The court peremptorily orders the parties to wait on the justices for their meeting to hear and examine the matter that there be no further delay therein but that justice may take place and Dick may be either cleared or condemned.

29. *John Gilbert constable hundred Branch and Dole about Calne money.*
John Gilbert heretofore one of the constables of the hundred of Branch and Dole has informed the court that he has demanded the moneys arrear for the relief of the poor people of Calne of such parties and places as are behind in payment thereof that is to say thirty four shillings and four pence out of Tilshead five shillings out of Wylye according to several orders of this court and that they refuse to pay the same. Whereupon the justices at this present Sessions assembled declare that the justices within or near the hundred are to grant forth their warrants for the levying of the moneys in arrear. Now ordered that Gilbert shall forthwith repair to the justices for their warrants to the now constables to distress the parties refusing to pay their rates in arrear.
(If any refuse to pay, to be bound over.)

30. *Henry Younge, John Watkin.*
Concerning all matters in difference between Henry Younge and John Watkin. Ordered by consent of parties that all differences between them be referred to the ordering and ending of Humfrye Norborne and William Kent arbitrators indifferently chosen who are desired to order and end the differences before the tenth day of May next. And in case the arbitrators do not then end the differences then the parties do by consent refer themselves to the umpirage of Edward Poore who is ordered to end the same between them before the twentieth day of May next. The court orders the parties to stand to and perform the award or umpirage.

31. *Calne money in the hundred of Malmesbury.* (Confirms the order in **2**. See also **52**))
Further ordered that the constables shall repair to the justices within or near the hundred for their warrants to the now constables to distrain the parties refusing to pay their rates in arrear and the justices are desired to grant their warrants accordingly.
(If any refuse to pay, to be bound over.)

32. *Mr Browne and Mr Cawley about Stephen Whithead.*
Upon hearing the matter in difference between Roger Cawley and Benedict Browne gent concerning Mr Stephen Whithead heretofore bound forth as an apprentice unto Mr Cawley deceased. It appeared to the court upon oath that Stephen at the time of his binding was of the age of sixteen years and that neither he or his parents had then or ever before any relief from the parish of Hilmarton where they always lived or were likely to be chargeable to the parish and that he was not bound apprentice with his own or his parents consent and

that at the same time there were divers other poor children on the relief of the parish fitting to be bound for the apprentice and it also appeared that the justices had not set their hands to the indenture of apprenticeship now produced in court as consenting thereunto and Sir William Button being the next justice affirmed that he never consented thereunto. The court therefore conceives that Stephen was not legally bound as an apprentice and therefore discharges Stephen of and from his apprenticeship with Mr Cawley. Ordered that the order made concerning the matter at Easter Sessions 17 Charles [1641] shall be revived and stand in force notwithstanding any order of the court made to the contrary thereof. And in regard Mr Cawley wants an apprentice the court therefore desires Sir William Button to call before him the overseers of the poor in Hilmarton and bind forth one of the poor children of that parish to Mr Cawley to serve him as an apprentice in husbandry.

33.   *Nicholas Flower constable of Whorwellsdown about Calne money.* (Recites **9**)
Now ordered that Nicholas Flower shall repair to the justices within or near the hundred for their warrants to the now constables to distress the parties refusing to pay their rates in arrear and the justices are desired to grant their warrants accordingly.
(If any refuse to pay, to be bound over.)

34.   *William Pynckney, Richard Bayly constables of the hundred of Swanborough , Calne money.*
William Pinckney and Richard Bayly late constables of the hundred of Swanborough were in arrear in payment of moneys due out of the hundred for the relief of the poor people of Calne the sum of two pounds and eight shillings which moneys the late constables paid into court at the last Sessions notwithstanding they had not collected the same. The late constables informed the court that divers persons refuse to pay their rates in arrear.
(Ordered as in **33.**)
(If any refuse to pay, to be bound over.)

35.   *William Wills and Osmund Martyn late constables of the hundred of Cawden and Cadworth.* (Recites **10.**)
(Ordered as in **33.**)
(If any refuse to pay, to be bound over.)

36.   *Arthur Estmeade and Walter Foreman.* (See also **66**)
The court is informed by Mr Yorke of counsel with Arthur Estmeade

and Walter Foreman two of the inhabitants of Calne that there has been levied on them by Peter Woodroffe bailiff for amercements on the inhabitants of Calne the sum of fifteen pounds three shillings and eight pence as by the acquittance thereof appears which sum ought by the law to have been paid by all the inhabitants and parish of Calne and not by those two particular persons only. Ordered that the moneys together with their charges expended in and about the matter shall be repaid them by all the inhabitants and parish of Calne and desires Sir John Ernle, Edward Hungerford, Charles Gore and Henry Bayliffe justices to make an indifferent rate on the whole inhabitants of Calne as well for the repayment of the sum of fifteen pounds three shillings and eight pence as of such charges and reasonable expenses as Estmeade and Foreman have laid forth and expended in the prosecution thereof.

37. *William Browne and his apprentice.*
William Browne was bound over to this Sessions for suffering of William Wheeler his apprentice son of Thomas Wheeler to depart from his service before the time of his apprenticeship was expired. The court is now informed by Mr Nicholas of counsel with Thomas Wheeler that William was illegally bound to Browne in regard it appears by the indenture of apprenticeship that the apprentice was to find himself meat drink and clothes during all the time of his apprenticeship and the master was to pay him wages and Mr Nicholas thereupon prayed the court that Wheeler might be discharged of his apprenticeship with the master. Ordered and declared that Wheeler was illegally bound to his master and discharged Wheeler of his apprenticeship with Browne his master.

(Browne of Tytherton Lucas, a clothworker, and Wheeler of Bremhill indenture. A1/110/1642E/157)

38. *Inhabitants of the county for not repairing the gaol.*
Upon reading of an order made at the last Assizes whereby it appeared that there was a fine of forty pounds set on the inhabitants of this county for the decay of the gaol and the fine is to be estreated unless the inhabitants shall show good cause at the next Assizes that they ought not to repair the same. The court now appoints the Clerk of the Peace or his deputies to take care of the matter and to retain counsel to move the judges of the Assizes for the discharge of the fine and clearing of the inhabitants from the reparations of the gaol and what fees they shall pay and what charges they be at in prosecution thereof they shall be allowed on their bill with a reward for their pains therein out of the stock of the county. And the court will appoint

some inhabitants to inform the Clerk of the Peace with such proof as shall be discovered and found out for the clearing thereof.

39. *Thomas Compton Longbridge Deverill inhabitants.* (Recites **18.**) Ordered that the former orders be continued and that Compton and his family be sent to Brixton Deverill and the inhabitants of Brixton Deverill are to suffer them to inhabit there and not to disturb them if they can get a house there and if he returns to Longbridge Deverill then the next justice is desired to commit him to the house of correction there to remain until the court discharges him. And this order is final.

40. *Appointments.*
Treasurers for the relief of maimed soldiers and mariners:
    North: William Quynten of Corton within the parish of Hilmarton, gent.
    South: Samuel Lynche of Downton, gent.
    Ordered that the rates shall remain and continue as they were the last year viz so as for every parish throughout the county there may be levied and paid three pence weekly and not above. The several rates of every parish to be apportioned and set down by the justices of every division according to their good discretions and by them to be delivered over to the new Treasurers before the next Sessions.

Treasurers for the relief of the prisoners of the King's Bench and Marshalsea and of such hospitals and almshouses as are within the county:
    North: Leonard Ferris of Sutton Benger, gent.
    South: Robert Edmonds of Britford, gent.
    Ordered that the rates shall continue and be as they were the last year viz. so as for every parish throughout the county there may be levied and paid one penny weekly and not above. The several rates of every parish to be proportioned and set down as in the former order.
    And the last Treasurers of both collections shall give up their accounts to the new elected Treasurers before Charles Gore, Henry Bayliffe, John Duckett and Edward Hungerford or any two of them for the north and Robert Hyde sergeant at law, John Penruddock, John Bowles and Francis Swanton or any two of them for the south before the next Sessions.

General Sessions of the Peace held at Warminster 12 July 18 Charles (1642). Thomas Hall, John Penruddock, John Farewell, Robert Drew.

41. *John Stone.*
It appears to the court by the testimony of the wife of William Style of Horningsham that John Stone now dwelling at Horningsham has there remained a covenant servant with Edward Francklyn of Horningsham and has been settled there by the space of half a year. Ordered that Stone shall be settled at Horningsham until the court shall see cause to alter the same. And touching the fourteen pounds which Mrs Ludlow of Baycliff [Horningsham] has in her hands of Stone confessed to be due unto him for wages the court desires and appoints Mrs Ludlow to pay the money unto Stone in ten days after the end of the present Sessions.

42. *William Morse.*
The court is informed by Mr Cusse on behalf of the inhabitants of Pewsey that William Morse of Pewsey alehouse keeper keeps a disorderly alehouse there and suffers many ill orders to be therein committed and entertains men's servants and suffer them to lie tippling and drinking there to the great grievance of their masters and to the ill example of others and prayed reformation thereof. Ordered that the examination of the disorders and abuses and of other complaints against him touching the alehouse shall be referred to the hearing and examination of the next justice unto Pewsey who is desired to call Morse before him and examine the matters complained of and certify the court thereof at the next Sessions that his alehouse may be suppressed if there be just cause for the doing thereof.

43. *George Jaques and Jeffery Barnes.*
The court is informed by George Jaques gent the late constable of the hundred of Malmesbury that at the last Easter Sessions Jeffery Barnes of Milborne was chosen constable of the hundred in the place of Jaques and ordered to take his oath before some justice within one week after the Sessions. The court is also now informed that Barnes refused to take the oath for the execution of the office six weeks after the order was tendered to him and three weeks after he had received the order in contempt of the court whereby Jaques was constrained to serve in the office longer than he ought to have done and thereby was put to great charges and expenses in execution of the office because Barnes refused and delayed to execute the same. The court desires Edmond Estcourt justice to call Barnes and Jaques before him and examine what

charges Jaques has been at in executing the office for longer time than he ought to have done and allow or disallow therein what he shall think fit and also bind over Barnes to the next Sessions to answer his contempt therein if he in his discretion shall think fit.

44.   *Wilcot and Oare inhabitants and Draycott inhabitants and Katheryn Manns.* (See also **496**)
Ordered upon the motion of Mr Nicholas that if the inhabitants of Wilcot and Oare shall receive Katheryn Manns and Elizabeth Manns two poor harbourless people the same shall not be prejudicial to them hereafter in point of right in case that difference shall arise between the inhabitants of Draycott and the inhabitants of Wilcot and Oare concerning the parties.

45.   *Nicholas Flower constable hundred of Whorwellsdown and Calne money.*
The court is informed by Mr Nicholas Flower one of the constables of the hundred of Whorwellsdown that he cannot obtain warrants to be granted from the justices in or near the hundred to the now constable for the levying of the moneys arrear for the relief of the poor people of Calne according to the order of the last Sessions and has made his return into the court of those places that are in arrear viz. from Edington five pounds and fourteen shillings, from Keevil three pounds and eight shillings, from Coulston three and twenty shillings, from Steeple Ashton three pounds and nine shillings, from North Bradley four and twenty shillings amounting in the whole unto fourteen pounds and eighteen shillings. Ordered that the now constables shall forthwith by power of this order levy the several sums of money of the several places returned in arrear and pay in the moneys into the Clerk of the Peace as soon as the same shall be received and Mr Flower promised in court that he will so prosecute the matter that the moneys shall be all levied in one month now next ensuing.

46.   *Samuel Clements.*
Samuel Clements was indicted at the Christmas Sessions last for erecting of a cottage at Pewsey contrary to the statute and at this present Sessions appeared to the indictment and submitted himself to the grace of the court and thereupon the court ordered that he should pay to His Majesty for a fine twelve pence and upon payment thereof was to be discharged. The court advises Clements forthwith to address himself to the Right Honourable the Lady Anne Beauchamp lady of the manor of Pewsey where the cottage is erected with his humble petition to her for the obtaining of her licence under her hand and seal for the continuance of the cottage and attend therewith at the next Sessions

that such order may be taken for the continuance of the cottage as to law and justice shall appertain.

(The petition explains that Clements was a cordwainer and had lived in Pewsey for 36 years. He explained that he had bought a piece of ground and had started to build a house on it with the permission of Lady Beauchamp. But 'one or two malignant enemies' had threatened to pull it down and had him indicted at the Salisbury Quarter Sessions. A1/110/1642H/156)

47. *Calcutt inhabitants, Daniell Browne for judgment.*
The inhabitants of Calcutt have been formerly indicted for decay of a highway called Dudgeemore leading from Rodbourne unto Cricklade to which indictment Daniell Browne one of the inhabitants being distrained appeared on the behalf of the inhabitants and disbursed fees in discharging the indictment besides his expenses in travail in prosecution thereof. Browne petitioned the court that the inhabitants might repay him the moneys by him disbursed for that the charge ought to be borne by the whole inhabitants. Ordered that the inhabitants of Calcutt shall repay Browne the money so by him disbursed or else show good cause to the contrary at the next Sessions.

48. *Martyn Scamell.*
It appears to the court that Martyn Scamell of the parish of Tisbury has with the consent of the parishioners obtained leave of the Right Honourable Thomas Lord Arundell Baron of Wardour and lord of the manor of Tisbury for the erecting of a cottage upon some part of Lord Arundell's land in the manor of Tisbury and that Lord Arundell has certified his consent under his hand and seal. Ordered that Scamell shall and may erect and build him a cottage in some convenient place within the manor and that the cottage shall remain and be a cottage without incurring the forfeitures of the statute.

49. *Thomas Marchant and Francis Whatly.*
The court is informed by Thomas Marchant the younger that Francis Whatly one of the waymen of Leigh Marsh [Westbury] would not accept of his service this year towards the reparations of the highways there with his plough but exacted of him fifteen shillings which Marchant paid unto him and conceives himself to be much wronged thereby. The court desires Sir Thomas Hall and John Farewell justices to send for Whatly and examine the matter complained of and also the abuse thereby and the justices are desired to do therein as to law and justice shall appertain.

50. *Thomas Harvy, Bradford overseers.*
The court is informed that Thomas Harvy of Bradford father of a
bastard child born of the body of Joan Daynton of Bradford refuses
to pay unto the overseers of the poor of Bradford the sum of 12d per
week towards the maintenance of the bastard child according to an
order made and according to the condition of a bond of £40 entered
into by him together with Richard Harvy and Edward Dick of the
same parish his sureties. The court desires Sir Thomas Hall to send for
Harvy and the overseers to come before him and if Harvy shall then
refuse to pay the 12d per week with the arrear then the court desires
the overseers to put the bond in suit against Harvy and his sureties.

51. *Borough, abbey and parish of Malmesbury about the tax for relief of
persons infected.* (See also **67**)
It appears to the court by an order made under the hands and seals of
Henry Baylye, John Duckett and Charles Gore justices that the sum of
thirty pounds was to be rated and taxed weekly upon the inhabitants
of the county within five miles of the borough for the relief of the
persons infected. The court resolved that the parishes hereunder
written were within five miles and were to be taxed towards the
relief. The court confirms the former order and further orders that
the arrearages due upon the order be forthwith levied and paid. And
the weekly rate of thirty pounds to continue and be paid so long as
the infection shall continue.

(The petition explained that the rate of £30 a week was to last for
six weeks but the overseers received only £68. When the money ran
out, the infected people 'did rise and make a tumult'. The overseers had
to spend their own money to provide relief. Most of the people affected
were tradesmen and dealers in wool and yarn and they were barred from
the markets in other towns because of the fear of the infection spreading.
A1/110/1642H/160)

52. *Edward Sumner and William Erle constables of Malmesbury for Calne
money arrear.* (Recites **31**.)
The court is now informed by Edward Sumner and William Erle
heretofore constables of the hundred that they have repaired unto Mr
Bayliffe and Mr Duckett justices for their warrants to levy the arrears
who by reason of the infirmness of their bodies could not meet to do
the same whereby the order became fruitless. The court now desires
Sir Nevill Poole and Sir Theobald Gorges justices to grant out their
warrants to the now constables for the levying of the moneys arrear
on such places and persons as Sumner and Erle shall return unto them
under their hands to be in arrear and the money so to be levied is to be

paid into court at the next Quarter Sessions to the Clerk of the Peace. And the justices assembled at Easter Sessions last having taken mature consideration of the statute declared that the justices within or near the hundred where the distresses are to be taken to grant forth their warrants for the levying of the money in arrear as aforesaid.

53. *William Lever.*
It appears to the court that William Lever of Tisbury clothworker by and with the consent of the parishioners of Tisbury has obtained leave of Lord Arundell for the erecting of a cottage upon some part of Lord Arundell's land in Tisbury for the habitation of himself, his wife and children.
  (Ordered as in **48**.)

54. *Henry Andros, overseers of Whatley and William Corpe.*
It appears to the court that Henry Andros one of the constables of the town of Warminster having a warrant directed and delivered to him from Sir Thomas Hall justice for the apprehending of William Corpe the reputed father of a bastard child born of the body of Alice Smithfield widow which bastard child is now chargeable to the parishioners of Whatley in the county of Somerset. It also appears that Andros having by virtue of the warrant taken Corpe and afterwards suffered him to escape. Ordered by consent of Andros and the churchwardens and overseers of Whatley that Andros shall from the date of this order pay weekly to the overseers of Whatley the sum of 12d until Andros shall cause Corpe to be apprehended and taken again.

55. *Robert Burge and Burton Hill.*
The court is informed that Robert Burge was heretofore sworn tithingman of the tithing of Burton Hill in the parish of Malmesbury for one year which year was expired two years since and that there has been no court kept ever since he was sworn tithingman. Ordered that he shall be discharged of his office and the court desires the next justice to choose a fitting man within the tithing to be tithingman there and swear him forthwith to execute the office. And the justice is desired to consider what is fitting to be allowed to Burge for his charge in serving in the office since his year was expired.

56. *Mr Marshall, Mr Swayne, Mr Batt and Milford inhabitants.*
The inhabitants of Milford within the hundred of Underditch have been formerly indicted and presented at the Sessions for decay of the highways within the parish and that Mr Marshall, Mr Swayne and Mr Batt three of the inhabitants of the parish have appeared on the

behalf of the whole inhabitants and discharged the indictment and presentment and in discharging thereof have disbursed some moneys in paying the fees of the court and otherwise amounting to the sum of 28s which charge ought to be borne by the whole inhabitants of Milford. The court is now informed that Mr Marshall etc have caused an indifferent rate to be made on the whole inhabitants of Milford for the repayment of the moneys so by them disbursed and that divers of the inhabitants refuse to pay their rates. Ordered that the inhabitants shall forthwith pay their rates or else show good cause to the contrary before Francis Swanton justice.

General Sessions of the Peace held at Marlborough Tuesday next after feast of St. Michael Archangel 4 October 18 Charles (1642). William Button, John Glanville, John Danvers, Theobald Gorges, Edward Hungerford, Robert Drew, James Long, Edward Ernle, Walter Norborne, William Wallis, Francis Swanton.

57. *The form of warrant for Calne money.*
It appears that Thomas Sloper and William Hunt heretofore constables of the hundred of Potterne and Cannings have not collected and paid in three pounds eight shillings and five pence being the moneys arrear within the hundred for the relief of the poor people of Calne. These are therefore to will and require you that forthwith you apprehend and take the bodies of Sloper and Hunt and bring them before the next justices to be bound over to the next Quarter Sessions.

58. *Mr Browne and Mr John Mayo for Calne money.*
Ordered that Benedict Brown of Calne gent and John Mayo of the same shall join together in the prosecution of the matter against those constables of the hundreds and liberties who have not collected and paid in the moneys arrear towards the relief of the poor people of Calne and they are to be assistant each to other in the prosecution thereof that the moneys may be collected and paid into court with all convenient speed.

59. *John Looker alias Davis, William Gray.*
The court is informed that John Looker alias Davys a baseborn child begotten on the body of Joan Davis by John Looker of Purton as it is supposed being placed an apprentice with William Gray of Swindon blacksmith and having served his apprenticeship is now become impotent and so chargeable to the parish of Swindon. The court

desires Sir William Button, Sir John St John and Sir George Ayliffe justices to call Gray and all other persons before them and to examine and find out whether Looker is the reputed father of the baseborn child which if the justices shall adjudge Looker to be so then the court desires the justices to make some order therein accordingly for the future maintenance of the baseborn child and for the freeing and discharging and satisfaction of the parish of Swindon from the bastard child thereafter and for the discharge and satisfaction of all such charges as they have been at heretofore if there can be no former order found to be made therein. And that the overseers of Swindon shall in the meantime provide for and keep the said bastard.

60. *John Elborrowe.* (See also **78**)
There are divers differences and controversies depending betwixt John Elborrowe, John Browne, Edmond Browne and John Mills and one Thomas Hawkes concerning a tenement in Purton. Ordered that by consent of all the parties that the hearing and determining of all the differences be referred unto Mr Nevill Masklyn and Mr John Sadler of Chilton for the ending thereof which the court desires accordingly and that between this and All Hallows tide (1 November) there may be a meeting concerning the same.

61. *Swindon constables.*
It appears to the court by the oath of Samuel Lane constable of the town and Liberty of Swindon that the constable has disbursed and been at the charge of thirty shillings for the keeping of watching and warding within the town in these dangerous and troublesome times. Ordered that Lane should make an indifferent rate upon the inhabitants for the raising of the thirty shillings together with ten shillings for his counsel's fee.
    (If any refuse to pay, to be bound over.)

62. *Lacock inhabitants, Thomas Ballard.*
Thomas Ballard one of the inhabitants of Lacock has been distrained on behalf of the inhabitants upon presentment for decay of the King's highway leading from Lacock to Marshfield between a certain bridge called Reybridge and Notton unto which presentment Ballard has appeared on behalf of the inhabitants and in prosecution thereof has been at charges in paying the fees of the court and for his travail and expense. Ordered that an indifferent rate shall be forthwith made on the inhabitants for the reimbursing of the moneys laid out and expended and also for the payment of such moneys to the supervisors of the highways there as they have expended about the repairing of

Reybridge and the way.
(If any refuse to pay, to be bound over.)

63. *Alexander Townsend.*
The court is informed by Alexander Townsend of Hardenhuish that upon the twentieth day of September last past there happened a great fire to arise in the house of Joan Brewer widow in Hardenhuish where Townsend lived as an undertenant and had consumed in the fire of corn and household stuff to the value of ten pounds and upwards tending to the utter undoing of Townsend and his poor wife which value was proved to be true by oath taken in open court. Ordered that the Treasurer shall forthwith pay to Alexander the sum of five marks in regard of his great necessity.

64. *Anthony Cue and Wroughton inhabitants.*
Anthony Cue one of the inhabitants of Wroughton has disbursed the sum of three pounds and ten shillings for the inhabitants of Wroughton for amercements, fees and his reasonable expenses in the prosecution of an indictment against the inhabitants for the default of their highways in Wroughton leading from Swindon to Marlborough. Ordered that Cue shall cause an indifferent rate to be made on the inhabitants for the satisfying of himself the three pounds ten shillings.
(If any refuse to pay, to be bound over.)

65. *John Mayo and inhabitants of Calne.*
The inhabitants of the parish of Calne have been indicted for decay of a certain bridge called Blackbridge to which indictment Mayo being distrained has appeared on behalf of the inhabitants and has discharged the indictment and paid the fees of the court and expended moneys in the prosecution thereof amounting in the whole to the sum of twenty and eleven shillings at the least which charge ought to be borne by the whole inhabitants of Calne. Ordered that an indifferent rate be made on the whole inhabitants for the repayment of the twenty and eleven shillings.
(If any refuse to pay, to be bound over.)

66. *Calne inhabitants and Arthur Estmeade and Walter Foreman.* (Recites **36**.)
The court is now informed by the oath of Estmeade that Henry Blake gent, Thomas Orrell, Roger Scott, John Fry and others refuse to pay their rate.   The court desires Sir John Ernle justice to bind over to the next Quarter Sessions, Blake etc if they shall not pay their rates upon demand and all others refusing to pay their rates.

67. *Malmesbury Abbey relief about the sickness of the plague.* (Recites **51**.)
The court confirms the former orders and further orders and declares
that the parties refusing to pay their arrearages be forthwith distrained
and their goods sold for payment thereof by the constable of the
hundred. Forasmuch as the court is informed that divers constables
have become negligent in levying the moneys, the court desires the
next justice to examine the same and to bind over to the next Quarter
Sessions such constables as they shall find faulty therein.

(This entry includes a list of parishes within five miles of Malmesbury.)

68. *Pouchers occupiers.* (See also **82**)
The jury of the hundred of Highworth, Cricklade and Staple have
presented the occupiers and farmers of the land called Pouchers Ragge
in the forest of Braydon for stopping of a cartway there leading from
Purton to Cricklade and whereas there has been an appearance made
to the presentment this Sessions and the court moved by Mr Hyde
counsel with the parties presented informed that the way is sufficiently
repaired but substantially proved neither was it made appear to the
court what charges had been laid out about the repair of the way
nevertheless the counsel desired the court that process might stay against
the parties presented and that the presentment should be quashed for
insufficiency which the court refused to grant. Ordered that the way
shall be sufficiently repaired before the feast of All Saints next on pain
of ten pounds and oath is to be made at the next Quarter Sessions
for the repairing thereof and also then they are to make appear to the
court what charges they have been at about the repair of the way.
And the surveyors of the highways of Purton and Cricklade are to
have notice thereof fourteen days before the Sessions that they may
view the way and then inform the court whether the same may be
sufficiently repaired or not.

69. *Broad Hinton parishioners.*
The court is informed by the parishioners of Broad Hinton under divers
of their hands and otherwise that Giles Gilham having about three
years since taken into his house a woman great with child delivered
shortly after of a bastard which to this day is chargeable to the parish.
Gilham now lately took Edith Younge another woman with child into
his house whereof complaint being made and Edith accusing William
Rogers of Cirencester (a man who cannot be had) to be the man that
begot her with child. Gilham after admonition given him to provide
for the indemnity of the parish has shifted of Edith who is gone to a
poor man's house in the parish and is like there to be delivered and

her child also being a bastard may become further chargeable to the parish which if it should happen. Ordered that Gilham shall be rated weekly to the relief of the parish ten shillings and the same rate shall continue on him until he shall secure the parish from the charge of keeping and relieving of the bastard child.

(The full petition reveals a story of fraud and intrigue. The first woman was a servant to William Penn, Gilham's brother and the second was his sister's (who lived in Cirencester) servant. Gilham reported the name of the reputed father in the first case but went to a magistrate in a far part of the county, having already deliberately warned the father who then had time to flee. The mother was sent to Bridewell and the child became chargeable on the parish. In the second case the woman was expelled from the parish but five weeks later, when the child was almost due, she crept back into the parish to a house owned by John Reeve who lived near Gilham. They described Gilham's actions as 'crafty, wilful and dishonest practices'. A1/110/1642M/169)

70. *John Durram and Thomas Heyward supervisors of Brinkworth.*
It appears to the court that John Durram and Thomas Heyward supervisors of the highways of the parish of Brinkworth (1640) and Richard Lewen and Thomas Stratton (1641) have disbursed and laid forth several sums of money for the repairing of the highways in the several years. It also appears that divers of the inhabitants are behind in their rates. The court desires the next justice to bind over to the next Sessions all such persons as refuse payment of their rates.

71. *Foxham and Avon, order for highway rate.* It appears to the court upon the motion of Mr Nicholas of counsel with the inhabitants of the tithings of Foxham and Avon[Bremhill] that the tithings have for the more better repairing of the highways lying within the tithings by the consent of the inhabitants there made by law a rate that the several persons hereafter named for their several and respective tynings and so the several occupiers of the tynings from time to time and shall and will yearly from henceforth and for ever thereafter carry and lay upon the highways at such places as the surveyors shall direct and appoint so many loads of stone and in such manner as are hereafter particularly mentioned and agreed upon.

Foxham tithing: Edward Hungerford (4 load of stone), Fridswith Gale widow (6), Edward Scott (4), George Sellman for that which was Strattons (4), Robert Kylie (3), George Cooke (3), Elizabeth Hammons (3), John Kylye (3), Elizabeth Gale (3), John Saunders for the mill (3), John Scott for Broadhedge (2), Robert Hawkins (2), William Scott (2), Thomas Sellman (2), Thomas Harris (2), William Scott for Holbrookes

(2), Joan Shepherd (2), Edward Button (1), Henry Hammons (1), John Jenkins (1), Edward Sparkman (1), Margery Hammons (1), Robert Kylie for Hathaways (1), George Hellier (1).

Avon tithing: Edward Hungerford (4), Thomas Tramplyn (4), John Gale (3), William Sellman (3), Joan Cliffe (3), Thomas Truman (2), Richard Baylie for Collers (2).

(Signed): Robert Kylie, Edward Scott, George Cooke (his mark), Edward Sperman (his mark), John Jenkins (his mark), William Scott, Thomas Sellman, Richard Baylie, George Hellier, William Sellman.

72. *Anthony Loveday.* (See also **100**)
The court is informed by Anthony Loveday of Liddington that whereas one Elias Edwards last tithingman of the tithing of Liddington who served in the office of one Agnes Edwards of the same place widow the sixteenth and seventeenth years of His Majesty's reign [1640-1642] collected and received of the inhabitants the Sheriff's aid and lawday money imposed on and due from the inhabitants for those years, Edwards afterwards becoming insolvent and not able to answer the Sheriff the same moneys, the Sheriff then being by William Yewen his bailiff distrained Loveday's goods for the whole money due from the inhabitants and received of Loveday the sum of forty shillings whereby the whole burden thereof is cast upon Loveday. Ordered that the constable of the parish of Liddington is to examine how much money has been levied on Loveday and shall cause an equal rate to be made on the whole inhabitants for the repayment of the forty shillings to Loveday or so much thereof as he shall make appear that he has disbursed and if any of the inhabitants shall refuse to pay their rates the next justice is desired to bind them over to the next Sessions unless the inhabitant shall make it appear to the justice that either Elias or Agnes Edwards for whom he served as tithingman are sufficient and able to repay Loveday the moneys levied on him. And if it appears to the justice that either Elias or Agnes are sufficient and refuse to pay the same then the court desires the justice to bind the parties refusing to pay the same to the next Sessions.

73. *Order to grant warrants for Calne money in arrear.*
Concerning such moneys as are in arrear for Calne when it was infected with the plague the court now orders that the Clerk of the Peace shall grant out his warrants against all constables of hundreds and liberties who have not collected and paid in their moneys due and the court renews the order in all parts and also further orders that the Clerk of the Peace shall also grant out warrants against all such constables who have been formerly questioned for the money and have not collected

and paid in the same into the court all which warrants shall be for the binding of them over to the next Quarter Sessions.

1643

General Sessions of the Peace held at Salisbury Tuesday after feast of Epiphany 12 January 18 Charles (1643). William Button, Robert Hyde, John Penruddock, Robert Drew, Francis Swanton.

74. *Nathaniel Cantloe.*
The court is informed by a certificate under the hands of divers of the parishioners and inhabitants of Tisbury that Nathaniel Cantloe of Tisbury a very poor man there born and bred is destitute of an inhabitation for the succour of himself his wife and children has obtained leave of the Rt Hon Thomas Lord Arundell lord of the manor of Tisbury under his hand and seal to erect him a cottage on some part of the waste ground there for his habitation and dwelling. Ordered that Cantloe may erect a cottage there on some part of the waste without incurring the forfeiture in the statute.

75. *Stapleford inhabitants, John Moorton.*
The court is informed by Mr Hyde counsel with the inhabitants of Stapleford that John Moorton and his wife are lately come to inhabit in Stapleford and are likely to be chargeable to the inhabitants there and that it will be made appear at the next Quarter Sessions that they by law ought to be settled at Alton or Woodborough and prayed the court that if Moorton and his wife shall remain at Stapleford till the next Quarter Sessions the same may not be prejudicial to the inhabitants of Stapleford in point of settlement. Ordered the same accordingly and further ordered that the inhabitants of Stapleford shall give notice unto the inhabitants of Alton and Woodborough of this order that they may attend at the next Quarter Sessions with their proofs that the matter in difference may be heard and settled according to law and justice.

76. *Nicholas Flower constable hundred of Whorwellsdown about Calne money.*
(See also **104**)
The court is informed by Mr Yorke of counsel with Nicholas Flower heretofore one of the constables of the hundred of Whorwellsdown that he cannot gather the moneys arrear in Edington and Keevil toward the relief of the poor people of Calne heretofore infected with the plague: from Edington five pounds and fourteen shillings and from Keevil

three pounds and eight shillings. Ordered that the now constables shall forthwith levy the arrears in Edington and Keevil that the same may be paid in to the Clerk of the Peace and if the now constables shall be remiss and negligent therein then the next justice is desired to bind the constables over to the next Quarter Sessions.

77. *Great Durnford and Boscombe inhabitants, Joan Shorley.*
Upon hearing of the matter in difference between the inhabitants of Great Durnford and the inhabitants of Boscombe in the presence of counsel learned on both side concerning the settling of Joan Shorley who was lately a covenant servant with Mr William Kent of Boscombe and during the time of her covenant being lunatic and distracted and was sent to Great Durnford the place of her birth contrary to law. The court declares that Joan ought not to be settled at Great Durnford and orders that the parish of Durnford shall be discharged of Joan. Further ordered that Joan shall be settled at Boscombe there to remain and be provided for as an impotent poor of the parish. And the overseers of Boscombe are required and ordered to receive her and provide for her accordingly.

78. *Thomas Hawkes, John Elborrowe and others, an order made at the last Quarter Sessions.* (Recites **60**)
The court is now informed that Mr Staples of counsel with Hawkes that Hawkes has attended the referees and that there is nothing done upon the order. Ordered that if the parties shall not attend the referees that the difference may be composed before the next Quarter Sessions that then the court will grant restitution upon the indictment of forcible entry confirmed at the last Sessions unless good cause shall be then shown to the contrary. Further ordered that Hawkes shall leave a copy of this order at one of the other parties' house and the same shall be deemed a sufficient notice of this order.

79. *Wilton burgesses, Purton inhabitants, Elizabeth Davis alias Orpen.*
It appears to the court upon full debate and examination of the business and upon hearing of counsel of both sides that Elizabeth Davis alias Orpen being and dwelling with Mr Reade of Purton as a covenant servant for a year and there continued by the space of three quarters of a year or thereabouts and being in that time found to be gotten with child and thereupon was illegally put away before the end of her term and the afterwards came to her mother to Wilton where she is likely to be chargeable to the parish. Ordered that Elizabeth shall be forthwith sent back again to the parish of Purton there to be provided for by the overseers and churchwardens as an impotent person and

that the parish and borough of Wilton shall be freed and discharged from Elizabeth.

80. *Mr Robert Chivers and others, inhabitants of Burford* [Britford] *and East Harnham.*
Whereas Robert Chivers gent, Anthony Turvy, William Phillipps, John Shuter, John Adams and John Whatly stand indicted at this Sessions for a riot and stopping of an ancient watercourse between Harnham Marsh and a place called Entersheels to the common nuisance of the inhabitants of Burford and East Harnham. And whereas it appears now by the testimony of John Kingman and John Jellicoes examined on oath that the inhabitants of Britford and East Harnham have had the quiet and peaceable possession of the watercourse by the space of four years last past and whereas the court is informed that the inhabitants have heretofore erected and set up flood hatches in the watercourses and have made trenches for carrying and conveying of the water into their meadows there to improve them which was done with a general consent both of the inhabitants of Britford and West Harnham and moreover Mr Joseph Bates landlord to Mr Chivers of the ground which Chivers holds within the parish affirmed in court upon oath that the hatches and trenches for drowning of the grounds were set up and made with the consent of him, Bates, before he had granted any estate to Mr Chivers. And that Mr Chivers etc have cast earth into the watercourse before the hatches and have cast earth into the trenches and have spoiled the waterworks therewith which tends to the hindrance of the improvement. Ordered that if any disturbance shall be made hereafter against the inhabitants by Chivers or the other persons indicted or by any other person or persons whatsoever by the procurement of Chivers in removing of the nuisances or after the nuisances are removed in throwing down the trenches or flood hatches or any other works made for the improvement until there shall be a legal trial had concerning the same that then the next justice is desired to bind over to the next Sessions Chivers and all other parties indicted and all other persons which shall hinder the inhabitants by the procurement of Chivers in the reforming of the nuisances or after the nuisances are reformed shall spoil and throw down the same there to answer their contempt therein.

81. *Richard Stoakes, a soldier paid £4.*
The court is informed that Richard Stoakes was heretofore impressed out of the parish of Burcombe in the Spanish voyage to Cales [Calais] and from that time continued a soldier in His Majesty's service until after the expedition to Rochelle and the Isle of Rhe in France and

in the wars received a wound in the knee and two other wounds in each hand one and thereupon Stoakes desired the court to grant him a pension in regard of his hurts which the court refused to grant yet nevertheless taking into consideration the great necessity of Stoakes orders that the Clerk of the Peace shall pay unto Stoakes out of the county money for maimed soldiers remaining in his hands the sum of four pounds.

82. *Powchers Ragge occupation.* (Recites **68**)
The court was now informed by Mr Hyde counsel with the occupiers of Powchers Ragge that the way by reason of the times and seasons of the year could not be amended according to the former order but desired time for the repair thereof until the next Sessions which was granted accordingly. And it was thereupon ordered that the pain of ten pounds should be respited until Easter Sessions next and that if the way was not then sufficiently amended and so made appear to the court then the pain of ten pounds to be estreated.

83. *Misentered and pacat* [satisfied]. [Entry crossed through]
Ordered that John Freeland now keeper of the gaol of Fisherton Anger shall be master of the house of correction there and that he shall correct all such prisoners as shall be thither sent and set them to work and that William Croome now collector for the relief of the poor prisoners which now are in the gaol or shall be hereafter thither sent and committed shall pay unto John fifty pounds per annum in full satisfaction of the relief of the prisoners and in consideration thereof John accepts of the same to relieve the prisoners. Further ordered that John shall be bound in a bond of one hundred pounds to the Clerk of the Peace with two sufficient sureties as well for the due execution and discharge of his office of being master of the house of correction as for the answering redelivery and satisfaction as well of the county's stock committed to his charge as of all such goods and implements of the county's as are now remaining in the house of correction or which shall hereafter be delivered to his custody and Freeland is to continue master of the house of correction until the county shall alter the same.

84. *Amesbury hundred, John Day, John Smart constables.*
It appears to the court that at Christmas Sessions last John Smart was chosen constable of the east part of the hundred of Amesbury in the place of John Day and that Day then affirmed in court that Smart's means was worth at least thirty pounds or forty pounds per annum. And whereas Mr William Bowles and John Smart at this present Sessions affirmed severally in open court upon oath that Smart's living

is not worth above twelve pounds per annum and no stock thereon. Declared that Smart is a very insufficient man to undergo the office of a constable for so great a hundred and therefore discharges him of the office. Ordered that John Day for his abuse to the court in naming such an insufficient person shall again take upon him the office of constable of the east part of the hundred of Amesbury in the place of Smart and shall undergo the office by the space of one whole year and that he shall repair to some justice within or near the hundred within one week now next ensuing and be sworn for the due execution of the office upon pain of twenty pounds.

(If he refuses, to be bound over.)

85. *Thomas Biston versus Edmond Rabbetts and wife.*
Thomas Biston of Ebbsbourne Wake clerk affirmed in open court at this present Sessions upon oath that Edmond Rabbetts of Ebbsbourne Wake and Elianor his wife have violently assaulted and beaten him and that she gave Thomas very foul and opprobrious speeches and threw stones at him in a most abusive manner and with all Biston required surety of the peace against Edmond and affirmed that he required the same not for any malice hatred or evil will but simply that he is afraid of his life or the hurting or maiming of his body or the doing him some other private mischief. These are therefore to will and require you in His Majesty's name that forthwith upon sight hereof you apprehend the bodies of Edmond and Elianor and bring them safely before one of the justices, Edmond to find sufficient sureties for his personal appearance at the next Quarter Sessions and in the meantime to keep His Majesty's peace towards His Majesty and all his liege people and especially towards Biston, and Elianor to find sufficient sureties for her personal appearance at the Quarter Sessions and in the meantime to be of good behaviour. And if they or either of them shall refuse to do that then you are to convey them or either of them so refusing to His Majesty's gaol at Fisherton Anger there to remain until they shall do the same.

86. *Mr William Biggs Treasurer £31 2s.*
The court is informed that there is remaining in the hands of William Biggs late Treasurer for the relief of maimed soldiers for the south the sum of thirty one pounds and two shillings of the county's money which the court orders Biggs shall pay in before the Feast of the Purification of the Blessed Virgin Mary now next ensuing unto Mr Francis Bennett for the use of the county. The court sets a fine of five pounds on Biggs for not passing his account according to the statute which fine is to be estreated against him if he shall make default of

payment in of the moneys according to this order.

87. *Mr Francis Topp Treasurer £39 10s 7½d.* (See also **103**, **121**)
The court is informed that there is remaining in the hands of Mr
Francis Topp late Treasurer for the relief of maimed soldiers for the
south of the county the sum of thirty nine pounds ten shillings seven
pence halfpenny of the county's money which the court orders that
Topp shall pay in before the Feast of the Purification of the Blessed
Virgin Mary now next ensuing unto Mr Francis Bennett for the use
of the county. The court sets a fine of twenty nobles on Topp for
not passing his accounts according to the statute which fine is to be
estreated against him if he shall make default of payment of the moneys
according to this order.

88. *William Croome deputy for several Treasurers £15.*
The court is informed that there is remaining in the hands of William
Croome of the county's money the sum of fifteen pounds which
the court orders that Croome shall pay in before the Feast of the
Purification of the Blessed Virgin Mary now next ensuing unto Mr
Francis Bennett for the use of the county. The court sets a fine of
five pounds on Croome which fine is to be estreated against him if he
shall make default of payment in of the money according to this order.

89. *To prosecute for the decay of Milford bridge, Mutton bridge and St Thomas
bridge* [Salisbury] *at the Assizes.*
The repair of diverse decayed bridges in the county have of late been
laid upon the inhabitants of this county by reason no particular person
has been appointed to solicit the same to free the county from the
repair thereof and to find out what villages, hamlets and bodies politic
or other persons ought to repair the same. The court is informed that
Muttons bridge, St Thomas bridge and Milford bridge are grown into
much decay for want of reparations. Ordered that Francis Bennett and
William Coles gent Clerks of the Peace in the behalf of the county
at the next Assizes and shall then prefer bills of indictments against
the inhabitants of Milford and such other inhabitants as they shall
have evidence that ought to repair the bridges and shall indict them
or any of them for the decays of the bridges or any of them and shall
prosecute the same on the behalf of the inhabitants of the county from
time to time and shall retain counsel from time to time for advice
direction and defence concerning the same as needs shall require and
Mr Bennett and Mr Coles shall from time to time have the help and
assistance of this court concerning the prosecuting thereof. And if any
person or persons shall be hereafter found out to be evidence to find

such bills of indictment as shall be preferred on behalf of this county for the decays and reparations of the bridges then all such parties are to attend at the Assizes to give their evidence to the Grand Jury and petty juries concerning the bridge. And Mr Bennett and Mr Coles are to be allowed their charges in prosecution thereof with recompense for their pains and the same to be paid them out of the county's stock upon delivery of their bills of account into this court.

(The constables of the hundred had presented that St Thomas Bridge, Milford Bridge and Muttons Bridge were in decay and ought to be repaired by the whole county. A1/110/1643H/116)

90. *To sue forth a commission for charitable uses.*
Ordered that Mr Bennett and Mr Coles shall renew the commission for charitable uses the next Easter term and shall attend the same commission from time to time and shall be allowed their charges and disbursements therein with recompense for their pains out of the county's stock.

91. *For custody of County records.*
The court taking into consideration how the Sessions records of the county may be preserved and kept safe in this time of danger orders and appoints that Mr [Francis] Bennett and Mr [William] Coles deputy Clerks of the Peace shall with all convenient speed cause a strong chest to be made at the county's charge with two locks and keys for the safe keeping of the records and that the records shall be put into the chest and the chest placed in the vestry house of Warminster church and the keys kept by the deputy clerks that they may have recourse thereunto as occasion shall require. The court thinks fit that two or three years of the later bundles and the later books shall remain in their custody for the making up of the Sessions book and for the granting forth of the process of the court against such persons as are or shall be indicted or presented.

[*There is no record in the Order Book for the Sessions normally held at Easter and in the Summer, neither are there Great Rolls for these times. It is most likely that Quarter Sessions were not held because of the upheavals in the country.*]

General Session of the Peace held at Marlborough Tuesday after Feast of St. Michael the Archangel 30 October 19 Charles (1643). William Button, John Glanville, Walter Norborne, Francis Swanton and Edward Ernle.

92. *Jonathan Scott Treasurer.*
The court is informed that Leonard Ferris gentleman late Treasurer for the north died about Easter last. Now ordered that Jonathan Scott of Chippenham gent shall be nominated elected and chosen Treasurer for this year to commence from the Feast of Easter last and he shall forthwith take upon him the execution of the office and collect and pay all such moneys as are due and payable by virtue thereof. He is likewise ordered to attend Edward Hungerford and Walter Norborne justices at such time as they shall appoint to take the account of the executors or administrators of Ferris the last Treasurer for his further instruction therein.

93. *Mr Ferris late Treasurer, his executors.* (See also **108**)
Leonard Ferris gent was in Easter Sessions 17 Charles [1642] elected and chosen Treasurer for the north part and died without giving up his account. The court desires Edward Hungerford and Walter Norborne justices to call before them the executors or administrators of Ferris and to cause them to account and to certify the same to the next Sessions. And if they shall refuse so to do then the justices are desired to bind them over to the next Sessions. Further ordered that the executors or administrators shall forthwith pay all such moneys as are due from him towards the relief of the hospital of East Harnham and also such moneys as are due to the masters of the houses of correction of Devizes and Marlborough in regard of their great necessity.

94. *Mr Quynton Treasurer versus constables et al.*
The court is informed by Mr Quynton Treasurer for the north that many constables of hundreds are behind in payment to him the moneys due out of their several hundreds and do sleight the payment of the same when they are demanded and that churchwardens are also negligent in paying in the same to the constables whereby poor pensioners go away unsatisfied their pensions to their great impoverishment and loss. Ordered that if the constables shall not forthwith collect and gather all such moneys due out of their several hundreds towards the said relief and pay in the same to the Treasurer that the pensioners may be satisfied or if they shall refuse to pay in the same or be negligent therein then such justice to whom complaint thereof shall be made is desired by the court to bind over such constables to the next Quarter

Sessions and if any churchwardens within their hundreds shall be remiss and negligent in collecting levying and paying in to the constables the moneys due from their several parishes then the churchwardens are to be bound over to the next Quarter Sessions.

95. *William Croome Treasurer versus constables et al.*
(Same as **94** for Treasurer for the south.)

96. *Nicholas Peirce £10 relief for fire.* It appears to the court by the petition of Nicholas Peirce of Homington and also by the certificate of divers of the inhabitants of Homington that Nicholas by reason of a fearful fire which happened upon the 25th day of January last past which burnt not only his dwelling house and all his goods there but also his barn and all his corn therein being all the maintenance he has to maintain him and his wife being both of them very aged and past labour which losses of his amounted to the value of forty pounds or upwards. Ordered that Mr Francis Bennett clerk of the court shall forthwith pay the sum of ten pounds to Nicholas out of the moneys remaining in his hands of the surplussage of the Treasurer's accounts for the south part of the county.

(Peirce had said that he was nearly 80 years old and a cripple while his wife was nearly 70. A1/110/1643M/137)

97. *Anthonie Greenaway £10 relief for fire.*
It appears to the court by the petition of Anthonie Greenaway of Preshute and also by the certificate of divers of the inhabitants of Preshute that Anthonie by reason of a sudden fire which burnt and consumed his dwelling house and household stuff and divers other goods to the value of thirty pounds being his whole estate by means whereof both he his wife and family are grown into great need and poverty. Ordered that there shall be paid unto him the sum of ten pounds out of the surplussage of moneys remaining in the hands of Mr Gabriell Goldney (if there remain so much in his hands) or otherwise out of the surplussage of such moneys as remain in the hands of Mr William Sherston both late Treasurers for the north. The court desires John Ernle, Edward Hungerford and Walter Norbonne justices or any two of them to call the said Treasurers before them to pass their accounts and the justices are desired to certify the same to the next Sessions and to bind over the Treasurers to the next Quarter Sessions if they shall refuse to do the same.

(Greenaway said the fire happened on the Sabbath in the time of divine service. He listed some of the goods he had lost: one stack of hay; one bed with all furniture to it with 3 bedsteads and mattresses; one coffer full of linen; of brass and pewter, chairs and stools leather and wood together with my shopbook wherein I had many debtors which I cannot call to mind; and many other things which would be too troublesome to set down in particular; the loss of which goods amounts to £30 besides the state of my house which was worth £3 per annum for one life. And not many years ago I bought a house in Marlborough from the rent of which I received £10 per annum which house was likewise burnt to the ground for which losses I never received any help. A1/110/1643M/139)

98. *Collector gaol versus constables.*
Upon consideration by the court of the distress and want that the poor prisoners remaining in His Majesty's gaol at Fisherton Anger are now in by reason that divers constables of hundreds have not paid in to the collector for the gaol prisoners the moneys already due for the relief of the prisoners. It is desired by the court that the justices or some of them will call before them all such constables as they shall be informed are now behind towards the relief and bind them over to the next Quarter Sessions if they shall refuse to pay to the collector the moneys in arrear within their several hundreds.

99. *Abraham Hall and Thomas Peirce.* (See also **109**)
There have been several petitions now preferred to the court by Abraham Hall and Thomas Peirce both of Devizes for the office of being master of the house of correction at Devizes. The court desires Robert Drew and Edward Ernle justices who are desired to send for Hall and Peirce before them and examine and consider which of them is fittest to execute that place of being master of the house of correction as well in respect of the ability of person and understanding as of their trade and sufficiency of the security tended for the due execution of the office and for the correcting of such persons as shall be thither send and for setting of them to work and answering of such stock of the county as now is in the house of correction or hereafter shall be thither sent or placed. And the court desires the justices to certify their opinion therein to the next Quarter Sessions that the court may then determine the same.

100. *Antonie Loveday against Agnes Edwards.* (Recites **72.**)
Ordered that Agnes shall forthwith repay to Loveday the forty shillings with such reasonable charges as Loveday has been at in prosecution of this matter the same charges are to be allowed and approved by the next justice.
    (If she refuses, to be bound over.)

101.   *Order for respiting of recognisances.*
It appears to the court that divers persons bound by recognisances to this Sessions being often called have not appeared and now the court is informed that no proclamation of this Sessions has been made in divers parts of the county whereby divers persons bound over might not have notice of this Sessions to appear according to the tenor of their recognisances and that the ways are now very dangerous to travel in by reason of the interruptions of soldiers. Ordered that no defaults shall be entered on any recognisance for the present and that every recognisance of persons bound to this Sessions which have not appeared shall be called at the next Quarter Sessions and if they shall then appear and show good cause for their not appearing at this Sessions, the court orders that their appearances shall be received and entered of record tunc pro nunc [literally then for now] and if any such persons bound by recognisance being called at the next Sessions shall not appear but make default the court further orders that their defaults shall be entered of record tunc pro nunc.

102.   *Wick and Nursteed* [Devizes]*, Woodford inhabitants and Margaret Frye.* (See also **107, 151**)
Upon hearing the matter of difference between the inhabitants of Woodford concerning the settlement of Margaret Frye and her bastard child in the presence of counsel learned on both sides. Ordered that the matter shall be heard at the next Sessions and both sides shall attend the court with their witnesses and the inhabitants of Wick and Nursteed are to give notice of this order to the churchwardens or overseers of Woodford or to some of them a fortnight before the Sessions at least that they may then come prepared to the court concerning that matter and Margaret and her bastard child are to remain in the meantime where now they are and if it shall fall out at the hearing that Margaret or her bastard child ought to be settled at Woodford then consideration shall be had for recompensing and discharging the inhabitants of Wick and Nursteed touching the charge already sustained and hereafter to be sustained concerning Margaret and her child.

103.   *Francis Topp Treasurer £39 10s 7½d.* (See also **87, 121**)
The court is informed that Mr Francis Topp has not paid unto Mr Bennett the £39 10s 7½d mentioned in the order of Christmas Sessions last past. Ordered that there shall be a fine of £20 set on Topp and that the fine of £6 13s. 4d. mentioned in the order shall be levied on him unless Topp shall pay in the said sum unto Mr Bennett before the Feast of All Saints [1 Nov] now next and upon payment thereof the court will take into consideration at the next Sessions the several fines

and make some order therein if Topp shall desire the same.

104.   *Nicholas Flower constable hundred of Whorwellsdown about Calne money.*   (Recites **76**)
The court is now informed that nothing was done on the order and Nicholas prayed that the order might be renewed which the court now taking into consideration again orders that the now constables of the hundred shall forthwith levy on Edington the sum of five pounds and fourteen shillings and from Keevil three pounds and eight shillings that the same may be paid to the Clerk of the Peace at the next Sessions.
(If they refuse, to be bound over.)

1644

General Sessions of the Peace held at Salisbury Tuesday next after Epiphany 9 January 19 Charles (1644).   Robert Hyde, Richard Goddard and Thomas Bennett.

105.   *Hundred of Dunworth and Liberty of Donhead.*
Upon hearing of the matter in difference between the inhabitants of the hundred of Dunworth and the inhabitants of the Liberty of Donhead within that hundred it appears to the court that the Liberty of Donhead have time out of mind borne a fourth part in all rates and payments against all the other parts of the hundred which was not gainsaid by Mr Yorke of counsel with six tithings part of the same hundred.   Ordered and declared that they see no cause to alter the same proportion of rating within the Liberty of Donhead and that the same Liberty shall only bear a fourth part hereafter in all rates and payments against the hundred as anciently it has done unless the court shall hereafter see good cause to alter the same.

106.   *Richard Shotter.*
The court is informed by Richard Shotter of Whaddon in the parish of Alderbury as by a certificate made under the hands of divers if the most substantial persons of the parish that upon the 18th day of November last past about eight of the clock in the morning Richard Shotter had his house and almost all his goods and apparel consumed and burnt with fire accidentally there arising whereby he indemnified to the value of forty pounds at the least and by his petition prays the court to commiserate his distressed estate and to allow him some thing out of the treasury of the county towards the building up of his house and repair of his losses.   Ordered Mr Francis Bennett the clerk

of this court to pay unto Richard five pounds of the county's money remaining in his hands of Treasurers' accounts towards his losses in regard of his great necessity.

107. *Wick and Nursteed* [Devizes] *inhabitants versus Woodford inhabitants and Margaret Frye.* (Recites **102.** See also **151**)
Upon reading of an order made therein by Robert Drew and Edward Ernle justices and upon examination of witnesses upon oath, it was proved that Margaret was delivered of a child at Woodford (which the court adjudges to be a bastard) and therefore orders that Margaret shall be committed to the house of correction at Fisherton Anger there to remain the residue of one whole year according to the statute and afterwards until she shall give security unto the parish of Woodford to perform the order of the justices. Further ordered that the bastard child shall be forthwith sent to the mother to be kept and relieved and that the overseers of Woodford shall pay weekly to the mother of the bastard child during the time aforesaid the sum of 12d towards the keeping and relieving of the bastard child for the space of seven years or until the father be found out the time of which weekly payment shall commence from this commitment of Margaret. Also ordered that if the overseers of Woodford shall refuse to pay the weekly payment or make default in payment thereof by the space of one month then the bastard child shall be sent to Woodford to the overseers by them to be kept and relieved and provided for as a poor of the parish. Further ordered that the inhabitants of Wick and Nursteed shall be discharged from Margaret and her bastard child from henceforth.

108. *Leonard Ferris Treasurer and East Harnham hospital and masters of the Devizes and Marlborough houses of correction.* (Recites **93**)
The court is now informed that there has been nothing done upon the order since the last Sessions. Again ordered and the court desires the justices and Charles Seymour, Charles Gore and Robert Chivers three more justices or any two of them to call before them the executors or administrators of Leonard Ferris and cause them to account before them of the receipts and payments of Ferris during the time he continued in the office.
(If they refuse, to be bound over.)
And the justices are also desired to certify the account to the next Quarter Sessions that the same may be entered of record. The court thinks fit to order and appoint that the hospital of East Harnham and the masters of the several houses of correction at Devizes and Marlborough shall be satisfied and paid all such moneys as shall be justly due unto

them out of the surplussage of the said account as soon as the same shall be given up in regards of their great want and necessity.

109. *Abraham Halle master of the house of correction at Devizes.* (Refers to **99**)
It appears to the court by the certificate of Ernle and Drew that the justices thought Abraham Halle to be the better spirited man to execute the office. Ordered that Abraham Halle shall be master of the house of correction and shall correct all such prisoners as shall be thither sent and set them to work and that Abraham with his securities named in the certificate shall be bound to the Clerk of the Peace in such a sum of money as the justices shall think fit as well for the due execution and discharge of his office as for the answering redelivery and satisfaction of the county's stock delivered over to him as of all such goods and implements of the county's as are now remaining in the house of correction or which shall hereafter be delivered to his custody. And Abraham is to continue master of the house of correction until the court shall see cause to alter the same and shall receive the usual fees for his pains therein.

(The full certificate gave other details saying that both candidates were suitable and had satisfactory securities. Halle had been a dealer in cloth and spinning yarn but was then a cardmaker. His securities were Thomas Clarke, an ancient burgess of Devizes, and John Stevens now constable for the town. Peirce was a spinner of yarn. His securities were Richard Peirce, mayor of Devizes for the last year, and William Brookes, his father-in-law now living at Rowde. A1/110/1644H/98)

110. *Oliver Horsey constable of hundred of South Damerham and Mr Hollis.*
The court is informed by Oliver Horsey of Martin now constable of the hundred of South Damerham that he has executed the office by the space of a year at Michaelmas last past and ever since, the custom of that place being not to execute that office but only one year and not more and then a new constable be chosen and sworn at the leet and lawday of Denzill Hollis lord of the manor of Damerham who the last year kept no leet or lawday there according to the ancient custom by reason whereof Horsey was overburdened by reason of the execution of the office and prays the court that he might be discharged of the office and another chosen in his place. The court taking into consideration the great troubles that officers are put unto in regard of the troublesome times, thinks fit to order that Richard Yardly of Damerham gent shall be elected and chosen constable of the hundred in the place of Horsey and orders and appoints Yardly to repair to some justice within or near the hundred within one week next after

the receipt hereof there to take his oath for the execution of his office upon pain of twenty pounds. And the court declares that this order shall not be prejudicial to the right of Mr Hollis for the time to come concerning the election of officers in his leet.

111. *Mr Hunt constable of Elstub and Everleigh and John Vincent gent.*
It appears to the court by the oath of Mr John Hunt one of the constables of the hundred of Elstub and Everleigh that he is employed in special service for His Majesty in the county of Berkshire and is not able to perform the same and execute the office of constableship. Ordered that Hunt be discharged of and from the office of constableship and elects and chooses John Vincent the elder of Collingbourne to be constable of the hundred in the place and stead of Hunt and that Vincent shall within one week after notice to him given of this order repair to some justice and take his corporal oath for the due execution of the office upon pain of forty pounds.

112. *Inhabitants of Bower Chalke and Coombe Bissett and John Hobbes.* (See also **114**)
The court was this day informed that there was heretofore a difference between the inhabitants of Bower Chalke and the inhabitants of Coombe BIssett touching the keeping of John Hobbes a child now remaining at Bower Chalke. And it appears upon oath made unto the court that for the ending of the controversy it was theretofore agreed between the several inhabitants that the overseers of the parish of Bower Chalke should keep and relieve the child until the court should give further order therein. And that the overseers of Coombe Bissett should pay weekly from and after the first day of May last past unto the overseers of Bower Chalke the weekly sum of twelve pence for and towards the maintenance of the child. Now ordered that the inhabitants of Bower Chalke shall be discharged of the child and that the child shall be sent to Coombe Bissett. Also further ordered that the overseers of Coombe Bissett shall pay unto the overseers of Bower Chalke the weekly sum of 12d according to the agreement.
(If they refuse to pay, to be bound over.)

113. *Robert Dowse, Richard Hickman, Hackleston* [Fittleton] *tithing.*
It appeared unto the court on the information of divers of the inhabitants of Hackleston that Robert Dowse the now tithingman heretofore sworn to execute the same office as the deputy of Richard Hickman and that Hickman is very able of himself to execute the office and that Dowse is a man of a small estate and unfit to undergo the office. Ordered that Robert Dowse shall be discharged of and from

the office and Richard Hickman is ordered to serve in the office in the place of Dowse and that Hickman shall upon notice to him given of this order forthwith repair to some one justice and take his oath for the execution of the office upon pain of five pounds.

114. *Inhabitants of Bower Chalke, Coombe Bissett and Piddletrenthide, John Hobbes.* (Recites **112**)

It appeared to the court by proof upon oath that Elizabeth Hobbes was apprehended as a vagrant at Coombe Bissett having then the child being about three years of age with her and that Elizabeth at the time of her apprehension confessed that she was born at Piddletrenthide in the county of Dorset and that she had lived there with her husband and had done so for divers years. That thereupon she together with her child was duly sent and conveyed from Coombe Bissett unto Piddletrenthide according to the law. And it was likewise proved upon oath that Elizabeth whilst she was conveying from Coombe Bissett by virtue of the pass died at Bower Chalke in her passage through that tithing and that her child was conveyed unto Piddletrenthide according to the pass but was thence sent back to Coombe Bissett. The court upon proof concerning that by the law the child ought to be kept and provided for at Piddletrethide therefore declares that neither of the parishes of Coombe Bissett or Bower Chalke are by law chargeable or maintain the child. Ordered that the child shall be forthwith removed from Bower Chalke where he now is to Coombe Bissett and that the overseers there shall forthwith convey the child unto Piddletrenthide by virtue of this order there to be kept and provided for according to the law. The court requires the overseers of Piddletrenthide to receive the child and provide for him as one of the poor of that parish as they will answer the contrary at their peril.

115. *Stapleham and Northington tithings* [Damerham] *and Thomas Hunt and William Cozens.*

It appears to the court by the petition of Richard King the tithingman of the several tithings of Stapleham and Northington preferred to the Rt Hon His Majesty's Justice of Assizes and gaol delivery held at Salisbury the second day of December last past and referred unto this court by the Rt Hon Sir Robert Heath Lord Chief Justice of His Majesty's Court of King's Bench one of the judges of the Assizes that Richard King has served as tithingman by the space of twelve months at Michaelmas last past and that if there had been then any leet held for the manor of Damerham he should have been discharged. And for that this court is also informed there was no leet then or yet there held neither is there any likelihood of holding any leet therein in regard of the great troubles of the time. Ordered that Richard shall be discharged of being tithingman and that Thomas Hunt shall serve the office within the tithing of Stapleham and that William Cozens shall serve the office of tithingman for the tithing of Northington in the place of King and that they and each of them shall within one week next after notice to him or them to be given repair to some or one justice and take their several oaths for the due execution of the office on pain of five pounds apiece.

116. *Cawden and Cadworth hundred, John Scovell and Francis Nightingale.*
It appears unto the court as well by the information of Mr Hyde being counsel with John Scovell constable of the west part of the hundred of Cawden and Cadworth as also by the oath of Scovell that he is much indebted and very unable to undergo the charge of the execution of the office and in these troublesome times has been at great charges already in the execution thereof wherefore the court thinks fit and so orders that Scovell shall be discharged of the office and Francis Nightingale of Fovant yeoman shall serve in the office in the place and stead of Scovell and shall within one week after notice given of this order repair to some one justice in or near the hundred and take his oath for the execution of the office on pain of twenty pounds.

117. *Chalke hundred, Simon White, Henry Good.*
It appears by the oath of Simon White one of the constables of the hundred of Chalke and John Williams alias Laurence that White is a man of a small estate not exceeding the value of £10 per annum and has charge of nine children and is not able to undergo the charge of the office. It also appears that White was chosen constable of the hundred at the last Sessions upon the information of Henry Good the last constable of the hundred that he was a man of sufficiency for the execution of the office. Ordered that White shall be discharged of the office and that Good in regard of the false information in court shall be constable again and that Good shall within ten days next after notice of this order to him to be given repair to some justice within or near the hundred to take his oath for the executing of the office upon pain of forty pounds and that he shall execute the office until the court shall see good cause to discharge him from the same.

118. *Westwood and Iford tithing, Mr Heyward versus John Godwin.*
It appears to the court by the petition of William Heyward the tithingman of the tithing of Westwood and Iford that he has served in the office by the space of 3 years last past. And that John Godwin one of the inhabitants of the tithing was at a leet held at Westwood about

Michaelmas last was twelve months elected and chosen tithingman in the place and stead of Heyward and was at the leet ordered to take his oath before the next justice for the due execution of the office and Godwin has ever since refused to undertake the same and that there has been no leet there held since (by reason of the troubles of the time) for the punishment of his contempt therein. Ordered that John Godwin shall forthwith upon notice hereof repair before one of the justices next residing to Westwood and take his oath for the due execution of the office.

(If he refuses, to be bond over.)

119. *Bradford hundred constables, Mathew Smith, George Graunt.*
The court was this day informed on the behalf of Mathew Smith and George Graunt the constables of the hundred of Bradford that the court leet of the hundred of Bradford has by reason of the troublesomeness of the times been of late left unkept and that the constables of the hundred have been anciently there chosen and that by reason of the not keeping of the leet Smith and Graunt have served in their offices longer than by the custom of the place they ought to have done. The court taking into consideration the extraordinary troubles of these times and of the great charge of constables in the execution of their offices orders that Robert Dicke of Midford yeoman and Daniel Deverell of Frankleigh yeoman shall be constables of the hundred in the places and steads of Smith and Graunt and that Dicke and Deverell shall within one week next after notice given to them of this order repair to some justice in or near the hundred and take their oaths for the due execution of the office upon pain of £20 by each of them making default therein. Further ordered that the choosing of these constables shall be not prejudicial to the lord of the leet for that the election is made only for the relief of the constables in these times of trouble courts being not held as usually have been.

120. *Inter inhabitants of Little Langford and Fisherton Anger.*
It appears to the court upon full hearing of the matter in difference between the inhabitants of Little Langford and the inhabitants of Fisherton Anger concerning Elizabeth Smyth and her bastard child now chargeable to the parish of Fisherton Anger that Elizabeth did run away from her bastard about four years whereby it became chargeable to the parish. These are therefore to will and require and in His Majesty's name straightly to charge and command you that forthwith upon receipt hereof you apprehend and take the body of Elizabeth and bring her before the next justice to find sufficient sureties to appear at the next Quarter Sessions next after her apprehension there to answer

to such matters as shall be objected against her on His Majesty's behalf concerning the misdemeanour. And after she shall be apprehended she is to keep and maintain her bastard at her own charges until the court of Sessions shall otherwise order the same. Given under the seal of office.

121. *Mr Francis Topp late Treasurer.* (Recites **103.** See also **87**)
It appears unto the court by the testimony of Mr Francis Bennett that Francis Topp gent heretofore Treasurer for maimed soldiers for the south has paid in to Mr Bennett the thirty nine pounds ten shillings and seven pence halfpenny remaining in his hands being the surplussage of his account. Ordered at the humble request of Topp that the several fines mentioned in the order made at the last Quarter Sessions and now openly read in court shall be discharged.

General Sessions of the Peace held at Devizes Tuesday after Easter 30 April 20 Charles (1644). Thomas Hall, Robert Eyre, Edward Ernle, William Wallis and Francis Swanton.

122. *Gabriell Goldney late Treasurer.*
Upon the confession of Mr Gabriell Goldney late Treasurer for the north that there is remaining in his hands upon his account the sum of £12 at the least. The court is informed that the master of the house of correction at Marlborough has due to him out of the north part of the county the sum of £3 6s 8d for his fee at Michaelmas last past. Also there is due to the hospital of East Harnham out of the north part the sum of £7 10s for one year and half ended this present Sessions. Ordered that Goldney shall pay upon sight hereof to the master of the house of correction at Marlborough the sum of £3 6s 8d and likewise to the hospital of East Harnham the sum of £7 10s and for the doing thereof this order shall be his discharge.

123. *John Marchant a maimed soldier.*
The court is informed by John Marchant the elder of Potterne that his son John Marchant the younger at Christmas last being then a servant and dwelling at Orcheston St. George was there impressed in the fight near Winchester by the treading of horses upon him so that he is utterly unable to work and get his maintenance and that his father is a very poor man and not able to relieve him. Ordered that Mr Francis Bennett shall forthwith pay unto Marchant the younger out of the stock of the county remaining in his hands for the relief of maimed soldiers the sum of forty shillings in regard of his great necessity.

124. *Easton Priory, Easton Warrens* [Easton], *James Whitehart and John Wyatt.*
It appears to the court that James Whitehart late tithingman of the tithing of Easton Priory and Easton Warrens deceased about three quarters of a year since whilst he was tithingman there and that since the death of Whitehart there has been no court kept for the hundred of Kinwardstone at which court the officer has been usually elected. The court is informed that by the custom of the place the office of right now falls upon John Wyatt. Ordered that John Wyatt shall be tithingman of Easton Priory and Easton Warrens in the place of Whitehart deceased. And Wyatt shall within one week next after notice of this order repair to the next justice to take his oath for the due execution of the office upon pain of ten pounds.
(If he refuses, to be bound over.)

125. *Milton Abbotts tithing* [Milton Lilbourne], *George Mortimer and Richard Peirce.*
It appears to the court by the petition of George Mortimer tithingman of Milton Abbotts that he has served in the office by the space of one whole year ended at Michaelmas last and that the leet and lawday court for the hundred of Kinwardstone has been of late neglected to be kept at which court the office has been usually elected. And that by the custom of the place the office goes from house to house which of right and custom now falls upon Richard Peirce who ought of right to undergo he office. Ordered that Richard Peirce shall be tithingman of Milton Abbotts in the place of Mortimer and that Peirce shall within one week next after notice thereof to him given repair to the next justice to take his oath for the due execution of the office upon pain of ten pounds.
(If he refuses, to be bound over.)

[Then follows a number of similarly worded entries for the appointment of tithingmen.]

126. *Easton Broadstock* [Bradenstoke] *tithing* [Easton], *James Mist and Francis Wise.*
James Mist has held the office for three years. To be replaced by Francis Wise.

127. *Down Pewsey tithing* [Pewsey], *Ralph Smyth and Walter Stratton.*
Ralph Smyth has held the office for one year. To be replaced by Walter Stratton.

(It was confirmed that the office of tithingman went from house to house and it was known what house should serve every year even though there was no election held. A1/110/1644E/62)

128. *Southcott tithing* [Pewsey], *Richard Winter and John Monday.*
Richard Winter to be replaced by John Monday.

129. *Kepnell tithing* [Pewsey], *Richard Bryne and John Alston.*
Richard Bryne to be replaced by John Alston.

130. *Wingfield tithing, Roger Hinton and William Baylie gent.*
Roger Hinton has held the office for one year. To be replaced by William Bayly gent.

131. *Marden tithing, William Lavington and William Holloway.*
William Lavington has held the office for two years. To be replaced by William Holloway.

132. *Colerne college tithing, John Jones and Thomas Greenway.*
John Jones has held the office for two years. To be replaced by Thomas Greenway.

133. *Somerford tithing* [Great and Little Somerford], *Thomas Alloway and John Merymonth.*
Thomas Alloway has held the office for one year. To be replaced by John Merymonth.

134. *Smithcott tithing* [Dauntsey], *Thomas Daye and John Spencer.*
Thomas Daye has held the office for one year. To be replaced by John Spencer.

135. *Atford tithing* [Atworth], *Robert Newman and George Street.*
Robert Newman to be replaced by George Street.

136. *Dauntsey tithing, William Skuce and Richard Pope.*
William Skuce to be replaced by Richard Pope.

137. *Burbage Turny* **[Sturmy]** *tithing* [Burbage], *Mary Rawlins.*
Mary Rawlins of Burbage Sturmy is ordered to find a tithingman for the tithing in the place of Thomas Piper. Further ordered that the tithingman shall repair to some justice in the tithing within one week to take his oath for the due execution of his office upon pain of twenty pounds.

138. *Elstub and Everleigh hundred, Thomas Hopkins and Thomas Bennett.*
At the last Sessions Thomas Hopkins of Stockton was elected constable of the hundred of Elstub and Everleigh in the place of Thomas Hart and in obedience unto the order then made Hopkins took upon him the office but now in open court Hopkins made oath that he had not above £10 per annum and can neither write nor read and therefore desired the court to discharge him of the office. The court conceiving Hopkins to be a very unfit man for that office orders that Thomas Bennett of Stockton shall be constable of the hundred in the place of Hopkins. And that he shall within one week next after notice of this order repair to the next justice to take his oath for the due execution of the office upon pain of £40.

139. *Elstub and Everleigh hundred, Richard Prater and Walter Stretch.*
The court is informed by Richard Prater constable of the hundred of Elstub and Everleigh that he was enforced by a party of horse to repair unto Sir Walter Smyth of Great Bedwyn justice to be sworn to execute the office of constable of the hundred by virtue of a warrant from the Lord Chief Justice as they pretended. And forasmuch as Prater has informed the court on his oath that his means is but £12 per annum and that he is above the age of seventy years and unfit and unable to execute the office. Ordered that Prater shall be discharged from the office and orders and appoints Walter Stretch of Fifield yeoman to be constable. Also ordered that Stretch shall within one week next after notice of this order to him given repair to some justice within or near the hundred there to take his oath for the due execution of his office upon pain of forty pounds.

140. *Bromham Liberty, John Webb and William Baylie.*
John Webb has been constable for 2 years and upwards. To be replaced by William Baylie.

141. *Bradford borough, John Smyth and Henry Plumpton.*
John Smyth of Bradford clothier was elected to be one of the constables of the borough of Bradford at the last Quarter Sessions and has been by the order of the court since sworn for the execution of the office. Now forasmuch as it appeared to the court by the information of Smyth that he is no way able to undergo the office and follow his trade in clothing and that unless he is discharged of the office he must give over his trade which would tend to the extraordinary damage of all those poor people which he now sets on work and on his promise to the court that he will follow the same trade and employ his work folks to

the utmost of his power and that Henry Plumpton of the borough is a man fit to execute the office. Ordered that Henry Plumpton shall be constable of the borough in the place of Smyth and that he shall within one week next after notice of this order to him given repair to the next justice to take his oath for the due execution of his office upon pain of twenty pounds.

(If he refuses, to be bound over.)

142. *South Damerham hundred, Richard Yardley and Oliver Horsey.*
Richard Yardley gent was at the last Sessions chosen constable of the hundred of South Damerham in the place of Oliver Horsey in regard that no court leet was the last year kept by the lord of the manor of Damerham at which court the constables have usually been elected which order was obtained and declared in defect of a court leet and that it should be in no prejudice to the lord of the manor. Also Richard Yardley before Robert Hyde and Richard Goddard justices on 16th day of January last past undertook that a leet should be kept within fourteen days after Easter last past and that then there should be a new constable chosen according to the usage of the court whereupon they declared and directed that the execution of the order touching the oath to be taken by Yardley for the office should be suspended until that time should be passed and in the meantime Oliver Horsey to execute the office, the order notwithstanding. And that in case there should be no court held and constable chosen then the order was to be pursued and Yardley to serve in the office. Now forasmuch as the court is informed by Mr Hyde of counsel with Yardley that Yardley has laboured to have had a court to be held for the manor according to his undertaking but could not yet procure the same but well hopes to get a court to be held before the twentieth day of May next and that Yardley being a tenant of sequestered lands unto the King's Majesty cannot without much prejudice execute the office and in case he cannot procure the court to be held Yardley desires, he procuring a sufficient man to undertake the office, that he may be excused thereof. The court respects the former orders until the twentieth day of the month of May next and that Horsey shall in the meantime execute the office and that in case Yardley shall not procure the court to be held before the 20th day of May and a new constable to be there elected and sworn or in default thereof shall not procure a sufficient man and such as some or one of the justices shall approve and allow of to be sworn for the due execution of the office, then the court further orders that the former orders shall in all things stand and be pursued anything in this present order notwithstanding.

143. *Trowbridge tithing, John Pickeringe and John Barton.*
John Pickeringe tithingman to be replaced by John Barton.

144. *Leigh and Woolley tithing, Anthonie Rogers and Richard Estcourt.*
Anthonie Rogers to be replaced by Richard Estcourt.

145. *William Barnes.*
William Barnes one of the inhabitants of Beechingstoke has at this Sessions appeared unto a presentment in the court against the inhabitants of Beechingstoke for default of the highways within the parish and has discharged the same presentment. Ordered that forthwith there shall be an indifferent rate made on the inhabitants for satisfying Barnes as well such fees as he has disbursed in the discharge of the presentment and the King's fine as all such charges and expenses as he has been at in the prosecution thereof.
(If any refuse to pay, to be bound over.)

146. *Pinnell constable of Calne hundred.*
The court is informed by Jefferie Pinnell one of the constables of the hundred of Calne that there are divers petty constables and churchwardens within the hundred who are behind in payment of the moneys for the relief of maimed soldiers and mariners, etc. and do deny the payment thereof. Ordered that the said moneys shall be demanded of the petty constables and churchwardens.
(If any refuse to pay, to be bound over.)

147. *William Gale constable of Malmesbury hundred.*
The court is informed by William Gale one of the constables of the hundred of Malmesbury that he has served in the office by the space of three whole years. Ordered that John Oven of Dauntsey shall be elected and chosen constable. The court is also informed that Gale has not collected and paid in such moneys for the relief of poor prisoners and for the relief of maimed soldiers as are due to the Treasurer out of his part of the hundred but has been negligent therein. The court desires Sir Theobald Gorges and Edward Hungerford or one of them to examine the truth thereof and if the constable be found faulty therein then he is to continue in his office until further order but if not faulty the justices are desired to send for Oven forthwith after examination and swear him constable of the hundred.
(If he refuses, to be bound over.)
Further ordered that if it should appear upon examination of Gale that the petty constables and churchwardens have refused or neglected the payment of the moneys due they shall be bound over.

148. *Malmesbury hundred constables, Jefferie Barnes and John Newman.*
Jefferie Barnes constable of the hundred has served for two years. To
be replaced by John Newman of Escott.
(Provision as in **147** if Barnes has not paid moneys in.)

149. *John Whittaker, Edward Moore, Phillipp Sutton.* (See also **274,
396, 686, 717**)
The court is informed by John Whittaker of Devizes, Edward Moore
and Phillipp Sutton of the same that on Monday the fifteenth day of this
instant April about one of the clock in the morning there happened a
fearful fire in Devizes beginning at the house of Edmond Burges and in
a short time burnt the house wherein Whittaker, Moone and Sutton
dwelt together with all their foods and household stuff amounting to
the sum of £24 or thereabouts viz of the goods of Whittaker to the
value of £14 or thereabouts, of Moone twenty nobles or thereabouts
and Sutton three pounds and ten shillings or thereabouts to their utter
undoing. The court is informed that divers of those who have been
Treasurers for the north have not given up their accounts and there
are divers moneys of the county's stock remaining in their hands. The
court commiserating the distressed estates of Whittaker, Moone and
Sutton and for the relieving of them desires Mr Norborne, Mr Duckett
and Mr Hungerford to call before them Mr William Sherston, Mr
Henry Graye, Mr Richard Jaques and the executors of John Sale all of
them late Treasurers for the north and to take their accounts and orders
that the Treasurers shall pay unto Michael Tidcombe of Devizes gent
forth of the moneys remaining in their hands of the surplussage of their
accounts the sum of ten pounds to remain in his hands until the court
shall be certified of the truth of the petitioners losses and if in case the
petitioners be true the court orders that the £10 be proportionately
paid unto the petitioners according unto their several losses. Further
ordered that the residue of the surplussages shall be paid unto the Clerk
of the Peace at the next Quarter Sessions to remain in his hands to be
disposed by the court for the use of the county.
(If Treasurers refuse, to be bound over.)
(It was explained that the houses in that part of Devizes were old and
thatched and the time was very dry. The fire ran swiftly from house to
house and within three hours seven tenements had been burnt down. The
petitioners had not actually lost their own houses but had lost all their goods.
A1/110/1644E/68)

150. *Edward Tidcombe and Thomas Dick.*
The court is informed by Mr Edward Tidcombe late one of the

constables of the hundred of Swanborough that Thomas Dick his fellow constable has not paid the moneys which he promised in court the last Michaelmas Quarter Sessions payable from Dick for the relief of poor prisoners out of his part of the hundred. Ordered that if Dick does not pay the same to Tidcombe within short time after sight of this order he is to be bound over.

151. *Margaret Fry and Woodford inhabitants.* (Recites **107**. See also **102**)
Now the court is informed that the overseers have not paid the 12d per week and the arrears according to the order. Now ordered that they shall be bound over to the next Sessions. Further ordered that the bastard child shall be forthwith sent to Woodford according to the last order unless they pay the said 12d a week.

152. *Mr John Ferris.*
The court was this day informed by the account of John Ferris clerk guardian to Thomas Ferris and Charles Ferris executors of Leonard Ferris gent deceased late Treasurer that divers constables of hundreds are behind in paying in of such moneys as are due from them to the Treasurer by means whereof John Ferris cannot make a perfect account of the office as by the particulars thereof hereunto annexed more plainly appears. The court desires Edward Hungerford justice to call before him as well John Ferris as also all such constables as are mentioned in the account to be in arrear and examine the account. And if upon the constable's account any petty constables and churchwardens shall be in arrears and omitted the payment of his and their part and portion unto the constables then Hungerford is further desired to bind over all such high constables, petty constables and churchwardens as he shall find to be faulty and negligent in not collecting and paying in of their proportionable parts due from them and Hungerford is also desired to certify the court at the next Sessions the remissness as well of the constables of the hundreds as of the petty constables and churchwardens.

Mr Ferris account. The account of John Ferris clerk guardian to Thomas Ferris and Charles Ferris executors of Leonard Ferris deceased late Treasurer for the north 1642 during the time that Leonard Ferris was in office.

Receipts	£	s.	d.
Henry Stevens and Stephen Hyde constables			
Kinwardstone	1	8	2
Robert Webb and Thomas Smyth constables			
Selkley	1	1	8
David Shewring constable North Damerham	0	17	4
Richard Terrell alias Maditch and Robert			
Jenkins constables Chippenham	6	9	4
Jefferie Pynnell and John Reynolds constables			
Calne	1	3	10
Robert Banks constable Ramsbury	0	2	6
Robert Hippsly and Robert Pyke constables			
Highworth, Cricklade and Staple	1	16	10
Antonie Kemm and Edward Haggard constables			
Kingsbridge	1	0	8
Total sum	9	14	4

Disbursements. The several sums of money paid by
the hands of Leonard Ferris Treasurer 1642
in the north part of the county.

	£	s.	d.
Paid to John Purrier and Edward Webb			
October 4th 1642 masters of the two houses			
of correction of Devizes and Marlborough	5	12	4
Paid to William Crome October 5th 1642 for			
the hospital of East Harnham otherwise			
called the Spittle	2	10	0
Item paid to the overseers of the poor and church-			
wardens of Standen [in Chute] October 5th			
1642 towards the maintenance of John Peter			
by virtue of an order made at the			
Sessions held at Marlborough 17 Charles	1	13	4
	9	15	8

Arrears. The several constables of the hundreds in the
north part of the county that are behind
in payment of their several sums of money
to the Treasurer for the year 1642.

	£	s.	d.
Henry Seymour and Stephen Hyde Kinwardstone	1	8	2
Robert Webb and Thomas Smyth Selkley	1	1	8
David Shrewring North Damerham	0	17	4
Richard Terrell alias Maditch and Robert Jenkins			
Chippenham	6	9	4
Jefferie Pynnell and John Reynold Calne	1	3	10
Robert Banks Ramsbury	0	2	6

Robert Hippsly and Robert Pyke Highworth	1	18	10
Antonie Kemm and Edward Haggard Kingsbridge	1	0	8
William Trymnell and William Chappell Potterne			
and Cannings	1	2	0
Thomas Pike and Edward Tidcombe Swan-			
borough the first half year	2	3	10
Edward Tidcombe and Thomas Pike the last half			
of the year	2	3	10
John Bryant and John Osdall borough of Devizes	0	10	0
Jefferie Barnes and William Gale Malmesbury	9	6	8
To receiving	29	6	8
Total sum received	9	14	4
Total sum paid out	9	15	8
Total of the arrears	29	6	8

John Ferris clerk

(Shewring had previously explained that the hundred of North Damerham was very small with only four parishes and the office of constable went from parish to parish. He had served as constable for two years, the first for Nettleton and he was willing for the second year to count for Grittleton as it was a poor parish with no one in it fit for the office. It was now the turn of Christian Malford. A1/110/1644E/69)

153. Chosen to be Treasurers for the year following:
    North: Benedick Browne of Calne, gent
    South: Richard Awbrey of Chalke, gent
Ordered by the justices at this present Sessions assembled that the rates shall remain and continue as they were the last year viz so as for every parish throughout the county there may be levied and paid three pence weekly and not above the several rates of every parish to be proportioned and set down by the justices of every division respectively according to their good discretion and by them to be delivered over to the new Treasurers before the next Sessions.
For the relief of prisoners, hospitals, etc.:
    North: Roger Cawley of Hilmarton, gent
    South: Thomas Poore of East Harnham, gent
[Rate as above but one penny weekly and not above.]

General Sessions of the Peace held at Warminster 16 July 20 Charles (1644). John Topp and Francis Swanton.

154. *Thomas Crouch, Edith Crouch.*
The court is informed by Edith Crouch of Upton Lovell widow that Thomas Crouch her son was heretofore impressed a soldier in His Majesty's service from Upton Lovell and was maimed in the service and is now remaining with her at Upton Lovell where she has kept him at her own charge by the space of fourteen weeks she being but a poor woman. Ordered that the overseers of the poor of Upton Lovell shall from henceforth keep and relieve Thomas until the court shall think fit to allow unto him a pension out of the Treasury of the county for maimed soldiers. Further ordered that Mr Francis Bennett shall forthwith pay unto Edith the sum of forty shillings out of the surplussage of former Treasurers' accounts remaining in his hands in regard of her great necessity.

155. *John Phillipps, William Phillipps.*
At the last Quarter Sessions there was a recognisance certified into the court against William Phillipps to appear at the next Sessions after the birth of a bastard child begotten on the body of Ellen Gane. And whereas Phillipps being then called did not appear neither did it appear to the court that Ellen was delivered of the child whereupon the court thought fit to respect the default of the recognisance until the next Sessions. And whereas at this present Sessions John Phillipps father of William appeared in court on behalf of his son and alleged that his son was a soldier in His Majesty's service whereby he could not appear and that Ellen was delivered of her child and that he knew not where his son was and that he would endeavour to bring him in at the next Sessions. Ordered that the recognisance shall be further respected until the next Sessions and that John shall be bound to the next Sessions and then to bring forth his son or prove that he is then in His Majesty's service. Further ordered that in the meantime John shall attend two justices for their warrant to apprehend Ellen and bring her before them to be examined concerning the reputed father of her bastard and the justices are desired to send for her and such witnesses as shall be pertinent to discover the truth of the matter and make such order therein as shall be agreeable to law and justice. And if upon examination of the matter it shall appear that William is the reputed father of the bastard then John is to give security to perform such order as the justices shall make therein and the order is to be returned to the next Quarter Sessions.

156.   *Little Woodford, Richard Mackerrell and William Davis.*
The court is informed by Richard Mackerrell tithingman of Little
Woodford that by reason the lord of the manor of Little Woodford
has neglected the keeping of the leet and lawday he has been enforced
to serve tithingman longer than of right and by custom he ought to
have done and that by custom and course William Davis of Woodford
should have sworn tithingman in the place of Richard at Our Lady
day last. Ordered that William Davis should be tithingman of Little
Woodford in the place of Mackerrell and that William should within
one week next after notice of this order to him given repair to the
next justice to take his oath for the due execution of the office upon
pain of ten pounds.
     (If he refuses, to be bound over.)

1646

General Sessions of the Peace held at Warminster 14 July 22 Charles (1646). William Hussey, William Eyre, Edward Tooker, Thomas Bennett, George Ivy.

157.   *No constables of hundreds to be discharged until they have paid in their
moneys to the Treasurer.*
The moneys for relief of maimed soldiers etc remain due and
uncollected in most of the parishes within the county by means
whereof the several constables of hundreds have not paid the same into
the several Treasurers for the time as they have been constables. And
for that the churchwardens and petty constables in every parish who
ought by the statute to collect the moneys and pay the same over to
the constables of their hundreds have not collected the moneys and
pay the same but do slight and neglect the collecting thereof. Ordered
that no constables of hundreds be discharged of their office until they
have paid unto the several Treasurers the moneys due for both the
collections in their time of constableship. Further ordered that if the
churchwardens and constables in any parish shall not forthwith pay the
same in unto the constables of their several hundreds upon demand
thereof to be made, then they are to be bound over.

158.   *Watches to be duly kept in every parish.*
By reason of these troublesome and dangerous times there are divers
thieves, rogues and other malefactors suspicious and dangerous persons
wandering about the country by whom divers felonies, offences and
misdemeanours have been of late and daily are committed and yet

they escape and pass away without punishment or questioning for want of watchers and wards which should be kept in the country for preservation whereof for time to come. Ordered that the constables and tithingmen of every hundred town and village within this county warn and take care that the inhabitants of every parish and tithing shall from henceforth until further order given to the contrary keep constant watches and wards in the several towns and villages and at the bridges, crossways and other needful places both by night and by day within the same country where watches and wards have been usually kept upon other occasions. And that such watch and watchmen apprehend all wandering soldiers and mariners, rogues, vagabonds and suspicious persons that they shall meet with who cannot give good account of their travel and having apprehended them bring them before the head constable or chief officer of the town hundred or liberty where such dangerous persons shall be apprehended to be examined. And if there shall be cause to be brought before one of His Majesty's justices by him to be sent to the prison or otherwise ordered according to the law. And that every town and village neglecting their duty in performing the premises shall forfeit forty shillings and every person neglecting his duty in watching upon summons shall forfeit ten shillings for every default and the same watches and wards are to be kept and performed either by the householders in person or supplied by such able men as they will be answerable for.

159. *Alehouses suppressed throughout the county.*
The court taking into consideration the manifold abuses inconveniences and mischief which arises by reason of the multiplicity of alehouses in this county orders that all the alehouses within this county shall be and are suppressed.

Ordered that no alehouse keepers shall be hereafter licensed but such as the justices shall think fit upon the certificate testimonial and desire of most of the chief inhabitants and the constables of the place where such alehouse keeper desiring such licence shall inhabit and dwell.

160. The court is informed by the several petitions of the inhabitants of Fugglestone and Quidhampton that by reason of the contagiousness and infection of the plague now amongst them the inhabitants there are not able of themselves to relieve the persons infected and other poor people within their parish by reason of their poverty but desired the relief and assistance of other the neighbouring parishes adjoining. The court taking the miserable conditions of the poor inhabitants of the parish of Fugglestone and the tithing of Quidhampton by reason of the infections into consideration orders according to the statute that all and every the parishes and places hereunder named being within the compass of five miles of Fugglestone be rated and taxed towards the payment of three pounds by the week for and towards the relief of the infected persons and poor people of Fugglestone and Quidhampton. The court requires the several constables and persons hereunder named equally and indifferently to tax and assess the inhabitants of the several parishes and places hereunder mentioned for the raising of the weekly sum of three pounds the same to continue until the next Assizes to be held for the county and then to be altered or continued as the justices shall see cause. And that Henry Blake constable of the hundred of Branch and Dole to receive the tax and dispose thereof for the relief of the infected people of Fugglestone and Quidhampton.

161. *Ann Gunston apprentice to Grace Pulley.*
The court is informed that Ann Gunston the daughter of Ann Gunston of Corsley being a poor child and fit to be put forth an apprentice and having lived with Grace Pulley of Chapmanslade for two years last past with whom Ann is to be bound apprentice and Gunston is likewise contented to take Ann as an apprentice. Ordered that the churchwardens and overseers of the parish of Corsley forthwith bind Ann apprentice with Grace until she shall come to the age of one and twenty years.

162. *Richard Anley and others of Bradford.*
The court is informed by Richard Anley, Robert Baylie, Francis Yerbury, William Bayley of Bradford and Jane Rogers widow that Richard Anley in the time of the infectious disease of the plague within the town of Bradford delivered so much ware for the use of the infected as amounted unto the sum of six pounds eight shillings and six pence, Francis Yerbury as much bread to the sick as amounted to the sum of thirty six shillings, Robert Baylie as much bread to the sick as amounted to twenty shillings and nine pence, William Bayley as much butcher meat to the sick as amounted unto thirty shillings six pence and Jane Rogers widow as much bread as amounted to thirty seven shillings and two pence and never received any recompense for the same. Ordered that the matter be referred to the consideration of the two next justices who are desired to call the petitioners before them and examine the truth of the petitions and take such course for the petitioners relief therein as shall be agreeable to law and justice.

163. *Edward Dick.*
The court is informed by Edward Dick heretofore portreeve of the

town and borough of Bradford that about three years last past he was commanded by Sir Edward Hungerford and other justices for to keep watch and ward in the cold winter time and was enforced to buy wood coals and candle for the watch as much as amounts unto the sum of forty three shillings eight pence and that he could never be paid by the town any part of his charge although promised by the constables and allowed of by the justices for to have the same. Ordered that the matter shall be referred to the consideration of the two next justices unto Bradford who are desired to call the petitioner before them and examine the truth of the petitioner and take such course for the petitioner's relief therein as shall be agreeable to law and justice.

164. *Elianor Parsons.*
Upon hearing of the matter complained of by Elianor Parsons against Edward Croome her master and upon consideration had of the indentures of apprenticeship. Ordered that Croome pay unto Elianor his servant the ten shillings mentioned in the indenture and give her double and apparel.
(If he refuses, to be bound over.)

165. *Jeffery Hellier.*
The court is informed by Jeffery Hellier of Warminster that he lived a covenant servant with William Sydnall late of Warminster deceased until his wages amounted unto thirty shillings who promised to make payment thereof and died intestate without paying the same after whose death Ann Payne wife of William Payne sued forth letters of administration of the goods of the deceased but still refuses to pay unto Jefferie his wages. It is agreed by them that Ann shall pay twenty shillings by two shillings six pence a week in full satisfaction of the thirty six shillings the first payment to begin on Monday next.
(If she refuses, to be bound over.)

166. *West Knoyle inhabitants.*
The court is informed by Mr Hyde counsel with the inhabitants of West Knoyle that William Willoughbye one of the inhabitants of that place has always heretofore borne the third part against the whole parish in all rates and payments for his demesnes valued at three hundred pounds per annum and that he has an impropriate parsonage some other means in the same parish to the value of six score pounds per annum and upwards besides his old rents which are of a great value for all which he refuses to be rated. Ordered upon hearing of the matter and the allegations of Willoughby's son present in the behalf of his father that the parishioners shall meet together and make an equal and

indifferent rate over the whole parish and that they shall give notice to old Mr Willoughby of such their meeting who is desired to be present at the rate making but if he shall refuse to come or dissent thereunto then the parishioners are to attend the two next justices with their rate who are desired to examine the same and if they find it to be just and equal then they are desired to confirm it or else to alter it as they shall think fit upon hearing of the parties interested in the same rate.

167. *Woolston Foster.*

Woolston Foster of Mere the younger has made complaint at this Sessions that his father Thomas Foster late of Mere deceased being about two years since constable of the town of Mere and that during his constableship he had disbursed for the town and the inhabitants thereof the sum of twenty two pounds whereof he accounted to the parish and the parish was allowing thereof. But Thomas shortly afterwards dying before he was paid the twenty two pounds whereupon Woolston his son suing for the letters of administration and having demanded the twenty two pounds from the inhabitants of Mere they in a slighting way neglect and refuse the payment thereof. Ordered that the now constables of Mere with some of the inhabitants there upon sight of this order cause a rate to be made within the parish for payment of the twenty two pounds and forthwith collect and gather the same and make payment thereof to Woolston without further delay or otherwise show good cause for the contrary at the next Sessions.

168. *Richard Harry.*

The court is informed by Richard Harry of Burton Hill that about two years and a half since he being hired as the tithingman for the tithing of Burton Hill in the hundred of Malmesbury for one year has divers times since the year ended endeavoured to be freed from the office but cannot and is yet continued therein to his great charge and trouble. Ordered that Harry shall be discharged of his office and nomination and appoints John Bleeke of the tithing of Burton Hill to serve as tithingman there in the place of Harry for one year. Further ordered that Bleeke shall repair to the next justice within one week after the receipt of this order to take his oath for the due execution of the office on pain of five pounds.

169. *Lawrence Boulter.*

Upon the petition of Lawrence Boulter and the certificate of the inhabitants of Swallowcliff the court is informed that Boulter is a poor man and not able to maintain himself and family and did in the life time of his wife receive a sister's child of five years of age and twenty shillings in money with her of the parish of Dinton for the keeping of her until such time as either Boulter or his wife should die since which time Boulter's wife is dead Boulter is not able to undergo the charge of keeping of the child. It appears to the court that John Mogridge an overseer of the poor of Dinton was a means for placing of the child with Boulter at Swallowcliff of purpose to lay the charge of keeping the child on the parish of Swallowcliff and to free the parish of Dinton from the same. The court desires the next justice to send for Mogridge and John Shepperd of Dinton and examine the contents of the petition and if he finds the petition to be true then the court orders that Mogridge shall pay unto Boulter such weekly pay for the keeping of the child as the justices shall think fit. And if Mogridge refuse the payment of the same then the child is to be sent to Dinton to be provided for as a poor of that parish.

170. *Jeffery Barnes constable of hundred of Malmesbury.*
The court is informed by Jeffery Barnes one of the constables of the hundred of Malmesbury that he has served constable by the space of four years and upwards to his great loss and prejudice and desires the court to release him of his office. The court desires Charles Gore and George Ivy justices to examine the accounts of Barnes concerning the collection of relief of maimed soldiers etc. and if they find that Barnes has levied his accounts then the court further desires the justices to elect one of those whose names are under written or one other whom they think fit to serve constable in the place of Barnes.
[Similar entry relating to John Oven having served as constable for two years and upwards.]
Jeremy Goodwyn   Robert Hort   Leonard Atkins

171. *Thomas White.*
The court is informed by Thomas White that he keeping a tavern in Potterne about three years since Sir William Waller coming to the petitioner's house required the officers of the same place to take up for the Parliament service from the petitioner as much beer strong water and sack as come to the sum of twelve pounds or near thereabout and carried the same to a place called Roundway Hill with promise to pay for the same since which time the same has been demanded but the petitioner cannot receive any satisfaction from the officers by reason of the backwardness of the parishioners who refuse to contribute towards the same. The court desires the justices of that division or some of them to take the petitioner into their consideration and examine the truth of the petitioner and if they shall see cause they are desired to take such order therein for the petitioner's relief as to law and justice shall appertain.

172. *Thomas Hanniball and others of Mere.* (See also **839**)
The court is informed by Thomas Hanniball, Alexander Stronge, James Trasye, Phelip Hill and Roger Forward poor craftsmen of the town and parish of Mere about three years since they were set on work by the parishioners of Mere for the new building of a cottage there for Christopher Acrigge who had his house burnt by misfortune of fire and not able to new build the same their work about the building of the cottage amounting in all to the sum of five pounds and some odd moneys as by their work will appear and that the inhabitants have not yet paid the same. The court advises the parishioners of Mere to meet together and to make a rate for the payment of the poor men that this court be not further troubled therein.

173. *John Rogers apprentice to Thomas Harris.*
It appears to the court upon complaint of John Rogers apprentice unto Thomas Harris of Warminster range weaver that Rogers has received divers abuses and hard usage from Harris in the time of his apprenticeship and prayed the court that he might be discharges from his master. Ordered by the court upon hearing of the difference between the parties and with the consent of Harris that Rogers shall be discharged of his apprenticeship. In witness whereof the justices assembled at the Sessions have hereunto set their hands and seals the day and year above said.

(Harris made 'ranges' i.e. sieves. Rogers was to be paid for weaving every dozen plain range bottoms 14d, every dozen twilly bottoms 20d, every dozen trainer bottoms 12d and for setting up every dozen ranges 6d; Harris had to find the hair and tackling. The main issue was that Rogers was impressed into the Parliamentary army before he finished his apprenticeship. When he came back two years later, Harris refused to accept him. A1/110/1646T/144)

174. *Thomas Hanniball.*
The court is informed by Thomas Hanniball of Mere that Jasper Coward and Henry Clarke constables of the hundred of Mere did take from Hanniball two hundred cheese at the price of sixteen shillings a hundred and commanded him to carry the same with his three horses to Faringdon near Oxford for His Majesty's provision. And that he and his three horses were wanting from his house eight days and for which travail the constables had promised him like payment as others which they hired for the like travail and paid them but not Hanniball to his great losses he being a very poor man and craving only twelve pence per day a piece for himself and his three horses. The court desires the two next justices unto Mere to call the parties before them

and to examine the truth of the matter and to do therein according to law and justice.

(Hanniball was originally a mason but, because there was little work during the period of the war, he had taken to buying cheeses and selling them from market to market. A1/110/1646T/169)

175. *Inhabitants of Devizes.* (See also **192**)
The court is informed by Mr Hyde counsel with the inhabitants of Devizes that the inhabitants of that place are much impoverished by relieving of the infected people during the time that the sickness of the plague remained in that place in regard the adjacent villages towns parishes and other places within five miles compass have not collected and paid in their several rates for relief of the same poor infected people. Ordered that the consideration thereof shall be referred to Sir John Ernle and William Eyre justices who are desired to call before them all constables collectors and all other officers formerly appointed to collect and gather the rates within five miles compass for the relief of the poor infected people of Devizes who are hereby required to attend the justices with their rates (except the officers within the parish of Potterne). And the justices are also desired to examine what moneys have been paid upon the rates and what moneys are in the constables and collectors and other officers hands not paid over for the relief and what moneys are in arrear and uncollected on the rates and also examine what moneys have been expended by the inhabitants of Devizes for the relief of their poor infected people and what moneys are justly due unto them concerning the same. And it is further ordered that the moneys collected and remaining in the constables hands shall be forthwith paid over unto such officers in Devizes who have laid out more money about the relief then they have received at the discretion and appointment of the justices and if such moneys will not satisfy the officers their just demands therein then the justices are desired to grant forthwith their warrants for the levying of the arrears on the rates and to do further therein as to law and justice shall appertain.

176. *Edward Yates, Robert Huggins.*
The court is informed by Edward Yates and Robert Huggins constables of Malmesbury in the year 1642 that they were enforced the same year to lay out and engage themselves for divers sums of money to several persons there amounting in the whole to the sum of thirty pounds at the least and that for a great part thereof they are often threatened to be sued which money was disbursed watching and warding, for arms for trained soldiers and mending of other arms, for attendance on prisoners and carrying others to prison and for divers other occasions.

Ordered for the relief of the petitioners that the matter be referred to the consideration of Charles Gore and George Ivy justices who are desired to examine the truth of the petition and take such order therein for the petitioners relief as to law and justice shall appertain.

177. *Edward Bull.* (See also **210, 246, 272, 324**)
Complaint has been made to the court by Edward Bull marshal of the garrison at Malmesbury that divers prisoners have been committed to his charge and custody for felonies and other misdemeanours which did properly belong to the gaoler of the county for the keeping of which prisoners Bull has been at great charge and has had not allowance from the county for the same. The court desires that Charles Gore and George Ivy examine the premisses and the time of the taking unto prisons and the time of discharging of the prisoners and to allow such reasonable allowance to Bull as they shall think fit and order the payment thereof to be made by the Treasurer for the north.

178. *Benedict Browne, Treasurer.*
The court is informed by Benedict Browne gent Treasurer for the north part of the county that all constables of hundreds are behind in payment to him the moneys due out of the several hundreds for the said relief and do slight the payment of the same when they are demanded. And that the churchwardens are also negligent in paying in the same to the constables as he is informed whereby poor pensioners go away unsatisfied therein to their impoverishment and loss. Ordered that if any of he constables in the north part of the county shall not forthwith on sight of this order collect and gather all such moneys due out of their several hundreds towards the said relief and pay in the same to the Treasurer that he pensioners may be satisfied.
[Same order for churchwardens.]
(If any refuse to pay, to be bound over.)

179. *Constables, churchwardens and overseers of Malmesbury.*
Complaint has been made to the court by the constables churchwardens and overseers of the poor of Malmesbury for the year 1642 that they have disbursed out of their own purses and are engaged to divers persons in the borough for provision for the poor people which were then infected with the pestilence and other the poor there divers sums of money more than they have received. And whereas there was allowed weekly the sum of thirty pounds to be collected within the several parishes within five miles next adjoining to the borough and parish of Malmesbury for the relief of the infected persons and other poor people there. The court is informed that divers of the constables

of the parishes are behind in their weekly payment of thirty pounds and that the sum of ninety pounds and upwards remains unsatisfied and unpaid unto them which they were to receive of the weekly pay of thirty pounds. Ordered that the constables churchwardens and overseers of Malmesbury shall make up their accounts both of their receipts and of their disbursements and shall attend Mr William Eyre , Mr Gore and Mr Ivy or any two of them who are desired to consider of the said account and also of the former orders and warrants in that business and to call before them the several constables and such others as they shall think fit and examine the premises and order and relieve the constables churchwardens and overseers as they shall see cause.

(The overseers should have received £180 12s 6d for the first six weeks but received only £87 17s 2d leaving £92 15s 4d to be paid

Hundred	Levy			Paid			Owing		
Malmesbury	80	0	0	76	13	8	3	6	4
Chippenham	49	15	10	7	14	0	2	1	10
Kingsbridge	20	0	0	0	0	0	20	0	0
Highworth	17	10	0	3	9	6	14	0	6
Damerham North	13	6	8	0	0	0	13	6	8
	180	0	0	87	17	2	92	15	0

A1/110/1646T)

180. *Robert Pope.*
The court is informed by a certificate under the hands of Robert Longe and Ambrose Hunt overseers of the poor of Potterne during the time the same place was infected with the plague that Roger Pope then the tithingman of Potterne in the time of the sickness laid forth seven pounds and nine shillings for beer and tobacco to relieve the then infected people and that he is yet unsatisfied the same and that there is moneys uncollected on the rate made for the relief of the infected people. Ordered that the arrears of the rate shall be forthwith collected and the sum of seven pounds and nine shillings shall be paid unto Pope out of the same. And if any person rated shall refuse to pay their rates then the two next justices are desired to grant forth their warrants for levying the same.

181. *Radigan Crandon.*
The court is informed by Radigan Crandon of Westbury widow that there are divers controversies and fallings out between Radigan and John Amiatt of Westbury about turning of a watercourse into her backside with violence and that Amiatt threatens to beat and kill her and her cattle. Ordered that the constables of the hundred or town of Westbury carry Amiatt before the next justice who is desired to

examine the truth of the matter and bind Amiatt to the peace if he shall find cause or to do further therein as to law and justice shall appertain.

182. *Overseers of Purton.* (See also **193**)
The court is informed by John Elborowe and Richard Gleed overseers of the poor of Purton that by former orders of the court there has been yearly allowed unto the overseers towards the relief of the poor people there out of the parish of Blunsdon [St Andrew] the sum of five pounds and five shillings. And that Alexander Cleeve a tenant unto the Lord Lovelace is behind in arrears seven pounds seventeen shillings and six pence for one year and half towards the yearly pay of five pounds and five shillings. Ordered that Cleeve shall forthwith pay unto the overseers the arrears and that the yearly pay of five pounds and five shillings be from henceforth paid by the inhabitants unto the overseers of Purton for the time being according to the former orders until the inhabitants of Blunsdon shall show good cause to the contrary. (Purton was described as being a very poor place and there were no poor at all at Blunsdon). A1/110/1646T/140)

183. *Overseers of St James Chapel Bishops Cannings.*
The court is informed by Thomas Ruddle and Roger Wheeler overseers of the poor of the several tithings belonging to the chapel of St James [Southbroom] within the parish of Bishops Cannings that they have been kept in their office three years and upwards during which time they have laid out thirty pounds of their own moneys and above in relieving the poor of those tithings and that they can gather no moneys upon their rates every parishioner utterly refusing to pay towards the relief of the poor there. Ordered that the churchwardens and overseers of that place together with the minister of Bishops Cannings calling unto them some of the sufficient inhabitants of that place shall forthwith make an indifferent rate on the inhabitants of the tithings for the repayment of the thirty pounds and the rate is to be presented to the two next justices to be confirmed by them.

184. *Henry Langfyer.*
Henry Langfyer of Lyneham has made complaint that he has served in the office of a tithingman both for Lyneham and Preston above three quarters of a year longer than he ought of right to do. Ordered that election be forthwith made of other fitting men both for Lyneham and Preston according to the ancient custom and usage. And that such persons so to be elected do within one week after such election repair to the next justice to take their oaths upon pain of ten pounds to him that shall make default therein.

185. *Clerk of the Peace to make forth his warrant against persons presented.* It is thought fit and so ordered that the Clerk of the Peace shall send forth warrants under his hand and seal of office against all persons presented at this Sessions and shall direct the same warrants to the constables of such hundreds and liberties wherein the persons presented shall inhabit and dwell requiring them in His Majesty's name to apprehend and take the bodies of such persons and bring them before the next justice to find sufficient sureties to appear at the next Quarter Sessions there to answer to all such matters and offences whereof they stand presented. And if the same parties or any of them shall refuse to do the same then the justice is desired to send such party or parties so refusing to His Majesty's gaol at Fisherton Anger there to remain until they shall willingly do the same. Further ordered that the Clerk of the Peace shall hereafter by virtue of this order grant out warrants against all persons presented at any Quarter Sessions hereafter to be held according to the manner and form before on this order mentioned and expressed without expecting any further order to be made in this behalf.

General Sessions of the Peace held at Marlborough 6 October 22 Charles (1646). Anthony Ashley Cooper, Edward Tooker, William Eyre, William Hussey, George Howe, Thomas Bennett, George Ivy and Francis Swanton.

186. *Inhabitants of Wilton, Fisherton, Maiden Bradley and Horningsham.* The court is informed by the mayor, aldermen and other inhabitants of the borough of Wilton as also by the petitions and complaints of the inhabitants of the several parishes of Fisherton Anger, Maiden Bradley and Horningsham being infected with the noisome and contagious disease of the plague so that they are not able to relieve the infected persons there and other the poor people of the parishes occasioned by reason of the infection and prayed the assistance and help of the court. And as concerning the infection in Fisherton Anger which God be praised it is hoped that place being in reasonable health and condition except such as are yet at the pesthouse who if let go among fresh people are likely to endanger them again and increase the infection. And therefore prayed the court that course may be taken that the arrears of the rate formerly granted them within five miles compass being £49 5s 5d may be satisfied and that order may be taken for them until they shall be thought fit to come to their houses which the court orders accordingly and desires Mr Edward Tooker and Mr Francis Swanton justices to appoint them such further allowance and for such time as they shall think fit. Ordered that there shall be raised throughout the county the sum of one hundred marks weekly as well for and towards the relief and maintenance of the poor infected persons and places as for watching and warding in all the places infected (that is to say for the borough of Wilton the sum of thirty five pounds weekly and for the poor of Fisherton Anger the sum of £13 6s 8d or any lesser sum as the justices shall think fit and for the relief of the poor infected people of the parishes of Maiden Bradley and Horningsham the sum of £13 6s 8d weekly) which weekly sum of one hundred marks is to be raised in the several hundreds according to the rates and proportions to be set upon each hundred by Mr Tooker and Mr Swanton to commence from the sixth day of October being the first day of this present Sessions and continue until the next Quarter Sessions unless the infections shall in the meant time cease. And what shall remain of the rate of one hundred marks per week undisposed of by this order shall be retained in the receivers hands hereafter named until the justices shall dispose thereof to the like use. And the court nominates and appoints Christopher Bell of Wilton gent, William Able of the same gent and George Sadler of the same gent or either of them to be receivers of the weekly payment of one hundred marks who are to pay over weekly to each of the several places and parishes infected the several sums allotted them by this order. Further ordered that all the constables of the hundreds within the county shall forthwith make out their warrants to all petty constables and to tithingmen within their hundreds as well for the raising of all such weekly payments within their hundreds to the use aforesaid as for the collecting and paying in of the same to the receivers monthly by virtue of this order. And in all places within the county rated towards this payment where there is neither petty constable or tithingman there the constables of the hundred shall collect the same. And all persons refusing to pay their rates are to be distrained by their goods for the same by warrant of two justices. Ordered the receiver to account monthly before Mr Tooker and Mr Swanton of the receipts and payments concerning that matter. And if it shall please Almighty God to cease the infection in all or any of the places infected before the next Quarter Sessions then Mr Tooker and Mr Swanton upon information thereof given unto them are desired to take such course for the cessation of the weekly payment as they in their discretion shall think fit. And last of all the court desires all the justices to further the execution of this order. And all constables of hundreds and other officers herein interested are hereby required carefully to execute their offices herein as they will answer the contrary at their peril. And all the receivers are hereby required to be earnest and careful in the prosecution of this order that all places and persons infected may be speedily relieved and the county cured by God's mercy from all future danger concerning that matter. And all the rates and taxes made therein are to be certified to the next Quarter Sessions.

(At Michaelmas, Wilton said they had been infected with the plague for the last five months with about 30 houses affected. A1/110/1646M)

187. *Edward Yates and Robert Huggins constables of Malmesbury.* (See also **225**)
The court is informed by Edward Yates and Robert Huggins constables of Malmesbury in the year 1642 that they were enforced the same year to lay out and engage themselves for divers sums of money to several persons there amounting in the whole to the sum of thirty pounds at the least and that for a great part thereof they are often threatened to be sued which money was disbursed for watching and warding, for arms for trained soldiers and mending of other arms, for attendance on prisoners and carrying others to prison and divers other occasions. Ordered for the relief of the petitioners that the matter shall be referred to the consideration of William Eyre, Charles Gore and George Ivy justices who are desired to examine the truth of the petition and take such order therein for the petitioners relief as to law and justice shall appertain.

188. *Constables, churchwardens and overseers of Malmesbury.* (See also **224**)
Complaint has been made by the constables churchwardens and overseers of the poor of Malmesbury for the year 1642 that they have disbursed out of their own purses and are engaged to divers persons in the borough for the provision for the poor people which were then infected with the pestilence and other the poor there divers sums of money more than they have received. And whereas there was allowed weekly the sum of thirty pounds to be collected within the several parishes within five miles next adjoining to the borough and parish of Malmesbury for the better relief of the infected person and other poor people there according to the form of the statute in that case made. And forasmuch as the court is informed that divers of the constables of the parishes are behind in their weekly payment of thirty pounds and that the sum of thirty pounds and upwards remains unsatisfied and unpaid unto them which they were to receive of the weekly pay of £30. Ordered that the constables churchwardens and overseers of Malmesbury shall make up their accounts both for their receipts and of their disbursements and shall attend Mr Eyre, Mr Gore and Mr Ivy who are desired to consider of the account and also of the former orders and warrants in that business and to call before them the several

constables of the several parishes and places in arrear and all such others as they shall think fit and examine the premises and order and relieve the constables, etc of Malmesbury as they shall see cause.

189. £30 of Calne money in Mr Bennett's hands to be paid to Wilton. The court is informed that the poor people of the borough of Wilton now grievously infected with the plague are in exceeding great necessity for want of present relief and maintenance. Ordered that Mr Francis Bennett shall forthwith pay unto Mr Christopher Bell, Mr William Abell and Mr George Sadler of Wilton to the use of the poor infected people of that place the sum of thirty pounds out of the moneys remaining in his hands called Calne money.

190. *Mrs Webb to find a tithingman in the place of Robert Michell for Wroughton.*
The court is informed that Robert Michell now tithingman of Over Wroughton having served the office a far longer time than of right or custom he ought to have done by reason of the keeping of the leet there has been neglected and not kept as by law it ought to have been whereby a new tithingman ought to be elected and sworn. The court is informed that Mrs Grace Webb widow ought by due course to find the next tithingman to serve in the office. Ordered that Mrs Webb forthwith provides a fitting man to serve as tithingman in the place of Michell and that he repair to the next justice to take his oath for the execution of the office within one week after notice of this order upon pain of forfeiture of ten pounds.

191. *Constables for Purton.*
The court is informed that Anthony Morgan and Richard Bath now constables of Purton by reason that the leet or lawday has not been of late kept there they have served in the office two years and above and that William Bath and John Goodderidge of Purton are fit men to serve in the office in the place of them. Ordered that William Bath and John Goodderidge shall be constables of Purton in the place of them Morgan and Bath and that William Bath and John Goodderidge shall within one week after the receipt hereof repair to some justice to take their oaths for the due execution of their offices on pain of twenty pounds.

192. *Inhabitants of Devizes for moneys in arrear.* (Recites **175**)
At this Quarter Sessions the justices have returned into the court a certificate of their doings and proceedings therein and by the certificate it appeared that there is in arrear to the inhabitants out of the six

hundreds mentioned in the certificate the sum of one hundred eighty five pounds one shilling and two pence halfpenny (that is to say in the hundred of Potterne and Cannings the sum of forty nine pounds, Swanborough threescore and one pounds ten shillings and nine pence halfpenny, Melksham twelve pounds seven shillings and two pence, Elstub and Everleigh four pounds and nine shillings, Whorwellsdown thirteen pounds seven shillings and eight pence, Calne forty four pounds six shillings and seven pence). Ordered that the arrears shall be forthwith levied and collected in every of the six hundreds respectively and that out of the same money the inhabitants of Devizes shall be satisfied and paid the sum of one hundred and five pounds eleven shillings and six pence halfpenny which they have disbursed in the time of their visitation with the sickness more than they have received. And that the inhabitants of Urchfont shall be allowed so much moneys out of the remainder of the arrears (Devizes being satisfied) as John Ernle and Mr Eyre shall think fit and that the inhabitants of the parish of Potterne shall be allowed by the justices out of the arrears so much money as their part comes to in regard they are excepted in the order of the last Sessions. And forasmuch as it appeared by the certificate that the hundred of Calne was reduced to the payment but of forty marks for the full three months of relief. Ordered that they shall be repaid out of the remainder of the arrears what shall be due unto them over and above the forty marks which they are to pay. Further ordered that what moneys shall remain of the arrears of one hundred eighty five pounds one shilling and two pence halfpenny (Devizes, Urchfont, the parish of Potterne and Calne hundred being satisfied as aforesaid) shall remain for the use of the county to be disposed of as the court shall think fit. The court further orders and requires all the constables of the six hundreds forthwith to levy and collect all the arrears and pay the same over as aforesaid.

(If they refuse to pay, to be bound over.)

193. *Overseers of Purton and inhabitants of Blunsdon* [St Andrew]. (See also **182**)
The court is informed by John Elborowe and Richard Gleed overseers of the poor of the parish of Purton as also upon the reading of former orders of the court that there has been yearly allowed unto the overseers of Purton towards the relief of the poor people there forth of the parish of Blundson the sum of seven pounds and five shillings viz. from the Lord Lovelace and his tenants yearly six pounds and five shillings and from Mr Phetiplace ten shillings per annum and that there remained due upon arrears from Alexander Cleeve a tenant to the Lord Lovelace the sum of three pounds and also three pounds two shillings and six

pence for the half year due at Michaelmas last. Ordered that Cleeve shall forthwith pay unto the overseers of Purton as well the arrears of three pounds as also the three pounds two shillings and six pence due for the half year ended at Michaelmas last. And that the yearly pay of seven pounds and five shillings be from henceforth paid by the inhabitants of Blunsdon to the overseers of Purton for the time being according to the former orders until the inhabitants of Blunsdon shall show to the court good cause to the contrary. And if they shall refuse the payment thereof the next two justices are desired to grant their warrants for the levying thereof according to law and to do further therein as to law and justice shall appertain.

194. *Thomas Miller.*
The court is informed by Thomas Miller that he being under the command of Major Pausey has received many dangerous wounds while he was in service within the county and for that he has not wherewithal to pay his surgeon for the recovery of his wounds and lameness. Ordered that Mr Benedict Browne collector for maimed soldiers, etc. for the north forthwith pays to Miller the sum of fifty shillings.

195. *Richard Burt of Cricklade.*
The court is informed by Richard Burt of the parish of Cricklade that whereas about three years since a fine of four pounds was imposed on the inhabitants of Chelworth within the parish of Cricklade for not repairing the highways there and whereas the fine with nineteen shillings and eleven pence for redemption of Burt's cattle which was distrained and driven away by Edmond Brunsdon was satisfied to Brunsdon by Burt within the whole cost of Burt £4 19s 11d which sum ought to be borne proportionately by all the inhabitants there. Ordered that Burt shall cause an equal and indifferent rate to be made on the inhabitants of Chelworth for the raising of the sum of £4 19s 11d which rate is desired to be confirmed by the two next justices.
(If any refuse to pay, to be bound over.)
And the inhabitants if they see cause are to attend His Majesty's Commissioners for the Revenue to have the fine allowed to them back again towards the repairing of their highways.

196. *Nicholas Greene and Thomas Hopkins for a cottage.*
The court is informed that Nicholas Greene and Thomas Hopkins lived in a cottage erected on a plot of ground in the manor of Elston in the parish of Orcheston St. George which cottage was suddenly on fire which happened the one and twentieth of September last and burnt the cottage to the ground by reason whereof Greene and Hopkins

are now destitute of an habitation. And whereas Edward Tooker lord of the manor of Elston has certified the court his consent under his hand and seal that Greene and Hopkins should erect and build them another house for their habitation and dwelling in some convenient place upon the waste ground in the manor of Elston. Ordered that Greene and Hopkins should erect and build them a new house or cottage for their habitation and dwelling on some convenient place within the manor of Elston and shall continue the house or cottage for the succour of themselves and their wives without incurring the forfeitures in the statute.

197. *May Flower and the inhabitants of Warminster.*
The court is informed by May Flower of Warminster that the major part of the inhabitants of Warminster out of malice have from time to time and at all times ever since the unhappy differences first began in this kingdom rated him exceeding disproportionable to his ability insomuch that he is brought to a very mean condition and that upon often complaints he has received many fruitless promises yet could receive no redress of his just grievances. And to bring Flower to utter ruin have imposed offices upon him which he is no ways able to perform not only through want of estate but also by reason of his infirmity. The court desires the two next justices to examine the rates of the parish of Warminster both to the church and poor whether he is overrated or not. And if they find the same to be true according to the petition then they are desired to relieve Flower therein. And if not true, then to bind him over to the next Quarter Sessions to answer the scandalising of the inhabitants.

198. *Thomas Withers and Elizabeth Hobbes of Coombe in the parish of Enford.*
The court is informed by Thomas Withers that he has served tithingman of the tithing of Coombe in the parish of Enford by the space of three years last past by reason that there has been no court there kept by the Dean and Chapter of Salisbury at which court the tithingman of that tithing has been usually chosen. And whereas Withers informed the court that the office according to the custom there used goes from house to house and that it is now come to the turn of Elizabeth Hobbes widow to find a tithingman for the tithing and for that it cannot be known when any leet will be there kept. Ordered that Elizabeth Hobbes shall forthwith find a sufficient man to execute the office and that he shall within one week next ensuing repair to the next justice to take is oath for the due execution of the office. (If she refuses, to be bound over.)

199. *William Pound and Robert Rolfe.* (See also **284**)
Whereas William Pound and his wife and Robert Rolfe were now
convicted upon the testimony of two witnesses sworn in court for that
they have torn taken and carried away five hundred lugg of Sir Anthony
Ashley Cooper's hedge to the value of twenty nobles. Ordered that
Pound and Rolfe shall pay unto Cooper for his damage in that case
sustained the sum of twenty nobles before the 17th day of this instant
month of October and if they shall make default in payment thereof
at or before the said day then the court orders that Pound and his wife
and Rolfe shall be openly whipped at Lydiard by the officer there for
the said offence according as the statute in that requires.

(The offence probably occurred in Lydiard Millicent where Sir A. Cooper
had an estate. V.C.H. vol 18 p.196)

200. *Inter Mr Foyle and the inhabitants of Chute.*
Upon hearing of the matter in difference between Mr Foyle a freeholder
of the manor of Chute and the inhabitants of Chute concerning the
bearing the office of tithingmanship there and also upon reading of an
order of the court made at the Sessions held at Marlborough the 4th
of October 17 Charles [1641] concerning the matter. Ordered that
both sides shall attend at the next Quarter Sessions for the settling of
the same and in the mean time the former order is to stand and the
now tithingman to continue in the office until the next Sessions and in
case it shall be then ordered that the office ought to be borne by Foyle
then he is to satisfy the tithingman for serving in the office longer than
he ought to have done but if any of the three copyholders ought to
execute the office then they are to satisfy the tithingman for his service.

201. *Thomas Stone.*
Upon reading of the petition of Thomas Stone now prisoner in
His Majesty's gaol at Fisherton Anger concerning the cause of his
commitment to the prison. Ordered and desired that the two next
justices to Fisherton shall take sufficient bail of Stone for his appearance
at the next Assizes to answer the cause for which he now stands
committed.

202. *The parsonage of Dinton and Teffont.*
The court is informed that the parsonage of Dinton and Teffont has
heretofore been always rated at four yardlands to all rates and payments
and that now of late as the court is informed by Mr Hyde that the
parsonage is raised to nine yardlands for and towards all rates and
payments. Ordered that the old rate shall stand and that the parsonage

shall be rated to church and poor and other ancient rates and payments but at four yardlands as anciently it has been.

203.   *Hannington Bridge.*
The court is informed by the inhabitants of the parish of Hannington that the bridge of Hannington is built part in the county of Wiltshire and part in the county of Gloucestershire and that heretofore the bridge was by the command and directions of the garrison of Cirencester broken down and the planks and other timber thereof disposed to some particular persons. And that there are lands in the parish of Hannington appointed and leased out to William Harper for the repairing and maintaining of that part of the bridge which stands in the county of Wiltshire and that Harper during the time that the bridge has been broken down has taken the profits of the lands without doing anything towards the repairing of the bridge and still continues therein. And that the inhabitants of Hannington were at the last Assizes at Salisbury presented for the decay of the bridge. The court desires the two next justices to Hannington with what convenient speed they can to send for Harper the occupier of the land and cause him to give in his accounts before them what profits he has made of the lands. And the inhabitants of Hannington are to have notice thereof and to be present at the time when he shall pass his accounts to take their exceptions thereunto (if they see cause) and the same profits to be employed towards the repairing of the bridge. And the justices are likewise desired to send for those particular persons in whose custody the planks or other timber of the bridge are and to cause them to be responsible for the same.
(If Harper or any refuse, to be bound over.)

204.   *Alehouses in Pewsey suppressed.*
At the last Quarter Sessions it was ordered that all alehouses within the county should be and were suppressed by the order and whereas the court is informed by Mr Hyde of counsel with the inhabitants of Pewsey that the officers of that place had no notice of that order and that there are divers alehouse keepers in that place (that is to say Cristian Smith widow, Symon Lane, William Canninges, Robert Yeday, Robert Bennett, William Allen and David Monday) who continue selling of ale notwithstanding the order. Ordered that the constables of that place shall give notice to the foresaid of the order of Sessions and the parties are hereby required to observe the same as they will answer the contrary at their perils.

205. *Inter Elizabeth Blake and the inhabitants of Mildenhall.*
The court is informed by Elizabeth Blake of Marlborough spinster that about five years and a half since the churchwardens and overseers of the poor of Mildenhall placed one Alice Smyth a poor and lame impotent maid of the said parish with her to be by her kept and maintained and promised her 14d per week so long as she should keep her which maid Elizabeth Blake has ever since kept and there is now due to her for keeping the maid £4 6s in arrear. The court desires the two next justices to send for the churchwardens and overseers of Mildenhall and examine the truth of the petition and make such order for Blake's relief as in their discretions they shall think fit and whatsoever the justices shall do therein the court will confirm the same.

206. *Inter William Head and the inhabitants of Upavon.*
William Head of Wootton Rivers has been bound over from Sessions to Sessions for a long time for suffering of one Monday a bastard getter to escape he being tithingman of Wootton Rivers at that time when the escape was made and there has been no prosecution against Head by any of the parish of Upavon who at first complained against him. Ordered that Head shall forthwith give notice to the churchwardens and overseers of the poor of Upavon that they appear at the next Quarter Sessions there to show cause unto the court for the further continuance of Head if they have any cause to show and Head is to deliver a copy of this order to the churchwardens and overseers that they may attend accordingly and in default of their prosecution Head is to be discharged at the next Quarter Sessions.

207. *Constables and churchwardens to pay Treasurer the money in arrear.*
The moneys for the relief of maimed soldiers etc. remain due and uncollected in most of the parishes within the county by means whereof the several constables of hundreds have not paid the same into the several Treasurers for the time they have been constables. And for that the churchwardens and petty constables in every parish who ought by the statute to collect the moneys and pay the same over to the constables of their hundred have not collected the same but do sleight and neglect the collecting thereof. Ordered that no constables of hundreds be discharged from their office until they have paid unto the several Treasurers the moneys due for both the collections in their time of constableship.
  (If any neglect to pay in the money, to be bound over.)

208. *Inter Webb and Gardiner.*
The court is informed by Robert Webb tithingman of Liddington that

he has served in the same office above a year by reason that there has
been no court kept for the hundred of Kingsbridge for a long time
and that by custom one Joyce Gardner widow ought to provide a man
to serve in the same office in her stead. Ordered that Gardner shall
forthwith upon receipt of this order provide a sufficient man to serve
in the office in place of Webb and go before the next justice within
one week there to take his oath on pain of ten pounds.

209. *Inter Richard Madderinge and the inhabitants of Chiseldon.*
The court is informed by Richard Madderinge of Chiseldon that he
is a blind man having an impotent woman to his wife and not able to
do anything towards their maintenance and relief. Ordered that the
churchwardens and overseers of the poor of Chiseldon shall forthwith
upon sight of this order provide for Madderinge and his wife and give
them such fitting relief as their age and impotency requires as they will
answer the contrary that the court be no further troubled therewith.

210. *Edward Bull.* (Se also **177**, **246**, **272**, **324**)
Complaint has been made by Edward Bull marshal to the garrison of
Malmesbury that divers prisoners have been committed to his charge
and custody for felonies and other misdemeanours which did properly
belong to the gaoler of the county for the keeping of which prisoners
Bull has been at great charge and has had no allowance from the county
for the same. The court desires that Charles Gore, George Ivy and
William Eyre or any two of them examine the premises and the time
of the taking into prison and the time of discharging the prisoners and
to allow such allowance to Bull as they shall think fit and order the
payment thereof to be made by the Treasurer for the north.

211. *Edward Middlecot.*
At the last Sessions the court was informed by Edward Middlecot
gent late constable of the hundred of Warminster that when he was
discharged of his office he was enforced by the court to pay unto the
Treasurer all such moneys as were charged on him for the time he was
in office of constable. And that he had not then neither yet has the
same from all the churchwardens of the hundred but some of them
are yet behind in the payment as follows, that is to say: Anthonie
Thresher, Norton Bavant 13s 4d, Edward Baylie and Robert Weeks,
Sutton 25s 4d, Leonard Newe and Nicholas Danyell, Dinton and
Teffont 29s 6d and the churchwardens of Fisherton and Bapton 19s.
Ordered that the several and respective sums shall be demanded of the
several churchwardens.
    (If any refuse to pay, to be bound over.)

212. *John Stoaks of Seend.* (See also **249, 310**)
It appears unto the court that John Stoakes of Seend is bound over to this Sessions for being accused to be the reputed father of a bastard child borne of the body of Ann Salter. And forasmuch as it also appears to the court upon examination of the matter about the bastard of Elizabeth Somner that Stoakes is a man of scandalous life and conversation. Ordered that his alehouse shall be suppressed and by this order stands suppressed any licence heretofore granted to him by the justices to the contrary hereof in any wise notwithstanding.

213. *John Thorpe master of the house of correction of Fisherton.*
Ordered that John Thorpe now keeper of the gaol at Fisherton Anger shall be master of the house of correction there and that he shall convert all such prisoners as shall be thither sent and set them to work. Further ordered that Thorpe shall be bound in a bond of one hundred pounds to the Clerk of the Peace with two sufficient sureties as well for the due execution and discharge of his office of being master of the house of correction as for the answering redelivery and satisfaction as well of the county's stock committed to his charge as of all such goods and implements of the county as are now remaining in the house of correction or which hereafter shall be delivered to his custody. And that Thorpe is to continue master of he house of correction until the court shall alter the same.

214. *Constables and churchwardens for the arrears of maimed soldiers and mariners.*
Forasmuch as the moneys for relief of maimed soldiers and mariners etc. are not all collected by means whereof the several constables of hundred have not paid the same into the several Treasurers for the time as they have been constables. And for that the churchwardens and petty constables in every parish who ought by the statute to collect the moneys and pay the same over to the constables of their hundred have not collected the same but do sleight and neglect the collecting thereof. Ordered that no constables of hundred be discharged from their office until they have paid unto the Treasurers the moneys due for both the collections in their time of constableship. Further ordered that if the churchwardens and constables in any parish shall not forthwith pay the same in unto the constables of their several hundreds upon demand thereof to be made (then to be bound over).

215. *John Oven constable of the hundred of Malmesbury.*
Forasmuch as it appears to the court by an order made at the last

Quarter Sessions that the court was then informed by John Oven one of the constables of the hundred of Malmesbury that he had served constable of the hundred by the space of two years and upwards to his great loss and prejudice and desired the court to release him of his office which the court desired Charles Gore and George Ivy justices to examine the accounts of Oven concerning the collection of the relief of maimed soldiers, etc. as by the order among other things therein contained more at large it appears. And whereas the court is now informed that there has been nothing done upon the order. Now ordered that Oven shall within two weeks after the end of this present Sessions give his account to the justices of his receipts and payments of the moneys concerning the collections for the reliefs. And the court desires the justices to meet together to take and examine the account of Oven concerning the collections. And the court orders Robert Hort of Turtlebridge gent to be constable of the hundred in the place of Oven. And if Oven shall not give his account to the justices according to this order then he is to be bound over to the next Quarter Sessions.

216. *Jeffery Barnes constable of Malmesbury hundred.*
(As for **215.** Jeffery Barnes had served for four years and ordered to be replaced by Robert Parker of Chedglow in the parish of Crudwell.)

217. *William Hawkes.*
The court is informed by William Hawkes of Coate that by unhappy accident of fire his house was consumed with all goods therein to the value of twenty pounds and thereby is utterly undone and destitute of an habitation for the succour of himself his wife and children. It is therefore thought fit and ordered that the overseers of the poor of the parish of Liddington shall forthwith make a charitable collection for him over the parish for to relieve and comfort him and his family in his great want and misery and to provide for him and his family as the poor of that parish as the law in that case requires.

218. *Elizabeth Tayler of East Bedwyn* [Little Bedwyn].
The court is informed by the petition and complaint of Elizabeth Tayler who shows that she having lived in the parish of East Bedwyn for all the time of fourteen years and upwards where she has had three children who are still with her and that her husband being departed from her and she having no house or habitation or any other subsistence for herself or her children nor any relief from the parish but are all likely to perish for want of a habitation and other necessaries. Ordered that the overseers of the poor of the parish of East Bedwyn together with the churchwardens there take care and provide for the relief of Elizabeth

and her children according to their necessity and wants. And further that they bind forth apprentices such of her children as are fit to be placed out according to the statute in that case provided. (If overseers refuse, to be bound over.)

219. *Henry Cheate tithingman of Wilcot.*
The court is informed upon the complaint of Henry Cheate tithingman of Wilcot that he having disbursed 26s for the carrying of a prisoner to gaol being charged for murder and that there being a rate made for the payment thereof by the yardlands and assented thereunto by some of the chiefest of the parish and that many of the inhabitants have and do refuse to pay their rates and taxes. The court finding upon examination that the prisoner had no goods of his own to defray the charge, orders that the 26s be rated upon the parish of Wilcot together with such other charges as the tithingman has expended in procuring this order. (If any refuse to pay, to be bound over.)

220. *Elizabeth Coxe.*
It appears to the court by the testimony of John Russell tithingman of Easterton [Potterne] that Elizabeth Coxe wife of Joseph Coxe will not obey the warrant of the peace granted against her and her husband by Mr [Edward] Tooker and Mr [Francis] Swanton justices. And whereas the court is informed by Osmond Amor that she spoke contemptuous words of the justices. Ordered that the tithingman shall forthwith apprehend Elizabeth and if occasion be shall require the assistance of his neighbours therein and bring her before the next justice to be bound over to appear at the next Quarter Sessions and in the mean time to be of the good behaviour.

221. *Inter Whityeate and Pontinge.*
At this Sessions Thomas Whityeate of Axford in the parish of Ramsbury is presented by the jury of the hundred of Ramsbury for entertaining in his house George Pontinge an undertenant. And whereas Whityeate has informed the court that he stays there against his will and that he cannot get Pontinge forth of his house. Ordered that Pontinge shall within fortnight next coming depart out of the house of Whityeate. (If he refuses, to be bound over.)

222. *Robert Norrice.*
The court is informed that Robert Norrice the elder of Elcombe [Wroughton] is a very poor man and chargeable unto the parish and that Robert Norrice the younger of the parish of Brinkworth his son is a man of sufficiency and ability for to relieve his father. Ordered that

Robert Norrice the younger shall from henceforth pay unto Robert Norrice the elder his father the weekly pay of 12d for and towards his maintenance.

223. *William Dollery.* (See also **243** and **417**)
At the last Assizes William Dollery of Stratford [sub Castle] near Salisbury a poor distressed maimed soldier preferred a petition to Mr Justice Rolle for some maintenance for himself his wife and children he being not able to work. Mr Justice Rolle left the consideration thereof to the justice. Ordered that the Treasurer for the south shall upon sight of this order pay unto Dollery the sum of forty shillings out of the moneys of the county remaining in his hands for the said relief in regard of his great necessity.

224. *Constables, churchwardens and overseers of Malmesbury.* (Recites **188**)
The court is now informed that as yet nothing has been done upon the order. Ordered that the last order shall continue until the next Sessions and in the mean time the justices are desired to examine the premises and to order and relieve as they shall see cause according to the last order.

225. *Edward Yates and Robert Huggins.* (Recites **187**)
The court is informed that as yet there is not anything done upon the order. Ordered that the last order shall continue until the next Sessions and in the mean time the justices are desired to examine the truth of the premises and to relieve the parties as they shall see cause according to the last order.

226. *Roger Cunditt and Thomas Hulbert for a bastard.* (See also **592, 726, 800, 823**)
Roger Cunditt was bound over to this Quarter Sessions for being the reputed father of a female bastard child borne of the body of Elizabeth Somner of Seend. And whereas there was an order made by William Eyre, Thomas Bennett and George Ivy justices charging Cunditt to be the reputed father of the bastard which order is now returned into court and read and from which order Cunditt appealed. Whereupon the court upon full hearing of the same matter in open court and upon examination of all such witnesses as were produced as well on the behalf of the inhabitants of Seend as on the behalf of Cunditt in the presence of counsel learned on both sides being fully satisfied therein do repeal and nullify the order certified by the justices against Cunditt and declare order and adjudge Thomas Hulbert late of Seend to be the reputed father of the bastard and further orders that Hulbert

shall forthwith pay and deliver unto the churchwardens and overseers of the poor of Seend for and towards the relief and maintenance of the bastard child the sum of 12d weekly to begin from the birth of the child and to continue until the child shall accomplish the full age of seven years. Also ordered that the mother thereof shall also pay to the overseers the sum of six pence weekly. Further ordered that Hulbert shall forthwith put in sufficient security for the full discharge of the parish of all inconveniences and troubles and charges which may happen by means of the bastard child. And lastly Somner is to remain in the house of correction for the space of one whole year from the time of her commitment.

227. *For arrears of maimed soldiers, etc.*
There has been much complaint made unto the court by the Treasurer and constables of hundreds against churchwardens for not collecting and paying in of such moneys as are due of most parishes for and towards the relief of the poor prisoners, maimed soldiers, etc. for divers years last past whereby the collections are unsatisfied. Ordered that in all parishes where the moneys of the collections are in arrear the now churchwardens and petty constables in every several parish being in arrear in their payments shall forthwith meet in every several parish and call together the precedent churchwardens and petty constables if there be any and shall make an equal and indifferent rate on the inhabitants in every several parish in arrear to raise up so much moneys as are in arrear in their several parishes towards the reliefs. And the now churchwardens and petty constables in every several parish (if there be any petty constables) shall forthwith levy and collect the said rates and pay them in to the now constables of their hundreds. And if any shall be refractory and not pay their rates then the several churchwardens shall return unto the court at the next Quarter Sessions the names of all such persons within their parishes as shall refuse and be refractory to pay their rates that there may be an exemplary punishment inflicted on them.

228. *Almeshouse bridge in Warminster.*
The court is informed by the inhabitants of Warminster that the water at Almeshouse bridge is bayed up and the highway there is much decayed by reason that the arches of the bridge are not cleansed and divers of the inhabitants of Warminster do not scour and cleanse the water course running from the bridge to Lawrence mead but so suffer the banks to increase upon the water course whereby the water has not so broad a passage from the bridge as anciently it has had. The court is also informed that the water course out of the street running between

Robert Gardners and John Perryes houses and so behind the town is not cleansed and scoured by reason whereof the water has not his passage out of the street but is bayed up to the common annoyance of the passengers and prayed the assistance of the court for redress thereof. Ordered that the waymen of Warminster shall forthwith cause the arches of the bridge to be cleansed and shall make a rate on the town for the doing thereof and the waymen are forthwith to give notice to all those who have any land joining to the water between Almeshouse bridge and Lawrence mead that they do forthwith sufficiently scour the water course and cut the same water course as wide as anciently it has been that the water may have his free passage. And the court also orders the waymen forthwith to give notice to Gardner and Perry and all others who of right ought to scour the water course behind the town that they do forthwith scour and cleanse the same sufficiently that the water in the street be not bayed up.

(If any refuse, to be bound over.)

And the waymen are hereby required forthwith to cleanse the gutter in the street leading into the water course behind the town.

229. *For apprehending of tithingmen that refuse to be sworn being chosen in lawdays.*
The court is informed that tithingmen elected at lawdays to serve in that office refuse to be sworn to execute their office notwithstanding the orders of these courts. Ordered that the Clerk of the Peace ex-officio shall send out warrants to apprehend them and bring them before the next justice to bind them over to the next Quarter Sessions.

230. *Mr Croome to collect the arrears of the gaol money.*
The court is informed by William Croome collector heretofore of the moneys for relief of prisoners in His Majesty's gaol of Fisherton Anger that there is much moneys arrear in the several hundreds for the relief of the prisoners as by the note of the particulars in each hundred delivered into court and there remaining of record appears. Ordered that Croome shall continue collector thereof until the court shall alter the same and he is to collect all the arrears against the next Sessions that the court may take some order for the disposing thereof.

231. Wilts: Rate made by Edward Tooker and Francis Swanton justices according to an order of this Sessions for the raising of one hundred marks weekly within the county for the relief of the borough of Wilton, Maiden Bradley and Horningsham.

	Hundreds	Marks
Say division	Amesbury	4
	Branch and Dole	3
	Elstub and Everleigh	4
	Alderbury	2
	Chalke	2
	Cawden and Cadworth	2
	Downton	2
	Underditch	1
	Frustfield	1
	Salisbury City being taken off from the hundred	4
Warminster division	Dunworth	4
	Mere	2 and 3 quarters
	Damerham	2 and 1 quarter
	Heytesbury	3 and 2 quarters
	Warminster	3 and a half and a half quarter
	Whorwellsdown	3 and a half and a half quarter
Trowbridge division	Melksham with the liberty of Trowbridge	3
	Bradford	3
	Westbury	2
Chippenham division	Chippenham	6
	Malmesbury	6
	Damerham north	1
	Calne	2
Devizes division	Kinwardstone	6
	Swanborough	6
	Potterne and Cannings with the borough of Devizes and liberty of Bromham and Rowde	3
Marlborough division	Kingsbridge	5
	Selkley	4 and 1 third part
	Highworth	6 and 1 third part
	Ramsbury	1 and 1 third part

1647

General Sessions of the Peace held at Salisbury Tuesday after the feast of Epiphany 12 January Charles 22 (1647). Edward Tooker, William Eyre and William Hussey.

232. *Order for Wilton, Fisherton, Bradley and Horningsham.*
At the last Quarter Sessions there was a tax of one hundred marks a week laid on the inhabitants of this county for the relief of the poor infected persons of the borough of Wilton, of Fisherton Anger, Maiden Bradley and Horningsham which continued until this Sessions. And now the court taking into consideration that the sickness (by God's mercy) is ceased at Fisherton Anger and is ceasing at Wilton and Maiden Bradley and Horningsham orders that the weekly taxation of one hundred marks per week shall cease and determine. Ordered that Mr Bell, Mr Abyn and Mr Sadler receivers mentioned in the order forthwith to draw up their account as well of such moneys as they have received by virtue of the order as of all such moneys as are received upon the rate of five miles compass or sent unto them by way of any charitable benevolence from any places or persons whatsoever and also their disbursements thereof. And they are forthwith to deliver their accounts to Mr Coles Clerk of the Peace who is to survey the same and they are to give notice thereof to the parishioners that if any will except against the same account they have liberty to acquaint Mr Coles therewith. And Mr Edward Shoare and John Wansey and Thomas Shoare receivers of the moneys collected for the relief of the infected persons of Maiden Bradley and Horningsham are also ordered to make up their account to Mr Francis Bennett. And if the accountants shall not deliver exact accounts then Mr Coles and Mr Bennett are to direct the accountants in what form they shall make the same who are hereby injoined to draw up their accounts accordingly. And after Mr Coles has surveyed the account of Mr Bell, Mr Abyn and Mr Sadler he is to send the same to Mr Tooker and Mr Swanton justices who are desired to take and examine the accounts and cause the accountants to present the same. And Mr Bell and the other receivers are to attend the justices thereabouts. And after Mr Bennett has surveyed the accounts of Mr Shoare, John Wansey and Thomas Shoare he is to send the same to Mr Bennett and Mr Howe justices who are desired to take and examine the account and to perfect the same. And the accountants are to attend the justices to that purpose. And the justices are desired to return both the said accounts into the next Quarter Sessions to remain amongst the records. And for the future maintenance and relief of the infected places of Wilton and

Maiden Bradley and Horningsham ordered that all the arrears upon the weekly tax shall be forthwith levied and collected by the several constables of the hundreds and shall be paid in to the receivers to the uses intents and purposes aforesaid. And after Mr Shoare and the other accountants have paid their accounts to the justices and the new elected constables of Maiden Bradley are sworn to execute their office then the new constables are to undertake the provision for the poor infected persons of Maiden Bradley and Horningsham and to receive the moneys of the hundreds and places formerly allotted for the relief of those places. And last of all the court desires all the justices to further the execution of this order. And all constables of the hundreds and other officers therein interested are herby required carefully to execute their offices as they will answer the contrary at their perils. And all the receivers are hereby required to be earnest and careful in the prosecution of this order that all places and persons infected may be speedily relieved and the county secured (by God's mercy) from all future danger concerning that matter.

(Maiden Bradley said the plague had begun on 1st June last and had not yet ceased. About 33 persons had died and a greater number had been sick. Joan Underhill and Joan Addams, widows, of Fisherton Anger said in July last their houses had had the plague and six died. To stop the spread of the disease they were ordered to leave their houses and go into the pesthouse which was then newly erected. A1/110/1647H/191)

233. *Inter Winterslow and Enford.* (See also **755**)
Upon some difference between the parishes of Winterslow and Enford about the receiving and maintaining of Jane Carter late of Winterslow singlewoman and begotten with child by a man of Sussex (not to be heard of) for the settlement whereof the parishioners of Enford petitioned the Lord Chief Justice of the Common Pleas who referred the hearing and determining of the same to the Lord Gorges, William Ashburnham, Sir William Britton and Sir John Evelyn or any two of them and Wm Ashburnham and Sir John Evelyn calling the churchwardens and overseers of the said parishes before them 7th March 1636 at which time it was agreed by the consent of the parishes and ordered that the parish of Enford should suffer Jane Carter to remain with her father in law in Enford till she was delivered and that the child so born to remain there and that the parish of Winterslow should pay weekly towards the maintenance thereof nine pence for the space of seven years from the birth of the child. And the parish of Enford should pay weekly six pence during the same term which money was to be paid by the overseers of the parishes to the hands of Thomas Carter of Enford father in law of Jane monthly for the

use of the child. It was further agreed that at the end of the term of seven years there should be five pounds equally raised by and between the parishes for binding the child apprentice. And that the parish of Winterslow shall be from henceforth cleared and acquitted from any further charge of the child or mother. And that the payment of nine pence and six pence should begin from the last Sessions before the date of that order being 11th March 1636 as by the order now read under the hands of Mr Ashburnham and Sir John Evelyn appears which the court taking into consideration orders that the order shall stand in force until the next Sessions and then to be confirmed by the court if there shall be no cause presented to the contrary either to part or to all by Mr Hyde being of counsel for the parish of Winterslow.

234. *Abraham Halle, John Purryer masters of the houses of correction.*
The court is informed by Abraham Halle and John Purryer masters of the houses of correction at Marlborough and Devizes that there is two years wages due unto them from the Treasurer which come unto the sum of forty marks and desired the court that they may be satisfied the same which the court orders the Treasurer to pay them the sum of twenty marks out of the money remaining in his hands in regard of their great want and necessity which said twenty marks is for one half year's pay.

235. *Overseers for Milton* [Lilbourne].
Complaint has been made to the court by the inhabitants of the parish of Milton that there is great want of overseers of the poor there being none within the same parish. Ordered that Mr Henry Cusse, Anthony Mancks and John Chappell inhabitants within the said parish do join with the churchwardens there and do execute the office of overseers of the poor and make rates and take such care therein according to the statute and to continue until there shall be new overseers nominated for the same parish.

236. *Inter Edward May and inhabitants of Potterne.*
At the last Quarter Sessions held at Marlborough 6th October last past Edward May one of the inhabitants of the parish of Potterne appeared in the behalf of the inhabitants to a presentment against them for decay of a bridge between Worton and Marston and made oath for the reparation thereof and discharged the fees of the court and the fine set on the inhabitants. And at this Sessions May complained that he could not be paid the fees and fine disbursed for the said inhabitants and that he had been at expenses in travail in prosecution thereof. Ordered that the parishioners shall forthwith meet and make an equal rate that

Edward May may be resatisfied the moneys by him laid out on the behalf of the inhabitants as well for the fees and fine the court as for his charges and expenses in travail in prosecution of the discharge of the presentment in regard the same is not to be borne by any particular person but by the whole parish.

[If any refuse to pay, to be bound over.]

237. *John Evans.*

The court is informed by John Evans that he is very aged and impotent and that he and his family are in great distress for want of relief. Ordered that the churchwardens and overseers of the poor of Fisherton Anger shall forthwith take into their consideration his miserable condition and give him such relief as his age and impotency requires that the court be no further troubled therewith.

238. *For neglect of constables, churchwardens and other officers.*

The court taking into consideration the great neglect of officers of this county in execution of their offices orders that if any constables of the hundreds, churchwardens, petty constables and tithingmen shall be hereafter negligent in collecting and levying the three months arrears for the relief of Wilton and the other places infected in this county or in collecting and levying the rates for maimed soldiers, etc and the collection for the relief of the gaol prisoners and also if any of the overseers of the poor shall be remiss or negligent in collecting and levying of the rates for the relief of the poor and payment of the same, then the next justice upon complaint thereof to him made and proof of the truth of the complaint is desired to bind over such officers to the next Quarter Sessions.

239. *Highworth.*

The court is informed that the parish of Highworth is grievously infected with the noisome contagious disease of the plague so that they are not able to relieve the infected persons there and other the poor people of that parish. And to the intent that the spreading abroad of that noisome disease into other parts of this county may (by God's blessing) be timely prevented and the infected persons and the poor of that parish may be sufficiently relieved and kept in. Ordered that the sum of one hundred marks shall be forthwith raised throughout the county after the rate and proportion set down and agreed upon at the last Quarter Sessions for one week's pay for the relief of the infected persons of the borough of Wilton which sum shall be forthwith rated and collected, levied and paid unto Mr Thomas Thatch and William Forder of Highworth and Mr William Percival of Westrop and Richard

Humphrey of Eastrop or either of them within one week after the fourteenth day of January for and towards the relief and provision of the poor infected persons and poor people of Highworth over and above the arrears within the hundred of Highworth, Cricklade and Staple formerly allotted to that place. The court nominates and appoints Mr Thatch, etc to be receivers of the sum of one hundred marks and such other moneys as shall be raised by virtue of this order. And they are to pay over weekly towards the relief of the poor infected persons and other the poor of that parish the sum of ten pounds out of the sum of one hundred marks until the same be fully satisfied and paid out. Further ordered that all the constables of the several hundred shall forthwith make out their warrants to all petty constables and tithingmen as well for the raising of the hundred marks to the uses aforesaid as for the collecting and paying in of the same together with the said arrears to the receivers. And in all places in this county rated towards this payment where there is neither petty constable or tithingman there the constables of the hundreds shall collect the same. And the persons refusing to pay their rates are to be distrained by their goods for the same by warrant of two justices. The court orders and appoints the receivers to account before Edward Tooker, Charles Gore, George Ivy and Francis Swanton justices of their receipts and payments when and as often as the receivers shall be required. And if it shall please almighty God to cease the infection in part or in all before the one hundred marks be expended then Mr Tooker, etc upon information thereof given unto them are desired to take such course for the cessation or lessening of the weekly payment of ten pounds as they in their discretion should think fit. But if the infection shall increase and spread abroad so that the weekly sum of ten pounds shall not be sufficient to relieve the infected and other poor persons then Mr Tooker etc upon credible information thereof given unto them are desired to increase the allowance and to take such course for the speedy raising such sums over and above the sum of one hundred marks in such manner and for such time of continuance and place or places as they in their discretion shall also think fit. And last of all the court desires all the justices of the county to further the execution of this order. And all the constables of the hundreds and other officers herein interested are hereby required carefully to execute their office as they will answer the contrary at their peril. And the receivers are required to be earnest and careful in the prosecution of this order that all persons infected may be speedily relieved and the county secured by God's mercy from all future danger concerning that matter. And all the rates and taxes made therein are to be certified at the next Quarter Sessions.

(There had also been plague at Wootton Bassett beginning about 25th April 1645 and lasting for 16 weeks. About 60 persons died. A1/110/1647H/237)

240. *Constables of Maiden Bradley.*
The court is informed by diverse of the inhabitants within the Liberty of Maiden Bradley that John Wansey and Thomas Shoard have served in the office of constable for the liberty for three years and upwards and desired the court that John Toogood and Nicholas Moulton the younger might be elected constables in their place. Ordered that John Toogood and Nicholas Moulton be constables of the Liberty in the place of John Wansey and Thomas Shoard and that they repair within one week after notice of this order unto the next justice to take their oaths upon pain of twenty pounds a piece. Further ordered that Wansey and Shoard shall within one month next ensuing collect and gather all such moneys as are due and arrear to the collections of the King's Bench, etc and pay the same to the Treasurer.

241. *Inhabitants of Upton Lovell.*
The court is informed by William Blake, George Pashion, John Moody, John Seagram, Susan Andrewes, Marie Heyward and Thomas Mogg inhabitants of the tithing of Upton Lovell that by virtue of the several warrants from certain officers of the King's army there has been several sums of money, horses and provision levied on them for and in respect of the whole tithing amounting to the value of £49 8s as they are able to make appear. And George Pashion, John Seagram and Henry Curtis being tithingmen of the tithing of Upton Lovell being compelled to execute the warrants are sued by the said Moody. The court desires Mr Howe and Mr Bennett justices to call the parties interested before them and to examine and end the differences between them if they can. And the court will confirm their order if it be made before the end of the first week in the next term.

242. *Inter Dinton and Teffont.*
Upon reading of the matter in difference between the inhabitants of Dinton and Teffont concerning the manner of rating and the order made in that behalf at the last Quarter Sessions being read and witnesses upon both side now sworn and examined and divers rates on either side produced in court and counsel learned on both sides being heard. Ordered that Dinton and Teffont shall be again reunited and rated together in all rates.

243. *William Dollery.* (Refers to **223.** See also **417**)
It appears to the court that William Dollery of Stratford-sub- Castle
being a soldier under the command of Sir William Waller for the space
of three years and being wounded at Newbury fight last where he lost
the use of his right hand and thereby unabled to labour for his living.
Ordered that the Treasurer shall forthwith pay to William the sum of
forty shillings towards his relief.

244. *Inter Bower Chalke and Coombe.*
Upon reading of an order of Christmas Sessions 9 Charles [1634]
between the inhabitants of Bower Chalke and the inhabitants of
Coombe Bissett it was alleged that 35s of the weekly pay of 12d therein
ordered to be paid unto the overseers of the parish of Bower Chalke by
the overseers of Coombe Bissett remains unpaid and in arrear. Ordered
that the overseers of the poor of Coombe Bissett shall forthwith make
a rate on the inhabitants of the parish for the said 35s and collect the
same accordingly and the same unto the overseers of Bower Chalke.
      [If any refuse to pay, to be bound over.]

245. *Reybridge* [Lacock].
The court is informed that a great bridge called Reybridge is grown
into great decay for want of reparations and is very likely to grow into
utter ruin unless some speedy course be taken for the repair thereof.
Ordered that the four next justices meet together and enquire what
persons, lands, tenements and bodies politic ought to make and repair
the bridge and take speedy course for the repair thereof. And what
order the justices shall make therein the court will and does approve,
ratify, confirm and allow.

246. *Edward Bull.* (See also **177, 210, 272, 324**)
Whereas William Eyre, Charles Gore, George Ivy justices have returned
into the court their certificates made by virtue of an order of the last
Quarter Sessions concerning Edward Bull marshal of the garrison of
Malmesbury whereby it appears that the justices having fully examined
the business concerning Edward Bull that in these troublesome times
by reason that prisoners could not be conveyed to the common gaol
they were committed to the charge and custody of Edward Bull many
prisoners for felony and other great misdemeanours which ought to
have been sent to the gaol of the county whereby the inhabitants of
those parts have received great ease and benefit. And that Edward Bull
has been 'dempnified' and is out of purse at the least the sum of thirty
pounds for the keeping and relieving of the prisoners for which he has
received no satisfaction and that divers of those prisoners having lain a

long time in prison were released by the governor of Malmesbury and the residue of them were transmitted by George Ivy to the common gaol of Fisherton Anger the last Assizes where some of them were executed and the rest released after their trials. And therefore they did think fit and reasonable that the sum of thirty pounds should be forthwith paid unto Edward by the Treasurer if this court of Sessions should thereunto condescend and approve of which this court approves and condescends hereunto. Ordered the Treasurer shall forthwith pay unto Edward Bull the sum of thirty pounds according to the said certificate that the court may be no further troubled for non payment of the same.

247. *Thomas Collett.*
The court is informed by Thomas Collett tithingman of Wadswick [Box] that he in the execution of his office and conveying of prisoners to gaol has disbursed several sums of money amounting to the sum of six pounds. Ordered that Thomas Collett causes an indifferent rate to be made within his tithing and the two next justices are desired to make their warrants for the levying thereof.

248. *Matthew Waterman.*
The court is credibly informed that Matthew Waterman of Fonthill Gifford carpenter upon the seventh day of August last past sustained great loss by fire in burning his dwelling house and goods to the value of one hundred marks and upwards. Ordered that the Treasurer pay to Matthew towards his loss the sum of five pounds.

249. *John Stoakes, Inhabitants of Seend.* (See also **212**, **310**)
John Stoakes was bound over to this Sessions for being the reputed father of a bastard child born of the body of Ann Salter his servant and before this Sessions deceased. And whereas upon examination of the matter it appeared (upon the prosecution of some in the behalf of the parish of Seend) that between the time Ann Salter was discovered to be with child and the death of the bastard child the inhabitants of the parish were put to great charge in keeping and relieving Ann and her bastard and in prosecuting Stoakes touching the same and prayed the assistance of the court for their relief therein. Ordered that the matter shall be referred to the examination of two near adjoining justices who are desired to call the churchwardens and overseers of the poor and such of the inhabitants of that parish before them as they shall think fit and examine what charges the parish has sustained and been at concerning Ann and her bastard and make such order for the relief of the parish of Seend as in their discretion and as to law and justice shall appertain.

250. *Ogbourne St George.*
Complaint has been made by the inhabitants of Ogbourne St George that Alice Wooldridge a covenant servant with William Jones of Woodlands in the parish of Mildenhall and there had dwelt and continued by the space of near two years and her term not ended until Michaelmas next and William Jones finding Alice to be with child did about a week since put away Alice forth of his service who comes to inhabit with her father a poor man in the parish of Ogbourne where she is likely to be chargeable to the parish. Ordered that Alice Wooldridge shall be forthwith removed from Ogbourne St George and sent back again into Woodlands to William Jones where she was last a covenant servant there to remain.

251. *Richard Nott.*
The court is informed by Richard Nott of Winterbourne Earls that he has lost both his eyes by a corn pick so that he is a maimed man and no ways able to get his maintenance and he has a wife and two small children and prayed the court to take the same into consideration. Ordered that the overseers of the poor of Winterbourne Earls shall pay weekly four shillings unto Richard towards the relief of him, his wife and children. And in case there shall not be any overseers of the poor in the parish then the court desires the next justices to order and appoint two of the inhabitants of the parish to execute the office of overseer until Easter next and cause the parish to make an equal rate there for the relief of Nott and other poor and impotent persons there who shall have need of relief. And the two inhabitants are to collect and gather the same and pay Nott the four shillings a week for his relief until it shall be otherwise ordered.

252. *Monkton Bridge.*
The court is informed by Henry White and William Mathewe constables of the hundred of Melksham that the bridge called Monkton bridge being in decay the inhabitants of the hundreds of Bradford and Melksham were indicted to repair the same. And forasmuch as the constables of the hundred of Melksham have on behalf of the inhabitants of the hundred paid the sum of five pounds for the repairing of that part of the bridge which belongs to the inhabitants of the hundred of Melksham to be repaired. And has also been at 17s charges and expenses in discharging of the indictment. Ordered that the constables shall make a rate upon the inhabitants of the hundred of Melksham for the levying of the moneys by them disbursed.
[If any refuse to pay, to be bound over.].

253. *Thomas Browne.*
The court is informed by Andrew Browne of Collingbourne Kingston that his father Thomas Browne being a poor cripple was allowed 12d a week for his relief by the overseers of Collingbourne. And that Thomas has received but 6s and half a bushel of wheat of his allowance for almost three years past during which time the petitioner has relieved his father to the great impoverishing of the petitioner who not being able to relieve him any longer Thomas is likely to perish. The court desires the next two justices to examine the premisses and allow unto the petitioner towards his expenses in relieving his father out of the arrears due unto him so much as they in their discretion shall think fit and to take such course for the future maintenance of Thomas as to law and justice shall appertain.

254. *Inter Gleed and Webb.*
The court is informed by Bennett Gleed of Lydiard Millicent labourer that he lives in a cottage erected upon the highways side in the parish of Lydiard. And that William Webb alias Richman of Lydiard gent pretending himself to be lord of the waste of Lydiard requires rent of Gleed for the cottage and sues him for the same in Wilton court. Ordered that Gleed shall not pay any rent to William Webb alias Richman for the cottage.

255. *Churchwardens and overseers of Malmesbury.* (See also **269**)
Upon complaint made to the court by the constables, churchwardens and overseers of the poor of the borough of Malmesbury for the year 1642 that they had disbursed and were engaged to divers persons in the borough for provision for the poor people then infected with the pestilence and others there more money than they had received. And whereas there was allowed thirty pounds weekly to be collected in the several parishes within five miles next adjoining within the borough, abbey and parish of Malmesbury . The court was also informed that many constables of the said parishes were behind about ninety pounds of the weekly payment whereupon the examination of the accounts of the constables, etc. both of their receipts and disbursements was referred to Mr William Eyre, Mr Gore and Mr Ivy or any two of them who calling the several constables and other parties interested in the premisses before them have certified to the court that there remains uncollected and due from the several hundreds besides the sum of twelve shillings and six pence which is to be added the sum of seventy one pounds one shilling and sixpence viz from the constables of the hundred of Malmesbury five pounds six shillings, Highworth hundred

fourteen pounds and six pence, Kingsbridge hundred twenty pounds, Chippenham hundred twenty seven pounds seven shillings and five pence, hundred of Damerham North five pounds seven shillings and a penny which amounts in the whole to the sum of seventy one pounds fourteen shillings as by the certificate remaining in the court appears which certificate the court confirms and orders the several sums due from the several constables of the hundred to be forthwith collected and paid over to the constables, churchwardens and overseers of the borough of Malmesbury which were in the year 1642. And in default of payment thereof that they distrain within their hundreds according to the statute.

[If any default, to be bound over.]

256.   *Thomas Dowse and Chilton Foliat.*
Complaint has been made by Thomas Dowse of Chilton Foliat clothworker for and on the behalf of the five female children of one Robert Pleister late of Chilton Foliat who as the court is informed is run away from his children and left them upon the parish of Chilton Foliat destitute of all help or relief but only some small goods which the five children have spent since their father's departure and are now in great want. Ordered that the churchwardens and overseers of the poor of Chilton Foliat take care and provide for the relief of the five children by making a rate over the parish and get the same confirmed according to law. And further that they bind forth apprentices such of the children as are fit to be bound forth to masters and to take care for the relief of the rest.

257.   *Alice Dimond.*
The court is informed by Alice Dimond a poor widow woman dwelling at Horningsham that her husband was slain at Wardour Castle under the command of Colonel Ludlow and has left her three small children and nothing to maintain them they being all sick and struck with leprosy and likely to perish for want of food. Ordered that the overseers of Horningsham shall forthwith take care of them and make a rate to relieve them and get the rate to be confirmed by the justices.

[If any refuse to pay, to be bound over.]

258.   *William Smyth.*
Upon hearing the matter in difference between the inhabitants of Charlton and the inhabitants of Whiteparish concerning the settlement of William Smyth his wife and children lately sent from Whiteparish unto Charlton. It appears to the court upon examination of witnesses upon oath that William Smyth was settled at Whiteparish and had

a house there and lived there with his family above a year last past. Ordered that William Smyth his wife and children shall be removed from Charlton and sent to Whiteparish there to remain and be settled until the inhabitants of Whiteparish shall hereafter show good cause to the contrary.

259. *Thomas Clarke.*
The court is informed by Mr Whitfield minister of Lydiard Millicent that Thomas Clarke alias Tyler of Lydiard Millicent keeps a disorderly alehouse and sells beer without licence he being formerly suppressed by the justices and still continues the selling of ale in contempt of the justices order. Ordered that from henceforth Clarke be suppressed from selling of ale and that the tithingmen of Lydiard Millicent forthwith carry Clarke before the next justice who is desired to bind him to the good behaviour and to appear at the next Sessions to answer the premises.

260. *Thomas Feald.*
Thomas Feald of Ramsbury is a very poor aged and impotent person and past labour and not able to relieve himself but is in great want and necessity and likely to perish without some course be taken for his relief and has made complaint thereof to the court. Ordered that the overseers of the poor of Ramsbury forthwith give some weekly allowance to Thomas towards his maintenance.
[If they refuse, to be bound over.]

261. *Ann Elcock.*
The court is informed that Ann Elcock being suspected to be with child by Richard Hurste and was afterwards married to him a covenant servant with Mr Kent of Boscombe. The court is now informed that Ann is in great necessity for want of relief. Ordered that Ann shall be sent to Boscombe where Richard Hurste her husband dwelt and there settled as a covenant servant. And that the overseers of the poor shall receive her and relieve her as a poor of the parish until the inhabitants of Boscombe shall show good cause unto the court to alter this order.

262. *John Wansey and Thomas Shoare constables of Maiden Bradley.*
It appears to the court upon the oaths of John Wansey and Thomas Shoare constables of Maiden Bradley that William Mattock, Robert Dunkerton and Edward Annerly of Maiden Bradley sell ale or beer without licence. Ordered that the said alehouse keepers shall be suppressed and by this order do stand suppressed. And that they shall severally pay to the use of the poor of that parish the several fines of twenty shillings a piece to be levied forthwith.

263. *Marston inhabitants and Worton.*
The court is informed by Mr Yorke of counsel with the inhabitants of
the tithing of Marston within the parish of Potterne that when the late
infection of the plague was at Potterne the inhabitants of the tithing
of Marston were also then infected and that the tithing of Worton was
not at all infected and that there was a rate of five shillings the yardlands
made throughout the whole parish of Potterne whereof the tithings
of Worton and Marston are part and that the tithing of Worton have
not paid their rate of five shillings the yardlands and prayed that the
same rate may be levied on the inhabitants of the tithing of Marston.
And that the inhabitants of the tithing of Marston might have the
one moiety thereof toward the extraordinary charges they were at in
relieving the poor infected persons of that place and that the other
moiety might be paid to Potterne. The court desires the two next
justices unto Marston to examine the truth thereof and make such
order therein for the relief of the said tithing.
    (The plague had started about 24th July 1644 and had lasted for about
three months. A1/110/1647H/230)

264. A certificate granted this Sessions to the commissioners of the
Great Seal of England upon the petition of John Lee of Wylye for
the loss of the value of three hundred pounds in housing, goods and
provisions and a bond by him given according to former directions
from the Lord Keeper.

265. *Inter Edward Shoare and several constables of hundreds.*
The court is informed by Mr Edward Shoare receiver of the moneys
payable out of the hundreds hereafter mentioned appointed for the
relief of the poor infected persons of Maiden Bradley and Horningsham
that Nicholas Mylls and John Aldridge constables of the hundred of
Warminster, John Gaifford and Edward Martyn constables of the
hundred of Whorwellsdown, George Dyer and John Kinge constables
of the hundred of Heytesbury and Thomas Smyth one of the constables
of the hundred of Mere have been negligent in collecting the money
rated in their several hundreds and payable for the relief of the infected
persons of Maiden Bradley and Horningsham by virtue of an order
of this court made at the last Quarter Sessions held at Marlborough
whereby the infected persons are in great misery for want of relief
and the infection likely to spread further unless by the mercy of God
it be timely prevented. Ordered that if the constables of the several
hundreds shall not forthwith after sight of this order collect levy and
pay in the moneys due and arrears in their several hundreds to the uses

aforesaid then the next justice upon complaint thereof to him made is desired to bind them over to the next Quarter Sessions.

266. Thursday 11 March 1646. Order of Parliament.
Ordered by the Commons assembled in Parliament that Mr Recorder and Mr Selden confer with such judges as are in town and acquaint them from this house that if they shall have any persons brought before them upon any fact committed by them (in tempore et loco bello) [i.e. in time of war] in pursuance and obedience of any ordinance of Parliament that the parties be discharged and that the judges do give so much in charge and direction to the jurors. And that Mr Recorder and Mr Selden do prepare a letter to be sent to such other of the judges as they shall not meet within the town.
H. Elsynge Clerk of Parliament.

267. *Chaffield Orcheston St George.*
The court is informed by Mr Frederick Hyde being of counsel with the inhabitants of the tithing of Chaffield within the parish of Orcheston St George that the tithing has of late years been much overrated and burdened in their parish rates more than they ought of right to be and that the inhabitants of Uppington being another tithing within the same parish who have always before paid a fourth part more all rates than the tithing of Chaffield. Ordered that the inhabitants of both tithings shall upon notice given attend Mr Giles Eyre and Mr Francis Swanton the two next justices who are desired to hear and examine the difference between the tithings concerning the rates and to settle and order the same according to equity and justice and then the court will confirm the same. And in the mean time the old rate to stand.

268. *Thomas Hobbes and Richard Starr constables of Longbridge Deverill.*
The court is informed by the constables and inhabitants of Longbridge Deverill that Thomas Hobbes and Richard Starr now constables there by reason that the leet is not kept as usually it has been they have served in office much longer than of right and custom they ought to have done and that Thomas Hobbes is lately removed out of the parish which is to the great damage as well of the constables as of the inhabitants and Richard Starr prayed the court to be discharged from the office and have nominated John Oldis and Henry Baker able and fitting men to serve and execute the office in their place and stead. Ordered John Oldis and Henry Baker to be constables of Longbridge Deverill. And the court orders John and Henry to repair to the next justice within one week after the receipt of this order there to take their oaths for due execution of their office upon pain of twenty pounds.

General Sessions of the Peace held at Devizes Tuesday 27th April Charles 23 (1647). Robert Nicholas, Edward Tooker, William Eyre.

269.   *Constables and churchwardens overseers of Malmesbury 1642.*
(Recites **255**. See also **292**)
Now further ordered that the several parishes mentioned in the former order are within five miles distance of the borough and no further to be disputed of. And that the several constables of the several hundreds respectively shall peremptorily forthwith collect the several sums of money due from the several hundreds and pay the same over to the constables of the borough of Malmesbury. And that in neglect and default thereof the court will further proceed against them according to law and justice.

270.   *Edward Weste and Edward Halle.*
Whereas Edward Weste tailor was bound over to this Quarter Sessions for not bringing up his apprentice Edward Halle in the trade of a tailor whereunto he was bound and whereas it now appears unto the court by proof upon oath of several witnesses that the said Halle has lived with his master about six years and is able to do very little at his trade his employment having been for the most part about the household work and very little at the trade. And it was also proved that there was five pounds given with the boy by his grandfather Mr Thurman when he was bound apprentice to Weste. Ordered upon full hearing of the matter that Edward Halle shall be discharged from his apprenticeship with his master and that his master shall pay back unto Mr Thurman five pounds which Weste received with his apprentice which moneys are promised by Weste to be paid before Whitsunday next and in default thereof Weste is to be bound over to the next Quarter Sessions. And the five pounds is to be employed for the binding for the apprentice of Halle to some other man or otherwise employed for the best benefit and advantage of the boy.

271.   *John Rogers and Robert Trymnell constables of Calne.*
It appears to the court that John Rogers and Robert Trymnell now constables of the hundred of Calne have served in the same office above three years a piece and that they have not paid in the moneys due out of their hundred for the relief of maimed soldiers etc pretending they cannot receive the same. Nevertheless they desire to be discharged of their office. And whereas there are warrants to be granted now by the court for discharging them out of their office and for electing

of new constables in their place.   Ordered that the constables shall forthwith send out their warrants to the several petty constables and churchwardens for the several parishes and places within the hundred for the speedy levying collecting and paying in unto them all such moneys as are due and in arrear for the foresaid collections at such convenient time as they shall appoint in regard the constables of the hundred are ordered and appointed to pass their accounts thereof and other matters before Whitsunday next before Mr Eyre and Mr Ivy justices who are desired to take their accounts by that time or bind them over to the next Quarter Sessions in case they shall fail to do the same.   And all the petty constables and churchwardens are hereby strictly required not to fail in collecting levying and paying in of all such moneys as are due from them as they will answer the neglect thereof at their perils.

272.   *Edward Bull.*   (See also **177, 210, 246, 324**)
The court is informed by Edward Bull of Westbury Leigh that at the last Quarter Sessions held at Salisbury he obtained an order for the payment of thirty pounds by the Treasurer and that he has often required the thirty pounds but cannot receive one penny from him.   And prayed the assistance of the court for satisfaction of the same in regard of his faithful service to the state and his long forbearance thereof. All which the court taking into consideration and to the intent that Edward Bull may be speedily satisfied the thirty pounds do think fit, order and desire Sir John Ernle, William Eyre and George Ivy justices or any two of them to call before them Mr Roger Cawley and Mr Benedict Browne the last Treasurers for the north before Whitsunday next to pass their accounts of such moneys as they have received and disbursed concerning their several offices since their election thereunto and cause them to pay in the surplussage of moneys due upon their accounts and upon receipt thereof the justices are desired to cause thirty pounds to be paid unto Edward in the first place in satisfaction of the last order of Sessions in regard the same has been a long time out of his purse and disbursed for the service of the county.

273.   *Simon Lane of Pewsey.*   (See also **833**)
The court has been informed by Mr Staples that the parish of Pewsey is a great parish of extent and much travelled both by carriers and others and that there is but one inn there for entertainment of passengers. And that Simon Lane who is licensed to keep a common alehouse there by Sir John Ernle and John Norden two near justices to Pewsey to consider of the premises whether Simon Lane be a fit man for keeping an alehouse and to further license him if they shall think fit.

274. *John Whittaker, Edward Moore and Phillip Sutton.* (Recites **149** on which order nothing has been done. See also **396, 686, 717**)
The court now desires Mr Eyre, Mr Topp and Mr Ivy or one of them to call before them Mr Sherston, etc and take their accounts and certify the same at the next Sessions. Also ordered that the Treasurers shall pay unto the mayor of Devizes forth of the money remaining in their hands of the surplussage of their accounts the sum of ten pounds to remain in his hands until the court shall be certified of the truth of the petitioners losses. And if in case the petition be true the court orders that the ten pounds be proportionately paid unto the petitioners according to their several losses. And the court further orders that the residue of the surplussage shall be paid in unto the Clerk of the Peace at the next Quarter Sessions to remain in his hands to be disposed of by the court for the use of the county.
   [If they refuse, to be bound over.]

275. *Peter Godby, Edward Horne.*
The court is informed by Peter Godby and Edward Horne late constables of the borough of Bradford that in the time that the sickness of the plague remained in Bradford the parishes and villages lying within five miles compass thereof were by warrant from Sir Thomas Hall and Robert Eyre justices taxed to pay one hundred and twenty pounds for two months being fifteen pounds a week towards the relief of the poor infected people whereof forty nine pounds is already collected and paid in but the other seventy one pounds thereof residue they do refuse to pay during which time of infection the petitioners laid forth and engaged themselves to butchers and other tradesmen for sustenance for the poor infected people to the value of forty pounds more than they have received and are daily sued for the same. The court desires Mr Eyre and Mr Ivy justices to examine the truth of the petition and take speedy order for the petitioners relief.

276. *John Griffeth.*
The court is informed as well by John Griffeth of Urchfont as by a certificate under the hands of the most substantial persons and inhabitants of the parish of Urchfont that Griffeth has lived in the parish three score years or thereabouts and has honestly behaved himself towards his neighbours and is destitute of an habitation for the succour of himself and family. And whereas John Griffeth has obtained licence from the lord of the manor for to erect and build him a cottage upon some part of the waste of the manor. Ordered that Griffeth shall erect and build him a cottage for the succour of himself and family upon

some convenient place on the waste of the manor to be assigned unto him and the same to continue a cottage for the succour of himself and family without incurring the forfeiture mentioned in the statute until it shall be otherwise ordered by the court.

277. *John Goodwyn tithingman of Westwood and Iford.*
The court is informed by John Goodwin tithingman of the tithing of Westwood and Iford as by a certificate under the hands of ten of the inhabitants that the tithingman there has heretofore been usually chosen at the court held there by the Dean and Chapter of Winchester and that the same being now in sequestration there is no court kept. And that Goodwin has served in the office above three years last past and by the custom Christopher Cromwell ought to be the next tithingman. Ordered that Christopher Cromwell shall be tithingman and that he shall within one week after notice of this order repair to some justice to take his oath for the executing of the office upon pain of ten pounds.

278. *Inhabitants of Froxfield, Little Bedwyn and Chiseldon.*
Ordered that the overseers of the poor of the several places or parishes of Froxfield, Little Bedwyn and Chiseldon shall attend at the next Quarter Sessions with their witnesses that the business concerning the settling of William Fabian now remaining at Little Bedwyn may be heard and ordered. And the court declares and orders that the staying of Fabian at Little Bedwyn in the mean time shall not be prejudicial to the inhabitants of that place in point of right at the hearing thereof.

279. *Edward Yates and Robert Huggins.* (See also **291**)
Edward Yates and Robert Huggins late constables of Malmesbury in 1642 upon their information of the court that in the time of their constableship they had disbursed and were engaged for the use of the parish the sum of thirty pounds for watching and warding, for arms and mending of arms for the trained soldiers and for conveying of prisoners to gaol. And thereupon the court referred the examination of the truth of the premises and the relief of the constables unto Mr Charles Gore and George Ivy, justices. And now for that it appears to the court by a certificate under the hands of divers of the inhabitants of Malmesbury that they have made a rate for the satisfying of Yates and Huggins of the moneys and that many of them have paid to the rate but divers others do refuse the payment thereof.
      [If any refuse to pay, to be bound over.]

280. *Henry Spackman.*
The court is informed by Henry Spackman of Lydiard Millicent

coppersmith that he is a very poor man and was born and has always lived at Lydiard Millicent is destitute of an habitation for the succour of himself his wife and five small children and also for his mother who is relieved by the parish which petition is attested under the hands of some of the inhabitants of Lydiard Millicent. And whereas Sir Anthony Ashley Cooper baronet lord of the manor of Lydiard Millicent has likewise certified his consent unto the court under his hand and seal that Spackman should with the licence of the court erect and build a cottage for him and his wife to dwell in during their lives in some convenient place upon the waste within the manor. Ordered that Spackman shall or may erect and build him a cottage for the succour of himself his wife and family to dwell in upon some convenient place upon the waste of Sir Anthony Ashley Cooper's manor in Lydiard Millicent and shall continue the same cottage without incurring the forfeiture mentioned in the statute until it shall be otherwise ordered by the court.

281. *Thomas Ragland.*
The court is informed by Thomas Ragland keeper of the hospital otherwise called the spittle house at East Harnham near the city of Salisbury that there is allowed five pounds per annum to be paid by the Treasurer towards the relief of the poor people of the hospital whereof there is fifteen pounds behind for three years now last past and the poor people are like to perish for want of relief. And whereas the court is informed that Mr Roger Cawley heretofore and yet Treasurer refuses to pay the allowance and that for want thereof the poor people of the spittle house are like to perish unless some speedy course be taken therein. Ordered that Mr Francis Bennett shall forthwith pay unto Thomas the sum of five pounds out of the county's stock remaining in his hands for the present succour and relief of the poor people in regard of their great necessity.

282. *Roger Cawley.*
The court desires Mr William Sadler justice to bind over Mr Roger Cawley of Hilmarton to the next Quarter Sessions there to answer to such matters as shall be objected against there concerning the neglect of his office.

283. *Alexander Sessions.*
The court is informed that Alexander Sessions of Liddington carpenter having formerly erected a cottage for his habitation and dwelling in the lordship of Mr Sharrington Talbott in the parish of Liddington on part of the waste ground at the corner of the lane there has now

obtained licence from Mr Talbott lord of the waste under his hand and seal for continuance of the cottage. Ordered that the cottage shall remain continue and be a cottage for the habitation succour and dwelling of Alexander Sessions and Lettice his wife without incurring the forfeiture mentioned in the statute unless it shall hereafter otherwise ordered by the court.

284. *William Pound and wife, Robert Rolfe.* (See **199**)
It appears to the court that William Pound and his wife and Robert Rolfe were convicted at Michaelmas Sessions last by the testimony of two witnesses then sworn in open court that they had taken and carried away five hundred lugg of hedge of Sir Anthony Ashley Cooper of the value of twenty nobles. It was then ordered that Pound and Rolfe should pay unto Sir Anthony for his damage the sum of twenty nobles before the 17th day of October then next following and in default thereof it was then also ordered that Pound and his wife and Rolfe should be openly whipped at Lydiard Millicent by the officer there. Now for that this court is credibly informed that the twenty nobles is not paid and that Thomas Little being the titihingman of Lydiard Millicent has not only neglected the execution of the order but also utterly refuses the execution thereof. Ordered that the constable of the hundred of Highworth does forthwith and upon sight of this order apprehend Thomas Little and convey him to His Majesty's gaol of Fisherton Anger there to remain until he shall perform the order or cause the same to be duly executed.

285. *Inhabitants of Urchfont.*
The inhabitants of Urchfont have desired the court to confirm a rate by them made for the repair of their highways which rate is as follows: That all parishioners shall be charged at the rate of four shillings the yardland. That in case the four shillings the yardland shall not suffice for the repairing of the ways then we further charge other four shillings more upon every yardland within the parish. That this order and rate shall always continue for the repairing and maintenance of the highways. That every day labourer and other inhabitants there not herein charged by virtue of this rate shall either work according to the statute or pay 6d. a day for every day as he or any of them shall make default. The court confirms the rate unless good cause shall be shown to the contrary at the next Quarter Sessions.

286. *Milford bridge.*
The bridge called Milford bridge near Salisbury is grown into great decay for want of reparation and by reason it is not well known who

of right ought to repair the same. Ordered that the Treasurer shall forthwith disburse unto Benedict Swayne, Mr Marshall, John Evans and Edward Barnes inhabitants of Milford the sum of five pounds with a salvo iure [i.e. saving the right] the county. And that the same shall not hereafter be taken for any prejudice to the county in point of right. Further ordered that there be an indictment preferred against the inhabitants of Milford and Laverstock for the not repairing of the bridge that it may be known who of right ought to repair the same.

287. *Inhabitants of Westbury, Ann Greenhill, John Lane.*
The court is informed by a certificate under the hands of divers of the inhabitants of Westbury that Ann Greenhill widow being an aged and impotent person of Westbury by means of the death of her husband became destitute of an habitation and dwelling and hereupon with the assistance of John Lane her son-in-law and some other charitable people there have built a cottage for her habitation upon the waste ground within the parish of Westbury. And whereas Sir John Danvers lord of the manor of Heywood within the parish of Westbury where the cottage is built has certified unto the court his consent under his hand and seal that Ann Greenhill and John Lane shall continue their habitation in the cottage. Ordered that Ann Greenhill and John Lane shall continue the same cottage for their habitation without incurring the forfeiture mentioned in the statute until it shall be otherwise ordered by the court.

288. *Visitors of the house of correction.*
The court desires William Sadler and Richard Goddard of Clatford to be visitors of the house of correction at Marlborough, John Topp and John Norden at Devizes, Edward Tooker and Francis Swanton and Giles Eyre at Fisherton Anger.

General Sessions of the Peace held at Warminster 20th July Charles 23 (1647). William Hussey, Edward Tooker, William Eyre.

289. *Alice Bleathman.*
It appears to the court by a certificate under the hands of the most ablest and sufficient inhabitants within the parish of Homington that Alice Bleathman is a poor old lame impotent person and has no house to inhabit in neither is she anyways able to work to get her maintenance to pay any rent for a house if such house should be gotten. It also appears that Alice has obtained a licence from Richard Gorge and

Francis Swanton lords of the manor there and the assent of the whole inhabitants to erect and build her a house for her habitation and dwelling in a fit and convenient place upon the waste. Ordered that Alice shall erect and build her a house upon the waste which house shall be for her habitation and dwelling during her natural life without incurring the forfeitures mentioned in the statute.

290. *Jeffery Pope and Edward Younge.*
Jeffery Pope of Whiteparish was in Christmas Sessions last ordered and appointed to serve the office of constable of the hundred of Frustfield in the place of Edward Younge gent and he has neglected or refused to take his oath and the execution of the office. Further ordered Jeffery Pope forthwith upon sight of this order to repair to the next justice to take his oath for the due execution of the office which if he shall neglect or refuse then the next justice is desired to bind Pope to the good behaviour and to appear at the next Quarter Sessions.

291. *Edward Yate and Robert Huggins constables of Malmesbury.* (Recites **279**. See also **345**))
It now appears to the court by a certificate under the hands of divers of the inhabitants of Malmesbury that they have made a rate for the satisfying of Yates and Huggins of the money and that many of them have paid the rate but divers others refuse the payment thereof. The court desires the next justice to Malmesbury to bind over to the next Sessions all those who refuse to make payment of the rate.

292. *Constables, churchwardens and overseers of Malmesbury.* (Recites **269**)
Whereas upon the order of the last sessions on the neglect and refusal of the constables therein mentioned George Ivy justice granted his warrant for the binding over of the several constables to answer their neglect at this sessions which warrant was contemned by the several constables as the court is now informed by the oath of Robert Huggins. The court therefore confirms the order of the last Sessions and further orders that the £14 and 6d payable forth of the hundred of Highworth, Cricklade and Staple be also collected and paid into the court at the next Sessions and then the court will further consider thereof as touching the £14 6d. And for the rest to be forthwith collected and paid over unto the constables, etc of Malmesbury.
[If any refuse to pay, to be bound over.]

293. *Radigan Crandon and overseers of Westbury.*
Concerning the difference between Radigan Crandon and the overseers of the poor of Westbury about some money she pretends to

be due to her for keeping of a child. The court refers the matter to the hearing examination and ending of Thomas Bennett justice who is desired to call the parties before him and end the difference that the court may be no further troubled.

294.   *Susan Barter distracted.*
It appears to the court as well upon their own view as upon the information of some of the chiefest inhabitants of the town of Warminster that Susan Barter wife of John Barter of Warminster is a distracted woman and walks up and down the town in a distracted and distempered condition likely to hurt men women and children and to set the town on fire in her distempers if she is not prevented and being concerned that she may be recovered thereof if care be taken for her in time. Ordered that the overseers of the poor of Warminster shall forthwith take her into their care as one of the poor and take course that she is kept in and allowed fitting relief that she goes not abroad until she is well recovered that no hurt be done by her. The court orders and appoints the overseers to take course forthwith that she by the blessing of God may be cured of these distempers in regard her husband is a very poor man and unable to keep and relieve her himself. And whatsoever the overseers shall disburse or lay out for her in obedience of this order the same shall be allowed them again out of the rate for the poor.
   [If overseers are in default, to be bound over.]

295.   *Mary Foord.*
The court is informed by Mary Foord of Westbury widow that John Southery of Westbury sells ale without licence and that Sibbell his wife is often drunk and abuses her neighbours and has beaten Mary Foord her daughter and taken away her clothes from her and detains them and prayed the relief of the court therein. Ordered that the matter complained of shall be referred to Mr Bennett justice who is desired to call the parties before him and examine the matter complained of and do therein that which should be agreeable to law and justice.

296.   *Thomas Willoughby, William Baylie.*
Thomas Willoughby of Warminster gent and William Baylie of the same were distrained by the sheriff by virtue of a 'distringas' [distraint] of the court against the inhabitants of Warminster upon three several presentments against the inhabitants for decay of the highways within the parish. To which presentment Willoughby and Baylie have appeared at this court on the behalf of the inhabitants and made oath for the repairing of the ways and have discharged the presentments and

for their charges in the doing thereof have disbursed the sum of thirty nine shillings and four pence forth of their own purses. Ordered that forthwith there be a rate made on the inhabitants of Warminster for the payment of the 39s 4d unto Willoughby and Baylie and that the same be forthwith paid unto them accordingly.

[If any refuse to pay, to be bound over.]

297. *Against maltsters.*
There is now a great scarcity of corn and grain not only in this kingdom in general but also in this county in particular by reason whereof many poor people are driven into great want and many likely to perish for want of bread. And that without the mercy of God a dearth and scarcity of corn is much to be feared in the year ensuing and for preventing of converting of that small quantity of barley now remaining in this county into malt and so the poor to want bread. Ordered and declared that no maltster whatsoever shall or may from and after the present Quarter Sessions buy within this county in any market or elsewhere any barley to convert into malt until after the feast of St Michael the Archangel next upon such pain and punishment as by the laws and statutes of this kingdom is ordered. Further ordered and required that all constables and other officers shall duly look to the execution and due performance of this order and cause the same to be forthwith proclaimed and published in all market towns within this county.

298. *Charles Gunn.*
The court is informed by Charles Gunn of Warminster that he is near eighty years of age and has not any means not so much as a house of his own but formerly he had a small stock of money which he employed in making malt for which he was rated a penny a week to the poor and which stock one Innbarr with his associates robbed Charles which extends to the great impoverishing of him and his crippled wife. Nevertheless he is still rated at a penny a week and can have no redress therein. The court desires Mr Bennett the next justice to send for the overseers of Warminster and some of the chiefest of the inhabitants there that made the rate and Charles before him and examine the matter and make such order as shall be agreeable to law and justice.

299. *John Allwood.*
The court is informed by John Allwood of Norton Bavant that he has lost his sight and is near one hundred years of age and has received relief from the collection two years and upwards which has lately been detained from him about six weeks and more to his great hurt he being

not able to do anything for his maintenance. The court desires Mr Bennett justice to send for the overseers of the poor and the petitioner before him and examine the truth of the petition and make such order for the petitioner's relief as shall be agreeable to law and justice.

300. *Several constables and inhabitants of Devizes.*
The several constables of the several hundreds of Swanborough, Calne, Whorwellsdown, Potterne and Cannings and the tithingman of Patney were at Christmas Sessions last indicted for refusing and neglecting the execution of a warrant made for the relief of the poor inhabitants of Devizes in the time of their visitation of the plague to which indictment some of the constables have appeared and pleaded and were bound over to prosecute their traverses at this Sessions. Ordered by the consent of all parties that prosecution upon the indictment shall be stayed until the next Sessions and the examination thereof be referred to Mr Topp, Mr William Eyre, Mr Norden and Mr Yorke or any two of them who are desired to take such course and order therein as they shall think fit. And all the constables are to appear at the next Sessions there to be tried or otherwise discharged upon their indictment. And that their recognisances for prosecuting their traverses be in the mean time respited.

301. *Morris and overseers of Warminster.*
At the last Christmas Sessions the court was informed by one Morris a poor man of the parish of Warminster that the overseers of the poor owed unto him for the keeping of a young child by the space of one and twenty weeks the sum of 35s and that he was in great necessity thereof. It was then ordered that the overseers should forthwith pay the same money unto Morris in regard of his want and poverty. The court is now informed by Morris that the money is not yet paid. The court orders and desires the next justice to call the overseers of Warminster before him and to do Morris justice therein.

302. *William Lovell.*
William Lovell of Malmesbury has been convicted for selling ale without licence. Ordered that he repair within one fortnight next ensuing this present Sessions before Mr William Eyre and Mr George Ivy justices or one of them with two sufficient sureties to enter into recognisances to His Majesty's use not to sell ale any more according to the statute which if he shall neglect or refuse then the justices are desired to bind him over to the good behaviour and to appear at the next Sessions.

303. *Thomas Ragland.*
The court is informed by Thomas Ragland keeper of the hospital at East Harnham that the poor people of the hospital are in great necessity for want of relief and that he cannot get any money from the Treasurer of the arrears due mentioned in the order of the last sessions. The court orders and appoints Mr Bennett to pay Ragland the sum of five pounds out of the county's stock remaining in his hands for the relief of the poor people.

304. *Joan Neate.*
The court is informed by Joan Neate wife of William Neate of the parish of St Mary's in Devizes that she has a child of one John Griffen a soldier there when it was a garrison town of the Parliament and Griffen was slain in the same town and that the mother thereof ran away from her child. And the child being left with Neate's wife she has kept the same near three years since the mother ran away and that she is not able to keep the child any longer and has made her complaint thereof to the mayor of Devizes and can have no relief for the keeping and relieving the child. Ordered that the overseers of the poor shall forthwith take the child into their relief and provide for him as a poor of that parish. And if they shall refuse to do the same then the justice is desired to take such course for the relief of the child as law and justice shall appertain.

305. *Roger Hollis.* (See also **328, 348, 445**)
The court is informed by Roger Hollis that he has served the State service four years or thereabouts and by misfortune his horse fell with him and crushed his foot in so much that he is not able to help himself or to get his living. The court is also informed that he has lived in Heytesbury by the space of half a year with his father since he received his hurt and that his father is not of ability to relieve him any longer. Ordered that he shall remain at Heytesbury and that the overseers of the poor shall provide for him and give him fitting relief until he shall be recovered and able to get his maintenance.
[If they refuse, to be bound over.]

306. *Stephen Mattock.*
It appears to the court that Stephen Mattock and Luce his wife of the parish of Sutton Veny are very old and impotent people and in great want and poverty. Ordered that the overseers of Sutton do forthwith take care and provide for Stephen and his wife according to their wants and necessities.

307. *Inhabitants of Seend and Seend Row tithing.*
The court is informed by the inhabitants of Seend and Seend Row tithing that they have already made a rate of six shillings the yardland for repairing their highways the which have been to very good purpose disbursed by the supervisors and yet the ways want further reparations and desires the confirmation of the rate, the one being the rate of six shillings the yardland to which some certain refractory persons have not paid their rates and the other new rate of four shillings the yardland for the better amendment of the ways being as yet in great need thereof the same rates being attested with the hands of the chiefest inhabitants of those tithings. Ordered that both the rates shall be confirmed and shall be collected and employed for the repair of their highways until the court shall see good cause to alter the same.
[If any refuse to pay, to be bound over.]

308. *Katherine Hollis.*
Complaint of Katherine Hollis of Fonthill Gifford that she being a poor aged woman and has long lived in the parish of Fonthill Gifford and being destitute of a habitation and not able by reason of age and poverty to procure herself a house. The court taking the same into consideration and that the desmesnes and wastes of the parish being lately the Lord Cottyngtons and now sequestered by the State commends the consideration of the premises to Mr William Hussey being steward to the commissioners of the Prince Palatine's revenue desiring him to acquaint the commissioners herewith that Katherine may be provided for and relieved accordingly. And that the overseers of the poor of Fonthill take care that she be kept to work and be provided for in the mean time.

309. *Samuel Quynton.*
It appears to the court on the petition of Samuel Quinton vicar of Wilsford that he and his predecessors for many years past have been rated but at two yardlands for his vicarage towards all rates and payments within the parish until now of late within these four years last in the times of trouble wherein one John Hurd gent being overseer of the poor has lately raised the vicarage to three yardlands and so easing himself of one yardland. Ordered that the vicarage shall continue the ancient rate of two yardlands according to the old rate unless there be good cause showed to the contrary.

310. *John Stoakes and Ann Salter.* (Recites **249**. See also **212**)
It appears unto the court that nothing has been done. It is therefore now further ordered that the matter shall again be referred to the

examination of two near adjoining justices who are desired to take the matter in examination and consider thereof and make such order therein for the relief of the parish of Seend and punishment of Stoakes as in their discretion and as to law and justice shall appertain.

311. *Inhabitants of Leigh.*
It appears to the court by a petition under the hands of divers of the inhabitants of Leigh that there is a common bridge called Cow bridge lying within the parish which is in great decay and which ought to be repaired by the inhabitants of Leigh. Now for that the bridge being a common highway and rode for horses and other passengers leading towards Cricklade and Highworth and is at this present in great decay and very dangerous for passengers. Ordered that for the speedy and full repair of the bridge there shall be public warning given in the parish church by the constable and churchwardens and overseers there or by one of them for the making a general and equal rate. And if any of the parish shall be refractory thereunto and not submit themselves to the rates or refuse to pay the same then he or they refusing upon complaint made to some justice near adjoining shall be bound over to the next Quarter Sessions.

312. *Nathaniel Creeche.*
The court is informed by Nathaniel Creeche a maimed soldier and pensioner that about thirteen years last past he had a pension of four pounds per annum allowed him by the Court of Sessions and that there is four pounds due unto him for one year's pay at Easter last and although he has been often with Mr Browne the late Treasurer he could not get if of him in regard the country did not bring into him their pay for the same relief and now he is out of his office and the new Treasurer Mr Aylewoorth makes a scruple to pay the four pounds without the order of this court. All which the court taking into consideration and seeing Creeche is in great necessity for want thereof orders and appoints Mr Aylewoorth to pay the four pounds to Creeche upon sight of this order that the court be no further troubled therewith.

313. *Inter inhabitants of Hannington and Castle Eaton, Nicholas Curtys.*
There has been some difference between the inhabitants of Hannington and the inhabitants of Castle Eaton about the settlement of Nicholas Curtys. Upon hearing of counsel of both sides ordered that Curtys shall be and continue at Castle Eaton until there be further cause shown to the court to the contrary.

314. *Susan Weekes.*

The court is informed by Susan Weekes of Westbury that there was a child placed by the parish with her at a very low rate being but ten pence a week and having kept it a long time there is now eleven shillings due to Susan which the parish refuses to pay. Ordered that the overseers of the poor shall forthwith pay the eleven shillings to Susan. (If in default, to be bound over.)

315. *Harnham bridge, Arthur Poore and Thomas Poore.*

The court is informed that whereas Harnham bridge being a bridge of public travel from all the western parts towards London and grown into great decay for want of reparations and not known whether the same ought to be repaired by the county or any particular person and that for present necessity and repair of the bridge Mr Arthur Poore at Christmas Sessions 17 Charles was ordered to repair the bridge. And since that Mr Thomas Poore of Harnham was likewise ordered by the judges of Assize for the repair of the bridge who have both disbursed several sums of money for the repair viz Arthur the sum of three pounds and Thomas the sum of nine pounds and neither of them have had any satisfaction for the same. Ordered that Mr Edward Tooker , Mr Giles Eyre and Mr Francis Swanton or any two of them be desired to examine the disbursements and make order for the payment thereof forth of the stock of the county. And that the same shall not be any evidence or otherwise prejudicial against the county in time to come when it shall be found out who of right ought to repair the same.

316. *Robert Monday, Marston* [Potterne] *and Elston* [Orcheston St George].

The court has been informed that Robert Monday a poor man who lately lived and inhabited at Elston is now removed from thence and lives at Marston and has left behind him John Monday his son who was born and always living at Elston and about twenty years of age and is now very likely to be chargeable to the parish of Elston since the departure of his father who uses the trade and art of making beehives wherein John was and will be useful to his father. Now for the better easing of the inhabitants of Elston where John by law ought to be placed and provided for, ordered with the consent of his father that the overseers of the poor of Elston shall pay 12d weekly to Robert and he to keep his son at work with him in his trade and to look to him so long as he shall be of ability to use and follow trade and afterwards John to be settled at Elston again.

317.   *Certificate pro Robert Raynes for fire.*
To the Right Honourable.   May it please your honours that at the Quarter Sessions held at Warminster 20th July 23 Charles [1647] Robert Raynes of Keevil tailor humbly presented unto the court his humble petition therein setting forth that a sudden and lamentable accident of fire begun in the middle of the night upon 27th March last past at the house of Henry Jones gent, Robert had his dwelling house together with his barn stall and his other outhouses together also with all his hay and the greatest part of his goods and household stuff utterly thereby consumed to the loss and damage of one hundred pounds and upwards by means whereof Robert is utterly undone and altogether destitute of a habitation for himself his wife and three small children and likely to perish unless they may be relieved therein.   Which petition the court conceives to be true for that it did appear unto the court by the several oaths of William Hancock and Henry Spire two of the inhabitants of Keevil sworn and examined in open court who deposed the contents of the petition to be true.   And that Robert has given sufficient security in court for the true employment of such moneys as shall be collected by virtue of His Majesty's letters patent according to a letter of direction from the late Right Honourable Thomas Lord Coventry late Lord Keeper of the Great Seal of England sent unto the justices of this county and remaining amongst the records of the county.   Which we the justices whose names are subscribed present at the said sessions do humbly certify unto your honours leaving the premisses to your honours grave judgment and directions therein and have subscribed our names at the Sessions humbly taking our leaves of your honours at Warminster 20th July 23 year of His Majesty's reign [1647].

318.   *Bakers and alehouse keepers in Warminster.*
The court has taken into consideration the great abuse of bakers in not making their bread according to the assize to the great prejudice and deceit of His Majesty's subjects.   Ordered that from henceforth the constables of the town of Warminster shall take care that the bread as well of the town bakers as of the country bakers brought thither to the market to be sold be made according to the assize and see that their bread weighed every market day by the breadweighers of that place and present unto the next justice all such bread as they shall find to want weight and such other bread there sold for which there is no assize in the assize book together with the bakers' names that make such light bread and other bread that the bakers may be punished according to the law.   And Mr Francis Bennett is appointed to be assisting the constables in the execution of this order as often as his occasion will permit and take course also that the same be executed

in the tithing of Smallbrook within the town of Warminster. And for the better execution of this order the court orders that there shall be a just balance and troy weights provided forthwith for the weighing of bread by him that ought to provide the same. And the court taking also into consideration the great abuse of alehouse keepers in selling less than a full quart of the best beer for a penny and two quarts of small beer for a penny and in permitting and suffering of persons to remain tippling and drinking in their houses contrary to the law and at unseasonable times in the night. Ordered the officers forthwith to give notice to all alehouse keepers that they sell their beer and ale by the ale quart and a full quart of their best beer or ale for a penny and two quarts of small beer or ale for a penny and not otherwise as they will answer to the contrary at their perils and suffer such punishment as upon complaint and proof thereof shall be inflicted upon them according to the law.

[The like order for all other places in this county leaving out Mr Bennett's assistance.]

319. *Mr Bennett and Mr Markes supervisors of Steeple Ashton.*
The court is informed by Mr Bennett and Mr Markes supervisors of the highways of Steeple Ashton upon their oaths that these persons hereafter named have not paid their rates made by the yardlands towards the reparations of the highways: Mrs Pawlett widow six shillings, Edward Martyn for the parsonage twelve shillings, William Whitaker thirteen pence, Walter Markes thirteen pence, Edward Webb nine shillings, William Bremwich gent six shillings which tends to the hindrance of the repair of the highways. Ordered that the supervisors shall demand the several rates of the several parties.

(If any refuse to pay, to be bound over.)

320. *Robert Eagle.*
Robert Eagle of Quemerford [Calne]was bound over to appear at this Sessions and to keep the King's peace towards Susan his wife. And upon his appearance the court was informed that he has so miserable beaten his wife that she is not able to come to the Sessions to prosecute against him. The court is likewise informed by a certificate of the chiefest inhabitants of Calne that Robert is a person of very lewd and ill behaviour for that he having a wife of his own by whom he has two children both living has nevertheless by the space of five years now last past forsaken the company of his wife and accompanies one Dorothy Balle by whom he has had two bastards and that he maintains Dorothy and keeps the bastards as his own leaving his wife and children to themselves without allowing them anything at all for their relief they

having no other relief or maintenance than the bare labour of his wife. Ordered that Robert shall be committed to the gaol there to remain until he shall put in good sureties to appear at the next Quarter Sessions and in the meantime to be of the good behaviour. The court desires the two next justice to examine the truth of the certificate and to take such course with Robert for the relief of his wife and children and for the punishment of Dorothy as to law and justice shall appertain and to certify their doings therein at the next Quarter Sessions.

321. *Restraining of maltsters.*
The court has now restrained maltsters appearing before them from buying of excessive quantities of barley to convert into malt for that the scarcity of corn may be prevented and the poor people may have corn for their money. Ordered that all sellers of corn within the county shall bring forth all their corn into the open fairs and markets as they shall bring thither to be sold and shall not sell the same by sample within doors or out of the markets. And all maltsters not restrained are hereby ordered to be suppressed.

General Sessions of the Peace held at Marlborough Tuesday after feast of St. Michael Archangel 5 October Charles 23 (1647). Robert Nicholas, George Howe, John Norden, Richard Goddard, William Sadler, Robert Hippisley, Francis Swanton.

322. *Inhabitants of Kemble and Leigh.*
Upon hearing the matter of difference between the inhabitants of Kemble and the Leigh concerning the settlement of one Susan Styles. Ordered that the difference be referred to the examination of Mr Ivy and Mr Sadler justices who are desired to meet and examine the difference and to give notice unto the parties interested therein of their meetings and to certify the court thereof at the Sessions that a final order may be made therein. And both parties are to attend them at their perils. And Susanna shall remain in that parish where she was the first day of this Sessions without any prejudice to the settlement of her.

323. *Constables of the several hundreds.*
The court is informed that as well the late constables as the now constables for the time being of the several hundreds of Westbury, Warminster, Whorwellsdown, Heytesbury and Mere are all behind in payment as well as the five mile rate as of the weekly rate of one hundred marks a week towards the relief of the poor infected people

of Maiden Bradley and Horningsham. Ordered that the constables of the several hundreds do upon demand and notice of this order pay unto Mr Edward Shore of Maiden Bradley all the arrears due from the said hundreds upon both the rates before the feast of All Saints next or otherwise return such sufficient return in law as they will stand unto. (If in default, to be bound over.)

324. *Bull's order for £30. All constables and other officers to collect the arrears.* (Recites **246**. See also **177, 210, 272**)
The court is now informed that Edward Bull has received no benefit of that order but remains still unsatisfied the thirty pounds in regard that Mr Cawley has not taken upon him the said office and the county has not paid into Mr Browne the moneys due unto him and that much of the moneys for the collections remain in the constables, petty constables and churchwardens hands. Ordered that the matter shall be again referred unto the justices who are desired to send for the constables, etc in the north part of the county to appear before them and examine them what moneys thereof they have received and remain in their hands and what moneys are in arrear and cause the officers to pay in the money remaining in their hands to the now Treasurers and take order that the arrears may be speedily levied collected and paid in to the now Treasurers and cause the Treasurers to pay Edward the thirty pounds.
(If in default, to be bound over.)

325. *Inhabitants of Devizes against several constables of hundreds.*
It appears to the court upon complaint of the inhabitants of Devizes that the constables of the several hundreds of Potterne and Cannings, Swanborough, Elstub and Everleigh, Whorwellsdown and Calne are all of them behind in payment of the arrears due to the inhabitants in the time of their visitation with the sickness and as by the several orders heretofore made and a certificate returned into the court from Sir John Ernle and Mr William Eyre appears. Ordered that the constables do before the feast of All Saints [1 November] next pay unto Mr WilliamThurman of Devizes all such moneys as are behind and in arrear or else give sufficient return in law as they will stand unto.
(If in default, to be bound over.)

326. *Mr Hunt Treasurer of King's Bench.*
The court is informed that Richard Hunt of Dauntsey gent elected Treasurer of the King's Bench for the north at Easter Sessions last is since deceased and to the intent that the office may be served and the country satisfied with the account of Hunt of the moneys received

by him since his election and of his payments concerning the same. Ordered that Mr John Hunt of Dauntsey gent the executor of Richard be Treasurer for the remaining part of this year. Ordered that Mr John Hunt takes upon him the execution of the office and collect and get into his hands all the arrears of money due concerning the collections and all such other moneys as shall be due and payable to him or Mr Hunt the precedent Treasurer.

327. *Borough of Marlborough about the house of correction there.* (See also **398**)
The court is informed by the mayor and burgesses of the town of Marlborough that by order of Sessions held 13 July 6 Charles the sum of one thousand and two hundred pounds was to be raised throughout the county for the re-edifying the house of correction at Devizes and erecting three other houses of correction within the county. And the town of Marlborough to the end they might have the use and service of all such of those houses as by virtue of the order was to be built at Marlborough for that division in common with that part of the county did contribute the sum of eight pounds and expended twenty pounds at least in pulling down and removing poor cottages from the place where the house of correction is now built and further showed that the town being an exempt corporation from the county and holding Sessions by themselves cannot command the use and service of the house without further order from the court and prayed that an order may be made to that effect. The court in regard that there are none present to inform the court on behalf of the county appoint at Easter Sessions next to hear what can be alleged on both sides and to resolve thereto and determine the same. Further ordered that the master of that house shall in the mean time receive such persons as shall be sent thither by the mayor or other justices at their charges and shall observe their order and command touching such persons provided always that the doing thereof shall not be prejudicial to the inhabitants of the county in point of right in time to come.

328. *Hollis order against the overseers of Heytesbury.* (See also **305**, **348**, **445**)
Upon reading an order of the last Sessions Roger Hollis and the overseers of Heytesbury the court was now informed by Hollis that the overseers of Heytesbury viz William Deanes and Roger Snelgar refused to obey the order. Ordered the constables of the hundred of Heytesbury to convey Deanes and Snelgar before the next justice to be bound over to appear before the justices at Warminster on Saturday 16th October being the day and place that this Sessions adjourned unto.

329.   *Constables of Swindon for conveying rogues to prison.*
The court is informed by John Hath constable and Mathewe Wake
tithingman of Swindon that they having apprehended divers fellows and
carried them to His Majesty's gaol at Fisherton Anger and expended
in the same the sum of five pounds eleven shillings and three pence
and upon complaint made to Mr Jeanes and Mr William Sadler justices
they granted a warrant to levy the same upon the parish of Swindon.
Further informed that the petitioners since that time have sent John
Becket to the gaol and therein expended the sum of thirty shillings
more. And that notwithstanding the warrant the churchwardens and
inhabitants refuse to make a rate as the warrant requires. Ordered
that there shall be an indifferent rate made on the parish as well for
satisfaction of the £5 13s 3d as for the 30s. by such persons and in such
a manner as the statute in that case made.
    (If in default, to be bound over.)

330.   *Gabriell Bryan.*
The court is informed under the hands of the parishioners of the
parish of Collingbourne Kingston that upon the fifteenth day of
June 1646 there happened within the parish in the house of Gabriell
Brian inhabitant and clerk of the parish a sudden fearful and violent
fire whereby not only his dwelling house but also his barn stable and
other outhouses wherein lay a good competency of wheat barley and
other grain which was consumed he hardly escaping with his life
being dangerously hurt the total sum of whole losses together with
his childrens is estimated to amount to the value of six score pounds
at the least as by the certificate appears. Ordered Humfry Norborne
Treasurer to pay unto Gabriell the sum of forty shillings out of the
moneys of the collection for his present relief in regard of his great
necessity.

331.   *Holdwith.* (See also **538**)
The court is informed that Nicholas Holdwith is lately gone away from
Milton and has left a young child on the charge of the parish. Ordered
that the inhabitants of that parish shall forthwith send away the child
unto the father by him to be kept and relieved as the law requires.

332.   *Mr Bennett to pay £10 to the inhabitants of Mere.*
The court is informed by William Clement, Anne Hunt relict of
Christopher Hunt deceased, Christopher Hunt the younger, James
Tracie, James Westlie, Christopher Atrigge, Robert Barnes, Jasper
Coward, Dorothy Parrison, John Barnes, John Lacke and Dennys

Rawlins widow of Mere that in the month of August 1642 the petitioners by means of a sudden and lamentable fire happening in the town of Mere had their dwelling houses all burnt and consumed within the space of three hours and the fierceness of the fire was such (the houses being thatch houses and the season dry) that scarce any goods could be saved some of the petitioners had nothing at all left them and they being brought to this misery have continued therein ever since save only what has been afforded them by the charity of the neighbourhood there as by the petition (amongst other things therein contained may appear) and prayed the court to take their distressed condition into consideration. Ordered Mr Bennett to pay unto Mr Richard Greene and Mr William Barons of Mere to the use of the petitioners the sum of ten pounds of the county's stock remaining in his hands to be paid out and disposed of by the directions and appointment of Thomas Bennett and George Howe justices to such persons as they shall set down and appoint.

333. *Hancock concerning a bastard child.*
Upon complaint made unto the court that William Hancocke has conveyed away his daughter Grace Hancock who should keep and relieve her bastard child. Ordered that William shall keep and relieve the bastard child until he shall bring forth his daughter to be sent to the house of correction according to an order made by William Eyre and George Ivy justices and that John Dallimore the reputed father of the bastard child shall pay Hancocke 12d weekly until Grace shall be brought forth and sent to the house of correction and shall give security to perform his part of the order according as the order require.

334. *Mr Still to pay wages.*
Complaint made by William Gully, Nicholas Downton and Thomas Robbins all of Christian Malford against Mr Still of Brinkworth that Mr Still obtained from William Gullie (being a late covenant servant with Still) the sum of £8 for four years wages and from Downton for divers days work the sum of £16 19s and from Robbins for carpenters work at 12d per day the sum of four pounds six shillings which Still has often promised payment. The court desires the two next justices to send for Still and to hear and examine the premisses and end the same if they can or otherwise to bind over Still to the Sessions if they shall see cause.

335. *Inter inhabitants of Grittleton and Hullavington.*
There is a difference between the parishes of Hullavington and Grittleton about the settlement of William Hobbes late a covenant

servant with Mrs Gore widow of Grittleton. Ordered Hobbes and his wife shall remain and be at Grittleton until such time Mr Gore and Mr Ivy whom the court upon hearing all parties and examining the differences shall further order according to law and justice.

336. *Dixon for fire.*
The court is informed by a certificate under the hands of most of the inhabitants of Brinkworth and Charlton that Henry Dixon of Brinkworth by a lamentable and sudden fire happening upon the sixth day of August 1646 had his house burnt to the ground and the greatest part of his goods consumed to the value of £80 at the least to the utter undoing of himself his wife and poor children. Ordered the Treasurer shall forthwith pay unto Dixon the sum of five pounds out of the first money he shall receive in regard of his great loss and necessity.

337. *Brokenborough and Crudwell inhabitants.*
Ordered that the difference between the inhabitants of Brokenborough and Crudwell about the settlement of John Bevin and his wife shall be referred to the justices at the next Quarter Sessions where both sides are to come prepared with their witnesses that the court may make a full order therein. And in the meantime Bevin and his wife are to remain at Brokenborough and the same to be without prejudice in point of right and the overseers of the poor of the place are to take care that they have fitting relief in the meantime.

338. *William Hawkes for a cottage.*
The court is informed by Mr Hawkes of Coate in the parish of Liddington that by casualty of fire happening about Christmas last was a twelve months his house was burnt so as he is now destitute of a habitation and succour of himself and family. Ordered that Hawkes shall by and with the licence of the lord of the manor of Coate under his hands and seal erect and build him a cottage in some convenient place within the manor for the succour of himself and family and shall continue the same cottage for a habitation for himself and family without incurring the forfeiture mentioned in the statute.

339. *Joan Golding for fire.*
The court is informed by Joan Golding alias Vallentine of Devizes widow that her dwelling house and all her goods and household stuff therein with a mill house and malt mill and all her outhouses to the value of £220 were all burnt down to the ground by fire upon the last entering in of the Parliament forces into Devizes she having no means to live by but the house and malt mill which tends to the utter

undoing of the widow who prayed the assistance of the court for her relief therein. Ordered that the Treasurer shall forthwith pay unto Joan the sum of five pounds out of the first money he shall receive in regard of her great loss and present necessity.

(Her house stood opposite the castle. A1/110/1647M/193)

340. *John Mathew for a cottage.*
The court is informed by a certificate under the hands of most of the substantial inhabitants of the parish of Liddington that John Mathew of Liddington is destitute of a habitation for the succour of himself and family. Ordered that John shall and may by and with the licence of the lord of the manor of Liddington under his hand and seal upon some convenient place within the manor to be assigned by the lord of the manor erect and build a cottage for the habitation of himself and family and shall continue the same cottage without incurring the forfeitures mentioned in the statute.

341. *William Richardson for a cottage.*
[As in **340** for William Richardson of Liddington.]

342. *Vincent Dyper.*
The court is informed by Vincent Dyper of Aldbourne a poor man he has kept a child of the parish since Christmas 1642 at the intreaty of John Coleman and Stephen Barly churchwardens and Anthony Savery, John Martin and William King overseers of the poor and that they promised to pay him four pounds for keeping her six years which is almost expired and they have paid him but thirty four shillings thereof and deny to pay him the residue for want whereof Vincent is fallen into great misery. The court desires Mr Sadler and Mr Hippisley justices to call the parties before them and examine the truth of the complaint and make such order for the relief of Vincent as shall be agreeable to law and justice.

343. *Richard Hall apprentice discharged.*
At the Quarter Sessions at Marlborough the fifth day of October 23 Charles [1647] it appeared to the court that Richard Hall alias Baker has been formerly bound apprentice for 7 years which are not yet expired unto one Richard Clarke the younger of Malmesbury shoemaker. And it appears to the court that Clarke and his family about Whitsuntide last went forth of the county and left his apprentice unprovided for. We therefore the justices whose names are subscribed present at the Sessions discharge Richard of his apprenticeship.

344. *Malmesbury constables not to be discharged.*
Ordered that Robert Parker constable of the hundred of Malmesbury, John Shipway and Henry Bull constables of the liberty of the hundred of Chippenham, Richard Robbinson constable of the hundred of Highworth shall not be discharged out of their offices until they have paid the moneys due to Malmesbury out of their several hundreds by virtue of an order at the Quarter Sessions held at Warminster twentieth day of July last past. The court desires all stewards of leets in any of the hundreds not to discharge any of their constables in any of their lets unless it appears firstly that they have paid in their moneys due by the said order.

345. *Malmesbury rates.* (Recites **291**)
The court desires the next justice at large and the justice in the town of Malmesbury to bind over to the next Sessions all those that refuse to make payment of the rate.

346. *Ann Hewlett.*
The court is informed by Anne Hewlett widow inhabitant of Great Bedwyn that she is not able to maintain herself without some maintenance to be allowed her from the parish. The court desires Mr Richard Goddard and Mr William Sadler justices to examine the petitioners estate and if they find Anne fitting to be relieved by the parish that then they order that she may have fitting relief.

347. *Michael Hewstice tithing man of Corsley.*
The court is informed by Michael Hewstice tithingman of Great Corsley that he has served in the office longer by a year than he ought of right to serve by reason Sir James Thynne knight lord of the leet does not keep his leet (neither will it be kept as Michael is informed) to the great grievance of Michael. The court is further informed that Thomas Clace by the custom of the place is the next man that ought to serve in that office and prayed the court to take the same into consideration that he may be discharged of the office. Ordered that if Sir James Thynne does not keep his court there within one month after this Michaelmas that Hewstice may be discharged of his office then the court desires Mr Bennett justice to send for Thomas Clace to serve in the office for one year and swear him for the execution thereof.
     (If he refuses, to be bound over.)

348. *Hollis order.* (See also **305**, **328**, **445**)
Upon reading an order of Midsummer sessions last and upon hearing of the overseers of the poor concerning Roger Hollis of Heytesbury.

Ordered by the consent of the overseers that they shall pay to Hollis
2s a week for so much as is behind from Midsummer Sessions to the
present Sessions and 18d a week from this present Sessions till Hollis
is recovered of his lameness.

(If in default, to be bound over.)

349.   *Elizabeth Smyth.*
It appears to the court by the petition of Elizabeth Smyth of Ludgershall
widow that John Woodward of Ludgershall has in his house there a
cellar door which extends about five foot forth of his house into the
street very dangerous in the night time and a common nuisance for
all passengers going that way. And that Elizabeth passing in the street
fell into the cellar and bruised her body and broke her thigh by means
whereof she has been enforced to keep her bed near twelve months
and has spent and wasted all her means so that she is now fallen to
great want and poverty and thereby is become impotent. Ordered
that the churchwardens and overseers of the poor allow Elizabeth
some reasonable allowance weekly towards her maintenance or else
show good cause at the next Sessions. And the next justice is desired
to bind over John Woodward to his good behaviour and to appear at
the next Sessions.

350.   *A proportionable rate for the hundred of Malmesbury.*
There has been tendered to the court at this sessions a rate of £356
being allotted for a proportionable rate for the hundred of Malmesbury
for the raising of eleven thousand seven hundred and four pounds and
nineteen shillings through the whole county in the year 1642 which
rate of £356 was made by the constables of the hundred of Malmesbury
and divers other of the inhabitants within the hundred and is held
to be a just and equal rate and proportionably divided through the
several parishes and tithings and therefore desired to be allowed and
confirmed. A copy of which rate is hereunto annexed and which
this court ratifies and confirms accordingly until there shall be further
cause to show to the contrary.

351.   *Order for maltsters.*
The court has now restrained the maltsters appearing before them
for buying of excessive quantities of barley to convert into malt for
that the scarcity of corn may be prevented and the poor people may
have corn for their money. Ordered that all sellers of corn within this
county shall bring forth all their corn into the open fairs and markets
as they shall bring thither to be sold and shall not sell some by sample
within doors or out of the markets. And all maltsters not restrained are

hereby ordered to stand suppressed. And that no person whatsoever shall buy any corn in any market within the county until an hour after the ringing of the market bell there except the poor people and others which being for their own necessary provision who have liberty to buy immediately after the ringing of the bell. And no person whatsoever shall buy any corn or barley to convert into malt and sell again unless it be for their own provision without showing forth their licence unto the bailiffs constables or other officers who are hereby required and authorised to see the due execution of this order. And are also hereby authorised to make search in any loft or house for discovery of any corn or grain forestalled or bought out of the open market or ingrossed contrary to law and the true meaning of this order and to make stay of all such corn which shall be so unduly bought and cause the offenders to be brought before the next justice to be bound over to the next Quarter Sessions.

352. *Widow Gale.*
The court is informed by Mr Frederick Hyde that the widow Gale of Langley Burrell being grown aged impotent and very poor and not able to provide herself a house or place to live in or otherwise to relieve herself without some help and assistance of the parish of Langley Burrell where she has long lived. The court desires the two next justices to examine the premises and to take such further order and course therein for her relief as to law and justice shall appertain.

353. *Justice Bennett to bind over about Westbury petition.*
The court taking into consideration the scarcity and dearth of corn likely to ensue have with all care and faithfulness for the preventing thereof adjourned this Michaelmas Quarter Sessions to several quarters of the county and have there suppressed many maltsters and restrained others according to the statute yet many ill affected people have contrived and set their hands to a scandalous petition taxing this court with injustice and partiality in their proceedings. Ordered that a copy of the petition be sent to Mr Thomas Bennett being the next justice to the hundred of Westbury who is desired to bind to the good behaviour to appear at the next Quarter Sessions the chief actors and contrivers of the petition there to answer the premises.

1648

General Sessions of the Peace held at Salisbury on Tuesday 11 January 23 Charles (1648). William Stephens, Edward Tooker, Giles Eyre, John Norden, Richard Aubrey, William Yorke, Thomas Bennett, Barnaby Coles and Francis Swanton

354. *Calne money.*
The court is informed by the inhabitants of Calne that divers constables of the hundreds and tithingmen have much money in their hands of the collection for the relief of the poor infected people of Calne. The court desires Sir John Ernle and Mr Norden justices to examine the truth thereof and send for the constables and tithingmen and other officers who have any of the moneys remaining in their hands and cause them to pay the same to Mr Cole and Mr Bennett.
(If they refuse to pay, to be bound over.)

355. *Inhabitants of Burbage.*
The court is informed by the freeholders and other the inhabitants of the parish of Burbage that they have been very much oppressed by reason of the inequality of rates imposed on them in regard the yardlands are rated and not the bordlands and prayed the assistance of the court for their relief. Ordered that the matter should be referred to the examination of Mr John Goddard of Upham and Mr Goddard of Clatford justices who are desired to make such order as shall be agreeable to law and justice and certify their doings at the next Quarter Sessions that if they shall not rest themselves satisfied with such order as the justices shall make then both sides are to attend at the Sessions that the court may then hear and determine the same.

356. *John Head.* (See also **473, 636**)
The court is informed by John Head of Easton that he has served in the State service under the command of His Excellency Robert Earl of Essex in which service it pleased God to visit him with long and grievous sickness insomuch that he and his family are not yet recovered and prayed the court to commiserate him in this deplorable condition and allow him something for his relief. Ordered Mr Francis Bennett to pay Head twenty shillings out of Calne money remaining in his hands.

357. *To suppress tumultuous assemblies.*
At the Quarter Sessions now held at Salisbury great care has been taken for relief of poor people by directing a course for the raising

of rates of each parish where need is and by other means whereby appropriate relief will accrue to the poorer people which we have advised should extend as well to the labouring poor during this hard times as to the impotent chargeable on the parish by law so as the labouring poor contribute the uttermost of their own labour and industry towards their maintenance. And finding that the high prices of corn are chiefly occasioned by interruption of the markets disturbing the highway these are therefore in His Majesty's name to require you that if at any time thereafter any poor people shall tumultuously assemble within the hundred for the prosecution of any unlawful act whereby the peace is disturbed or interrupted that you forthwith raise the power of your hundred and apprehend the persons so assembled or as many of them as you can and then cause to be carried to the next justice to be dealt withal according as the law and their demerit shall require.

358. *George Reynolds.*
It appears to the court that at the Sessions held at Marlborough the fifth day of October last, George Reynolds of Everleigh was appointed to be constable for the hundred of Elstub and Everleigh in place of Walter Stretch and a penalty of £20 was laid on him in case he did not take his oath within a fortnight. Reynolds not being then present has petitioned the court to be discharged from undertaking the office. And appearing in court in person the court seeing his disabilities by reason of lameness and other imperfections discharges him of the office and fine as thinking him very unfit to undertake that office wherein his personal service and attendance is required.

359. *Constables of Malmesbury.*
Edward Yeates and Robert Huckinges late constables of Malmesbury (1642) informed the court that in the time of their constableship they had disbursed and were engaged for the use of the parish the sum of thirty pounds for watching and warding and for arms and mending of arms for trained soldiers and for conveying prisoners to gaol. The court referred the examination of the truth of the matter and the relief of the constables unto Mr Charles Gore and Mr George Ivy, justices. Now it appears by a certificate under the hands of divers of the inhabitants of Malmesbury that they have made a rate for the satisfying of Yeates and Huckinges and that many of them have paid but divers others refuse to pay.
[If any refuse to pay, to be bound over.]

360. *Farmers and cornsellers.*
The farmers and cornsellers who frequent the markets of Hindon and Warminster have generally agreed that they will sell and allow one bushel of barley at the rate of 4s the bushel for every quarter which they shall expose to sell in the several market towns the same to be for the benefit of the poor people of Hindon and Warminster and the country thereabout which course of charity we very much commend and approve and being now informed that some few cornsellers have of late endeavoured to obstruct if not utterly frustrate this agreement. Ordered that in regard the agreement is of so great concern to the poor of those parts no maltsters or barley buyers shall from henceforth buy or contract for any barley in either of the market towns until the cornsellers with whom they deal shall have delivered him one bushel for every quarter exposed to sale according to the agreement, the bushel to be of the same sort and measure as the barley they sell which shall be delivered and brought into the common storehouse provided for that purpose. If any of the barley buyers shall buy any barley before the seller has served in his bushel for every quarter then the same shall be supplied and made good by the buyer. Further ordered that all such cornsellers shall bring forth their corn to be sold in the open fairs and markets and shall not sell by sample in the houses. The court declares that such people shall take benefit of this order that shall bring a certificate under the hand of the minister and four or five of the chiefest inhabitants where they dwell that they are laborious and painful and by reason of their hard charge of children they are not able to maintain their family by their hard labour or that they are infirm and not able to work. In which certificate consideration is to be had what quantity of corn the family must of necessity spend to relieve them. Further ordered if any maltster or corn jobber shall not perform this order then he shall stand suppressed and the next justice is required to proceed against them if they shall afterwards buy. If the barley brought in shall not be worth 5s. a bushel, then the party that receives the same shall abate him so much of the price by 12d a bushel as the corn is truly worth to be sold in the market.

361. *William Head tithingman.*
William Head of Wootton Rivers, tithingman there, apprehended Thomas Monday a bastard getter by virtue of a warrant from a justice and suffered him to escape. Therefore Head was ordered to discharge the parish of the bastard until he could bring in Monday who is fled forth of the county. It is desired that if Head can find out where Monday is, that the justices of that county would be pleased to grant

their warrant for his apprehension and to bind him to appear at the next Sessions.

362. *William Gardner.*
The court is informed that William Gardner of Escott and his wife are very poor people and destitute of a house for their habitation and dwelling. The court desires Mr Yorke and Mr Norden to send for the overseers of the poor for Urchfont and to cause them to build a cottage in Escott for their habitation which cottage shall remain and be for a habitation and dwelling without incurring the forfeiture in the statute unless the court shall hereafter see good cause to alter the same.

363. *William Bennett and Ralph Bristowe.*
Complaint has been made by William Bennett and Ralph Bristowe, occupiers of land in Badbury within the parish of Chiseldon, who find themselves much grieved for that the ancient manner and custom of rating within the parish has been based by the yardlands until of late years since then these times of trouble whereby many of the inhabitants have, by altering the former way of rating, took occasion to undervalue and ease themselves and overrate others in the parish to their great grievance. Ordered that the examination of the premises be referred to Mr Jenner, Mr William Sadler and Mr Hippisley justices and to settle the rate according to the ancient way of rating and according to equity and law and they shall see cause or otherwise to certify their proceedings herein and in whom the default is at the next Quarter Sessions and then the court will further consider thereof.

364. *Castle Eaton bridge , the River Isis.*
Complaint has been made to the Judges of Assize of the decay of the great bridge over the River Isis called Castle Eaton Bridge. It was ordered that the four next justices should view the decay of the bridge and inquire who ought to repair the same and what the charge thereof will amount unto and what places and lands ought to join in repair thereof and to return a certificate to the court that a speedy course may be taken for the repair thereof. Robert Jenner, John Goddard, William Sadler and Robert Hippisley justices have viewed the bridge and made their certificate that the charge will amount unto one hundred pounds and that the tithing of Castle Eaton ought of right to repair the same. But conceiving that in this extraordinary case the whole parish of Castle Eaton, i.e. the tithings of Castle Eaton and Lushell and two meadows lying the other side of the river adjacent to the bridge called Bosteeds and the lordship of Water Eaton lying next adjoining to the parish of Castle Eaton may be equally charged towards

the repair without prejudice to the future. All which the court ratifies and confirms and orders the same.

(If any refuse to pay, to be bound over.)

(The bridge had been destroyed by Lt Col Carr to safeguard the Cirencester garrison from possible attack by the King's army at Faringdon. The bridge was said to be about 70 yards long, built of timber on stone arches. The timber had been thrown into the river and the stone arches damaged by flood. A1/110/1647E/275)

365. *Inhabitants of Dinton, Mr Earth.*
It appears to the court upon the information of the overseers of the poor and divers other of the inhabitants of Dinton that about twenty years since there was twenty nobles in money given by Mr Goddard to be put forth at interest from time to time by the overseers and the interest to be yearly paid and distributed to the poor of the parish. It also appears that Mr Joseph Earth about nine years since being overseer having the money in his hands and for many years continued the same and paid the interest thereof until his death. And afterwards Mr Gifford his son-in-law who married his daughter and now holds Mr Earth's farm in Dinton has for some years since Earth's death paid the interest and also promised to pay the principal. It appears that there is about four years interest now due and unpaid. Ordered that the overseers of Dinton shall rate the twenty nobles together with so much interest as is behind and unpaid upon their rate to be made for the relief of their poor and cause the same to be levied on the occupiers of Mr Gifford's farm in Dinton and the interest to be disposed to the poor according to the donor's will and the principal to be secured.

366. *William Edwards.*
The court is informed that William Edwards tithingman of Burbage has disbursed thirty shillings in carrying Francis Barber and George Woornall two felons to gaol they having no goods of their own which charge ought to be borne by the whole tithing. Ordered that the inhabitants of the tithing forthwith meet together and make an indifferent rate for the satisfaction of the thirty shillings and such reasonable charges as the tithingman has expended on prosecution thereof.

(If any refuse to pay, to be bound over.)

367. *Michael Stanmore.*
Michael Stanmore of Ford in the parish of North Wraxall mealman is licensed at this Sessions for the buying of thirty bushels of wheat and barley weekly to be sold out to the poor people. Stanmore has

promised in court in granting of the licence that he will sell the same
to poor people and take for the carriage and grinding thereof but six
pence a bushel profit for wheat and four pence a bushel profit for
barley and sell the same measure as he buys.

(Stanmore was to use his own mill in Ford. A1/110/1648H/241)

368. *Mr Thomas Earle, parish of Shorncote* [Somerford Keynes].
Mr Hyde, counsel with Mr Thomas Earle now minister and parson of
the parsonage of Shorncote, has informed the court that the ancient
general course of rating within the parish has always been by the
yardlands and that the parsonage has always been rated but at two
yardlands until within three years last past. The parishioners have of late
altered the usual course of rating by the yardlands and therein much
overrated Earle for his parsonage and underrated themselves. Ordered
that the former manner of rating by the yardlands shall continue until
the rest of the parishioners of Shorncote shall show good cause to the
court for the contrary.

369. *William Smith,   constable hundred of Kinwardstone for assessments.*
The court is informed by a letter from the Honourable James
Herbert, Mr Edward Poole and others commissioners appointed for
Wiltshire by an ordinance of Parliament for the assessment of 60,000
per month for the army that William Smyth late of Wootton Rivers
one of the constables of the hundred of Kinwardstone is now gone
forth of the hundred and lives in the county of Somerset whereby
there is obstruction in carrying on of the collecting of the six months
assessment in the hundred for want of the constable and that Thomas
Peeck of Wick [Wootton Rivers] in the same hundred gent is a fit
person to serve constable in place of Smyth. Ordered Peeck forthwith
to attend the next justice to take his oath for the due execution of
his office upon pain of forty pounds so that the assessment and other
services may be duly performed.

370. *Inhabitants of Alderbury, Richard Colborne.*
It appears to the court by the petition from the inhabitants of he parish
of Alderbury that there have been two cottages lately erected within
the parish upon the common waste wherein there inhabited the widow
Draper and the widow Maior who being both lately dead have left five
small children chargeable upon the parish. Also that Richard Colborne
has likewise lately erected and set up within the parish one other
cottage upon the commons in a very dangerous and unfitting place for
receiving and entertaining of lewd disposed persons. Ordered (at the
instance of the inhabitants) that the tithingman, churchwardens and

overseers of the poor forthwith remove Colborne from that cottage wherein he now dwells and place him in the cottage lately the widow Maior. And also pull down and demolish the cottage lately erected by Colborne and also the cottage lately the widow Draper and that the overseers provide for the five children according to law.

371. *Mr Edward Shoare, hundred constable.*
The court is informed by Mr Edward Shoare receiver of the moneys appointed for the relief of the poor infected people of Maiden Bradley and Horningsham when they were lately infected with the contagion of the plague that Edward Martin and John Gaifford now or late constables of the hundred of Whorwellsdown, Ralph Aldridge and Nicholas Milles now or late constables of the hundred of Westbury, William Wright and John King constables of the hundred of Warminster, George Drew and John King constables of the hundred of hundred of Heytesbury, John Combe and Henry Fricker constables of the hundred of Dunworth and the constables of Mere have not collected and paid in the moneys in arrear now given in their returns according to a former order of Sessions. The court desires Mr Topp and Mr Bennett justices to give out their warrants to the now constables for the speedy levying collecting and paying in of the arrears to Mr Shoare and the late constables who should have collected the arrears and did not are hereby required to aid and assist the now constables in execution of the warrants levying collecting and paying in of the arrears to the receiver. And if the now constables or the late constables shall be remiss or negligent in execution of the warrants then the justices are desired to bind them over to the next Quarter Sessions. And whereas Mr Shoare, John Wansye and Thomas Shoare, late constables of the hundred of Maiden Bradley, have not fully passed their accounts according to the order of Christmas Sessions last since which time Mr George Howe one of the justices there mentioned in the order to take the account is deceased. Further ordered Mr Topp and Mr Bennett to send for the accounts to pass their accounts before them who are herby required to attend them for that purpose and the justices are desired to allow or disallow therein what they shall think fit.

372. *Robert Morris.*
Upon complaint made by Robert Morris, a very poor man of the parish of Warminster, concerning 35s. detained from him by Mr Edward Middlecott, John Butcher, Christopher Willoughby and Thomas Toomer, the last overseers of the poor, for the keeping a child by the space of 21 weeks which was placed with him by the overseers to be kept and relieved they pretending they have not so

much money in their hands of the parish. Ordered that the overseers shall within one week after notice of this order pass their accounts before the parish of their receipts and payments for their year and give public notice of the time and place appointed to do the same that it may appear whether there are any moneys in their hands or remaining in arrear upon their account. And if the overseers shall not pass their accounts to this order, the next justice is desired to bind them over to the next Quarter Sessions to answer their contempt and the rather because it is alleged that they have heretofore promised at several times the payment thereof before Mr Hussey and Mr Bennett, justices, but have not performed the same to the great loss and charge of the poor man, the same being required to be paid unto him by former orders of the court made long since. And if it shall appear on their account that there is money in their hands, then Morris is to be paid out of the same if there be so much money in their hands but if not to be satisfied out of their arrears and the now churchwardens and overseers are forthwith to levy the same arrears by warrant from the justices and pay the poor man so much of the 35s as is not paid him by the last overseers and detain the residue of the arrears to be employed for the present relief of the poor of the parish.

373. *Roger Ballard.*
Roger Ballard, late one of the overseers of the poor in the parish of Westbury, was bound over to this Sessions by Mr Bennett for his abusive carriage in execution of that office in threatening and starving the poor people which was now proved in court by divers witnesses but the same not being fully discovered, the court orders Roger Ballard to attend Mr Bennett with his accounts for the time of his office and Mr Bennett is desired to examine the accounts and to require Mr Selfe and the other presenters to attend him at the examination thereof who are to except against the accounts if they see cause and Mr Bennett is desired to certify his doings therein at the next Quarter Sessions so that the court may proceed against Roger Ballard for the abuses.

374. *The town of Bradford.*
The court is informed that heretofore when the town of Bradford was infected with the contagion of the plague, there was two months tax raised within five miles compass for the relief of the poor infected people which came to one hundred and twenty pounds or near thereabouts and there was but forty nine pounds thereof paid in and that part of the arrears was collected and remains in the constables and other officers hands for the time being and the other part is not yet collected whereby the constables and divers inhabitants who laid out

money and lent their goods for the relief of the poor infected people are unsatisfied and the officers sued at law for the same to the great damage. The court is also informed that Mr Eyre and Mr Ivy, justices, by virtue of an order of the Easter Sessions last have taken great pains therein and have discovered what officers have moneys in their hands of the tax and what officers have not collected and levied the tax. Ordered that Mr Eyre and Mr Ivy forthwith send for the constables and other officers who have any of the money in their hands and bind them over to the next Quarter Sessions if they shall not within one month pay over the moneys discovered to be in their hands unto such persons as the justices shall appoint for satisfaction of the officers and others who have money owing them. The justices are further desired to grant out their warrants to the now constables of the hundreds and other officers of the several places in arrear so that they, with the assistance of the old constables, may collect and levy the arrears and pay it into the justices for the satisfaction of the parties. And if the constables of hundreds and other officers, old or new, shall be remiss or negligent in execution of their warrants, then the justices are desired to bind them over to the next Quarter Sessions. And if there shall be any surplussage remaining, all parties being satisfied their just debts owing them, the justices are desired to take course that the same be paid into the court at the next Quarter Sessions there to be disposed of as the court shall think fit.

375. *Widow Shergall and others suppressed from malting.*
Ordered that Joan Shergall of Warminster widow, Elianora Rawlyns of the same widow a baker, William Presse of the same draper, William Adlam of the same shoemaker, Mr Payne a maltster in Hindon, Edward Tyse of Hindon chandler, William Hobbes of Deverell, Richard Starr of Crockerton, Christopher Gardiner of Tinhead gent, Ambrose Chappell of North Bradley baker, Edward Martyn of Steeple Ashton gent and Thomas Boorne of Mere all being maltsters and having sufficient means and trades to maintain them, are suppressed from buying of any barley to convert into malt from henceforth in regard of the great dearth and scarcity of corn.

376. *Worton inhabitants to contribute to the relief of the poor of Potterne.*
The court is informed by the inhabitants of the parish of Potterne that for these many years past and at this present time they are very full of poor people in so much that they are not able of themselves without the help of others to give them such relief as the law requires or as charity binds them unto. And that the tithing of Worton within the parish is not charged with many poor and the inhabitants there

for the most part are of very good worth and prayed that the tithing might contribute towards the relief of the poor of Potterne. The court thinks fit that the matter shall be referred to the consideration and examination of the two next justices who are desired to send for such inhabitants of both these places before them as they shall think fit and examine the truth of the complaint and set down such order therein as shall be agreeable to law and justice which order shall be binding unless good cause be shown at the next Quarter Sessions to alter the same.

(Potterne said that one of the reasons for increased poverty was that the fields were uncultivated and therefore the poor could not go gleaning as usual. A1/110/1648H/239)

General Session of the Peace held at Devizes on Tuesday 11 April 24 Charles (1648). Robert Nicholas, William Eyre, John Norden, Thomas Bennett, William Yorke, Richard Goddard, George Ivy, Francis Swanton, William Sadler.

377. *Robert Ricketts to discharge East Knoyle of his grandchild.*
It appears to the court that the daughter of Richard Ricketts is kept at East Knoyle at the charge of the parish and that Robert Ricketts of East Knoyle, grandfather of Richard's daughter, is a man of sufficient estate and able to relieve his grandchild and to take her from the charge of the parish. Ordered upon hearing of the matter and upon reading the certificate attested by most of the chiefest inhabitants of East Knoyle, that Robert Ricketts shall relieve and maintain his grandchild himself upon pain of twenty shillings for every month wherein he shall fail to do the same.

378. *Inter inhabitants of Bradford, South Wraxall, Holt, Winsley and Stoke Atworth.* (See also **435**)
The court is informed that there are differences arising between the inhabitants of Bradford, South Wraxall, Holt, Winsley, Stoke Atworth and Westwood concerning the rates to the poor. Ordered that the matter be heard at the next Quarter Sessions and that all the places aforesaid having notice of this order shall attend with their witnesses so that the same may be then heard and determined.

379. *William Howell, titihingman of Monkton Deverill.*
The court is informed that William Howell tithingman of Monkton Deverill has served in the same office for the space of four years during

which time he has received much money from the inhabitants but has never given an account for the same to the inhabitants. Ordered that the said tithingman shall account for the same. And the two next justices or one of them are to send for the tithingman and cause him to account for his receipts and payments of and concerning that tything business ever since he has served in that office.

(If he refuses, to be bound over.)

380. *John Rogers and Robert Trymnell constables of Calne hundred.*
The court is informed that there is much money in arrear in the hundred of Calne towards the relief of the poor people of Devizes when they were lately infected with the plague and that John Rogers and Robert Trymnell constables of that hundred having had several warrants from the justices for levying and collecting and paying in of the same, have altogether neglected the execution thereof to the great hindrance of the execution of justice whereby the poor people of Devizes suffer much for want of relief. Ordered that the matter shall be referred to the hearing and examination of Mr William Eyre, Mr Ivy and Mr Norden, justices, or one or two of them who are desired to meet together and send for the constables and examine what moneys were rated on the hundreds and what is collected and paid in and what is in arrear and from whom. The justices are desired to grant their warrants for the speedy levying, collecting and paying in of the same. And if the justices shall find that the constables or either of them or the tithingmen within that hundred have been remiss or negligent in levying, collecting and paying in of the moneys, then the justices are desired to bind them over to the next Quarter Sessions to answer the same and the justices are also desired to certify their doings therein to the said Sessions that the offenders may receive such punishment as their offences shall deserve.

381. *Cornelius Wyatt allowed £5 for fire.*
The court is informed by Cornelius Wyatt of Devizes, carpenter, that about St. James tide [25 July] last past, it being a very dry time, a great and fierce fire happened in the absence of Cornelius upon divers houses in the parish of St Mary being thatched houses beginning at the house next adjoining to the house wherein Wyatt dwelt which fire consumed his dwelling house and all the goods, wood and timber in and about the house which amounts in the whole to the value of forty pounds or thereabouts which tended to the utter undoing of Cornelius, he being indebted for the wood and timber and not able to give satisfaction for it and prayed the court for some relief. The court allows unto Cornelius the sum of five pounds to be paid to him

out of the money of the King's Bench and Marshalsea remaining in the hands of Mr Francis Bennett.

382. *Christopher Hill and John Shoard constables of Maiden Bradley.*
The court is informed by divers inhabitants within the liberty of Maiden Bradley that John Twogood and Nicholas Moulton the younger served in the office of constables in the liberty for one year and upward and desires that Christopher Hill and John Shoard might be elected constables in their place. Ordered that Christopher Hill and John Shoard be constables of the liberty and that they repair within one week to the next justice to take their oaths for the due execution of their office upon pain of £20 a piece. Further ordered that Twogood and Moulton shall within one month collect and gather all such moneys as are due and arrear to the collections of the King's Bench and Marshalsea and pay the same to the Treasurer.

383. *John Purrier master of house of correction at Marlborough.*
The court is informed by John Purrier master of the house of correction near Marlborough that there is four years pay and a quarter due to him from the Treasurer which amounts to the sum of £15 besides the sum of £4 15s which he has laid out in repairing the house of correction amounting in the whole to £19 15s and prayed the court for his relief therein. Ordered that the last Treasurer shall pay unto John Purrier the sum of £19 15s due unto him, the same to be paid him with all convenient speed in regard of his great necessity and that he may be the better enabled to set his persons on work.

384. *Abraham Halle master of house of correction at Devizes.*
The court is informed by Abraham Halle, master of the house of correction in Devizes, that there is four years and a quarter pay due which amounts to the sum of £15 besides the sum of £4 12s 8d which was laid out by Halle for repairing the house of correction which comes in the whole to £19 12s 8d. Ordered that the Treasurer forthwith to pay him the sum of £19 12s 8d due unto him the same to be paid him with all convenient speed in regard of his great necessity and present occasion for money.

385. *William Mathewe constable of hundred of Melksham.*
The court is informed by William Mathewe, one of the constables of the hundred of Melksham, that he has expended and laid out the sum of five pounds and five pence for the carrying of two felons to the gaol who had no goods of their own to satisfy the same. And prayed an order of the court for the repayment thereof which the court conceived

to be much. And whereas it now appears unto the court upon oath that the felons were apprehended and taken in the parish of Potterne, it is ordered that the inhabitants of Potterne shall forthwith pay unto William Mathewe the sum of three pounds.

386. *Aldbourne town.*
The court is informed that the town of Aldbourne was affected with the plague and that William Sadler and Robert Hippisley have made a weekly assessment towards the relief of the poor and infected people upon the places and parishes hereunder written being within the five miles compass which assessment was to begin from the 25th March last past and continue until further order. The court is now informed that Aldbourne is in great want and necessity regard the sickness continues and the moneys rated are not paid in for their relief. The court was moved that there might be speedy course taken for the levying and collecting of the assessment. Ordered that two weeks assessment shall be collected levied and paid into Thomas Haynes gent, John Coleman, Mark Fowler and Thomas Bacon of Aldbourne, appointed receivers, for the use of the infected persons. The court desires the justices forthwith to grant out their warrants for the levying, collecting and paying in of the two weeks assessment.
The parishes assessed weekly.

Ramsbury	20s.	Ogbourne St George	13s 4d
Bishopstone	13s 4d	Ogbourne St Andrew	13s 4d
Baydon	6s 8d	Marlborough	40s
Little Hinton	10s 8d	Mildenhall	10s 8d
Wanborough	20s	Chilton Foliat	10s 8d
Liddington	13s 4d	Froxfield	8s
Chiseldon	20s		

387. *William Bamfield.*
The court is informed by William Bamfield of Potterne that the overseers of the poor of Potterne put John Townsend a poor child unto Bamfield to be kept, promising him 15d per week for so long as he should keep the child and there is now arrear almost three years and a half which amounts unto the sum of £10 5s over besides money which he has already received. Ordered that the two next justices are to send for the overseers and examine the truth of the petition and if they find cause then to bind them over to the next Sessions there to answer their neglect therein.

388. *Inter Mr Grove and Mr North.*
Upon hearing the difference between Mr Grove, farmer, of Potterne

and Mr North, vicar, and the overseers concerning the rates of the poor in the presence of counsel learned on both sides and upon examination of divers witnesses upon oath and viewing of several rates produced in court, the court is of the opinion not to alter the vicar's ancient rate which is but after one yardland for the relief of the poor and declares that they are of opinion that the woods in question ought to be rated towards the said relief.

389.   *Benjamin Bristowe and Thomas Hort.*
The court is informed by Benjamin Bristowe that there has not been for a long time any court leet or lawday kept for the manor of Biddestone and by reason thereof he has served as tithingman by the space of five years at the least to his great grievance.   Ordered that (salvo iure to the lord of the leet) Thomas Hort of Biddestone shall be elected and chosen to tithingman for the next year. It is further ordered that Thomas shall within one week after notice of this order to repair to the next justice and take his oath for the due execution of the office upon pain of ten pounds.

390.   *Inter Hurd and Quinton.* (See also **478, 530**)
Upon hearing of a matter of difference between John Hurd gent, proprietor of the impropriate parsonage of Manningford and Wilsford, and Samuel Quinton, clerk, vicar concerning payment of rates, counsel learned on both sides being present, and also upon examination of divers witnesses upon oath and producing of rates formerly made in those places. Ordered that the parsonage shall be from henceforth rated at three yardlands for Manningford and the vicar rated at four yardlands for the vicarage as anciently they have been rated.

391.   *Inhabitants of Worton.*
The court is informed by the inhabitants of the tithing of Worton in the parish of Potterne that the highways in Worton are in decay and that there are not materials to be digged within the tithing for repairing thereof and that the fetching of stone from other places and the pitching of the ways cannot be done without money. Prayed the assistance of the court that there may be an indifferent rate made by the yardlands for raising of money to buy materials for mending their ways as they have none of their own. Ordered that an indifferent rate shall be made by the inhabitants accordingly for the reparation of their ways and desires the two next justices to confirm the same and bind over to the Sessions all such persons as shall refuse to pay the same.

392.   *Robert Sheppard for a cottage.*
The court is informed by a certificate under the hands of the most substantial inhabitants of Poulshot that Robert Sheppard, labourer, has erected a cottage upon the waste ground within the manor of Elizabeth Drewe, widow, lady of the manor, and has the hand and seal of Elizabeth for the continuance of the cottage. Ordered that Robert Sheppard shall continue in the cottage during his life without incurring the forfeiture mentioned in the statute.

393.   *Thomas Ragland.*
Thomas Ragland master of the hospital of East Harnham shows that there is due to him for two years pay the sum of ten pounds from the Treasurer at Ladyday last. Ordered that the Treasurer pays Thomas ten pounds.

394.   *Richard Glover.*
Upon hearing a matter of difference between the inhabitants of Foxley, Stanton St Quintin and Burton Hill [Malmesbury] concerning the settlement of Richard Glover now remaining at Burton Hill, it appears to the court that he was married at Burton Hill about Michaelmas last past and has lived there with his wife ever since. Ordered that Richard Glover shall be settled at Burton Hill there to remain without prejudice to that place in point of right until good cause shall be showed to alter the same.

395.   *Edward Godwyn, John Hiscocks constables of Rowde.*
Petition of Richard Harvest and Richard Filkes constables of the liberty of Rowde showing that no court has been kept in Rowde for five years or upwards at which court the constables have been usually chosen. Ordered that Edward Godwyn and John Hiscocks of Rowde be elected constables of the liberty and that they shall within one week repair to the next justice to take their oaths upon pain pf ten pounds apiece but it shall not be any prejudice to the lord of the manor in point of right in time to come.

396.   *John Whitaker and others for fire £10.*   (Recites **149**. See also **274**, **686**, **717**)
Upon which order nothing has been done. The court now desires Mr Eyre, Mr Topp and Mr Ivy to call before them Sherston etc and take their accounts and certify the same at the next Sessions. Ordered that the treasurers shall pay to the mayor of Devizes forth of the money remaining in their hands ten pounds to remain in his hands until the court shall be certified the truth of the petitioners losses. If

in case the petition be true, the court orders that the ten pounds be proportionately paid to them according to their several losses. The court further orders that the residue of the surplussage be paid unto the Clerk of the Peace at the next Quarter Sessions to be disposed of by the court. The court also desires the justices, if the Treasurers refuse to account before them, to bind the refusers over to the next Sessions to answer their contempt.

397. *Henry Chapman, tithingman of Holt.*
It appears to the court that John Beazer has executed the office of a tithingman for the tithing of Holt for one whole year and upwards and by the custom there used ought to serve not longer. There has not been any court or lawday kept there since nor in any short time like to be kept. The court thinks fit (salvo iure lord of the said leet) that Henry Chapman of Holt shall be tithingman for the next year and he shall repair to some justice to take his oath within one week.

398. *Inhabitants of the borough of Marlborough about the house of correction there.* (Refers to **327**)
By order of the sessions 13th July 6 Charles [1630] the sum of £1200 was to be raised throughout the county for the re-edifying of the house of correction at Devizes and erecting three other houses of correction. The inhabitants of Marlborough to the end that they might have the use of one of those houses as by virtue of the order was to be built at Marlborough for that division in common with that part of the county, did contribute the sum of eight pounds and expended £20 at least more in pulling down and removing poor cottages from the place where the house of correction is now built. All which now appears to the court upon oath by the testimony of Mr John Lawrence and Mr Thomas Hunt nevertheless the town of Marlborough, being an exempt corporation from the county and holding Sessions by themselves, cannot command the use and service of the house without further order from this court. This Sessions was appointed by order of 5th October last for hearing what might be alleged on both sides. The court on a full hearing and debating the matter by counsel on both sides orders that from henceforth the master shall receive persons as shall be sent thither by the mayor or other justices of the town of Marlborough and shall observe their order and commands touching such persons yet this court still reserves to themselves the survey and government of the house and the master of whom they will require an account of all such persons sent thither. And forasmuch as it is alleged on behalf of the county that the town of Marlborough has hitherto neglected to contribute towards the reparation of the house of correction and the

wages of the master, it is ordered that the town of Marlborough shall contribute and pay towards the reparation and wages now in arrear and to come, so much as their just share and portion shall amount with that division for which the house was erected.

399. *Henry Gibbs.*
The court is informed by Henry Gibbs, bailiff of Clack within the parish of Lyneham, that he has been at the charge of conveying Adam Holloway and Thomas Pockeridge to the gaol of Fisherton Anger upon suspicion of felony and has expended and laid out the sum of £3 10s more than he has received. The felons had no goods of their own to help defray the charge of conveying them thither and therefore the charge ought to be borne by the inhabitants of Lyneham. Ordered that Gibbs cause an indifferent and equal rate to be made over the whole parish of Lyneham for the raising of £3 10s.
(If any refuse to pay, to be bound over.)

400. *Thomas Tyllye.*
Thomas Tyllye one of the inhabitants of Colerne, having a distress taken upon him by process issuing out of this court, has now appeared on behalf of the inhabitants unto the presentment in this court against them for not setting up a convenient bridge between Colerne and Corsham and has made oath that now there is a sufficient bridge set up, and thereupon the presentment is discharged and Thomas Tillye has paid the fees of the court and the fine set on them and has been at charge in prosecution thereof which charge ought to be borne by the whole inhabitants not by Thomas in particular. Ordered that there shall be an indifferent rate made on the inhabitants for satisfying Thomas as well such fees as he has disbursed in discharge of the presentment and the King's fine as such reasonable charges and expenses which he has been at in prosecution thereof.
(If any refuse to pay, to be bound over.)

401. *William Ferris for a cottage.*
The court is credibly informed by a certificate under the hands of the most substantial inhabitants of Dauntsey that William Ferris of Dauntsey labourer has lately erected a cottage for his habitation in a certain ground within the lordship of Sir John Danvers and has now obtained licence from him under his hands and seal for the continuance of the cottage. Ordered that the cottage shall remain a cottage for the habitation, succour and dwelling of William, his wife and family during his lifetime without incurring the forfeiture of the statute.

402. *Thomas Kitch for a cottage.*
The court is credibly informed by a certificate under the hands of divers of the most sufficient inhabitants of Melksham that Thomas Kitch of Melksham carpenter being a very poor man and having eight small children whom he maintains by his labour without any charge of the parish is lately questioned for erecting a cottage on part of the waste ground within the lordship of Sir John Danvers in Melksham and now has obtained licence from him under his hand and seal. Ordered that the cottage shall remain a cottage for the habitation, succour and dwelling of Thomas and his children during his life time without incurring the forfeiture of the statute.

403. *Mr Sloper, William Rooke, Symon Ruddle constables of Potterne and Cannings.*
The court desires Mr Yorke and Mr Norden justices to send for William Sloper, William Rooke and Symon Rudddle constables of the hundred of Potterne and Cannings who are forthwith to attend them with their rates made in that hundred for the relief of the poor people of Devizes when they were infected with the plague. The justices are desired to examine the constables what moneys have been collected and paid on the rate and to whom and what remains in their hands and how much of the rate is in arrear. If the justices shall find that the constables or either of them have been remiss or negligent in collecting and levying of the rates then they are desired to bind such of them over to the next Quarter Sessions. The justices are desired to grant out their warrants for the speedy collecting and levying of the arrears and direct them to the now constables who are ordered forthwith to levy the same and pay it in to such persons as are appointed to receive the same.

404. *John Stevens constable of Swanborough Hundred.*
The court is informed by the borough of Devizes that there is yet fifty pounds and upwards by the inhabitants of Swanborough hundred charged with a rate made towards the relief of the poor people of the borough infected with the plague. It now appears upon examination of the matter and upon full debate and Mr John Stevens of Connock being now present in court was at the time of the rate made and is still constable of the hundred and that he has received several warrants from the justices to levy and collect the same and for want of payment to distrain for the sum rated. It likewise appears that John Stevens had not only neglected to execute the warrants but he did and now does in open court still refuse to do the same to the great scandal and contempt of justice and utter undoing of the poor and some of the

inhabitants of the borough. Ordered that John Stevens shall be rated and assessed and the court rates him at fifty pounds towards the relief of the poor people of the parish of St. John's in the borough of Devizes unless he shall within three weeks give due obedience to the respective warrants and execute the same. Upon John Stevens default, the court authorises and requires the High Sheriff to levy the fine upon his goods and the money paid to John Wintworth and John Trimnell of the borough of Devizes.

405. *John Hurle, Elizabeth Chamberlyn.*
It is certified an order under the hands and seals of Richard Goddard and William Sadler, justices, that John Hurle of Overton is the reputed father of a bastard child born of Elizabeth Chamberlyn of Milton [Lilbourne] by which order there is only provision made for the discharge of the parish of Milton from the bastard child which order the court confirms and further orders that Elizabeth be forthwith sent and carried by the constable or tithingman of Milton or in case she is gone from Milton she is to be sent by the constable where she now dwells to the house of correction at Marlborough there to remain and to be set to work in the space of one year.

406. *Susan Coles pension.*
The court is informed by Susan Coles, widow, and by certificate of Colonel Edmond Ludlow and Captain William Ludlow that Henry Coles late of Maiden Bradley being in actual service for the King and Parliament as a trooper in this county under their command, was slain in the same service at Salisbury and has left a wife and four small children behind him who are in very great want and need. And that Susan, wife of Henry, is now very weak and sick and so has continued a long time. Ordered that Susan be allowed for her present relief in her sickness from the Treasurer the sum of five pounds. Further ordered that Susan and her children shall have a pension of ten pounds a year allowed them for their future relief to be paid to them quarterly. The first payment to begin at midsummer next.

407. In the present Session, appointed and chosen as Treasurers are, for the north part, William Parry of Easton Grey, gent, and, for the south part, William Bennett of Berwick St John, gent.

408. Ordered that the rates for the relief of maimed soldiers and mariners in pursuance of several ordinances of Parliament shall be doubled in every parish for that there may be levied and paid weekly upon every parish six pence and no more, which rate so doubled to commence from the time of the present Sessions and shall be collected and paid yearly to the Treasurers.

409. Appointed Treasurers for the relief of prisoners of the King's Bench and Marshalsea and of such hospitals and almshouses as are within the county; north, Walter Coleman of Langley in the parish of Kington St Michael; south, Jasper Westly of Whitley, gent.

410. Ordered that the rates for the same relief shall continue as they were last year viz for every parish throughout the county there may be levied and paid one penny weekly and not above, the several rates of every parish to be proportioned and set down as in the former order. And the last Treasurers of both the foresaid collections shall give up their accounts to the new elected Treasurers for the north part before Charles Gore, William Eyre, John Norden and George Ivy or any two of them, and for the south part before Anthony Ashley Cooper Baron, Giles Eyre, Richard Grobham Howe and Francis Swanton or any two of them.

411.   *Calne money.*
The court desires William Eyre, Mr George Ivy and Mr John Norden, justices, or any two of them to send for the constables of the hundred who have formerly received any money for the relief of the poor people of Calne when they were infected with the plague and do detain the same in their hands and also all other officers and persons who have any of the same money in their hands. The justices are desired to examine them concerning that matter what money they have in their hands and what they have received, collected or paid in, what is in arrear in any hundred and take course that the same be speedily levied, collected and paid in that the court be not further troubled therewith. And the court desires the justices to certify their doing therein at the next Quarter Sessions.

412.   *Inhabitants of Brokenborough against Thomas Hewett, Thomas Milles and William Uncles.* (See also **436**)
The court is informed by divers of the inhabitants of Brokenborough that Thomas Hewett, Thomas Milles and William Uncles, now or late tithingmen of Brokenborough, refuse to give up their accounts to the parish of their receipts of such money as they have received upon rates of carrying of prisoners to the gaol and other parish rates and how they have disbursed and paid away the same during the time that they have served in that office. Ordered that Thomas Hewett, etc shall within short time after sight of this order give up their several

accounts before the two next justices of their receipts and payments and such of the parishioners as will may attend the justices when the accounts are given up to except against the same if there be cause.

(If any refuse, to be bound over.)

General Sessions of the Peace held at Warminster on Tuesday 4 July Charles 24 (1648) William Hussey, William Eyre, William Yorke, George Ivy, Richard Grobham Howe, Edmund Ludlow, John Dove, John Long.

413. *Richard Cantloe.*
The court is informed that Richard Cantloe of Fonthill refuses to take the apprentice placed upon him by the churchwardens and overseers of the poor by and with the consent of the justices. Ordered that Richard Cantloe shall forthwith take and receive his apprentice according to the former order.

(If he refuses, to be bound over.)

414. *Augustine Perry, Edward Way, Thomas Yerbury.*
The court is informed by Augustine Perry of Trowle Magna in the parish of Bradford that he has served in the office of tithingman this two years or thereabouts and at Michaelmas last the lawday being kept there one Edward Waye was presented to be tithingman for Trowle Magna in the place of Augustine and accepted of by the stewards and ordered to come in and be sworn the next court upon pain of five pounds which he refused to do. Ordered that Perry shall attend the next justice near adjoining to examine the truth of the premises and if he cause to grant his warrant to bring the said Waye and Thomas Yerbury of Bradford who is next by course to serve in the said office to be sworn tithingman in the place of Perry provided it shall not be prejudicial to the lord of that leet in point of right in time to come.

415. *Fisherton Anger and Little Langford* [Steeple Langford].(See also **463**)
Complaint has been made by the inhabitants of Fisherton Anger within the hundred of Branch and Dole that they by reason of their late visitation of sickness and the great number of poor people inhabiting within the parish and which have weekly relief, and the small number of inhabitants there which are of ability to contribute to their relief and to bear the great burden and charge thereof, so that they are inforced to crave the assistance and help of some other parts of the hundred. Ordered that the inhabitants of the parish of Little Langford do make a rate within the parish for the raising of ten shillings monthly to be paid

to the churchwardens and overseers of the parish of Fisherton Anger towards the relief of the poor people there. The monthly payments to begin from the present Sessions and to continue until the court shall further order.

416. *William Beach.*
The court is informed by Mr Carter steward of the leet for the hundred of Heytesbury that William Beach of Brixton Deverill was chosen constable for the hundred at the last leet but refused to take upon him the same office and answers that he was exempted. Ordered that William Beach attends this court with his patent of exemption and being summoned to show the same as appears by witness sworn in court he made default. Ordered that William Beach shall be sworn within ten days after the end of these Sessions for the due execution of the said office.
  (If he refuses, to be bound over.)

417. *William Dollery.* (See also **223**, **243**)
The court is informed by certificate under the hand of William Waller, knight, that William Dollery of Stratford under the Castle has been employed in the service of the King and Parliament and served as a sergeant of a company of dragoons and that during his service he received a wound on the right hand by which he has lost the use of his right hand. Ordered that William shall be allowed a pension of four marks per annum to be paid him quarterly by the Treasurer. The first payment to begin at the feast of St Michael the Archangel now next ensuing. And for the better relief and maintenance of William in the mean time the court orders and appoints Mr Francis Bennett to pay him thirteen shillings and four pence.

418. *Constables of Bradford.*
The court is informed by Robert Holton and Henry Willett constables of the borough of Bradford that on 25th March 1647 they were elected constables of the borough by the committee substitute and ever since continued in the office by reason the royalty heretofore belonging to the Right Honourable the Marquess of Winchester is sequestrated and therefore no court kept that time. And whereas Thomas Kelston, Robert Baylye and Roger Deverell of the borough renominated in court to be fitting and able men for that office, the court desires Mr John Long, justice, to elect and choose two of the fittest men of those three to be constables and swear them for the due execution of the said office. The court declares that the doing thereof shall not be prejudicial to the lord of the leet in point of right to come. Ordered

that the new elected constables shall within one week after notice given them of their election repair to the next justice to be sworn for the due execution of their office upon pain of ten pounds.

419. *Town of Bradford.* (See also **618**)
The court is informed that when the town of Bradford was infected with the contagion of the plague there was two months tax raised within the five miles compass for the relief of the poor infected people which came to one hundred and twenty pounds or near thereabouts and that there was but forty nine pounds paid in and that part of the arrears were collected and remain in the constables and other officers hands and the other part is not yet collected whereby the constables of that town and divers inhabitants who laid moneys and lent their goods for relief of the infected people are unsatisfied and the officers sued at law for the same to their great damage. The court is informed that Mr Eyre and Mr Ivy, justices, by virtue of an order of Easter Sessions last have taken great pains and have discovered what officers have moneys in their hands of the said tax and what officers have not collected and levied the tax. Ordered that Mr Eyre and Mr Ivy forthwith send for the constables and other officers who have any of the said moneys in their hands and bind them over to the next Sessions if they shall not within one month after notice of this order pay over the same moneys discovered to be in their hands unto such persons as the justice shall appoint for satisfaction of the officers and others who have money owing them. And the justices are further desired to grant their warrants to the now constables of the hundreds and the officers of the several places in arrears that they with the assistance of the old constables may forthwith collect and levy the arrears and pay it into the justices. If the constables of the hundreds and other officers old or new shall be remiss or negligent in execution of the said warrant then the justices are desired to bind them over to the next Quarter Sessions and if there shall be any surplussage remaining of the said taxes, all parties being satisfied their just debts owing them, then the justices are desired to take such course that the same be paid into the court at the next Quarter Sessions there to be disposed of as the court shall think fit.

420. *Thomas Chipp.*
Upon hearing the matter concerning Thomas Chipp and William Payne, son of Hanna Payne, his apprentice it is ordered that Thomas Chipp shall keep his apprentice and allow him fitting clothes and victuals during his apprenticeship and in default thereof the next justice upon complaint to him made is desired to examine the matter and bind Chipp to the next Quarter Sessions.

421. *William Bisse.*

The court is informed that William Meggs of Horningsham being a very poor man was in the time of the last visitation of the sickness there shut up and spent that small means he had of his own. And that William Bisse by the appointment of the officers disbursed towards his relief thirteen shillings and four pence for which he threatens to sue the said Meggs for want of payment thereof by the said officers. The court, seeing the poverty of Meggs, orders that the overseers of the poor of Horningsham pay unto William Bisse the said thirteen shillings and four pence and also pay unto Meggs towards his expense and travel herein the sum of ten shillings.

(If they default, to be bound over.)

422. *John Whitaker, Edward Moore and Phillip Sutton for fire.*
(Repeats the information contained in **396**)

423. *The widow Stent pension.*

The court is informed by Colonel Ludlow on behalf of Josian Stent of Maiden Bradley, widow, that her late husband Richard Stent has performed good service in these late wars was grievously wounded in the same service and thereof died after he had lain a long time languishing with the same wounds which tends the utter undoing of her and her children. The court grants and allows unto Josian Stent one yearly pension of five pounds to be paid unto her quarterly by the Treasurer, the first pay to be made at Michaelmas next. Further ordered that Mr Francis Bennett shall pay unto Josian the sum of fifty shillings over and besides the foresaid allowance in regards of her great necessity.

424. *Richard Rickards 18d weekly of Ridge tithing* [Chilmark].
(See also **537, 576, 703**)

It appears to the court that Richard Rickards of East Knoyle, carpenter, being dwelling in Knoyle about four years since being at work at his trade of carpentry with one Ellice Lane in Ridge was there imprest by John Fessard tithingman there for a soldier into Langford garrison [Britford] where he was shot and maimed in his arm and thereby disabled to get his living. Ordered that the overseers of Rudge shall pay weekly to Richard the sum of eighteen pence weekly towards his maintenance (he being pressed from thence to save one of that tithing) to begin the day of the present Sessions.

(If they refuse, to be bound over.)

425. *Robert Hooker.*

It appears to the court by the complaint of Robert Hooker of Corsley that he being heretofore possessed of a yardland in Corsley containing two and thirty acres was constrained to sell away twenty three acres thereof and reserved to himself but only nine acres. And that the parishioners of Corsley do not withstanding impose on Hooker the half rate of the whole yardlands to all payments though he has but nine acres left in his own hands, which this court conceives to be very unreasonable and therefore desires the two next justices to examine the truth thereof and to order the same accordingly.

426. *John Stone.*

The court is informed by John Stone of Horningsham, husbandman, that he lived with Mrs Jane Ludlow of Baycliff [Horningsham], widow, for many years as a covenant servant and she was indebted to him for wages the sum of sixteen pounds ten shillings which she detained till he petitioned this court in 1640 for his relief therein, whereupon Mrs Ludlow paid him fourteen pounds thereof and there remains due unto him fifty shillings which she denies to pay. Ordered that Mrs Ludlow shall forthwith pay the sum of fifty shillings unto John Stone or show good cause to the contrary at the next Quarter Sessions.

427. *Julian Moore.*

The court is informed by Julian Moore of Devizes, widow, that her son Thomas Moore having been always a soldier in the Parliament army from the beginning of the wars was shot in his back in the Parliament service under the command of Sir William Waller in lying siege against Devizes. And being so maimed and sick he was kept and relieved by her three quarters of a year to her great costs and charges which tends to her utter undoing she being but a poor woman and not able to maintain herself. Ordered that there shall be allowance unto Thomas Moore the sum of four pounds for his relief and maintenance that he may be the better enabled to give his mother satisfaction for the charges she has been at in relieving him in his sickness and extremity, which money the court orders Mr Francis Bennett to pay her for her son's use out of the county's stock for the relief of maimed soldiers.

428. *Richard Quier.*

Complaint has been made by Nicholas Quier of Horningsham that his son living with William Langley the younger of Tytherington as a servant and being freed from thence by John Topp and Thomas Bennett, justices, and that William Langley refuses to deliver up his son's clothes. The court desires that Mr Topp and Mr Bennett or one of them call William Langley before them and examine the complaint and order and settle the same according to justice and as they shall see cause.

429. *Ann Burgis.*
It appears to the court that Ann Burgis lived at Devizes as a servant in the parish of St. John's and from thence removed and lived with Abraham Hales in the same parish and was there got with child by John Flowers and was afterwards committed to the house of correction there for one year since which time she has not been settled in any other place. Ordered that Ann Burgis shall go and remain in the parish of St John's in Devizes where she last dwelt and remained as a servant and where she was got with child there to be provided for and set to work by the overseers until it shall be further ordered by this court.

430. *Anne Jones to have 40s. of the money in Mr Bennett's hands.*
The court is informed by Anne Jones of Trowbridge, widow, that one George Erwyn a soldier under the command of Colonel Okeslye in his regiment of dragoons under the command of Captain Barrington who coming to Trowbridge on Whitsunday last past on a march happened to be sick and feeble that he could not follow his colours and is yet there very sick and not able to travel and is abiding at the house of Anne Jones and has not means to subsist nor yet to relieve himself or pay for what he is already engaged for to Anne and for what she has laid out for his succour and comfort and that he is likely to lie sick a long time on her charge to relieve and that he has been in the Parliament service these six years last past. Anne Jones prayed this court to take the miserable condition of the soldier and of her, being a very poor woman, into their consideration. Ordered that there shall be allowed unto Anne Jones the sum of forty shillings for the relief and maintenance of the sick and weak soldier and satisfying his engagements. Also ordered that Mr Francis Bennett to pay her out of the stock of money remaining in his hands for the relief of maimed soldiers.

431. *Joan Goldinge £5 for fire.*
The court is informed by Joan Goldinge alias Valentyne of Devizes, widow, that her dwelling house and all her goods and household stuff therein with a mill house and malt mill and all her outhouses to the value of one hundred and twenty pounds were all burned down to the ground by fire upon the last entering in of the Parliament forces into Devizes she having no means to live by but the house and malt mill which tend to her utter undoing and the widow prayed the assistance of this court for her relief therein. Ordered that Mr William Parry

of Easton Grey, Treasurer, shall forthwith pay unto Joan Goldinge the sum of five pounds out of the first money he shall receive in regard of her great loss and present necessity.

432. *Robert Kinge against the constables of the hundred of Branch and Dole.*
Upon complaint made by Robert Kinge that there was formerly upon the oath of John Reeves a warrant of the peace granted by Francis Swanton, justice, against John Blake and Richard Palmer of Woodford and others which warrant was directed amongst other officers to the constable of the hundred of Branch and Dole and Underditch for the apprehending of the said parties yet notwithstanding the constables have been remiss and negligent in the execution of the warrant. The court desires the next justice to Woodford to examine the truth of the premises and to bind over the constables for their remissness if he shall see cause and to take such further order as shall be agreeable to law and justice.

433. *To examine the arrears of Calne money.*
The court desires Mr William Eyre, Mr George Ivy and Mr John Norden, justices, or any two of them, to send for the constables of the hundreds who have formerly received any moneys for the relief of the poor people of Calne when they were heretofore infected with the plague and do detain the same in their hands and also all other officers and persons who have any of the money in their hands other than by order of court. And the justices are desired to examine them concerning that matter, what thereof they have in their hands and what they or any of them have received, collected and paid in and what is in arrear in any hundred and take course that the same be speedily levied, collected and paid in that this court be no further troubled therein. The court desires the justices to certify their doings at the next Quarter Sessions.

434. *Inhabitants of Seagry.*
Upon hearing the matter of difference between the inhabitants of Upper Seagry and the inhabitants of Lower Seagry concerning the manner of rating there, it is desired that the two next justices to Seagry would be pleased to call the parties interested before them and to examine the manner of rating there and to mediate an end if they can. And the justices are further desired to make such order therein as may be agreeable to law and justice which order the court (if they think fit) will confirm at the next Sessions.
     (Upper Seagry said that they used to pay for 14 yardlands and Lower Seagry for 18 but about 20 years ago Lower Seagry managed to lower their

assessment by 3 yardlands and had recently reduced it by a further half a yardland thus increasing the burden on Upper Seagry. A1/110/1648T/157)

435. *Inhabitants of Bradford and South Wraxall, etc.* (Refers to **378**) Upon hearing the matter in difference between the inhabitants of Bradford and South Wraxall, Holt, Winsley and Stoke. Ordered by consent of parties that the case shall be drawn up and agreed upon by counsel on both sides and presented to the honourable judges at the next Assizes and both parties with their counsel are to attend their lordships for their resolution and order therein.

436. *Inhabitants of Brokenborough.* (See also **412**) The court is informed by divers of the inhabitants of Brokenborough that Thomas Hewett, Thomas Milles and William Uncles now or late tithingmen of Brokenborough do refuse to give up their accounts to the parish of their receipts of such moneys as they have received upon rates of carrying prisoners to the gaol and their parish rates and how they have disbursed and paid away the same during the time that they have served in the office. Ordered that Thomas, etc shall within short time after this order give up their several accounts before the two next justices of their receipts and payments and such of the parishioners as will may attend the justices when the accounts are given up to except against the same if there be cause.
(If they refuse, to be bound over.)

437. *Arrears for King's and mariners maimed soldiers and mariners.* It appears to the court that there is much money in arrear for the relief of King's Bench and Marshalsea maimed soldiers and mariners and the gaol which remains in the hands of divers persons which have been churchwardens or petty constables or also is uncollected, levied and not paid into the several constables of the hundreds and by them to the Treasurers of those collections. Ordered that the now churchwardens or petty constables shall within one month after the end of this Sessions collect, levy and pay into the now constables of the several respective hundreds all such arrears and sums of money as are due to be paid out of several places and parishes that the same may be employed according as the statute requires. Further ordered that the Treasurers shall forthwith attend the Clerk of the Peace for copies of this order and they are required forthwith to send copies of this order to all the constables of the hundreds and the constables upon receipt thereof are also required to send out their warrants to all churchwardens and petty constables within their several hundreds for the speedy levying, collecting and paying in of the arrears and sums of money unto them, that they may pay the same over to the Treasurers according to the true intent and meaning of this order. The court desires the justices of the several divisions within the county or some of them in each division at their convenience and with as much speed as may be to meet together in each division and send out their warrants for summoning in of the Treasurers, constables of the hundreds, churchwardens or petty constables to appear before them and they are also desired to examine the due execution of this order. And if the justices shall find the Treasurers, etc. to have been remiss or negligent in the due observance hereof then the justices are desired to bind over all parties offending therein to the next Quarter Sessions.

438. *Edmond Lewes.*
The court is informed by Edmond Lewes tithingman of West Ashton in the hundred of Whorwellsdown that he has served in the same office one whole year before Easter last and could not be released by reason that there was no lawday held for the hundred and prayed this court that he might be released of the office and that John Fryer of the same place ought by the course there used to serve in that office which was likewise proved in court to be true. Ordered that John Fryer shall within fourteen days next after receipt of this order repair to the next justice to be sworn for the due execution of the office on pain of ten pounds and thereupon Edmond Lewes shall be discharged of his office.

439. *Robert Holton and Henry Willett.*
The court is informed by Robert Holton and Henry Willett constables of the borough of Bradford that on the five and twentieth day of March 1647 they were elected constables for the borough by the committee substitute and have ever since continued in the office by reason of the royalty belonging to the Right Honourable the Marquess of Winchester is sequestrated and therefore no court kept all that time. Thomas Kellston, Robert Baylye and Roger Deverell are nominated in court to be able and fitting men for that office. The court desires Mr Long, justice, to elect and choose two of most fitted men of these three to be constables for the borough and swear them for the due execution of their office. The court declares that the doing thereof shall not be prejudicial to the lord of the leet in point of right in time to come. The court also ordered the new elected constables shall within one week after notice given to them of their election repair to the next justice to be sworn for the execution of their office upon pain of ten pounds.

440. *Inhabitants of Devizes.*
The court is informed by the inhabitants of Devizes there is yet twelve

pounds and eight shillings unpaid by the inhabitants of the hundred of Calne being the arrears of a rate made towards the relief of the poor people of the borough infected with the plague. It now appears to the court upon examination of the matter and upon full debate thereof that John Rogers and Robert Trimnell, constables of the hundred, being now present in court have received several warrants from the justices to levy and collect the arrears and for want of payment to distrain for the same. And it likewise appears to the court that John Rogers and Robert Trimnell have not only neglected to execute the warrant but still do neglect to do so to the great scandal and contempt of justice and utter undoing of the poor and some of the inhabitants of the borough. It is now ordered that Rogers and Trimnell shall be rated and assessed.

441. *Eneas Gooddale cottage.*
The court is informed that Eneas Gooddale of Everleigh is re-edifying a cottage there upon an old foundation of an ancient cottage and that he is much hindered and disturbed in the re-edifying thereof. The court declares that Eneas Gooddale may erect a new cottage upon the old foundation without incurring the forfeiture mentioned in the statute made against the erecting of cottages and Eneas ought not to be hindered or disturbed in the re-edifying of the cottage.

442. *Ann Freeth.* Complaint is made to the court by Anne Freeth of Hindon widow that she is a poor woman and not able to pay anything for the relief of the poor nevertheless she is rated to her great impoverishment she not having wherewithal to satisfy the same. The court upon examination of the truth thereof in the presence of George Banister constable of Hindon orders with the consent of Banister on the behalf of the parish that twelve pence shall be accepted from her of all arrears until this Sessions which she paid to him in court. Further ordered that she shall not from henceforth be rated for the poor in regard of her great poverty until the court shall see cause otherwise to order the same.

443. *Thomas Still £4 pension.*
The court is informed by a certificate under the hands of Lieutenant Colonel John Blackmore, Captain William Browne and Richard Hinger surgeon to Colonel John Burch that Thomas Still of Warminster has served the Parliament in the regiment of Colonel Burch for the space of three whole years under the command of Captain Browne until the time of disbanding. At Gotheridge [Goodrich] Castle he received twenty eight grievous wounds to his utter undoing and the

loss of the use and benefit of his right arm. Ordered that there shall be a yearly pension of four pounds per annum granted and allowed to him in regard of the many wounds he received in the said service and his impotency thereby to be paid unto him quarterly by the Treasurer the first payment to begin at the feast of St Michael the Archangel now next ensuing. And for his relief and maintenance in the meantime the court orders Mr Francis Bennett forthwith to pay unto him the sum of twenty shillings out of the county's stock remaining in his hands.

444. *William Merriweather.*
The court is informed by William Gunstone together with the overseers of the poor of the parish of Westbury that William Merriweather, gent, formerly gained out of the hands of one Mary Kington while she was sole the full sum of three score and six pounds thirteen shillings and four pence and by his lease of indenture mortgaged his farm as by the deed appears for the payment of five pounds per annum towards the maintenance of Mary or her assigns for ninety years if Mary or William Stanton or Thomas Stanton or either of them so long live and Mary afterwards took to husband one Edward Smyth and having by him issue, about three years since Mary died since which time Mr Merriweather refused to pay the five pounds per annum for the relief of Edward Smyth or the issue of Mary who was sister to the now wife of Mr Merriweather but suffered them being in great misery to come to the charge of the parish. The court desires the two next justices to examine the truth of the petition whether any other children be on the relief of the parish or not. If they find they are on the relief of the parish, they are desired to take course for the petitioner's relief and the children's and make such order therein as to law and justice shall appertain and the court will confirm the same.

445. *Roger Hollis pension.* (See also **305**, **328**, **445**)
The court is informed by a certificate under the hands of Captain John Pausey, Humfry Buckler and Lieutenant Charles Buckler, a cornet, and William Davys, a quartermaster, that Roger Hollis has served in the Parliament service two years and upwards under the command of Major Pausey who was very faithful in that service and has been thereby insomuch that he is not able to work nor help himself but like to perish his friends being poor and he not able to relieve himself. Ordered that there shall be a yearly pension of four marks per annum granted to Roger to be paid unto him quarterly by the Treasurer, the first payment to be made at the present sessions in regard of his great necessity.

General Sessions of the Peace held at Marlborough on Tuesday after the feast of St. Michael the Archangel 3 October Charles 24 (1648). Robert Nicholas, Robert Jenner, Richard Goddard, William Littleton, William Sadler, Robert Hippisley, William Yorke, John Norden, Thomas Bennett and George Ivy.

446. *Edward Ricketts to have £6 13s 4d.* (See also **575**)
The court is informed by Edward Ricketts a maimed soldier in the parliament service and in the said service has lost the use of his right arm under the command of Captain Groave in the regiment of Colonel Banksteede as by his certificate appears. Ordered the Treasurer to pay unto Edward the sum of six pounds thirteen shillings and four pence for this year only in regard of his present necessity.

447. *John Harwell portreeve of Great Bedwyn.*
Complaint has been made by John Harwell portreeve of the borough of Great Bedwyn that he has disbursed out of his own purse several sums of money in carrying felons and other prisoners to His Majesty's gaol of Fisherton Anger. Ordered that John Harwell with some other of the inhabitants of the borough make an equal and indifferent rate and get the same confirmed by the next justice.
(If any refuse to pay, to be bound over.)

448. *Constables and churchwardens to pay their arrears to the Treasurers.*
The money for the relief of maimed soldiers are not collected by means whereof the several constables of hundreds have not paid the same into the Treasurers for the time as they have been constables. And the churchwardens and petty constables in every parish who ought by the statute to collect the said moneys and pay the same over to the constables of their hundreds have not collected the same but do sleight and neglect the collecting thereof. Ordered that no constables of hundreds be discharged from their office until they have paid unto the Treasurers the money due for both the said allowances in their time of constableship. Further ordered if the churchwardens and constables in any parish shall not pay the same forthwith in unto the constables of the hundreds upon demand thereof to be made, then the court orders the next justice to bind the churchwardens or constables who ought to collect the same to the next Sessions.

449. *Richard Helton a distracted person to be provided for.*
Complaint is made that Richard Helton, a distracted person, is permitted to wander about the country to the great annoyance of

people where he comes notwithstanding he has been several times sent home to Ludgershall being the place of his dwelling. Ordered that it be referred to the two next justices to Ludgershall who are desired to injoin the officers and inhabitants to distrain the said distracted person from wandering abroad and to provide for him as his case requires and to take such course as to them shall seem meet against such persons whom they shall find refractory or negligent in the premisses.

450. *Ayliffe Wayte, George Palmer.*
The court is informed that Ayliffe Wayte has served the office of tithingman for the tithing of Grittenham [Brinkworth] for one year last past and cannot be discharged of the office because the lord of the manor does not keep his courts and that George Palmer is the new elected tithingman by the inhabitants of the tithing. Ordered that Palmer shall repair to the next justice and take his oath for the execution of his office within one week after the receipt hereof with (a salvo iure) [i.e. saving theright] to the lord of the manor and in default thereof the next justice is desired to bind him over to the next Sessions.

451. *John Heath constable of Swindon.*
The court is informed by John Heath late constable of Swindon and Mathewe Wake late tithingman that they had several orders to levy the sum of seven pounds one shilling and three pence for charges expended in carrying felons to His Majesty's gaol of Fisherton Anger. And that notwithstanding the said orders of the inhabitants of Swindon and the several officers of the several tithings thereunto belonging do refuse to make any rate for the payment of the same. Ordered that the inhabitants of the borough with the constable and tithingman of the borough and several tithings together with the churchwardens shall forthwith meet together and make an indifferent and equal rate on the inhabitants for the raising of the sum of seven pounds one shilling and three pence and the two next justices are desired to confirm the rate and the now constables and tithingmen are desired to assist Heath and Wake in the levying and collecting thereof.
(If any refuse to pay, to be bound over.)

452. *The inhabitants of Fullway* [All Cannings] *and Stockton.*
There is some difference between the inhabitants of Fullway and the inhabitants of Stockton concerning the settlement of Francis Elwayes. Ordered that the inhabitants of Fullway shall give notice to the churchwardens and overseers of the poor of Stockton to attend at the next Sessions to be held at Salisbury whereupon hearing counsel

of both sides the court will further examine the differences and settle Francis according to law and justice.

453. *Thomas Leach £5 for fire.*
The court is informed by Thomas Leach of Devizes labourer that about midsummer 1646 it being a very dry time there happened a very fierce fire in the parish of St Mary in Devizes wherein divers houses were burned to the ground and the whole town endangered. At which time Thomas Leach's house was pulled down to the ground for the stopping of the fire and for the safeguard of other houses from burning has sustained great loss to the value of two and twenty pounds besides the damage which he sustained in the loss of his goods to the value of three pounds more amounting in the whole to the sum of five and twenty pounds to the utter undoing of Thomas and his wife they being both of them very aged, poor and impotent. Ordered Mr Francis Bennett shall pay unto Thomas the sum of five pounds in regard of his great necessity.
(Leach said that some of his goods were burnt in the fire, some broken and some looted by the multitude of people there. A1/110/1648M/203)

454. *New overseers of the poor in Bradford, South Wraxall. Holt etc. to execute their office.*
The court is informed that as well in Bradford as in the several hamlets within the parish viz. South Wraxall, Holt, Winsley, Stoke and Atworth there were new overseers of the poor elected and chosen in Easter week last in the several hamlets was alleged to be contrary to the ancient custom there used and the last overseers have given up their accounts and the new elected overseers do neglect the execution of their offices whereby the poor are not relieved. Ordered that the new elected overseers shall forthwith take upon them the execution of their offices and that they with the churchwardens do make equal and indifferent rates in the several hamlets for the relief of the poor people. The court desires Mr Bennett and Mr John Goddard justices to confirm the said rates and grant their warrants for the levying of the same upon the refusers. And the doing thereof shall not be prejudicial or destructive to any ancient custom there used concerning that matter.

455. *Robert Webbe, …Burges, … Eyres and Legge alehousekeepers in Great Bedwyn suppressed.*
The court is informed by Edward Hungerford esq that Robert Webbe, … Burges, …Eyres and John Legge all of Great Bedwyn do sell ale and common tippling houses and suffer menservants to lie there tippling at unseasonable times and suffer many disorders in their houses contrary

to the laws in that case made. The court desires Mr William Littleton and Mr Richard Goddard justices to call the said Robert etc before them and to examine the premises and to suppress them and do therein as they see cause.

(The manuscript leaves gaps where first names should appear.)

456. *Thomas Jones to be whipped or pay 20s.*
It appears to the court upon the oath of two witnesses that Thomas Jones of Broad Hinton has sold ale without licence. Ordered that Thomas shall pay twenty shillings or be whipped according to the form of the statute in such case made and provided.

457. *William Hobbs and his wife.*
Ordered that the churchwardens and overseers of the poor of Grittleton shall suffer William Hobbs and his wife to live at Grittleton and provide for them as the poor of that parish.

(If they refuse, to be bound over.)

458. *Inhabitants of Marston.*
The court is informed by the inhabitants of the tithing of Marston in the parish of Potterne that the tithing being a great roadway from Frome and Westbury and many other places to Devizes and having three stoneing bridges in the tithing and have not materials in that place to repair the same but what they are constrained to buy at other places and the most part of the inhabitants have agreed upon a rate by the yardlands and there are three of the inhabitants which now rent the parsonage which is to pay for three yardlands in all manner of payments and these three do refuse to pay their rates towards the reparation of the highways neither will they do their service with their ploughs for five days according to the statute. Ordered that the rate by the yardlands shall be confirmed.

(If any refuse to pay, to be bound over.)
(Marston said two of the bridges were for ploughs and the other a hackney bridge which cost £10 a time to repair. A1/110/1648M/207)

459. *John Scammell, Robert Hunt.*
It appears to the court that John Scammell of Netheravon chosen constable of the hundred of Elstub and Everleigh at the last Assizes and not yet sworn is an unfitting man for that office in regard his living is not worth above twenty pounds per annum and can neither write nor read as was proved upon oath in open court by the testimony of a sufficient witness. Ordered that Scammell shall be discharged from that office and the court elects and chooses Robert Hunt of Enford

gent to be constable of the hundred in place of Scammell and orders Mr Hunt to go before the next justice within or near the hundred within one week after receipt of this order to take his oath for the due execution of the said office upon pain of twenty pounds in regard of the special service which is to be performed .

(If he refuses, to be bound over.)

460. *Constables of Bromham and Rowde.* (See also **550**)
Whereas James Hughes, John Scott and William Bayly were presented at the last Easter Sessions for that they being constables of the Liberty of Bromham and Rowde refused to yield up their accounts and whereas Mr Hughes promised in court that they will account concerning that matter before John Norden justice within one month after the Sessions in the presence of such of the parishioners as upon notice of this order will be present at the doing thereof that they may except against the same if they see cause. Ordered that Mr Norden takes the said account and if it shall appear upon the account that the parishioners are indebted to the accountant then he is desired to take course that they may be satisfied the same but if the said accountant shall not pass their accounts then Mr Norden is desired to bind them over to the next Quarter Sessions.

461. *William Townesend discharged of William Axford his apprentice.*
At the Quarter Sessions held at Marlborough the third day of October 24 Charles [1648] upon hearing of the matter in difference between William Townesend of Warminster and William Axford his apprentice. Ordered that William Axford shall be discharged of his apprenticeship in regard of his master has given him immoderate commons being the cause of his running away from his master. In witness whereof the justices whose names are subscribed present at the Sessions have hereunto set our hands and seals the day and year first above written.

462. *For arrears of the money of King's Bench and Marshalsea.*
It appears to the court that there is much money in arrear for the relief of maimed soldiers, etc. which remains in the hands of diverse persons which have been churchwardens or petty constables of the several places and parishes within the same or else is uncollected and not paid into the constables of the hundreds and by them to the Treasurers. Ordered that the now churchwardens or petty constables shall within one month after the end of this Sessions collect, levy and pay in to the now constables of the hundreds all such arrears and sums of money as are due to be paid out of the several places and parishes that the same may be employed according to the statute. Ordered

that the Treasurers of the north and south parts shall forthwith attend the Clerk of the Peace for copies of this order and they are hereby required forthwith to send copies of this order to all constables of the hundreds and the said constables are also required to send out their warrants to all churchwardens and petty constables for the speedy levying collecting and paying in of the arrears unto them that they may pay the same over unto the Treasurers. The court desires the justices of the several divisions at their convenience and with as much speed as may be to meet together in each division and send out their warrants for summoning in of the Treasurers, constables of the hundreds, churchwardens and petty constables to appear before them. And they are also desired to examine the due execution of this order and if the justices find the Treasurers etc. to have been remiss or negligent in the due observance thereof then the justices are desired to bind over all parties offending therein to the next Quarter Sessions.

463. *Fisherton inhabitants to have the churchwardens and overseers of the poor of Little Langford bound to the next Sessions.* (Refers to **415**)
The court is informed by the inhabitants of Fisherton Anger that at the last midsummer Sessions they having received an order for the rating and levying of ten shillings monthly on the parish of Little Langford in the hundred of Branch and Dole towards the relief of the great number of poor people inhabiting within the parish of Fisherton Anger. The court taking into consideration their great necessity by reason of their late visitation and the poverty of the place and that the parishioners and churchwardens of Little Langford do utterly refuse to give their assistance towards their relief, the court desires the next justice to bind over the churchwardens and overseers of the poor of Little Langford to the next Quarter Sessions.

1649

General Sessions of the Peace held at Salisbury Tuesday 9 January 24 Charles (1649). William Stephens, William Yorke, William Littleton, William Eyre, Richard Grobham Howe, Barnaby Coles and Francis Swanton.

464. *Sir John Backhouse and inhabitants of Swallowfield* [now Berkshire]. (See also **506**)
The court is informed by Mr Frederick Hyde of counsel with Sir John Backhouse concerning some difference between Sir John and the inhabitants of Swallowfield about the rates and taxes to the poor

of Swallowfield being formerly rated but at two yardlands but now of
late he is rated to three yardlands wherewith he finds himself aggrieved
and overrated and for his relief appeals to this Sessions. Ordered that
the inhabitants of Swallowfield having notice of this order shall show
good cause to the court the next Sessions why Sir John should be
valued for more than two yardlands as he has been formerly rated
at. And in the mean time the rates to stand as they are now rated at.

465. *Roger Pope.*
The court is informed by Roger Pope that he has served tithingman of
the tithing of Milford [Salisbury] for Mr Thomas Hancock now deceased
one full year and a quarter. And by reason that at Michaelmas last the
usual lawday was not kept there he is not yet discharged. Ordered that
(salvo iure to the lord of the leet or lawday) James Watkinson (whose
turn it is next) shall be titihngman in the place of Pope.
      (If he refuses, to be bound over.)

466. *Edmund Potter.*
It appears to the court that Edmund Potter of Milford [Salisbury] being
a very aged man above fourscore years and his wife near seventy years
and sick and being formerly honest and laborious people and now by
reason of age and poverty are fallen into great want. Ordered William
Stephens and Francis Swanton or one of them to call the overseers of
the poor of Milford before them and to order such weekly allowance
unto Potter and his wife as they shall think requisite.

467. *Edith Willis to have 12d per week of the overseers.*
Upon complaint to the court by Edith Willis a poor widow who
having four female children and living in a cottage built upon the
waste ground belonging to the tithing of Ashton Gifford [Codford St
Peter] and being in great distress and poverty and not able to relieve
herself and children. Ordered the overseers of the poor of Ashton
Gifford pay weekly unto Edith the sum of twelve pence towards the
relief of her and her four children.
      (If they default, to be bound over.)

468. *Henry Lambert to have £6 3s 8d.*
Henry Lambert one of the inhabitants of Chippenham has heretofore
disbursed three pounds three shillings and eight pence for disbursements
about discharge of highways for the inhabitants which was to be paid
him by order of this court in Easter Sessions 17 Charles [1641] but is
yet unpaid. And for that he has informed the court hat he has since
disbursed for the inhabitants for distresses for the highways the sum

of three pounds being in all six pounds three shillings and eight pence
which the court desires the justices of that division or one of them to
examine the disbursements and to make a general rate upon all the
inhabitants of Chippenham for repayment thereof.

(If any refuse to pay, to be bound over.)

469. *The inhabitants of Nunton and the owners of the parsonage of Downton.*
Upon reading the petition of the inhabitants of the parish of Nunton
against the owners of the parsonage of Downton for refusing to allow
some relief towards the maintenance of the poor of Nunton (as time
out of mind they have done) the owners of the parsonage receiving to
the value of sixty pounds per annum at least in tithes out of the parish
of Nunton. The court desires Mr Howe and Mr Swanton justices to
call all parties interested before them and examine the contents of the
petition and to do therein as to law and justice shall appertain.

(The parsonage at Downton had maintained one poor man at Nunton
and allowed him twelve pence and his dinner every month on the Sabbath
day. The last one to be so relieved was Emanuel Dallery who died about ten
years previously. A1/110/1649/H/205)

470. *An order for binding forth apprentices.*
At the last Assizes held for the county the court was informed that
divers masters refused to take their apprentices bound to them by the
churchwardens and overseers of the poor with the consent of the
justices according to the statute in such case made and provided which
is a great disturbance of the execution of that statute. Ordered that if
any such masters of apprentices shall refuse to take their apprentices
bound to them by the churchwardens and overseers of the poor with
the consent of the justices then the justice are desired to bind over all
such masters refusing to take their apprentices to the next Assizes or
Quarter Sessions as they shall think fit there to answer the same and
that all apprentices which shall refuse to be bound forth should be
sent to the house of correction there to remain until they shall serve
their masters according to their indentures. And whereas the justices
at this Quarter Sessions have taken the same order into consideration
and finding by experience that divers constables churchwardens and
overseers of the poor in most parishes within this county are very
remiss and negligent in providing masters for apprentices and binding
them forth whereby many prove vagrants and take idle courses which
might be prevented if they were bound forth apprentices according to
the law. Ordered that in all parishes within this county the constables
churchwardens and overseers of the poor shall forthwith consider
what boys and maids are fitting to be bound forth apprentices and

provide fitting masters for them and bind them for apprentices by and with the consent of the justices of the same division or some of them. And to the intent this order may not prove fruitless the court appoints the Clerk of the Peace to send copies of this order to the constables of the several hundreds and all constables of hundreds are required forthwith to send out copies of the same order after receipt hereof to the constables and churchwardens of the several parishes within their hundred as they will answer the contrary at their perils and all constables churchwardens and overseers of he poor of all parishes are required to give obedience to this order and execute the same according to the interest and meaning of this order. And if it shall appear to the justices that the constables churchwardens and overseers of any parish shall not bind forth their apprentices accordingly but shall be remiss and negligent therein then the justices are desired to bind them over to the next Quarter Sessions there to answer the same and the justices are desired to appoint meetings in their several divisions concerning the execution of this order and punish the neglect of the officers if any shall be found negligent herein.

471. *Susan Candy recommended to the master of St Thomas hospital.*
The court is informed of the lamentable condition of Susan Candy a poor maid who is visited as is supposed with a disease called the King's Evil the maid having been under the hands of some surgeons of this county and can receive no cure but grows worse and worse in so much that none will harbour her for fear of infection and she being a loathsome creature and like to perish by reason thereof. And whereas the court is desired to take her into their consideration it is therefore thought fit and the court recommends Susan to the charitable consideration of the master of St Thomas in Southwark desiring him that he will be pleased to receive her into that hospital and that she may remain there for her cure if it shall please God to bless the work.

472. *Fisherton Anger, Little Langford and the pay reduced to 5s per month.* (See also **707, 765**)
It appears to the court upon reading an order of Midsummer Sessions last that the inhabitants of the parish of Little Langford were to pay monthly to the churchwardens and overseers of the poor of the parish of Fisherton Anger the sum of ten shillings per month towards the relief of the poor people of Fisherton Anger and the court is now informed that there is not money paid according to the order but they refuse to pay the same pretending they are not able to pay it. The court thinks fit to alter the payment and reduce it to five shillings per month and orders that the inhabitants of Little Langford shall pay all the arrears

from last midsummer Sessions to this Sessions after the rate of five shillings per month and from thence to pay five shillings per month for the relief until the court shall see cause to alter the same.

473. *John Head his pension for 10s quarterly.* (See also **356**, **636**)
It appears to the court by petition and certificate that John Head of Easton being a very poor man and having a charge of a wife and three children and being lame in his limbs by reason of hurts and bruises he took in the Parliament service under the command of the Earl of Essex whereupon the court by virtue of an ordinance of Parliament in that behalf made order that the Treasurer for maimed soldiers for the north forthwith pay to Head the sum of twenty shillings formerly allowed him by Richard Goddard, William Sadler and William Littleton justices. And that he further pay to Head ten shillings quarterly from this present Sessions to continue until the court shall otherwise order the same.

474. *John Stephens.*
Ordered that the Treasurer for the south shall upon sight hereof pay unto John Stephens, Mr Swanton's clerk, the sum of forty shillings for his pains for making and sending abroad divers warrants for the getting in the arrears of the moneys due for the relief of maimed soldiers, etc. and the sum of forty shillings shall be allowed upon the Treasurer's account.

475. *Mary Watts to be sent to Whiteparish.*
It appears to the court that Mary Watts an infant of the age of five years lately left and remaining at Whiteparish was punished as a vagrant and sent away from there by a pass under the constables hands of that place to be conveyed from tithing to tithing unto the city of Bristol from whence she is sent back again and now remains at the city of Salisbury. The court declares that the same is contrary to the law and orders that Mary shall be sent back to Whiteparish and there settled in regard she was there made a vagrant and the overseers of the poor of that place are hereby required to receive her and provide for her as a poor of that place as they will answer the contrary.

476. *John Brinde elected constable and John Duck tithingman for the tithing of Wroughton.*
Forasmuch as a constable and tithingman have heretofore been elected and sworn at the Court Baron held for the manor of Wroughton belonging to the church of Winchester and by reason the court has not been of late kept there, there have been no officers elected or sworn. Now for that Mr Chadwell bailiff of the manor with some of

the tenants there have elected John Brinde to server as constable and John Duck as tithingman within the tithing of Wroughton for the year ensuing. Ordered that Brinde upon pain of twenty pounds and Duck upon pain of ten pounds shall either of them within one week after notice of this order repair to the next justice either of them to take their several oaths for the due execution of their respective offices.

477. *Edmund Fettiplace.*
Complaint has been made by Edmund Fettiplace of some abuses offered unto him and Henry Comynge servant to Fettiplace by Thomas Pound, Thomas Dyer, Edward Kyett, William Richardson and Mrs Mary Fisher spinster by following and pursuing them and crying out kill the rogues which was affirmed in open court by the oath of Henry Comynge. Ordered and desired William Sadler and Robert Hippisley or one of them to call the parties before them and to re-examine the premisses and do therein as they shall see cause.

478. *Inter Hurd and Quinton.* (See also **390, 530**)
At Easter Sessions last it was ordered by the court about the difference of the rate between John Hurd the impropriate person of Manningford and Wilsford and Samuel Quinton the vicar of the same place that the parsonage should be from thence forwards rated at three yardlands for Manningford and the vicar at four yardlands for his vicarage. Now the court is informed by the petition of Quinton that he has some witnesses to examine for proving the ancient rates both for the vicarage and parsonage which were not formerly produced or examined neither then known unto him. Ordered that both parties shall attend at the next Sessions to be held at Warminster with all their witnesses and proofs and that this difference concerning the rates shall be examined and heard again that a final order may be made therein. And that Quinton in the mean time give notice to Hurd of this order and till then the rates to continue as they were ordered by the last order.

479. *Robert Blanket for erecting a cottage.*
Robert Blanket of Tockenham Wick being long living within the same parish and being a poor man and now destitute of an habitation for him his wife and children to live in and having the consent of many of the inhabitants of the parish for erecting of a cottage within the parish as by their certificate appears. Ordered that he may erect a cottage within the parish in some convenient place for his habitation with the consent of the lord of the manor under his hand and seal which shall continue for an habitation during his life without incurring the penalties in the statute.

480. *The inhabitants of Hungerford.* (See also **505, 521, 546**)
The court is informed by the petition of the inhabitants of Hungerford in the county of Berkshire that they being much burdened with multiplicity of poor people within the parish of Hungerford and are not able of themselves to relieve their poor. And therefore did desire that the tithing of Charnhamstreet (being a tithing within the parish of Hungerford but lying within the county of Wiltshire) might contribute towards the relief of the poor there being many inhabitants within the tithing and very few poor people. The court taking into consideration upon the certificate of the truth of the petition under the hands of Humfry Doleman and Roger Knight justices of the county of Berkshire orders that the inhabitants of the tithing of Charnhamstreet upon notice of this order show cause to the court the next Sessions why they should not contribute with the rest of the parish of Hungerford towards the relief of their poor that order may be made therein according to law and equity.
(Hungerford was said to have many poor because of several accidents of fire and the late wars. Charnhamstreet had many men of great estates and very few poor. A1/110/1649H/203)

481. *Anne Adlam.* (See also **514**)
The court is informed by Anne Adlam widow late wife of John Adlam of Dilton deceased together with the churchwardens and overseers of the poor of the same parish that John Hynton of Sutton Veny father of Anne being a man of a great estate promised unto John Adlam a good portion with her in marriage part whereof paid but thirty pounds parcel of the promised portion he still detains in his hands promising that when her husband should purchase some estate wherein she might enjoy her widowhood he would lay down the thirty pounds towards the same but after many years when her husband had obtained the price of a tenement wherein he lived worth about twenty marks per annum and had his own life in he entreated Hynton pay the thirty pounds towards the fine and preferred security to repay the money if he did not settle the tenement on Anne during her widowhood and the life of her son if they should happen to outlive him but Hynton not regarding the good of his daughter refused to pay the money by reason whereof her husband was put besides the purchase and being since dead Anne his wife and eight children are out of doors and re like to perish for want of relief and prayed the assistance of the court in this behalf. Ordered that Hynton her father being a man of estate shall forthwith keep and relieve Anne his daughter and her eight children and provide for them as the law requires unless he pay her the thirty pounds.
        (If he refuses, to be bound over.)

482. *Overseers of Shrewton.*
The court is informed by William Smyth junior of Shrewton that there
a base child borne of the body of Joan Bollen in the parish of Shrewton
and that the parishioners of Shrewton take no care for the relieving
maintaining and breeding up of the bastard child. Ordered that the
overseers of the poor of Shrewton shall take care for the relieving
maintaining and breeding up of the base child as a poor of that parish
until they shall show good cause to the court to the contrary.

483. *Mr Soper's Account.*
The account of John Soper Treasurer of maimed soldiers and mariners
for the south part of the county for one whole year beginning
midsummer 1641.

The several sums of money received of the several constables of hundred
in the south part of the county for the year 1641 for maimed soldiers
and mariners.

	£	s.	d.
Heytesbury	8	0	0
Branch and Dole	9	2	6½
Alderbury	5	10	10
Amesbury	6	19	4
Frustfield	0	19	4
Cawdon and Cadworth	7	8	6
Chalke	3	4	6
Elstub and Everleigh	7	15	6
Downton	1	2	4
Warminster	5	4	0
Liberty of Hindon, Knoyle and Fonthill	1	6	0
Liberty of Bishopstone	0	11	4
Damerham south	3	5	0
Liberty of Trowbridge	0	13	0
Dunworth	7	2	4
Mere	3	4	0
Whorwellsdown	3	5	0
Underditch	1	9	0
Westbury	1	14	8
Melksham	2	5	4
Bradford	2	9	10
Sum	82	12	4
Received of Francis Topp late Treasurer 19 July 1641	10	0	0
The total sum received	92	12	4

The several sums of money paid by the hands of John Soper Treasurer for maimed soldiers and mariners to divers pensions for one whole year 1641.

Mr Knowles	13	6	8
John Allen	2	0	0
William Tulse	2	13	4
Bise Humfrye	2	0	0
William Webb	2	0	0
Lawrence Ghost	4	0	0
Edmond Penn	2	0	0
William Batter	3	0	0
John Phillips	2	13	4
John Skinner	2	0	0
Walter Muntigue	2	0	0
James Leach	3	6	8
Thomas Snooke for three quarters	1	10	0
John Brundile for three quarters	1	10	0
John Brundile more when he had his patten at the Quarter Sessions at Warminster 29 July 1641	2	0	0
Sum total	46	0	0

Given more to travelling soldiers in this year 1641 as appears by certificates	12	10	0
Paid to Thomas Ragland master of the hospital of East Harnham by order of court for two years as appears by acquittances	10	0	0
Paid more to Edward Ricketts by order of court and by the appointment of Mr Swanton 28th October 1648	6	13	4
The whole sum of disbursements	75	3	4
The whole sum of receipts	92	12	4
For there remains in this accountants hands	17	9	0

This account allowed this Sessions in open court and the £17 10s ordered to be paid on to Mr William Bennett now Treasurer for maimed soldiers and mariners for the south part of the county.

484. *Francis Rawlins.*
The court is informed by the inhabitants of Great Cheverell that Francis Rawlins of the same place husbandman is a married man and of an honest life and conversation and lives quietly and orderly amongst them and is owner of a cottage there for the succour of himself and his family and the inhabitants are suitors to the court on his behalf for an order of court for the continuance of the cottage for his habitation

and dwelling according to the statute in such case made and provided. It appeared to the court by certificate under the hands and seal of John Hobbes who is lord of the land whereon the cottage was erected and built that he has given his full licence and consent for the continuance of the cottage. Ordered that the cottage shall remain continue and be a cottage for habitation and dwelling for Rawlins and his wife without incurring the forfeitures mentioned in the statute.

General Sessions of the Peace held at Devizes 3 April 1649. William Stephens, Edward Tooker, George Ivy, Thomas Eyre, John Long, William Littleton, Nicholas Green, Edward Stokes, Francis Swanton.

(William Sadler sent his apologies 'for we have with us a troop of soldiers and those none of the civillest that I have seen which makes me unwilling to be from home at this instant.' A1/110/1649/E/103)

485. *For repairing the gaol.*
The common gaol of the county is fallen into great decay for want of reparations and is not of strength to keep such prisoners as are sent thither but very likely to fall down unless timely prevented by speedy repair whereof the Lord Chief Baron Wylde being informed thereof at the last Assizes appointed some of the Grand Jury with other persons of the county to take with them some skilful workmen and to view the decay thereof and estimate what money will repair the same and make a certificate thereof to the justices at the next Easter Sessions who having viewed the particular decays thereof and by advice with workmen estimating the repair of the gaol will amount unto one hundred and eighty three pounds ten shillings which must of necessity speedily be disbursed to prevent the falling thereof. The court taking into consideration and finding the gaol has been formerly maintained and repaired by allowance forth of the Exchequer to the Sheriffs of the county order that the Under Sheriff or gaoler of this county forthwith attend the members of Parliament who serve therein for the county who are desired to move the Committee of Revenue to give order for the speedy allowance of moneys for the repair of the gaol whereby the same may be made of sufficient strength for the keeping of such prisoners as shall be sent thither.

486. *Roger Harding to be settled at Bremhill.* (See also **556, 596, 627**)
It was formerly ordered by the court upon full hearing that Roger Harding should remove from Calne to Bremhill the place where he

last dwelt by his own confession. The court now again further orders that as well Harding as also his wife and children shall forthwith be all removed from Calne to Bremhill where they ought to remain and that the churchwardens and overseers of Bremhill permit and suffer them there to remain until there be good cause showed to the court to the contrary.

487. *Jane Cloude.*
It appears to the court by the petition of Joan Cloude of the parish of Bishops Cannings widow that she is so poor and impotent that she cannot help herself and that Mr Sergeant Nicholas and Mr Norden justices ordered and appointed her to have eight pence per week and her house rent paid by the overseers of the poor of Bishops Cannings. All which the court confirms.
    (If overseers refuse, to be bound over.)

488. *Inhabitants of Calne, Ramsbury, Warminster, Fisherton to have Calne money which is in Mr Bennett's hands.*
It appears to the court by the account of Mr Francis Bennett of such moneys as he received by order of the court of several constables for the arrears of Calne money taxed upon the county when the inhabitants of Calne were infected with the plague that besides the sums of money by him paid to several persons and places by orders of the court there remain in his hands due to the county the sum of fifteen pounds ten shillings and four pence. Ordered that Mr Bennett upon sight of this order shall pay out of the fifteen pounds ten shillings and four pence remaining in his hands to the churchwardens and overseers of the poor of Calne the sum of five pounds, of Ramsbury five pounds, of Warminster fifty shillings, of Fisherton Anger three pounds four pence residue of the sum of fifteen pounds ten shillings and four pence. All which sums of money are to be distributed by the several ministers churchwardens and overseers of the poor of the several parishes amongst the poor people of every the parishes respectively and the several churchwardens and overseers or the major part of them of every of the parishes are to give Mr Bennett acquittance for the sums of money which acquittance shall be sufficient discharge to Mr Bennett for the paying of the moneys.

489. *Devizes.*
Upon the humble petition of divers well affected of Devizes concerning the destructive inconveniences which attend the not giving of accounts by the constables and other officers with the borough of Devizes. The court recommends the content of the petition to the Mayor, Justices or

Chamberlains of the borough and desires them to call such constables and officers (as are meant in the petition) to pass their accounts before them and to do such therein on the behalf of the petitioners as shall be agreeable to law and justice.

490. *Margaret Weston.*
The court is informed by Margaret Weston of Coate in the parish of Bishop Cannings widow that Robert Trewman a poor old blind impotent man and his wife being relieved by the parish have dwelt in a house of hers by the space of thirteen years last past or thereabouts without paying rent for the same. And yet notwithstanding she has been constrained by the overseers of the poor to pay her full rate towards the relief of the poor. And whereas also Margaret at two several petty sessions complained to Mr Norden and Mr Yorke thereof and the justices did think fit and order that Margaret should deduct yearly out of her rates in lieu of rent for her house the sum of fifteen shillings and yet notwithstanding the overseers of the poor refuse to allow thereof but have procured a warrant to distrain Margaret for the same. Ordered that Margaret shall detain the moneys remaining in her hands for the rates of the poor until the next Sessions and in the mean time the overseers upon notice of this order are required to forbear to distrain her for the same. And at the next Sessions the overseers are to show good cause why the moneys should not be allowed to Margaret in lieu of her rent.

491. *Edward Godwin, John Hiscock.*
The court is informed by Edward Godwin and John Hiscock constables of the Liberty of Rowde showing that no court has been kept in Rowde these six years or upwards at which court the constables of the Liberty have been usually chosen. Ordered that Edward Kinge and John Axford of Rowde be elected and chosen constables of the Liberty in the place of Goddin and Hiscock and that Kinge and Axford shall within one week after receipt hereof repair to the next justice there to take their oaths for the due execution of their offices upon pain of ten pounds a piece.

492. *John Barkesdale, inhabitants of Seend.*
The court is informed by Jane Barkesdale of Seend widow that John Barkesdale husband to Jane (now deceased) was in his life time seised in fee simple of a messuage, fulling mill and lands thereunto belonging which were anciently proportionately rated at half yardlands since which time John about eight years since sold away half of the messuage and yet the parishioners of Seend rate Jane as when John her husband

had the whole messuage in his hands,   The court refers the whole examination of the business to Mr Long and Mr Green justices who are desired to make such order therein as shall be most agreeable to law and justice and to consider of the premisses before they allow the rates of the poor for that parish for the future.

493. *Mr Mitchell and Mr Earnlye.*
The court is informed by Mr Frederick Hyde of counsel with Mr John Mitchell of Calstone that the tenants of John Earnlye living in Calstone refuse to bear the office of tithingmanship within the tithing of Calstone pretending they of right ought to be exempted from that office by which means the whole burden of that service is borne by Mitchell and his tenants. Ordered that Karnlye and his tenants upon notice to them given of this order shall show good cause at the next Quarter Sessions why they should not in their turns undergo the office of tithingmanship as well as Mitchell and his tenants for the future.

494. *Anthony Whatly.* (See also **676**)
The court is informed by Mr Anthony Whatly of Semley husbandman that he has been in the service of the State for four years space and that he has been many times wounded and imprisoned in the service and since that time has rented a house in Semley and lived honestly and paid his rent truly but through the molestation of some of the parishioners was turned out of doors. Ordered that Whatly shall be suffered to have an habitation in Semley peaceably and that the parish of Semley shall keep him on work. And the lord of the manor of Semley is desired to grant his licence to Whatly for the erecting of a cottage in some convenient place for the habitation of Whatly and his wife and child which licence the court will afterwards confirm and that Whatly may in the mean time quietly be suffered to rent a house within the parish.
(Whatly said he would be happy to have a house in Semley or in Tisbury where his wife was born and had an interest in a poor cottage set up on the waste and burnt by the Cavaliers. A1/110/1649E/124)

495. *Portreeve, bailiff and other officers of Great Bedwyn.*
The court is informed by the portreeve, bailiff and other officers within the parish of Great Bedwyn they have been at great charge in carrying of felons to the gaol of Fisherton Anger and that divers of the inhabitants refuse the payment thereof unto them. Ordered that the portreeve, bailiffs and other officers shall forthwith meet together and make an indifferent and equal rate over the whole parish for the

raising thereof.
(If any refuse to pay, to be bound over.)

496. *Katherine Mans.* (See also **44**)
The court is informed by Katherine Mans of Oare within the parish of Wilcot widow that she has formerly maintained herself by her hard labour and industry and has been a woman of honest life and conversation but now through age and by reason of many infirmities she is unable to maintain herself and likely to perish except some charitable course be taken for her relief therein. The court refers the examination thereof to the next justice to Oare who is desired to call the overseers of the poor of that parish before them and cause them to pay to her the arrears due for her weekly relief for some weeks past and to allow her more than formerly she was allowed if they shall see cause to do the same.

497. *Richard Matthew.*
Upon reading the humble petition of Richard Matthew of Melksham who has a wife who is distracted and six small children who are in no way able to subsist without some weekly relief from the parish. The court desires Mr Long and Mr Green justices or one of them to call the overseers of Melksham before them and examine the truth of the petition and (if they shall see cause) they are desired to take course for the relief of Matthew his wife and children according to law.

498. *Ambrose Gay his petition.*
It appears to the court as well by the certificate under the hands of Colonel Thomas Hamond and Lieutenant Colonel Robbinson as by the petition of Ambrose Gay of Figheledean that Gay has served in the Parliament service as a soldier under the command of Thomas Lord Fairfax in which service he lost the use of his left leg at the leaguer [a military camp involved in a siege] before Faringdon whereby he is utterly disabled to get his maintenance. Ordered that Gay shall be allowed yearly the sum of four marks to be paid him quarterly by the Treasurer for the south.

499. *William Hobbes.*
The court has this present Sessions been fully satisfied that William Hobbes, Margaret his wife and their children are to be settled at Grittenham alias Grettlington [Brinkworth] and to be provided for by the churchwardens and overseers of the poor of that parish as inhabitants and poor of the parish. Ordered that the churchwardens and overseers of the poor of Grittenham shall forthwith upon sight of

this order admit and suffer Hobbes, his wife and children quietly to be and inhabit in their parish and to set them to work provide them an house and other relief according to their necessities so as they may not be vagrant or perish for want.

(If refuse, they, with others who disturb this settlement, to be bound over.)

500. *James Swayne his allowance £3 6s 8d.*
It appears to the court by letters and certificates under the hands of Colonel Edmund Ludlow, Mr William Eyre and Mr John Ash that James Swayne lately of London having served the Parliament in this county as a soldier and has received several wounds and maims in both of his arms. Ordered that the Treasurer for the north forthwith pay unto Swayne towards his relief the sum of five marks.

501. *Christopher Coles his pension.*
Christopher Coles an inhabitant in Chippenham tiler has served the State as a soldier in the Parliament service and is now maimed in the service and has lost the use of his right arm and thereby disabled to get his living as by view and certificate appears. Ordered the Treasurer for the north to pay Coles yearly the sum of six pounds thirteen shillings and four pence to be paid quarterly to begin from the present Sessions and to continue until the court shall otherwise order the same.

502. *William Pound.*
Upon reading the petition of William Pound of North Lydiard [Lydiard Millicent] a poor aged and impotent person and one that is in want. The court desires the two next justices to Lydiard Millicent to send for the overseers of Lydiard to take such course for the maintenance of Pound his wife and four children as to law and justice shall appertain.

503. *Inhabitants of Box, South Wraxall.*
The court is informed by the inhabitants of Box that John Woodman who lately lived at Atworth and Mary Longe widow who lately lived at South Wraxall are now come into the parish of Box without giving any security to the parish, Woodman having a wife and Mary Longe having a child which are likely to come upon the charge of the parish of Box. The court desires Mr Long and Mr Green justices to examine the truth thereof and make such order therein as shall be most agreeable to law and justice.

504. *Thomas Hort.*
The court is informed by Thomas Hort of Biddestone that there has

not been for a long time any court leet or lawday kept for the manor of Biddestone and Hort has served tithingman of the tithing of Biddestone by the space of one whole year by the order of this court. Now ordered that Charles Cottle of Biddestone shall be elected and chosen tithingman for the next year in the place of Hort. Further ordered that Cottle shall within one week after notice of this order repair to the next justice to take his oath for the due execution of his office.

(If he refuses, to be bound over.)

505. *Inter inhabitants of Charnhamstreet and Hungerford.* (Recites **480;** See also **521, 546**)
It now appears to the court that the inhabitants of Charnhamstreet had notice of the last order yet nevertheless have not appeared nor showed any cause to the court for the not contributing to the relief of the poor. Ordered that for the future the inhabitants of Charnhamstreet shall contribute proportionately towards the relief of the poor of Hungerford until the court shall alter the same upon good cause to be shown by the inhabitants of Charnhamstreet.

506. *Inter Sir John Backhouse and the inhabitants of Swallowfield* [Berkshire]. (Recites **464**)
It now appears to the court by the oath of Thomas Mudde that the inhabitants of Swallowfield had notice of this order and that he gave a copy thereof to Francis Deane one of the overseers of the poor of the parish of Swallowfield yet nevertheless the inhabitants nor any of them have appeared to show any cause to the contrary at this Sessions. Ordered that Sir John Backhouse for the future shall not be rated by the inhabitants of Swallowfield at more than two yardlands towards the rates and taxes for the relief of the poor of Swallowfield until the court shall otherwise alter the same upon the complaint of the inhabitants.

507. *Inhabitants of Wraxall and St Tweenes* [St Ouens)
There are differences concerning the rates for the poor of Wraxall and that it was questioned whether St Owens should pay to the poor of Wraxall as part of the parish of South Wraxall. Ordered (the same being a case decidable at common law) that the differences be referred to the examination of Mr Long, Mr Green and Mr Thomas Eyre or any two of them who are desired to call all parties interested in the premisses and to examine the same and to determine and settle the same according to justice and equity.

508. *Richard Smyth discharged of apprenticeship.*
The court is informed by Lucye Smyth that about five years since her

son Richard Smyth became bound as an apprentice to Thomas Longier a tailor then dwelling in Mere where the boy continued in service until Longier his master was arrested and carried to prison for debt which was about six months past where he has continued ever since having no wife nor place of habitation and is so poor that his thee children are kept by alms one of them by the parish and the other two by the charity of friends and her son forced to come to her for relief which she is not able to allow by reason of her poverty having nothing to maintain herself but the labour of her hands and prayed to court that her son may be discharged of his apprenticeship with his master and may be at liberty to serve any other man. Ordered that Smyth shall be discharged of his apprenticeship with Longier his master unless Longier upon notice to him given of this order shall show good cause to the contrary at the next Quarter Sessions.

509. At this present Sessions of the Peace are appointed and chosen to be Treasurers for the relief of maimed soldiers and mariners:
> For the north part: James Hulbert of Corsham gent.
> For the south part: Maurice Green of Shrewton gent.

Ordered the rates for the relief of maimed soldiers etc shall remain in every parish so that there may be levied and paid weekly upon every parish three pence and no more to commence and begin from the time of the present Sessions and shall be collected and paid yearly to the Treasurer.

510. And for the relief of prisoners of King's Bench and Marshalsea and of such hospitals and almshouses as are within the county are appointed and chosen to be Treasurers:
> For the north part: Robert Hawkins of Hardenhuish clothier
> For the south part: Henry Bigges of Woodford gent.

Ordered that the rates for the same relief shall be and continue as they were the last year viz so as for every parish throughout the county there may be levied and paid one penny weekly and not above, the several rates of every parish to be proportioned and set down as in the former order.

And the last Treasurers of both collections shall give up their accounts to the new elected Treasurer for the north before William Eyre, Charles Gore, George Ivy, William Littleton and Edward Stokes or any two of them. And for the south part before Edward Tooker, William Stephens, Richard Howe and Francis Swanton or any two of them.

511. *John Tarrant to continue tithingman.*
It appears to the court by an order made at Christmas 24 Charles that

John Duck of Wroughton was elected and chosen to be tithingman for the tithing in the place of John Tarrant and that Duck was bound over to this Sessions by Mr William Sadler justice for disobeying of the order. It further appears by Mr Frederick Hyde of counsel and by the oath of Leonard Morton that freeholders of Sir Thomas Wroughton's land ought not to serve as tithingmen for the tithing of Wroughton. Ordered that John Tarrant shall continue tithingman until he shall present some fitting man who ought by the custom there used to serve as tithingman for the tithing of Wroughton unless he show better cause to the court why the freeholders of Sir Thomas Wroughton's land should serve as tithingmen.

512. *Daniel Drake to be master of the house of correction at Fisherton.*
Ordered that Daniel Drake now keeper of the gaol of Fisherton Anger shall be master of the house of correction there and that he shall from time to time duly correct all such prisoners as shall be sent thither and set them to work and that Drake shall receive all such moneys as are to be collected and paid forth yearly of several hundreds for relief of the poor prisoners which now are in the gaol or shall be hereafter thither sent or committed and shall duly timely and honestly from time to time relieve the prisoners. And in consideration thereof Drake accepts the same and undertakes to relieve the prisoners accordingly and to give due account thereof to the court. Further ordered that Drake shall be bound in a bond of one hundred pounds to the Clerk of the Peace with two sufficient sureties as well for the due execution and discharge of his office of being master of the house of correction as for the answering redelivery and satisfaction as well of the county's stock committed to his charge as of all such goods and implements as are now remaining of the county's in the house of correction or which shall hereafter be delivered to his custody whereof he is to return in an inventory to the Clerk of the Peace and Drake is to continue master and receive the gaol money until the court shall alter the same.

General Sessions of the Peace held at Warminster 26 July 1649. William Hussey, Edward Tooker, John Long, William Littleton, Richard Grobham Howe, Nicholas Green, Walter South, George Ivy and Francis Swanton.

513. *John Mattershed.*
Complaint has been made by John Mattershed of Maiden Bradley, cook, that about three years since when the parish of Maiden Bradley was visited with the plague he delivered by the command of the officers

of the parish towards the relief of the infected of the parish in victuals to the value of five pounds four shillings and two pence as by his bills appear. Ordered that a rate be forthwith made upon the inhabitants of the parish by the churchwardens and overseers there and by them to be collected and paid unto Mattershed for his victual. Further ordered that Mr Edward Shoard and the constables of the parish shall forthwith pass their accounts before the two next justices of all such moneys as they have received from the county in the time of the visitation. And thereupon the parish shall be repaid the sum of five pounds four shillings and two pence which they shall pay to Mattershed.

514. *Anne Adlam.* (Recites **481**)
Upon full hearing of the matter in difference between the parties and what could be said or alleged on either side it appears to the court that John Hinton is of sufficient ability to relieve Anne his daughter and her children. Ordered that he shall relieve them accordingly and assesses Hinton at eighteen pence per week to be paid to Anne for the relief of her and her children from the day of the date of the order being the ninth day of January last past and to continue until the court shall see cause to alter the same. And if he shall make default of payment thereof then the court desires the two next justices to grant their warrants from time to time for the levying thereof and imprisoning the party according as the statute in that case made and provided requires.

515. *Nicholas Shoard, William Shoard in loco Christopher Hill and John Shoard.*
It appears to the court by an order made in Easter Sessions 24 Charles that Christopher Hill and John Shoard of Maiden Bradley were ordered to be constables of the Liberty of Maiden Bradley for this last year who have faithfully executed the office accordingly. And that Nicholas Shoard and William Shoard ought to be constables of the Liberty for the year following. Ordered that Nicholas Shoard and William Shoard shall be constables of the Liberty in the places of Christopher Hill and John Shoard and that they repair within one week next after notice of this order to the next justice there to take their oaths for the due execution of the office upon pain of ten pounds. Further ordered that Christopher Hill and John Shoard shall within one month now next ensuing account for all such moneys as they have been charged with during the time that they have executed the office of constableship for the Liberty.

516. *Inter inhabitants of Idmiston and Bretiza Miller.*
Upon full hearing of the matter in difference between the inhabitants of

Idmiston and Bretiza Miller grandmother to the children of Alexander Miller her son late deceased which children are upon the relief of the parish of Idmiston and it appears to the court that the mother of the children at the time of her death left in goods to the value of four pounds and that Bretiza is of ability to keep and relieve her grandchildren. Ordered that Bretiza shall take her grandchildren from the charge of the parish and shall keep and relieve them according to the law and that she shall have the remainder of the stock and goods now remaining in the overseers hands towards the keeping and relieving and breeding up of her grandchildren.

517. *Jeremy Ballard his pension.*
The court is informed by Jeremy Ballard as also by certificate under the hand of Colonel Thomas Eyre that he has served the State as a foot soldier under his command and has done very good service for the State and was maimed in that service by receiving a shot in his hand with a common bullet whereby he is disabled to relieve himself by his labour. Ordered the Treasurer for the north to pay unto Ballard the sum of four pounds per annum to be paid quarterly and to begin from this present Sessions and to continue until the court shall otherwise order the same.

518. *William Hellier in loco Robert Curtis.*
The court is informed by Robert Curtis of Kingston Deverill that he has served in the office of tithingman by the space of one whole year ending the five and twentieth of March last by reason no leet nor lawday have been kept there and according to the usual custom William Hillier ought to have served next in the office but refuses so to do. Ordered that Hellier shall within one week after notice to him given of this order repair to the next justice to take his oath for the due execution of his office.
(If he refuses, to be bound over.)

519. *Inhabitants of South Wraxall and inhabitants of Chalfield.*
It appears to the court by the petition of the inhabitants of South Wraxall that they are over burdened with poor people and are not able to bear the charge for their relief themselves without the help and assistance of some neighbouring parishes within the same hundred. Ordered that the parishes or tithings of Great Chalfield and Little Chalfield and Cottles shall by an equal rate to be made pay weekly the sum of twenty pence to the overseers of the poor of South Wraxall towards their relief from the date of this order until the court shall alter the same.
(Those who refuse to pay, to be bound over.)

520. *William Allworth to be tithingman of Westwood in loco Christopher Cromwell.*
The court is informed by the certificate under the hands of divers of the inhabitants of Westwood and Iford that Christopher Cromwell has served as tithingman by the space of one whole year and upwards and that William Allworth of the same place ought by the custom there used to serve ass tithingman for the year following. Ordered that Allworth shall be tithingman for the year following and that he shall forthwith upon sight hereof repair to the next justice to take his oath for the execution of his office upon pain of ten pounds.
(If he refuses, to be bound over.)

521. *Inter inhabitants of Charnhamstreet and Hungerford and the former orders void.* (Recites **505**; see also **480, 546**)
Now for the reasons shown to the court by Mr Hyde of counsel for the tithing of Charnhamstreet. Ordered that the inhabitants of the tithing of Charnhamstreet lying in Wiltshire shall not be enforced to contribute towards the relief of the poor of the parish of Hungerford in the county of Berkshire by any of the former orders and that the former orders therein made maybe null and vacated.

522. *Inter Mr Mitchell and Mr Earnley's tenants.* (See also **557**)
The court is informed by Mr Hyde of counsel with Mr John Mitchell of Calstone that the tenants of Mr John Earnley living in Calstone refuse to bear the office of tithingmanship within the tithing of Calstone pretending that they or right ought to be exempted from that office by which means the whole burden of that service is borne by Mr Mitchell and his tenants. Upon notice given to them of this order shall show good cause at the next Quarter Sessions why they should not in their turns undergo the office of tithingmanship as well as Mr Mitchell and his tenants fro the future.

523. *Inter freeholders and copyholders of Biddestone, Thomas Dart to be tithingman in loco Thomas Hort.* (See also **542**)
The court is informed by the freeholders inhabitants of the parish of Biddestone that there are differences between the freeholders and copyholders of the parish who should serve tithingman for the tithing. Ordered that the difference between them shall be heard the next Sessions by consent of both sides and that Thomas Dart of Biddestone shall serve in the office of tithingmanship in the place of Thomas Hort for the next year and Dart immediately upon sight of this order shall repair to the next justice there to take his oath for the execution of his office upon pain of ten pounds.

524. *Nicholas Spencer and inhabitants of Box.*
The court is informed by Nicholas Spencer of Box that he has disbursed
for the parish (in the time the parish was infected with the contagious
disease of the plague) the sum of forty six shillings which the parish
utterly refuses to make satisfaction. Ordered that the inhabitants of Box
shall make an equal and indifferent rate for the paying of Spencer the
sum of forty six shillings which he disbursed for the inhabitants of Box.
(If any refuse to pay, to be bound over.)

525. *Warrant against Lovell.*
It appears to the court by the information of Mr George Ivy justice that
William Lovell of Malmesbury has been three several times committed
for selling of ale and beer without licence. Ordered that forthwith
upon sight hereof you apprehend and take the body of Lovell and him
safely convey to the house of correction at Devizes there to remain
until he shall be released from thence by order of the council.
(To the High Sheriff of the county, constables of hundreds and
to all other officers whom these may concern.)

526. *Inter John Brimesdon, Christopher Batt and the inhabitants of East
Grafton.*
John Brimesdon and Christopher Batt of East Grafton have been
distrained for not repairing a bridge called Heath Bridge by virtue of
a warrant issuing forth of the court of Sessions and have laid out in
discharging the presentment the sum of nineteen shillings and four
pence besides their expenses. Ordered that there shall be an equal
and an indifferent rate made on the whole inhabitants of Grafton for
the collecting thereof and paying Brimesdon and Batt the said sum.
(If any refuse to pay, to be bound over.)

527. *John Wanlye to be tithingman of Bradley in loco Andrew Bayly.*
The court is informed by Andrew Bayly of Maiden Bradley that he has
served tithingman within the Liberty about two years and a quarter and
that there is no court kept there for the swearing of another tithingman
by reason the manor of Maiden Bradley is in sequestration and that
John Wanlye of Maiden Bradley ought of right and course to serve as
tithingman. Ordered Wanlye shall forthwith upon sight hereof repair
to the next justice there to take his oath for the due execution of the
office upon pain of ten pounds if he make default.

528. *Agnes Younge her pension.*
The court is informed by Agnes Younge of Westbury widow that about
five years since Roger Younge her late husband was a soldier in the

garrison of Woodhouse [Horningsham] under the command of Major Henry Wansey and upon resigning the garrison Sir Francis Dodington hanged her husband with 13 other soldiers of the garrison by reason whereof Agnes and five single children are like to perish for want of relief and prayed the assistance of the court redress therein according to an ordinance of Parliament in that behalf made. The court thinks fit to allow her towards her relief and maintenance the sum of four pounds per annum to be paid her quarterly and to commence at this Sessions. The court orders and appoints the Treasurer for the south to pay her the sum accordingly until the court shall see cause to alter this order.

(In her petition Agnes Young adds in brackets after Sir Francis Doddington, 'that bloody tyrant'. A1/110/1649T /166 See also **622** and **713**)

529. *Arrears of maimed soldiers and mariners.* (See also **562**)
The court is informed that since the year of our Lord God 1642 there are many Treasurers for the collection of maimed soldiers, etc behind in giving up their several accounts. And whereas great complaint has likewise been made by the Treasurers and other that there is much money of the several collections behind and unpaid from most of the parishes in the county in default of the constables of hundreds and the churchwardens and petty constables of the several parishes and that divers orders have been made by the court for the collecting and bringing in of the arrears and for binding on such constables churchwardens and petty constables as have been faulty and negligent therein and that there is but little fruit gained thereby for want of due prosecution of the orders by reason whereof the maimed soldiers and pensioners within the county are in great want. The court desires Mr George Ivy for the north part of the county and Mr Francis Swanton for the south part make forth their warrants as well to the constables of hundreds as to the churchwardens and petty constables for collecting and bringing in to them all the arrears of the several collections due for the time aforesaid who are likewise desired to bind over to the next Quarter Sessions as well all such Treasurers who shall neglect or refuse to account as the constables of hundreds churchwardens and petty constables of any parish which shall refuse or neglect to collect or pay in all such arrears due for the time aforesaid whereby the moneys so in arrear may be paid into the court to be disposed of as the court shall order. And the court also orders that William Croome formerly deputy Treasurer for the south attends Mr Ivy and Mr Swanton for the better collecting and bringing in of the arrears and dispensing their warrants for which he shall have such allowance as the court shall think fit.

530. *Inter John Hurd and Mr Quinton.* (Recites **390** and **478**)
It now appears to the court that Hurd had no notice of the order. Ordered that the witnesses and proofs on both sides shall be heard at next Christmas Sessions and that Quinton give Hurd notice thereof at his house in Wilsford by leaving a copy of this order that he may provide his witnesses accordingly that there may be a final order made therein and till then the rates to continue as they were ordered by the first order of Easter Sessions.

531. *Thomas Harris, William Coles and inhabitants of Orcheston St George.*
It appears to the court by the petition of Thomas Harris and William Coles that for want of a pair of stocks within the tithing of Orcheston St George the inhabitants were amerced at two several lawdays held at Heytesbury the sum of ten pounds and that a distress was taken upon the cattle of divers of the inhabitants of the tithing for the amercement. And Harris and Coles were enforced for redeeming of the cattle to disburse the sum of ten pounds and also twenty shillings for charges. Ordered an equal rate to be made amongst the inhabitants throughout the whole tithing of Orcheston St. George both for raising the amercement of ten pounds as also for the expense and charges disbursed by Harris and Coles.
    (If any refuse to pay, to be bound over.)

532. *Robert Holloway.*
Robert Holloway was bound over to this Quarter Sessions being supposed to be the reputed father of a bastard child begotten on the body of Margery Phipp and forasmuch as it appears to the court that the child is born and no order made therein. Ordered that Holloway shall be bound over to the next Quarter Sessions and in the mean time he is to attend two justices who are desired to examine the matter whether he be the reputed father or not and if they shall be satisfied that he is the reputed father then they are desired to make an order therein as well for the security of the parish where the bastard child was born as for the punishment of the parties according to the statute in such case made and provided requires but if the justices upon examination of the matter shall conceive him not to be the reputed father then they are desired to make their order of acquittal and Robert is to attend at the next Quarter Sessions with such order as the justices shall make therein.

533. *Thomas Potticary, Thomas Butcher overseers of Warminster.* (See also **682**)
The court is informed by Mr Thomas Potticary and Thomas Butcher two of the overseers of the poor of the parish of Warminster that Simon

Elye an inhabitant of the same place ran away from thence and left behind him four little children who have been upon the charge of the parish for a long time. And Potticary and Butcher understanding the Elye had left behind him some of his goods they seized upon the goods and have detained them for the use of the children and prayed the directions of the court what should be done with the goods. Ordered Potticary and Butcher with the now churchwardens and overseers shall cause the goods to be inventoried and appraised by some honest and indifferent man of Warminster and the goods shall be sold for satisfying of such moneys as the parish have already been at or shall hereafter lay out for the keeping relieving and breeding up of the children.

534. *Alice Jones.*
The court is informed by the overseers of the poor of Warminster that Alice Jones wife of Thomas Jones being servant to Sir James Thynne possessed herself of a cottage in the parish of Warminster where she has been delivered of a child and to prevent charges to the parish the overseers procured a warrant from Mr Nicholas Green to remove Alice forth of the parish but she shut her doors against the officers and her husband came to the house armed with a great long staff so that the warrants could not be executed. The overseers prayed the order of the court concerning the matter. Ordered the overseers of Warminster to carry Alice unto her husband unto Longleat which is within the parish of Longbridge Deverill as was affirmed there to be provided as the law requires.

General Sessions of the Peace held at Marlborough Tuesday after Michaelmas 2 October 1649. George Ivy, William Littleton, William Sadler, Robert Hippisley, Thomas Eyre, Francis Swanton, Henry Martin, John Read, William Shute.

535. *Inter Mr Langton , inhabitants of Highworth.*
Mr Langton late vicar of Highworth has made complaint to the court that divers of the inhabitants of Highworth are behind with him in payment of their tithes. The court desires that Mr Martin, Mr Hippisley and Mr Sadler or any two of them justices to call the parties before them to hear and examine the differences and do therein according to law and justice.

536. *Inhabitants of the eastern part of the hundred of Amesbury.* (See also **709**, **729**, **788**)
The court is informed on behalf of the inhabitants of the eastern

part of the hundred of Amesbury that they are overrated in taxes and
payments against the inhabitants of the western part of the hundred in
regard they are now rated at the eighth part of the hundred whereas
they were anciently rated at the fourteenth part. And whereas there
was none of the inhabitants of the western part of the hundred present
that could answer the complaint. Ordered that the rates shall stand as
they now are till the next Sessions and then both parties are to attend
that they may be heard and the inhabitants of the western part are to
have a copy of this order left with them in some convenient time after
this Sessions that they may come provided to the next Quarter Sessions
where the court will hear the matter and make such order therein
as shall be agreeable to law and justice. But if the western part shall
fail in their attendance at the next Quarter Sessions concerning that
matter the court thinks fit that after that Sessions they of the eastern
part shall pay after the fourteenth part against them to all rates and
payments within the jurisdiction of the court.

537. *Richard Rickards.* (Recites **424**. See also **576, 703**)
It now appears to the court that the tithing of Ridge [Chilmark] are
much in arrear for want of payment of the eighteen pence per week.
Ordered that the inhabitants of the tithing of Ridge shall pay all the
arrears of the eighteen pence per week from the date of the order of
Trinity 24 Charles until the present Sessions. Further ordered that the
overseers of the poor of the parish of Chilmark shall from the day of
this present Sessions pay weekly the sum of eighteen pence.
   (If overseers refuse, to be bound over.)

538. *Inter inhabitants of Milton and Nicholas Holdwith.* (See also **331**)
The inhabitants of Milton [Lilbourne] have made complaint that
Nicholas Holdwith gent is removed from Milton to Rowden in the
parish of Haldwell (Halwell) near Totnes in the county of Devon
and left a young child on the charge of the parish. Ordered that the
inhabitants of Milton shall forthwith convey the child to Rowden to
the father there to be and relieved as by law is required.

539. *Gifford Hayward pension.*
The court is informed by Gifford Hayward of Melksham that for three
years space he has been in service for the state wherein he has received
two dangerous wounds by reason whereof he is utterly disabled to
use any way for his subsistence all which was affirmed to be true by
Captain Thomas Goore in whose troop he served. The court allows
Hayward for his relief and maintenance a pension of three pounds six
shillings and eight pence per annum and orders the Treasurer for the

north to pay the pension unto Hayward quarterly the first payment to begin at St. Thomas day next and to continue till further order.

540.   *Thomas Eyres, John Clifford, Thomas Miller fined £10 a piece.*
Thomas Eyres, John Clifford and Thomas Miller were committed at this Quarter Sessions upon the indictment for trespassing in the close of James Dewart esq called the Forest of Bradon and cutting and carrying away of a thousand loads of oak to the value of three hundred pounds of the goods of James Dewart as by the record appears. It is therefore adjudged by the court that Eyres, Clifford and Miller shall pay ten pounds a piece fine and be committed to the gaol where they shall be imprisoned by the space of two months unless they pay their fines sooner and for default of payment to remain afterwards until they pay their several fines.

541.   *Inter Thomas Buckland inhabitants of Brinkworth.*
It appears to the court that Edward Brunsedon the bailiff has levied upon Thomas Buckland of Brinkworth the sum of twenty shillings as issues estreated against the whole inhabitants and has also paid thirty five shillings for the meat of the said distress besides other charges and expenses which he has been put unto by reason thereof which issues ought to have been paid by all the inhabitants of Brinkworth. Ordered that an equal rate be made forthwith upon all the inhabitants of Brinkworth for the repayment of the sum of three pounds five shillings together with his charges of expenses.
     (If any refuse to pay, to be bound over.)

542.   *Inter the freeholders and copyholders of Biddestone concerning the office of tithingman.* (See **523**)
Upon hearing of the matter in difference between the freeholders and copyholders of Biddestone concerning the office of tithingman in that place it appears unto the court that the lord of the leet has kept no court there a long time whereby the tithingman kept in the office longer than of right he ought to be. And whereas there has been several orders now read in court concerning these differences and the court being informed that there will be a lawday kept there within a month after Michaelmas next. The court therefore thinks fit to nominate and appoint Isaac Hill to be tithingman in the place of Thomas Hort in case there shall be no lawday kept there within the time aforesaid and if he is not able to serve in the office himself then he is to find a sufficient deputy to serve for him in that office and orders and appoints Isaac Hill that he or his deputy shall repair to the next justice within one month after receipt hereof to take his

oath for the due execution of the office and in failure thereof Hill is
to forfeit ten pounds. But if the lord of the leet shall keep a lawday
there within the time aforesaid then the tithingman is to be elected
according to the ancient custom there used.

543. *Inter inhabitants of Atworth, inhabitants of Great Chalfield, Little
Chalfield and Cottles.*
It appears to the court by the petition of the inhabitants of Atworth
that they are over burdened with poor people and are not able to bear
the charge for their relief themselves without the help and assistance
of some neighbouring parishes within the same hundred. Ordered
that the parishes or tithings of Great Chalfield, Little Chalfield and
Cottles shall by an equal rate to be made pay weekly the sum of twenty
pence to the overseers of the poor of Atworth towards the relief from
the day of the date of this order until the court shall alter the same.
(If any refuse to pay, to be bound over.)

544. *Margery Robbinson.*
The court is informed by Margery Robbinson that she has lived at
Wootton Rivers about five years and that she is now come into such
poverty by reason of her age that she is not able to provide for her a
house to inhabit or dwell in and desires some relief from the court.
The court desires the next justice to send for the churchwardens and
overseers of the poor of Wootton Rivers and take such order for her
relief as shall be agreeable to law and justice.

545. *Edward Bull is to apprehend all suspicious persons in the county.*
The court taking into consideration the daily robberies, felonies,
burglaries and other misdemeanours committed and done in many
places of this county by robbers and idle lewd and wandering persons.
And that for want of putting the law in execution by officers and by
means of their negligence the said persons continue in their lewd and
wicked courses and are not apprehended to answer the law and honest
men are deterred from their lawful occasions. Ordered Edward Bull
of Westbury to apprehend in any place within the county all thieves,
robbers wandering lewd idle and suspected persons. And as often as
Bull apprehends or takes any such persons to convey or cause them
to be conveyed and brought before some justice and near unto the
place where they shall be apprehended to be examines concerning the
premisses and to be dealt withal according to law. The court further
hereby requires all constables tithingmen bailiffs and other officers to
be aiding and assisting Bull in performance thereof as they will answer
the contrary.

546. *Inter inhabitants of Hungerford and inhabitants of Charnhamstreet.*
(Recites **521**; see also **480, 505**)
Ordered that the inhabitants of the parish of Hungerford or some of them and the inhabitants of the tithing of Charnhamstreet or some of them shall attend at the next Quarter Sessions with their counsel and witnesses that the differences concerning that matter may be fully heard and determined. Further ordered that the inhabitants of that tithing shall have a copy of this order timely left with them that they may come provided to that Sessions that the differences may be fully heard and determined and in the mean time all things to stay as it now does.

547. *Richard Yerrington in loco Edward Harrold.*
The court is informed by Edward Harrold tithingman of Cloatley [Hankerton] that he has served in that office by the space of two years last past and that he is like to continue a long time in that office in regard the lord of the leet is dead by reason whereof no court leet will be kept there and prayed the assistance of the court that he may be discharged of that office and that Richard Yerrington may be tithingman in his place he being the next man to serve in that office by the custom there used. Ordered that Richard Yerrington to go before the next justice to take his oath for the due execution of the office within one week after receipt of this order.
    (If he refuses, to be bound over.)

548. *Alice Browne.*
It appears to the court by the petition of Alice Browne of Easterton that about five years since she had a bastard child begotten by a soldier in the late troubles and that she has inhabited and dwelt in Easterton in a house with Thomas Browne and forasmuch as the court is informed that the inhabitants endeavour to put Alice out of their parish. The court taking into account the poverty of Browne orders that she shall continue at Easterton without any disturbance until they shall show good cause to the court to the contrary.

549. *Elizabeth Laggatt to be sent to Inglesham.*
Upon hearing the matter concerning Elizabeth Laggatt widow it appears to the court that she lived at Latton and after married her husband at Inglesham where she lived with him till his death and after her husbands death the inhabitants of Inglesham sent her to Latton again where she is now remaining to her great prejudice. And the inhabitants of Latton prayed the assistance of the court for their relief therein. Ordered that Elizabeth shall be sent back to Inglesham in regard it appears to the court that she has had no quiet settlement at

Latton since her coming thither. Further ordered that she shall remain at Inglesham until they shall see good cause to alter this order.

550. *James Hughes, John Scott and William Bayly to account before Mr Eyre.* (Recites **460**)
It now appears to the court that James Hughes, John Scott and William Bayly have not yet accounted whereby the order is become fruitless. Now ordered that the parties shall yield up their accounts before Mr Thomas Eyre justice within one month after notice of this order and Mr Eyre is desired to take the account and if it shall appear upon the account that the parishioners are indebted to the accountants then he is desired to take course that they may be satisfied the same.
(If they refuse to present their accounts, to be bound over.)

551. *Inter overseers of Ogbourne St Andrew, Sir John Glanville.*
It appears to the court that John Bullock son of Alexander Bullock of Ogbourne St Andrew was bound apprentice by the churchwardens and overseers of the same parish unto Sir John Glanville knight for his means in Ogbourne with the allowance of George Ivy and William Littleton justices and that Glanville refuses to take the said apprentice. Ordered that the overseers of Ogbourne provide for the apprentice till the next Assizes and then the opinion of the Judges of Assize is to be desired herein and all parties interested herein then also to attend.

552. *Inter inhabitants of Pewsey and John Winter.*
Forasmuch as the inhabitants of the tithing of Down Pewsey were indicted for not scouring a water course within the tithing and whereas John Winter one of the inhabitants of the tithing appeared to the indictment and traversed the same and that upon trial the jury found against the tithing whereby the tithing was fined at twenty shillings and pained to amend the water course by All Hallowstide [1 November] next on pain of ten pounds for which trial suit and other expenses Winter has disbursed the sum of four pounds and two shillings. For the reimbursing whereof, ordered an equal rate to be made over the whole tithing.
(If any refuse to pay, to be bound over.)

553. *William Hathaway to be tithingman of Stanton in loco Benjamin Power.*
Forasmuch as it appears to the court that Benjamin Power has served tithingman for the parish of Stanton St Quintin by the space of a year and half and cannot get forth by reason the keeping of the leet is neglected and that William Hathaway of Stanton ought to serve next

in the office. Ordered that in default of keeping the leet between this and All Hallows next, Hathaway shall within one week after All Hallows repair to the next justice to take his oath for the execution of the office or else to be bound over to the next Sessions.

554. *Inter Ralph Smyth and inhabitants of Pewsey.*
Upon hearing the matter against Ralph Smyth for refusing to take an apprentice formerly placed with him by the justices for a roofless tenement in Pewsey which he rented of Mr John Woodland deceased and whereas it appeared to the court that Smyth's term in the tenement was expired at Michaelmas last past and that as yet he has not taken a further estate therein. Ordered that Smyth shall be discharged for the present and that if he shall take a further estate in the tenement then he shall take the apprentice and in refusing thereof the next justice is desired to send him to the gaol of the county there to remain until he shall do the same but if Smyth shall not take the tenement for longer term then he is to pay the parish their charges they have been at concerning the same matter.

555. *Henry Crumpe.*
Whereas Henry Crumpe was sent to the gaol of Fisherton Anger for want of sureties to answer the peace to Richard Lawence at this Sessions he being now discharged informs the court that he has a brown gelding with four white feet a white patch in the neck, three pounds ten shillings in money and other things taken from him at the time he was sent to the gaol by Mr Thomas Powlton. Ordered that Mr Powlton or any other who have any of the goods shall deliver the gelding, money and all other things whatsoever which Mr Powlton took from him when he was sent to the gaol.

556. *Roger Harding be removed from Calne to Bremhill.* (Recites **486**; see also **596, 627**)
It further appears to the court by the oath of John Newman that he tendered the wife and children of Harding with a copy of the order to Robert Kinge one of the overseers of Bremhill and that he refused to receive them. Now again ordered that the churchwardens and overseers of Bremhill should receive Harding his wife and children or any o them so tendered and provide for them as poor of that parish.
(If they refuse, to be bound over.)

557. *Inter Mr Earnly's tenants and Mr Mitchell's.* (Recites **522**)
Ordered and desired that the steward and jury of the leet whereunto the tithing belongs do at the next lawday equally hear and examine

the proofs on either side and certify the truth thereof at Easter Sessions next that the court may make some settlement therein.

558. *Inter inhabitants of Calne and Mr Lowe.*
Whereas there are some differences within the parish of Calne about the rates of the poor there betwixt the parishioners and Mr Lowe about rating the late King's park now in possession of the State to the poor.   Ordered Mr Lowe's rate for the parsonage shall continue at thirty five shillings per month for the poor as anciently he has paid and that touching the rate of the park the parish shall forbear to rate the same until after the next Assizes that the opinion of the judges might be had therein.

559. *John Aylesopp allowed £5 for present relief.* (See also **584**)
It appears to the court as well by the petition of John Aylesopp as by the certificate of Colonel Edmund Ludlow that Aylesopp has served as a trooper in his regiment and in the said service at Salisbury received a dangerous wound in his face by reason whereof he has lost his eyesight and thereby utterly disabled to get his livelihood.   Ordered that the Treasurer for the south forthwith upon sight of this order pay unto Aylesopp for his present relief the sum of five pounds.

560. *Thomas Champion his pension.*
The court is informed by the petition of Thomas Champion of Downton that he has served in the Parliament service by the space of five years and in the same service against Maidstone in Kent was shot and maimed in both his legs as by the certificate under the hand of Lt Col Axtell appears whereby he is disabled to get his maintenance he being a poor man and having a wife and three children and nothing to maintain them.   The court allows Champion a pension of four pounds per annum to be paid him quarterly by the Treasurer for the south the first payment to begin and commence from this present Sessions and to continue till the court shall alter the same

561. *John Simkins allowed £5.*
The court is informed by the petition of John Simkins of Warminster that he is utterly disabled in body and ruined in goods through imprisonment beating and plundering for acting for the good of the State's soldiers in the time of the late war by reason whereof he and his family (being in distress and for the reasons aforesaid is not able to get his own living much less unable to again maintenance for his household) are like to perish through want and prayed the assistance of the court for his relief herein.   And whereas the justices at this

Quarter Sessions are certified under the hand of Col Ludlow of the sad condition of Simkins occasioned by his imprisonment for his activity in the service of the public and his willingness to relieve those who were engaged for the Parliament. It is therefore thought fit and the court orders Simkins shall be allowed five pounds towards his relief and maintenance in regard of his sufferings. And that Maurice Green now Treasurer for the south shall upon sight of this order pay Simkins five pounds out of the moneys collected and paid for the said relief in regard of his great want and necessity.

562. *For gathering and collecting the arrears of maimed soldiers and mariners.* (Recites **529**)
Which said orders have not produced so good effect as was expected by reason that some justices thought themselves not so fully interested by this order in binding over such persons as were brought before them for the neglecting the performance of the same order because they were not particularly named therein wherefore the court the court hereby confirms the former order. And now again orders that the same continue in force from time to time until all the arrears of the several collections be duly and fully paid into the court whereby the maimed soldiers may be relieved according to the ordinances of Parliament without burdening the county in doubling the rates. And the court again desires that all and every justice will be aiding and assisting in the due execution of this order and in binding over to the Sessions such persons as shall be any way remiss and negligent in the due performance thereof.

1650

General Sessions of the Peace held at Salisbury 15 January 1650. William Hussey, Anthony Ashley Cooper, Edward Tooker, William Eyre, Richard Grobham Howe, William Littleton, Thomas Eyre, Richard Green, Barnaby Coles, Walter South, Giles Eyre, Francis Swanton, Gabriel Martin, William Shute, John Read.

563. *Inter John Rugge and inhabitants of West Knoyle.*
It appears to the court that John Rugge clerk has continued and inhabited in the parish of West Knoyle by the space of eleven years and upwards and has served as a curate there and is of late put forth from serving the cure there being grown impotent by reason of age and sickness and having no means or other maintenance whereby to relieve

himself is likely to perish for want. Ordered that the churchwardens and overseers of the poor of West Knoyle do forthwith pay weekly unto Rugge from the date of this order the sum of two shillings and six pence to relieve him he being an impotent person of the same parish. (If they refuse, to be bound over.)

564. *Inter Henry Jones and Henry Sheappard.*
Upon reading of the petition of Henry Jones of Keevil against Henry Sheappard of the same place, the court refers the examination of the truth of the petition to William Eyre and Nicholas Green justices or to either of them who are desired to send for the witnesses at the prosecution of Jones and to examine the contents of the petition and if Jones proves not the petition to be true then the justices are desired to bind over Jones to appear at the next Quarter Sessions and in the mean time to be of the good behaviour. But if Jones shall prove the petition to be true then the justices are desired to bind Sheappard to appear at the next Quarter Sessions and in the mean time to be of the good behaviour.

565. *Thomas Field.*
The court is informed by Thomas Field of Amesbury a very aged man and having a wife and that about half a year since he had his house burned to the ground and all his goods spoiled whereby Field is fallen into great want and poverty. The court refers the whole examination of the premisses to Mr Littleton justice who is desired to do therein according to law and justice.

566. *Inter Richard Reynolds and Richard Reynolds junior.*
Richard Reynolds the younger was bound over to this Quarter Sessions for refusing to relieve Richard Reynolds his father an aged and impotent person he being of ability to do the same. Now upon full hearing of the matter in open court the justices assembled at this Sessions do conceive Richard Reynolds to be of ability to relieve his father. Ordered with the consent of Richard Reynolds that he shall pay unto his father for his relief and maintenance the sum of four marks per annum during the life time of his father and if Richard Reynolds shall so long live to be paid to his father quarterly the first quarter's pay to be made at this Quarter Sessions and afterwards every quarter's pay to be paid to his father at the beginning of every succeeding quarter.

567. *Roger Foord allocated £5.*
He court is informed by Roger Foord of South Wraxall that he has served as a soldier in the Parliament service in Ireland under the

command of the Lord Killomegee [?Kilmeage] in which service he has undergone many hardships by reason whereof he has lost the use of his limbs as by the certificate of Mr John Ash more at large appears. Ordered that the Treasurer for the north shall forthwith pay unto Foord the sum of five pounds in regard of his poverty and present necessity.

568.   *The inhabitants of Hungerford and inhabitants of Charnhamstreet.* (Refers to **546**)
Upon hearing of the matter in difference between the inhabitants of Hungerford in the county of Berkshire and the inhabitants of Charnhamstreet. Ordered that the counsel on both sides shall draw up the case and agree thereupon and set their hands and seals thereunto and that the solicitors on both sides shall attend the honourable Judges of this Circuit with the same at the next Assizes with their counsel that their Lordships may give their resolutions therein.

569.   *Inter Mr Marvyn and inhabitants of Chicklade.*
The court is informed by Mr Marvyn one of the churchwardens of the parish of Chicklade that he has disbursed for the parish in building and repairing their parish church since the year 1640 the sum of seventeen pounds one shilling and eleven pence. And that he with other of the parishioners have made a rate for the reimbursing thereof and that there are some of the parishioners who refuse to pay their moneys according to the rate. Ordered and desired the two next justices to call the parties so refusing before them and to examine the accounts and determine the same according to justice and equity and according to the ordinance of Parliament in that case made.
(If any refuse to pay, to be bound over.)

570.   *Walter Beade his pension of five marks per annum.*
The court is informed by Walter Beade of Devizes that he has served the Parliament in the late wars as a gunner under the command of Sir Edward Hungerford and Col Fynes in which service against Wardour Castle in this county was shot with a common bullet and was much plundered as by the letter of Col Edmond Ludlow and certificate of the Mayor and divers others of the chief inhabitants of the borough of Devizes appears. Allowed Beade a pension of five marks per annum to be paid him quarterly from this Sessions by the Treasurer for the north and to continue till the court shall alter the same.

571.   *Solomon Hillman his pension of 4 marks per annum.* (See also **935**, **958**)
The court is informed by Solomon Hillman of Warminster that he

has served the Parliament in actual service under the command of Col
Ludlow where he received many grievous wounds as by a certificate
under the hand of Col Ludlow more at large appears. Ordered that the
Treasurer for the south pay Hillman the sum of four marks per annum
the same to be paid him quarterly towards his relief and maintenance
in regard of his great necessity and the many wounds he has received
in the service the first payment thereof to begin at Lady day next and
to continue till the court shall otherwise order the same.

572. *John Scutt his pension of 40s per annum.*
The court is informed by John Scutt of Warminster as also by the
certificate under the hand of John Warren major of the City Regiment
of dragoons for the relief of Taunton as also the hand of George Dunne
surgeon to the same regiment that he has served the State and was
maimed in that service by receiving a wound in his left arm whereby he
is disabled to relieve himself by his labour. Ordered that the Treasurer
for the south pay Scutt the sum of forty shillings per annum to be
paid him quarterly the first payment to begin at Lady day next and to
continue until the court shall otherwise order the same.

573. *Colonel Chester.*
The court is informed by Colonel Henry Chester a prisoner now
remaining in the gaol of Fisherton Anger that the constables of
Chippenham took from the said Colonel at the time of his apprehension
at that place two fine holland shirts, eight new holland bands and cuffs,
one pair of new worsted stockings, one pair of riding stockings, six
handkerchiefs, one sword and one belt and forty shillings in money,
one shirt, two bands and cuffs of his boys and that he now wants them
for his necessary subsistence in the prison and prayed the court for
some relief therein. Ordered that the sword shall be forthwith sold
to the best value and the rest of the goods shall be sent and delivered
to Chester or his assigns for his necessary relief and accommodation
in prison, the Colonel paying all such moneys as the constables have
been at in carrying him to the gaol and the next justice is desired to
consider what the constable is fit to have for carrying of him to prison.

574. *Inter Anne Hutchins and her husband.*
The court is informed by Anne Hutchins of Laverstock that John
Barnes of Laverstock husbandman has persuaded her husband to depart
from her and to live with Barnes and to allow her but ten pounds per
annum towards the relief and maintenance of herself and two children
her husband having forty pounds per annum. The court desires Mr
Swanton and Mr Tooker justices or either of them to call the parties

before them and examine the truth of the matter complained of and end the difference between them and what order or award the justices shall make therein the court confirms the same.

575. *Edward Ricketts allocated 40s.* (See also **446**)
The court is informed by Edward Ricketts a maimed soldier in the Parliament service in which service he lost the use of his arms under the command of Captain Croome as by his certificate more at large appears. Ordered the Treasurer for the south to pay unto Ricketts the sum of forty shillings in regard of his present necessity.

576. *Richard Rickards.* (See also **424, 537, 703**)
Whereas there have been several orders made in the court against the parish and tithing of Chilmark and Ridge for the allowance of some relief unto Richard Rickards a poor maimed man. And whereas it now appears that Rickards is a very poor man and quite out of clothes and lives within the parish of East Knoyle and being maimed and grown impotent. Ordered that all former orders made heretofore against Chilmark and Ridge concerning the premises be vacated and made void. Further ordered that the churchwardens and overseers of the poor of East Knoyle shall forthwith upon sight of this order provide for Rickards as a poor and impotent person of that parish and provide him clothes whereof he is now wholly destitute and give him a weekly allowance of eighteen pence per week.
    (If they refuse, to be bound over.)

577. *Inter inhabitants of Wishford and inhabitants of St Giles* [Dorset].
Upon reading of an order of Assizes held at Salisbury the ninth day of July last and likewise upon reading the Judges of Assizes opinion concerning the settlement of Thomas Combes and his wife. Ordered that the overseers of the poor of Wishford shall forthwith send and convey Combes and his wife to St Giles in the county of Dorset and deliver them to the churchwardens and overseers of the poor there together with this order and the copy of the Judges opinion hereunto annexed where Combes and his wife are to remain and to be provided for according to law.

578. *William Cantloe suppressed from selling ale.* (See also **607**)
The court is informed by the inhabitants of Tisbury that whereas William Cantloe and William Skevington of Tisbury being licensed for selling ale and beer in their houses for ease and refreshing of many travelling people which shall pass that way and by means thereof have and do suffer very much disordered courses to be used in their houses

by excessive drunkenness and in suffering divers poor men of that parish to continue drinking contrary to the law to the utter undoing of many of them their wives and children the same being done not only on the week days but also upon the Sabbath days in the sermon time and that the same is no roadway many travellers do not pass by to lodge there. All which was proved to be true upon the oath of Humfry Card of the same parish sworn in open court. Ordered that Cantloe his alehouse shall be suppressed and if he shall hereafter sell ale without licence he is to be proceeded against according to the statute in such case made and provided.

579. *Robert Lawes allocated £10.*
Robert Lawes of Chillington [Chilhampton, South Newton] yeoman has taken great pains and travail for the discovering and apprehending of John Knight a robber upon the highway causing him to be apprehended and committed to prison for which robbery Knight was this Quarter Sessions convicted as has judgment of death accordingly. And now he humbly desires the benefit of the orders of Parliament of the eighth of November last for his reward of ten pounds according to the same orders together with a certificate thereof under our hands to the Sheriff of the county which we do hereby certify accordingly. And do desire the Committee of Revenues to give allowance to the Sheriff of the ten pounds according to the same orders.

580. *Walter Keynton allocated £4.*
Whereas Walter Keynton of Corsham husbandman has taken great pains and travail for the discovering and apprehending of John Brickett, John Falkner, Thomas Keynes and William Keynes robbers on the highways and causing them to be indicted at this Quarter Sessions where they have been tried for the same. And Keynton humbly desires the benefit of the orders of Parliament of the eighth of November for his reward and our certificate under our hands to the Sheriff of the county for the certifying of the same which we hereby do certify accordingly. And desire the Committee of Revenues to give allowance to the Sheriff the sum of four pounds in regard of his pain and care therein.

581. *Inter inhabitants of Knoyle and inhabitants of Chilmark.* (See also **612, 633**)
Forasmuch as it appears to the court that the parish of Knoyle is a parish much oppressed and over charged with poor people and that there are very few poor people in Chilmark. Ordered that Chilmark inhabitants shall contribute towards the relief of the parish of Knoyle the sum of five shillings per week for the space of one month and that

afterwards they shall pay them two shillings six pence per week until the court shall cause to alter the same.

(If churchwardens refuse, justices to grant their warrants for levying the rate.)

582. *Daniel Drake for £50 about the expense of the gaoler.*
The court is informed by Daniel Drake of the gaol of Fisherton Anger that by reason of the several desperate insurrections and mutinies of the fellows committed to his charge and employ in serving of them for the good of the Commonwealth and his own trust in bringing them to a lawful trial for their facts and offences has been at great charge, loss and expense amounting in the whole to the sum of three score pounds four shillings and six pence as appears by a bill of particulars thereof annexed to the petition which he is ready to certify upon oath the charge whereof Drake is unable to bear or be at more for the future in case he fail of redress herein. And prayed the court to take the same into consideration and to settle away for his allowance of the charge and expense there having been never the like attempts of prisoners to make their escapes which enforced Drake to be at that charge. All which the court taking into consideration and knowing the faithful service Drake has performed in securing of the prisoners committed to his charge therefore thinks fit and orders that Drake shall be allowed the sum of fifty pounds towards his charges and expenses to be paid him by the Sheriff. And the court humbly desires the honourable Committee of Revenue to be pleased to give allowance thereof to the Sheriff and also to give their order to the Sheriff for the paying thereof accordingly.

583. *Mr George Ivy to pay John Story, Edward Jones and William Gilbert 50s a piece.*
The court is informed by John Story, Edward Jones and William Gilbert all of Snap [Aldbourne] that in May last past at Snap there happened a sudden and lamentable fire which consumed and burned to the ground their dwelling houses and stables with the greatest part of their household goods all which losses amount to the value of four hundred eighty four pounds by reason whereof they are utterly disabled to rebuild their house and maintain their wives and families. Ordered Mr George Ivy to pay unto Story, Jones and Gilbert the sum of fifty shillings a piece out of the money of the county remaining in his hands.

584. *Aylesopp for 5 marks.* (See also **559**)
The court is informed by John Aylesopp that he has served the Parliament as a trooper under the command of Col Ludlow in which

service at Salisbury he received a dangerous wound in his face by reason whereof he has lost his eyesight. Ordered the Treasurer for the south forthwith to pay unto Aylesopp the sum of five marks in regard of his great necessity.

585. *House of correction at Marlborough.* (See also **611**)
The court is informed by John Purrier master of the house of correction at Marlborough that the house is in great decay. The court desires Mr William Littleton, Mr William Sadler and Mr Robert Hippisley justices or any two of them to view the decays of the house and estimate what will repair the same and certify their opinion therein at the next Quarter Sessions that then the court may make an order for the speedy disbursing of a sum of money for the repair of the house of correction before it falls into further decay.

586. *Joan Smith placed with Mr Joles of Fisherton.*
The court is informed that Joan Brown placed her daughter Joan Smith with Mr Joles of Fisherton Anger for five years where she remained three years and afterwards fell lame and then was taken home to her mother to whom Mr Joles gave some satisfaction towards the relieving of her for one year and since she is become chargeable to the parish of Fisherton Anger. The court desires William Stephens, Edward Tooker, Richard Grobham Howe, Barnaby Coles and Francis Swanton justices or any two of them to call all parties interested therein and to examine and settle Smith and order the same as shall be agreeable to law and justice.

587. *John Davis and William Sealy.*
The court is informed by John Davis tithingman of Warminster that he has served in the same office by the space of whole year ended the twenty ninth of September last past and has continued the same office ever since by reason of the last default of keeping of the last court leet at the time accustomed and prayed the court that he might be discharged of this office and that William Sealy of Warminster who was formerly nominated by the constables of the town of Warminster to be tithingman of that place might serve in the office. Ordered that the examination thereof shall be referred to Mr Nicholas Green justice who is desired to send for the parties and examine the truth of the matter and if he finds it to be true then to send for Sealy and swear him to serve in the office.
(If Sealy refuses to be sworn, to be bound over.)

588. *Joseph Bennett.* (See also **631**)
The court is informed that Joseph Bennett late of Warminster being a soldier as he was taking ship for the service of Ireland fell down and broke his leg and now he is at Warminster with his mother in a sad condition for want of relief. Ordered that Mr Francis Bennett shall pay forty shillings for his present relief and defraying such charges as he has been at since his lameness, the same to be paid out of the county's stock for the relief of maimed soldiers as remaining in his hands.

General Sessions of the Peace held at Devizes 23 April 1650. Robert Nicholas, Edward Baynton, Edward Tooker, William Littleton, William Eyre, William Sadler, Thomas Eyre, Walter South, Richard Green, Edward Stokes, Francis Swanton, Gabriel Martin, William Shute, John Read.

589. *Robert Martyn.*
The court is informed by Robert Martyn the younger tithingman of Coate in the parish of Bishops Cannings that he has disbursed for the tithing in carrying Mary Akerman to the gaol of Fisherton Anger the sum of eighteen shillings. Ordered that the constables and churchwardens of the parish of Bishops Cannings with some other of the inhabitants there make an equal and an indifferent rate throughout the whole parish as well for the payment of the sum of eighteen shillings as all other charges he has been at concerning the business.
(If any refuse to pay, to be bound over.)

590. *Margery Bateman.*
The court is informed by Margery Bateman of Devizes widow that Robert Bateman her late husband deceased did in is life time pawn to Phillipp Smyth of Chippenham a mare bridle and saddle which was worth seven pounds and ten shillings for forty shillings to be redeemed upon payment back of the money which money her husband did afterwards tender the same day unto Smyth for the redemption of his mare bridle and saddle but he refused to receive the money and so does as yet fraudulently detain the mare bridle and saddle in his hands. The court refers the examination thereof to the two next justices to Devizes and desires them to examine the truth of the complaint and mediate the differences between them and make such order therein as shall be agreeable to law and justice.

591. *Thomas Maundrell and Richard Stevens elected constables of the Liberty of Rowde in place of Edward King and John Axford.*
The court is informed by Edward King and John Axford constables of the Liberty of Rowde that no court has been kept in Rowde these seven years and upwards at which court the constables of the Liberty have been usually chosen. Ordered that Thomas Maundrell and Richard Stevens of Rowde be elected and chosen constables of the Liberty in the places of King and Axford and that Maundrell and Stevens shall within one week after receipt hereof repair to the next justice there to take his oath for the due execution of their office upon pain of ten pounds a piece.

592. *Inhabitants of Seend and Langley Burrell, Elizabeth Somner.* (See also **226, 726, 800, 823**)
The court is informed by the inhabitants of Seend that Elizabeth Somner widow has had one child by her late husband and one bastard child since his death both which children have been kept and maintained by the tithing of Seend by the space of two years last past and about twelve months since Elizabeth departed from Seend and went into the parish of Langley Burrell where she lived as a covenant servant by the space of six months and there became great with another bastard child and so finding herself with child returned again to Seend of her own accord but by a justice warrant was conveyed back again to Langley and by misinformation to the justice she was by a warrant from the justices brought back again to Seend where she was delivered of that last bastard child. Ordered that the two next justices to Seend call all the parties interested before them and examine the business complained of and to make such order therein as shall be agreeable to law and justice.

593. *Inter William Button knight and Thomas Lewington.*
The court is informed by Thomas Lewington of Wilcot mason that he was employed by Sir William Button about many occasions of building belonging towards the reparations so much that his work amounted to the sum of four pounds one shilling and six pence whereof he received forty eight shillings so there remains due to him two and thirty shillings and six pence which Button utterly refuses to pay. The court desires the two next justices to Wilcot to treat with Button and examine the truth of the petition and make such order therein as shall be agreeable to law and justice.

594. *Inter Thomas Parsons, Philip Wingeham.*
Philip Wingeham was apprehended at the Bell in Southbroom in the

parish of Bishops Cannings for suspicion of felony by him committed whereupon Thomas Parsons bailiff of the manor of Cannings seized upon a bay mare of the goods of Wingeham in the behalf of the lord of the manor and carried Wingeham to the gaol of Fisherton Anger. And whereas Wingeham has been indicted for the mare at this Quarter Sessions and acquitted for the same and prayed the court that the mare might be restored to him again. Ordered that Parsons shall deliver the mare unto Wingeham, Wingcham paying him all such charges as he has been at in carrying of him to the gaol and for the meat of the mare during the time he has been in his custody.

595. *Inter inhabitants of Poulshot and inhabitants of Worton, John Andrewes.* The court upon hearing of counsel as well on the behalf of the parish of Worton about the settlement of John Andrewes. And likewise upon rendering of a former order of the court made at Marlborough Sessions last concerning that business. And for that it now appears upon the oath of Roger Lye and Thomas Stevens late overseers of the poor of Poulshot that Andrewes was disturbed and warned by them to remove out of the same parish within one month after his coming and settlement in the same parish. Ordered Andrewes with his family be forthwith removed forth of the parish of Poulshot to the parish of Worton where he formerly remained and was settled and there to continue as an inhabitant of that parish.

596. *Inter inhabitants of Calne and inhabitants of Bremhill, Roger Harding.* (Recites **556**; see also **486, 627**)
In truth Harding his wife and children were settled last in Calne for divers years together as appears to the court upon oath of Sarah Diston. Now ordered that the order of Michaelmas Sessions last shall be vacated and that Harding with his wife and children shall be forthwith sent back to Calne there to remain and be provided for as the poor of that parish and that the overseers of the poor there shall receive them accordingly. But if the inhabitants of Calne shall find themselves grieved therein then the inhabitants are to appeal at the next Quarter Sessions and to give notice thereof to the inhabitants of Bremhill and both sides are to come fully prepared to the Sessions that the matter may then receive a final order. And if it shall then upon hearing of the matter fall out that Harding is to be settled at Calne with his wife and children then the inhabitants of Bremhill are to be repaired in damage by the inhabitants of Calne for the keeping and relieving of Harding his wife and children ever since they were sent to Bremhill by virtue of the last surreptitious order if the court of Sessions shall then see cause to do the same.

597. *Overseers rates of Bromham confirmed.*

It appears to the court upon a due examination that divers inhabitants of the parish of Bromham are behind in payment of their rates for the relief of the poor of the parish according to a rate made and agreed upon by most of the parishioners under their hands and afterwards confirmed by two justices whereof one of them is of the quorum according to the statute in that case made. And whereas it also appears that a warrant was made under the hands and seals of two justices to the churchwardens and overseers of Bromham according to the statute for distraining of such of the inhabitants as refused to pay their rates and the churchwardens and overseers distrained accordingly but the distresses were afterwards replevied. Whereupon the court upon full examination of the premises orders that the churchwardens and overseers of Bromham do forthwith according to their warrant distrain the goods and chattels of such of the inhabitants as are so behind in their rates and taxes and make sale thereof rendering to the party the overplus according to the statute in that case made and provided.

598. *Inter Henry Davis and William Druce.*

The court is informed by Henry Davis of Woolley that he inhabited there in a tenement with his wife and eight female children in which tenement he has an estate for term of his life paying the yearly rent of one pound and twelve shillings being a poor man and failing of his rent at the very day of payment to William Druce who is the next taker to the tenement after the decease of Davis, Druce understanding him and his wife to be from home took the children of Davis and threw them out of doors took possession of the tenement so that if their neighbours had not had compassions on them they should have perished in the streets. The court desires the next justice to send for the parties before them and examine the truth of the petition and make such order therein as shall be agreeable to law and justice.

599. *Francis Morse accused to be the reputed father of a bastard.*

The court is informed that there is a bastard child born of the body of Jane Pannell in the parish of Rodbourne Cheney and that Francis Morse of the same place is accused to be the reputed father of the bastard child and that there is no order made therein. The court desires the two next justices to send for Pannell and Morse and examine the matter and make such order concerning the mother and the reputed father and discharge of the parish as shall be agreeable to law and justice and certify the same at the next Quarter Sessions.

600. *Inter inhabitants of Chilworth and inhabitants of Charlton.*
Upon hearing the matter in difference between the inhabitants of Chilworth in the county of Southampton and the inhabitants of Charlton concerning the settlement of Anne Salter and her bastard child born at Charlton as was alleged and now remaining there and upon reading of an order made at the Quarter Sessions of the county of Southampton held at the castle of Winchester the Tuesday after the feast of St John the Baptist 1649 [24 June] concerning Salter and the bastard child. Ordered that the order shall stand confirmed and the bastard child shall remain and be settled at Charlton according to the order of Sessions unless good cause be shown to the court at the next Quarter Sessions and the keeping of the child by the inhabitants of Charlton between this and the next Sessions shall not be prejudicial in point of right.

601. *Inter inhabitants of Brinkworth and inhabitants of Tockenham.*
It appears to the court that John Sherrar late of Brinkworth deceased was the reputed father of a bastard child begotten on his maid servant at Tockenham Wick where the child was born and where Sherrar then lived. And Sherrar afterwards removed to Brinkworth and carried the child with him and so kept it with him and provided for it till his death but now since the death of Sherrar the child is likely to be chargeable to the parish of Brinkworth. Ordered that the child be sent to Tockenham where it was born there to be provided by the churchwardens and overseers as a poor of that parish until the court shall further order the same.

602. *Richard Sherborne and John Wake.*
It appears to the court by the petition of Richard Sherborne of Ashley [now Glos] that he has been tithingman there by the space of three years now last past and that there has been no court leet kept there for that manor since the death of Sir Theobald Gorges knight late lord of that manor by reason whereof he cannot be eased of that office but is constrained to undergo it to his great prejudice and trouble and that John Wake of Ashley is the next man to serve in that office. The court desires the next justice to send for Wake and to examine whether he ought of course to serve in the office and if he ought to serve then the justice is desired to swear him for the due execution of the office.
(If he refuses, to be bound over.)

603. *Richard Davis and Richard Blake.*
The court is informed by Richard Blake of Manningford Bruce that he has served tithingman of his tithing for the space of three years last

past and that Sir Oliver Nicholas knight being lord of that leet has not kept any court there in the space aforesaid and that the office of right belongs unto Richard Blake of the same parish. Ordered that the next justice upon sight hereof should send forth his warrant for Blake to take his oath for the undertaking and executing the office.
(If he refuses, to be bound over.)

604. *Hugh Downynge and inhabitants of Quemerford* [Calne].
The court if informed by Hugh Downynge of Quemerford that he has appeared on behalf of the inhabitants of the tithing to five several presentments for decays of diverse highways within the tithing in prosecution thereof Downynge has disbursed the sum of three pounds. Ordered that an equal rate be forthwith made upon all the inhabitants of the tithing and pay unto Downynge the sum of three pounds.
(If any refuse to pay, to be bound over.)

605. *Richard Phelps and the inhabitants of Langley Burrell.*
Richard Phelps of Langley Burrell has disbursed the sum of four pounds nine shillings and ten pence in repairing the highways at Hennynge hill and the inhabitants of Langley Burrell have not as yet paid him the same. Ordered that an equal rate be forthwith made upon all the inhabitants of Langley Burrell for the reimbursing the said sum of money for the paying of Phelps.
(if any refuse to pay, to be bound over.)

606. *John Kember, alehouse suppressed.*
It appears to the court that John Kember of Ham keeps a common alehouse and sells ale without licence and likewise keeps two of his daughters in house with him being women suspected for light and loose living. Ordered that the alehouse be suppressed and that Kember (being a poor old man) be not suffered to sell any ale or beer in his house hereafter. Ordered that Jane Fisher one of Kember's daughters with her child be forthwith sent to her husband Humfry Fisher to Peasemore in the county of Berkshire where he now lives there to remain with her husband.

607. *William Cantloe.* (Recites **578**)
There are now at this present Sessions many of the most sufficient inhabitants of the parish of Tisbury together with the vicar there who desire the continuance of the alehouse and the necessariness of the same. The court therefore refers the fitness or unfitness of Cantloe's licensing for selling ale and beer unto the two next justices

of Warminster division who are desired to consider thereof and to do therein as they shall see cause.

(There was clearly some alehouse rivalry in Tisbury. Skevington maintained that Cantloe was ill-affected to the state, had a son in the King's army and entertained papists. But a petition signed by about 50 people explained that Tisbury was a large parish with the church in the middle. People coming from the outskirts needed a place for their horses and generally a public meeting place was required at the centre of the parish. They had persuaded Cantloe to develop his alehouse to meet these needs and also to provide quarters for soldiers who had been billeted on people who really did not have room to accommodate them. A1/110/1650E/158,190,200)

608. *Alexander Peircy and Edward Kinge.*
The court is informed by Alexander Peircy of Longbridge Deverill that he has served in the office of tithingman in the tithing of Longbridge Deverill for the space of two years and upwards and that there being no court leet kept there he is constrained to continue in the office and that according to the custom there used Edward Kinge of the same place is the next man who ought to serve in the office. And that Peircy has been at great charge in carrying felons to the gaol besides other expenses he has been at on the behalf of the tithing and that the parishioners refuse to make a rate for the payment of the moneys which are by him disbursed. The court desires the next justice to Longbridge Deverill to send for Kinge and swear him for the due execution of the office.

(If he refuses, to be bound over.)

Further ordered that there shall be an equal and indifferent rate made on the inhabitants according to the statute in such case made and provided for the raising of the moneys which are by him disbursed for the carrying of prisoners to the gaol and for other necessary charges and expenses which rate is to be allowed under the hand of a justice.

(If any refuse to pay, to be bound over.)

609. *Thomas Jones to erect a cottage.*
The court is informed by Thomas Jones of Steeple Ashton that he is a very poor man having a wife and four small children and not able to rent a house for to succour himself and children and that Mr John Bennett of Steeple Ashton commiserating the sad condition of Jones has given leave unto him to erect and build him a cottage on a plot of ground of Mr Bennett's without Sand Pittes gate being his land by inheritance. And Jones prayed the court to commiserate his poverty and grant him an order for the erecting and continuing of the cottage.

The court allows Jones to erect and build him a cottage on the plot of ground and orders that the cottage shall continue and be a cottage for his habitation and dwelling during the life time of Jones without incurring the forfeitures mentioned in the statute.

610. *Abraham Hall.*
It appears to the court by the petition of Abraham Hall master of the house of correction at Devizes that he was compelled to take a bastard child into the house with her mother and that he has kept the child a year and three quarters at his own charge to his great loss and trouble he being a poor man and not having any allowance either from the parish or the reputed father whose name is John Flower of Melksham for the doing thereof. The court desires Mr Eyre, Mr Long and Mr Green justices or any two of them to send for the churchwardens and overseers of the poor of Melksham and Flower and examine the truth thereof and consider of a way the master of the house of correction may be satisfied for his charges and expenses laid out and make such order therein as shall be agreeable to law and justice.

611. £22 allocated for the repair of the house of correction near Marlborough. (Recites **585**)
It now appeared to the court that according to the judgment and opinion of honest workmen upon view of the decays of the house the repairing thereof will amount to the sum of two and twenty pounds twelve shillings and eight pence. The court desires George Ivy justice upon sight of this order to pay the sum of two and twenty pounds towards the reparations of the house of correction out of the arrears of the county's money remaining in his hands to Mr Sadler or to such a man as he shall appoint to receive the same. And the court desires Mr Sadler to see the moneys disbursed and laid out for the repair of the house of correction with all convenient speed and take course that the house be speedily repaired.
(See Appendix 2/1 for a detailed account of the expenditure on repairs.)

612. *Inter inhabitants of Chilmark and East Knoyle.* (Recites **581**; see also **633**)
Ordered that the matter shall be heard at the next Quarter Sessions and that such order as shall be made shall be final and the inhabitants of Chilmark are to give reasonable notice thereof to the inhabitants of East Knoyle before the same Sessions and leave a copy with the churchwardens and overseers of the poor of that place that they may come thither provided with their witnesses that the matter maybe fully heard and finally settled accordingly.

613. *Inter inhabitants of Bishop's Lavington* [West Lavington] *and Devizes Green* [Bishops Cannings]. (See also **621**)
Concerning the matter in difference between the inhabitants of Bishop's Lavington and the inhabitants of Devizes Green about the settlement of Thomasin Smyth. Ordered that the matter shall be heard and settled at the next Quarter Sessions and to that end both sides are to come thither provided with their witnesses and that she shall remain where she now is till the next Quarter Sessions without prejudice to that place in point of right. Further ordered that that place against whom it shall be adjudged at the next Sessions shall pay the other place all such charges concerning Thomasin her child if shall have any as shall happen unto them between this and the next Quarter Sessions.

614. *John Aylesopp his pension of £8 per annum.* (Recites **584**)
The court allows him a pension of eight pounds per annum to be paid him quarterly by the Treasurer for the south the first payment to begin at midsummer next and to continue until the court shall see cause to alter the same.

General Sessions of the Peace held at Warminster 11 July 1650. William Hussey, Edward Tooker, Walter South, Richard Grobham Howe, Nicholas Green, Francis Swanton, John Read.

615. *Inter Mr Earnly's tenants and Mr Mitchell.* (Refers to **557**)
Ordered that the case be drawn up according to the examination of the steward and jury of the leet whereunto Calstone belongs and certified by them into the court and that the opinion of the Judges of Assize be humbly desired thereupon for the settlement of the tithingmanship.

616. *Simon Peirce.*
The court is informed by Simon Peirce of Stratford under the Castle [Salisbury] labourer that he has lived within the parish of Stratford by the space of twelve years where he has had four children and now being fallen into poverty and destitute of a house for the habitation of himself and family. The court desires the two next justices to send for the churchwardens and overseers of Stratford before them and make such order for the relief of Peirce as shall be agreeable to law and justice.

617. *Joseph Smyth pension of £10 per annum.*
The court is informed as well by Captain Joseph Smyth as by several certificates as well from the parishioners of Shalbourne as also by the

certificate under the hands of William Lenthall Speaker of the House of Parliament and divers other Parliament men of this county that Smyth was born and resided at Shalbourne and has since served the Parliament in the late wars and done very good service and has received at the siege of Reading and other places divers wounds whereby he is wounded and maimed and is not of ability to relieve himself. Ordered that Mr George Ivy justice forthwith pays unto Smyth the sum of five pounds for present necessity forth of such moneys of the arrears for maimed soldiers as remains in his hands. Further ordered that the Treasurer for the north pays unto Smyth a yearly pension of ten pounds to be paid unto him quarterly and to begin at Michaelmas next and to continue until the court shall alter the same.

618. *For collecting the arrears of the five miles tax near Bradford.* (Recites **419**)
The court was informed that the order has taken little or no effect in regard Mr Eyre and Mr Ivy justices have not executed the order and prayed the court that Mr Nicholas Green another justice may be joined with the said justices. Ordered Mr Eyre, Mr Ivy and Mr Green or any two of them speedily to meet together and put the order in execution.

619. *Edward Hill.*
The court is informed by Edward Hill of Westbury being a poor blind man and having a long time inhabited within the said parish and laboured hard in the calling of a fuller until now of late old age having overtaken him and being not able to work as he has done to get any relief to relieve himself and having but two pence a day allowed him from the parish. Ordered that the churchwardens and overseers of the poor of the parish shall forthwith sufficiently provide for Hill both in meat drink lodging and other necessaries by reason of his great want and necessity.

620. *Lady Beauchamp and others nominated to be feoffees in trust for the £50 given by William Tubb for the poor of Edington.* (See also **710**)
There has been some complaint made at this Sessions concerning the settlement and disposal of fifty pounds heretofore given by William Tubb late of Edington deceased. Now upon reading the certificate of the executors of Tubb which declares his intent and meaning for the settlement of the money and disposing the interest thereof accordingly. Ordered that the Rt Hon the Lady Beauchamp, John Carpenter, John Yorke and Thomas Sawe shall be feoffees in trust for the tithing of Edington and shall have the disposal and putting forth of the fifty pounds from time to time and when either of the feoffees

shall happen to die that the other surviving feoffees shall nominate one other of the inhabitants of Edington to be a feoffee in trust in the place of the feoffee deceased who shall join with them in the disposal of the fifty pounds. And that the interest of the fifty pounds be from time to time yearly disposed of by the churchwardens and overseers of Edington with the advice of the feoffees to the poor of the tithing of Edington for their better help and comfort without any definition of their parish rates made for the relief of the poor.

621. *Inter inhabitants of Bishop's Lavington* [West Lavington] *and the inhabitants of Devizes Green* [Bishops Cannings]. (Refers to **613**)
Upon full hearing of the matter in difference between the inhabitants of Bishop's Lavington and the inhabitants of Devizes Green concerning the settlement of Thomasin Smyth now remaining at Bishop's Lavington. It appears to the court amongst other proofs that she was married to Ralfe Barlowe and that she was last settled at Bishop's Lavington and that her husband was gone from her into Ireland. Ordered that Thomasin with her child shall remain and be settled at Bishop's Lavington until her husband come thither or it appears that he is settled elsewhere.

622. *Alice Carroway allocated £5, Treasurer of the south.*
Upon the petition of Alice Carroway widow late wife of John Carroway of Pewsey deceased that about six years since her husband was taken prisoner in Woodhouse garrison [Horningsham] in the county of Somerset by Sir Francis Doddington where he and thirteen more of his fellow soldiers were immediately hanged for their faithful service to the Parliament in consideration whereof the committee of this county allowed her towards her relief the sum of five pounds a year out of Sir Francis Doddington's estate and after a year and a quarter took it from her again by reason whereof she is brought into great want and misery. Ordered that according to an ordinance of Parliament in that behalf made Carroway shall be allowed five pounds towards her relief and maintenance in regard her husband being so barbarously hanged. And that the Treasurer for the south shall upon sight of this order pay Carroway the five pounds out of the moneys collected and paid for the said relief in regard of her great want and necessity.
(See also **528** and **713**)

623. *Edward Burford pension 40s a year.*
The court is informed by Edward Burford of Longbridge Deverill that he has served as a trooper in the Parliament service under the command of Colonel Ludlow by the space of two years in which service he

was maimed at Broad Chalke whereby he is disabled to get his living and by the certificate of Col Ludlow appears. Ordered and allowed Burford a yearly pension of forty shillings to be paid him quarterly by the Treasurer for the south the first payment to begin at this present Sessions and to continue till the court shall otherwise order the same.

624. *Andrew Smith allocated 3s 6d, inhabitants of Mere.* (See also **693**, **758**, **794**, **842**)
The court is informed by Andrew Smith of Mere that he has always been forth in arms under the command of the States of the Kingdom until about a year since at which time he was bound for the service of Ireland then it pleased God to inflict a grievous disease on him which compelled him to forsake his company and repair to his friends hoping there to find some relief but they not being of ability to relieve him in his great necessity was enforced to complain to Colonel Ludlow who gave order that he should receive two shillings per week of the parishioners for his relief and maintenance. And whereas Smith now complains unto the court that the allowance of two shillings per week is too little to relieve him he being old and infirm and prayed the court for an increase of his relief. Ordered that the churchwardens and overseers of the poor of Mere shall from henceforth pay and allow unto Smith the sum of three shillings and six pence per week for his relief and maintenance until the court shall see cause to alter the same.

625. *William Penry allocated a pension of £4 a year.*
The court is informed by William Penry late of Bratton also by his own affidavit made before one of the masters of the Chancery that at the time when Sir Edward Hungerford bore arms for the Parliament he took up arms under him at Devizes and was afterwards reduced under Colonel Ludlow at Wardour Castle where he was blown up and maimed with powder. It also appears to the court by a certificate under the hand of Colonel Ludlow that Penry has faithfully served the State under his command as a dragoon and in that service received certain maims viz that he has lost the use of his left arm and had the toes of his left foot broken and also his left leg by means whereof he is utterly disabled to get his living for himself and his wife. Ordered that the Treasurer for the south shall pay out of the stock of the county the sum of four pounds per annum to Penry towards his relief and maintenance in regard of his great necessity, the same to be paid quarterly and the first payment to begin at this present Sessions and to continue until the court shall see good cause to alter the same.

626. *Inter inhabitants of Maiden Bradley and inhabitants of Wincanton* [Somerset] *concerning Grace Toogood.*
Upon hearing of the matter in difference between the inhabitants of Maiden Bradley and the inhabitants of Wincanton in the county of Somerset concerning the settlement of Grace Toogood.   It appeared unto the court that she was last settled at Wincanton.   Ordered that Toogood shall be sent with her children to Wincanton there to be settled and provided for according to law until good cause be showed to the court otherwise to order the same.
    (See **659** and **699** where she is referred to as Alice)

627. *Inhabitants of Calne and Bremhill.* (Refers to **596**; see also **486, 556**)
Upon full hearing and examining of the matter in difference between the inhabitants of Calne and Bremhill concerning the placing and settlement of Roger Harding his wife and children and upon hearing of counsel on both sides upon the appeal of the parish of Calne according to an order of the last Sessions.   Ordered that Harding his wife and three of his children viz the elder boy and two of the younger children be forthwith removed from Calne to Bremhill there to remain and be provided for as parishioners of that parish by the churchwardens and overseers there.   And that Anne and Mary Harding two other of the children of Harding shall by the consent of the overseers of Calne remain in Calne there to be provided for or bound forth apprentices by the overseers of Calne.   And if the churchwardens and overseers of Bremhill refuse to receive Harding his wife and his said three children then further ordered that Anne and Mary be also sent to Bremhill there to continue and be likewise provided for with the rest of Harding's children.

628. *John Gray and Edward Kinge to have a rate made upon the inhabitants of Semley.*
The court is informed by John Gray and Edward Kinge of Semley that they have appeared on the behalf of the inhabitants of Semley to two several presentments whereof the inhabitants were presented for decays of several highways within their parish in prosecution thereof for fines and other reasonable charges and expenses Gray and Kinge have disbursed for the inhabitants the sum of five and forty shillings. Ordered that an equal rate shall be forthwith made upon all the inhabitants of Semley for the paying of Gray and Kinge the sum of five and forty shillings and all other reasonable charges which they have been at concerning the same business.
    (If any refuse to pay, to be bound over.)

629. *Robert Bayly to be tithingman in place of Thomas Fisher.*
The court is informed by Thomas Fisher of Stert that he has served in
the office of tithingman there by the space of two years and upwards.
And for that Mr Robert Bayly of Chilhampton [South Newton] gent
ought by the custom there used to serve as tithingman for the tithing
in the place of Fisher. Ordered that Bayly shall within one week after
receipt hereof repair to the next justice to take his oath for the due
execution of the office.
(If he refuses, to be bound over.)

630. (See also **640**) £10 allocated for repair of house of correction at
Devizes. It appears to the court by a certificate under the hands of Mr
Peirce mayor of Devizes and John Stevens of the same place gent that
they have viewed the decays of the house of correction there together
with some skilful workmen who have estimated that the repair thereof
will amount to the sum of thirty pounds. Ordered that Mr George Ivy
justice to pay unto Abraham Hall the sum of ten pounds towards the
reparations of the house out of the moneys of the county remaining in
his hands and this shall be his discharge for the same. And the court
desires Mr Peirce to see the same disbursed accordingly.

631. *Joseph Bennett pension allocated 40s per annum.* (See also **588**)
The court is informed by Joseph Bennett of Warminster that he was
pressed by the constable of Warminster to serve the State as a soldier
under the command of Colonel Eyre under whom he served about
four years in which service at the siege before Colchester he received
a bruise in his leg with a great shot by reason whereof Bennett is not
able to get his livelihood be being a poor man and having nothing
to relieve himself. Ordered and allowed Bennett a yearly pension of
forty shillings to be paid him quarterly by the Treasurer for the south
the first payment to begin at Michaelmas next and to continue until
the court shall otherwise order.

632. *Habbacock Holton allocated 5 marks.* (See also **653**)
The court is informed by the inhabitants of Warminster on the behalf
of Habbacock Holton of the same place that he has been a very
true and faithful servant to the Commonwealth ever since the first
engagement and constantly served them in all their wars and since his
disbanding has lived very quietly at home in his vocation and that he
behaved himself very civilly and quietly amongst his neighbours. And
that of late he has been dangerously shot and wounded by a soldier in
the face with a pistol charges with powder and hailshot without any
just provocation on his part as he was coming forth to his master's

assistance whose house was broken up by five soldiers under pretence of levying of arrears of contribution whereas in truth there was none due by reason of which wound he lies desperately sick and if he recover his life will never more receive his sight to the utter undoing of him and his family. And prayed the court for some allowance out of the public stock of the county for relief of maimed soldiers by way of yearly stipend might be granted unto him. Ordered and appointed the Treasurer for the south shall forthwith pay unto Holton the sum of five marks out of the county's stock for his present relief and in regard of his present great necessity.

(It appears that Holton had already upset the soldiers by laughing at them in the street and one of them vowed to kill him. A1/110/1650T)

633. *Inter inhabitants of Chilmark and East Knoyle.* (Recites **612**)
And now upon full hearing of the parties on both sides concerning the same, ordered that the inhabitants of Chilmark shall contribute towards the relief of the inhabitants of East Knoyle the sum of two shillings per week to begin from the present Sessions and to continue till the court shall see cause to alter the same.

634. The court is informed by Mr Ledesham one of the supervisors of the highways in the tithing of Seend and Seend Rewe that there was a rate made by the yardlands the 8th day of May 1648 for the repair of the highways within the tithing which rate was subscribed under the hands of William Somner, Richard Ledesham, Edward Michell, John Stoakes, William Stoakes, Jeffery Tipper and divers others inhabitants of the tithings which rate is also hereunto annexed. The court is informed by Richard Ledesham that by divers inhabitants therein mentioned refused to pay their rates whereby the highways within the tithings were unrepaired and Ledesham and James Stoakes another supervisor could not collect the rates and repair the ways as they intended to do. And prayed the assistance of he court for the obtaining and getting in the rates that the ways may be better repaired. Ordered Ledesham and Stoakes or either of them forthwith to demand the rate again and if they shall contemptuously refuse to pay their rates then the next justice upon complaint thereof to him made is desired to bind them over to the next Quarter Sessions there to answer the same. And Ledesham and Stoakes are hereby ordered to give their account to the parish what they have received of the rates and how they have employed the same.

General Sessions of the Peace held at Marlborough Tuesday 1 October 1650. Alexander Staples, Anthony Ashley Cooper, William Eyre, William Sadler, Robert Hippisley, Thomas Eyre, John Long, Nicholas Green, Edward Stokes, Gabriel Martin, Francis Swanton, William Shute and John Read.

635. *Staverton concerning the rates.* (See also **779**)
Complaint has been made by Oliver Chivers of Staverton Wick in the behalf of himself and the rest of the tithings of Staverton of the inequality of rates for the poor in the several tithings of Staverton, Studley and Trowle in the parish of Trowbridge. Ordered and desired that Mr John Ashe and Mr Nicholas Green or one of them call all parties interested before them in any of the said tithings and examine the equality of the rates and whether Staverton be more burdened that the rest of the tithings considering their several values and to certify the same or otherwise to make certificate thereof to the court.

636. *John Head his pension augmented to £4 per annum.* (See also **356**, **473**)
It appears to the court by a former order that John Head of Easton was allowed forty shillings per annum and then the court was certified of his faithful service to the State and of his hurts and bruises he has received there. The court thinks fit to augment his pension to four pounds per annum to be paid him quarterly by the Treasurer for the north, the first payment thereof to begin Christmas next and to continue till the court shall alter the same.

637. *Inhabitants of Wroughton and Westlecott* [Wroughton].
Edward Keate gent one of the inhabitants of the tithing of Westlecott was bound over to this Sessions at the prosecution of John Duck and William Smyth supervisors of the highways of the tithing of Wroughton for refusing to do his work towards the reparations of the highways of Wroughton. And now upon hearing of the matter and upon examination of witnesses upon oath in open court it appeared that the tithing of Westlecott have always joined with the tithing of Wroughton towards the reparations of the highways which was denied by Keate to be true. Ordered that Keate shall be discharged for the present from the court and that an equal and an indifferent rate shall be made on the inhabitants of Wroughton and the tithing of Westlecott. And that Keate shall be distrained for his rate that a trial may be had at common law whether the tithing of Westlecott ought to join with the tithing of Wroughton about the reparations of their

highways and the doing thereof is to be without prejudice in point of right on either side.

638. *William Verryer to erect a cottage.*
The court is informed by a certificate under the hand and seal of the lord of the manor of Winterbourne [Bassett] that William Verryer of the same place is destitute of a habitation for the succour of himself and family. Ordered that Verryer shall erect and build him a cottage for the habitation of himself and his wife in any convenient place where the lord of that manor will assign him. And it is desired by the court that the churchwardens and overseers of the poor of Winterbourne put their help in hand for erecting the cottage and that Verryer shall continue the cottage so erected without incurring the forfeitures mentioned in the statute.
(Parish identified by petition A1/110/1650M/214)

639. *John Upton allowed 6d weekly from the overseers of Shalbourne.*
It appears to the court as well by sight as by a certificate under the hands of divers of the inhabitants of Shalbourne that John Upton of Newton within the parish being a poor deaf broken and aged person and not able by his labour to provide sufficiently for his relief. Ordered that the churchwardens and overseers pay weekly to Upton the sum of six pence towards his relief and that also he be set to work for his better maintenance.
(If churchwardens and overseers refuse, to be bound over.)

640. *Thomas Eyre and Mr Sherston to view the house of correction at Devizes.*
(Refers to **630**)
The court is informed by Abraham Hall master of the house of correction at Devizes that the house of correction is in great decay and there has been ten pounds formerly allowed towards the reparations thereof by order of the court which is not all laid out as yet and informs the court that of late some workmen having viewed the other part of the house affirm that it will amount to ten pounds wholly to repair the house. The court desires Mr Thomas Eyre and Mr Sherston justices or one of them taking unto them some skilful workmen to view the decays of the house and make an estimate what will cost sufficiently to repair the house and to inquire how the ten pounds formerly allowed has been laid out and what remains and certify the court thereof at the next Quarter Sessions that some further order may be made therein.

641. *John Heath and Matthew Wake concerning the rates.*
The court is informed by John Heath late constable of Swindon and

Matthew Wake late tithingman of the same place that they had several orders to levy the sum of seven pounds one shilling and three pence for charges expended in carrying of felons to the gaol of Fisherton Anger. And that notwithstanding the order of the inhabitants of Swindon and the several officers in the several tithings thereunto belonging refuse to make a rate for the payment of the same. Ordered that the inhabitants of West Swindon borough and township with the constable and tithingman shall forthwith meet together and make an indifferent and equal rate on the inhabitants of the township and tithing for the raising of the sum of seven pounds one shilling and three pence and two next justices are desired to confirm the rate. And if any shall refuse to pay their rate then the justices are desired to make a warrant to distrain those who shall refuse payment of the rate.

642. *John Blundon allocated £5.*
The court is informed by John Blundon of London in the county of Middlesex that he was a soldier pressed from Idmiston to go against the Scots and has performed faithful service until such time he was wounded and maimed and having a wife and seven small children and not able to subsist without some relief. The court allows him the sum of five pounds to be paid by the Treasurer for the south and that he has promised never to trouble the county again for any more allowance. And the Treasurer is to pay the same immediately upon sight hereof and this shall be his discharge therefore.

643. *Henry Swaine.*
Henry Swaine was bound over to this Quarter Sessions for refusing to serve in the office of tithingman for the tithing of Broad Hinton although he was chosen in the court leet there and a pain set upon him by the steward of the leet to take his oath for the execution of the office which pain was forfeited long since. The court declares that Swaine shall be discharged for the present of further attendance of the court and that the matter shall be recommended to the steward of the leet that the pain may be levied and a greater pain set that Swaine may be compelled to serve in the office.

644. *William Liffelye to be sent to Eastleach Turville.*
It appears to the court upon the testimony of one witness upon oath that William Liffelye is a vagrant and apprehended at Inglesham as a vagrant and received punishment according to the law who confessed his place of birth to be at Eastleach Turville in the county of Gloucester. Ordered that Liffelye shall be sent by pass from tithing to tithing unto Eastleach Turville there to remain and be provided for according to law.

645. *Inhabitants of Highworth, Elizabeth Villier.*
The court is informed by the overseers of the poor of the parish of Highworth that there is a child of one Hintons chargeable on the parish of Highworth and that Elizabeth Villier of Hannington widow is grandmother to the child and that she is a woman of ability to keep and relieve the child her estate being worth twenty six pounds per annum as appears unto the court by the testimony of two witnesses upon oath. Ordered that Villier shall forthwith take upon her the keeping relieving and breeding up of the child and in default the court assesses Villier at two shillings per week to be paid to the overseers of the poor of Highworth towards the keeping relieving of the child the payment to begin at this present Sessions and to continue till the court shall see cause to alter the same.

646. *James Welch clerk and Thomas Baylye, John Gregory.*
Ordered by consent of parties that all matters in difference between James Welch of Hilmarton clerk and Thomas Baylye and John Gregory of the same parish shall be referred to the examination of Mr Stokes and Mr Shute justices who are desired to compose the differences and certify what they shall do therein at the next Quarter Sessions.

647. *Elianor Gest, inhabitants of Kemble.*
The court is informed by Elianor Gest wife of Richard Gest that she and her husband have lived at Kemble by the space of five years till of late her husband being much in debt was forced for fear of arresting to go with his wife and her child to Cradley in Worcestershire where the parishioners of Cradley would not permit them to settle there and that Richard not daring to return to Kemble whereupon the parishioners of Kemble refuse to suffer Richard his wife to abide there and provide for her a habitation. And for that it appears to the court by the oath of Elianor that the parishioners of Kemble had notice that she would appeal at this Sessions. Ordered that the overseers of the poor of Kemble shall provide for her as a poor of that parish until they show good cause to the court to the contrary.

648. *Henry Bailye to erect a cottage at Tytherton Lucas* [Bremhill].
The court is informed by a certificate under the hand and seal of Edward Stokes and divers others of the substantial inhabitants of Tytherton Lucas that Henry Bailye of the same place is destitute of any habitation for the succour of himself and family. Ordered that Bailye shall in some convenient place within the parish erect and build a cottage for the habitation of himself and his wife and shall continue the cottage without incurring the forfeitures mentioned in the statute.

649. *John Gale, Henry Shrapnell constable of Bradford, Nathaniel Smyth and Thomas Kellson.*
The court is informed that John Gale and Henry Shrapnell constables of the town of Bradford have served in that office one whole year and that the Marquess of Winchester lord of that manor is under sequestration whereby no court leet is likely to be kept and that they may be discharged of their office and prayed the court to take the same into their consideration that they may not be grieved in serving longer in that office than of right they ought to serve and to choose two other inhabitants of that town fitting to serve constables in their places and discharge them of that office. Ordered that they shall be discharged of their office and elects and chooses Nathaniel Smyth and Thomas Kellson of that town to be constables in their places and orders that Smyth and Kellson shall repair to the next justice within one week after receipt of this order to take their corporal oaths for the due execution of that office on pain of twenty pounds.
(If they default, to be bound over.)

650. *John Dowsewell.*
The court is informed by John Dowsewell of Minety that he has been formerly chosen tithingman and has continued in the office by the space of four years now last past whereas the custom of the tithing is and has always been to change the tithingman there at the end of one whole year and he being a very poor man and not able to undergo the office any longer it being to the utter impoverishing of Dowsewell. The court refers the same to Mr George Ivy justice to call before him William Paynter of the same place and see where he be a fitting man to serve in the office of tithingman and if he be it is desired by the court to swear Paynter in the place of Dowsewell.

651. *Churchwardens of Chiseldon.*
The churchwardens of Chiseldon have disbursed moneys about the repairing of their church and have made a rate for the payment thereof. Ordered that Mr William Sadler and Mr Gabriel Marten justices examine the particulars of the disbursements and whether the same be necessary and needful and whether the rates be equally laid and that they make certificate thereof to the next Sessions that the court may make further order therein.

652. *Mr Yerbury.*
Whereas the inhabitants of Bradford stand three several time presented in this court for decay of their highways and that Mr Thomas Yerbury one of the inhabitants has appeared to the presentment and for

discharging of them and for fines thereupon and for his charges he has been at in prosecution thereof has disbursed the sum of fifty shillings which charge ought to be borne by the inhabitants of the whole town. Ordered that there shall be an equal rate made on the inhabitants of the town of Bradford for repayment of the fifty shillings to Yerbury. (If any refuse to pay, to be bound over.)

653. *Habbacock Holton allocated £13 6s 8d.* (Refers to **632**)
Ordered that the sum of twenty marks shall be forthwith paid to Holton upon sight of this order out of the arrears of the north part of the county for relief of maimed soldiers remaining in Mr Ivy's hands in regard of the faithful service he has performed for the Parliament and also in regard of his present necessity. And the court desires Mr Ivy that the same may be forthwith paid accordingly.

654. *Stephen Guye, inhabitants of Urchfont.*
The inhabitants of Urchfont stand indicted in this court for the decay of a highway called Lydeway lying in the parish of Urchfont and that Stephen Guye of the same place being distrained for the inhabitants has appeared the indictment and confessed the same and made oath that it is sufficiently repaired and has disbursed for the discharging thereof the sum of thirty shillings which charge ought not to be borne by one particular person but by the inhabitants of the whole parish. Ordered that there shall be an equal rate made on the inhabitants for repayment of the sum of thirty shillings and all his other reasonable expenses which he has been at in the prosecution thereof.
(If any refuse to pay, to be bound over.)

655. *Order of Assizes concerning a freehold book.*
Whereas within this county of late years there has been great neglect as well in the under sheriffs and their deputies by impanelling of insufficient juries as by the several bailiffs of hundreds and other places in warning such jurors but by a general summons by the bailiffs only all the freeholders of the county are usually warned to come to the Assizes who are thereby forced to their great trouble and charge to attend during the whole Assizes albeit in truth they have no particular employment there. And those who are impanelled and returned by the Sheriff for want of particular summons do not know what his or their service is until they are called to the great grievance of the county and thereby many issues are unawares lost and many causes for defect of juries do either remain untried or are supplied by tales for the most part exceeding the number of those which appear upon the principal trial in most causes contrary to the ancient writs and forms

of law. And because an exact and perfect book of the freeholders names and of such as are fit to serve in juries would be a great help and direction to the Sheriff. And for that the Sheriff's books of late have been very unperfect and many men therein mentioned are aged impotent and very unable for the service yet are returned in juries. And for that inferior officers and bailiffs take upon them an illegal power and without warrant to spare or connive at whom they please as well from attendance as issues lost, whereby many of the most able and substantial freeholders and others although returned in hope of impunity forbear the service for the prevention whereof for time to come the court being advertised thereof by the grand jury and others taking the matter into serious after consultation therein has with the justices of the peace there present. And to the end that a grand jury upon life and death between party and party may be the better supplied with able and substantial men think it very fit and requisite that the justices of the peace within each division of the county every year with four of the most able and sufficient freeholders within every hundred shall cause the bailiffs of such hundred and places to attend them with a true and perfect list of the names of all the freeholders in every parish within such hundreds and places respectively that thereby the justices or four or more of such freeholders so meeting may in every division hundred and other places make such lists for the Sheriff to be entered and made up together by the Sheriff for a perfect and exact freeholders book omitting such as are aged decrepit or otherwise unfit to be impanelled thereby the better to enable the Sheriff in the execution of his duty for the ease and benefit of the country at the Assizes Sessions and other public places and that the Sheriff his under-sheriff and deputies after such jury or juries impanelled send to their bailiffs either notes on tickets of their juries names therein contained or their cause why they are returned and summoned. And that the bailiff and those to whom it belongs to give such notice or warning to deliver or send such note on tickets to all and every juror before the Assizes for the furtherance of the public service and if any neglect or default shall hereafter happen in the premises then the grand jury for the time to come are desired to inform the court thereof that such course may be taken against the offenders as to law and justice shall appertain . And the Sheriff to send copies of this order to the justices of the several divisions of the county.

656.   *The order of the Assizes above written is confirmed.*
Upon reading this order made at the Assizes held at Salisbury the sixth day of March in the three and twentieth year of the reign of the late King Charles[1648], the court ratifies and confirms the order

and further orders that the same be entered and remain amongst the records and orders of this Sessions.

657. £10 allowed for repair of the house of correction at Salisbury. The court is informed by Daniel Drake master of the house of correction at Fisherton Anger that the house is in great decay for want of reparations and the court being certified that the repair thereof will amount unto the sum of ten pounds. Ordered that the Treasurer for the south shall forthwith pay unto Mr Edward Tooker and Mr Francis Swanton justices the sum of ten pounds or to some other as they shall appoint to see the same disbursed about the reparations of the house of correction.

658. There has been a trial at this present Sessions against Charles Glover upon an indictment upon the statute made in the fifth year of the late Queen Elizabeth [1563-4] for using the trade of a woollen draper not being trained up as an apprentice in the same trade by the space of seven years according to the statute. And for that the jury upon the trial have found and given up a full verdict therein. Ordered that the special verdict be agreed upon and drawn up by the counsel on both sides and that they attend the Judges at the next Assizes that the opinion of the Judges might be had therein. And that afterwards this court will give judgment upon the verdict accordingly.

659. *Inter the inhabitants of Maiden Bradley and Wincanton* [Somerset] *about the settlement of Alice Toogood.* (Recites **626**)
The inhabitants of Wincanton now allege that they were not privy to the making of the order. Now upon further examination thereof and upon hearing of counsel as well on the behalf of the inhabitants of Maiden Bradley it appears that she first lived at Wincanton with her husband and had four children there born. And that in the year 1646 she came to maiden Bradley and lived in William Walter's house when the parish was visited with the sickness where she continued about half a year and Walter warned to remove her by the officers of the parish but by reason the sickness was in the town they did not complain to any justice but as soon as the sickness ceased she was removed to Wincanton and dwelt in Wilton's house where she continued about two years and had a child born and christened there afterwards she came again to Maiden Bradley and got into the house of Mary Stone where so soon as she was known she was warned by the overseers of the parish to rid her away but by reason that Toogood fell dangerously sick she could not be presently removed but so soon as she was in some measure recovered she was removed to Wincanton again. Ordered that

the parishioners of both parishes with their counsel attend the Judges of Assize who are humbly desired by the court to give their opinion upon which parish Toogood and her four children are to be settled.

1651

General Sessions of the Peace held at Salisbury 14 January 1651. William Hussey, Edward Tooker, John Dove, Richard Grobham Howe, Thomas Eyre, Richard Green, Giles Eyre, Walter South, Francis Swanton, Alexander Staples, Barnaby Coles, John Read, Edward Mannings.

660. *Nicholas Thring.*
It appears to the court that the inhabitants of Steeple Langford were indicted at the Christmas Sessions last for not repairing a gate within the tithing and that Nicholas Thring his cattle were distrained for the same and that Thring in appearing to the indictment to the bailiff, repairing the gate and other necessary charges has disbursed the sum of thirty and four shillings which charge ought to be borne by the whole tithing of Langford. Ordered that the churchwardens and overseers of the poor there shall make an indifferent rate throughout the whole tithing for the repaying Thring the sum of four and thirty shillings.

661. *John Ponting pension of £3 6s 8d per annum.*
The court is informed by John Ponting of Warminster tailor that he has served the State as a trooper under the command of Colonel Ludlow and that by reason of many wounds he received in the service he is utterly disabled to get his living (he being a poor man) and having a wife and children and all their maintenance depends upon his labour as by a certificate under the hand of Colonel Ludlow appears. Ordered that the Treasurer for the south shall forthwith pay unto Ponting the sum of forty shillings in regard of his present necessity. The court further allows him yearly a pension three pounds six shillings and eight pence to be paid him quarterly the first payment to begin at our Lady day next and to continue until the court shall see cause to alter the same.

662. *Tobias Blisse and Richard Cater.*
Tobias Blisse and Richard Cater are both committed to the gaol of Fisherton Anger upon the complaint of Jane Cowles for endeavouring the burning of her house. It appears to the court by several certificates that they are honest poor labouring men and never intended the burning the house but only to fire some of the thatch of the house

and put the same forth again for that they suspected Jane Cowles to be a witch. Wherefore the court conceives they are bailable and desires any two justices to take good bail for Blisse and Cater's appearance at the next Assize there to answer the premises.

663. *Edmond Stevens his pension of five marks per annum.*
The court is informed by Edmond Stevens of the city of Salisbury clothier that he has served the State under the command of the Earl of Essex as a conductor in the train of artillery and that by reason of many hardships he received in the service (he being a very aged man) has lost the use of his limbs and eyesight to his great impoverishment as by a certificate under the hand of Colonel Richard Deane appears. Ordered that the Treasurer for the south shall forthwith pay unto Stevens the sum of five marks in regard of his present necessity. And the court further allows him a pension of five marks per annum to be paid quarterly the first payment to begin at our Lady day next and to continue until the court shall see cause to alter the same.

664. *William Moore to erect a cottage.*
The court is informed by William Moore of Winterbourne Dauntsey [Winterbourne] labourer as also by the certificate under the hands of most of the substantial inhabitants of the parish that he is destitute of an habitation both for himself and family and having a brief under the hand and seal of William Bowles gent lord of the manor of Winterbourne for the erecting and building a cottage in some convenient place within the manor. Ordered that Moore shall erect and build him a cottage in some convenient place within the manor for the habitation of himself and family and the cottage shall continue and be a cottage during his lifetime without incurring the forfeitures mentioned in the statute.

665. *Inter Nicholas Aldridge, inhabitants of West Wellow* [now in Hampshire].
The court is informed by the inhabitants of West Wellow that Nicholas Aldridge of the same place has been overseer of the poor there for the space of three years or thereabouts and refuses to yield up his account. The court refers the whole examination of the premises unto Mr Giles Eyre and Mr Barnaby Coles justices who are desired to make such order therein as shall be agreeable to law and justice which order the court confirms.

666. *Jane Houndwell allowed £4.*
The court is informed by Jane Houndwell of Bromham widow that her husband being a trooper in the regiment of Colonel Horton died

in the service of the Parliament and left her in a very sad and miserable condition with a poor infirm child and not above seven pounds to maintain her and her family. Ordered that there shall be the sum of four pounds paid unto Jane out of the money remaining in the hands of Mr George Ivy for her relief and maintenance in regard of her present necessity.

667. *Inter inhabitants of Bapton [Wylye], Codford St Peter.* (See also **695**) The court is informed that Elinor Snowe about midsummer last was entertained by Robert Wansborough of Bapton as a covenanted servant where she continued until about Michaelmas last within which time she was in Wansborough's service begotten with child and so became impotent and is now come to the parish of Codford St Peter. Ordered that Elinor shall be forthwith sent back to Bapton there to remain and be provided for according to law until a better settlement can be proved to the court but the same to be with a salvo iure to the parish of Bapton.

668. *Abraham Hall.*
Abraham Hall master of the house of correction at Devizes has disbursed for the repairing of the house the sum of two and twenty pounds three shillings and eleven pence as by an account in this court appears. And whereas he has received ten pounds for that use, it is therefore now ordered that it shall be referred to Mr Thomas Eyre and Mr Sherston or either of them to examine the bills and to consider thereof and to allow him from the Treasurer of the north as in their or either of their discretions shall think fit.
(See Appendix 2/2 for a detailed account of the expenditure.)

669. *Concerning the settlement of John Phillips and others.*
Upon reading the petition of John Phillips the elder, John Phillips the younger, Edith Willis and others living in certain cottages erected upon the waste ground between Stockton and Codford St Mary near unto Sherrington and Alston Gifford of the parish of Codford St Peter but not owned by any or either of the parishes and being now in want and like to perish desire some relief. The court desires Mr Howe, Mr Mannings and Mr Swanton justices or any two of them to take the pains to view the place where the petitioners live and to inform themselves by examining some ancient and discreet persons to what parish or parishes the petitioners belong and to take such course for their relief as to law and justice shall appertain in regard of their great wants.

670. *Inter inhabitants of Semley and William West.*
The court is informed by the parishioners of Semley that William West of the same place entertains in his house a lewd woman of an ill name and fame and her son, she being called by the name of the widow Ledwyn and West entertains them as his servants and has neglected his own wife who is ready to starve and their usual course has been to wander the country together leaving his poor wife in a very bad condition. Ordered that if the parishioners of Semley take West and the widow Ledwyn any more together then the next justice is desired to send the widow to the house of correction and bind West to the good behaviour and not to be discharged but in open court.

671. *Inter inhabitants of Milton, inhabitants of Collingbourne.* The court is informed by George Annott that he was born bred and served his apprenticeship in the parish of Milton [East Knoyle] and there remained until such time he went into the State's service and after that he served as a covenant servant in Collingbourne and being now married and returned to Milton where he dwelt in a house which Steven Annott his father in law bought for him until such time he was disturbed and put forth of the parish by the inhabitants of Milton and carried him and his wife to Collingbourne where they are also desired to be entertained and notice being given both to the inhabitants of Milton and Collingbourne to appear at this Sessions for the settlement of Annott and his wife and for that the inhabitants of Milton did not appear. Ordered that Annott and his wife shall be settled at Milton for the present until the inhabitants show good cause to the contrary.

672. *Inter Henry Bealing, Henry Foster and inhabitants of Mere.*
The court is informed by Henry Bealing and Henry Foster overseers of the poor of the parish of Mere that in the year 1648 and upon passing their account at Easter according to the custom of the place there remained unto them the sum of four pounds five shillings and four pence as appears upon their account. Ordered that there shall be an equal rate made on the inhabitants of Mere for the repayment of the four pounds five shillings and four pence and all other reasonable charges they have disbursed in procuring of this order which charge ought to be borne by the inhabitants of the whole parish.
(If any refuse to pay, to be bound over.)

673. *Jane Jackman her pension of £4 per annum.*
The court is informed by Jane Jackman of Devizes widow that her husband and family went fourteen years since into Ireland into the city of Cork where he lived in good repute until that unheard of rebellion

broke forth there by reason whereof they were enforced to leave all that they had and to return again into England where they lived at the town of Devizes and being a surgeon dressed many soldiers there wounded under the command of Lord Fairfax and was likewise a surgeon unto that part of the army that lay against Faringdon and that her husband and eldest son went with the Lord General into Ireland where her husband lost his life shortly after the taking of Tredagh [Drogheda]so that she is not able to support herself and family any longer. Ordered that the Treasurer for the north shall upon sight of this order pay unto Jane the sum of four pounds in regard of her present necessity and allows a yearly pension of four pounds to be paid unto her quarterly by the Treasurer for the north.

(In this entry her name appears as Jukeman but it is clearly Jackman in the later entry **690**.)

674. *Inter Robert Morris, Alexander Barrett, John Turner.*
The court is informed by Robert Morris of the parish of Warminster that Alexander Barrett late of the same place assigned over a plot of ground unto Robert Morris towards the keeping of a child of Alexander's and that John Barrett and John Turner of Warminster pretended right to the ground. The court desires Mr Green justice to call Barrett and Turner before them and examine the truth of the petition and to make such order between the parties as he shall think fit.

675. *Alexander Sanders.*
The court is informed by Alexander Sanders of Damerham South [now in Hampshire] that he has served tithingman for the tithing of Northington in the parish of Damerham by the space of one whole year and a quarter and that by the custom he ought to serve but one year. And because the lord of the leet has not kept no court for the manor at Michaelmas last to the great prejudice of Sanders and that by custom Richard Shabeen of the same place ought to serve in his room ever since Michaelmas last and for the year ensuing. Ordered that it shall be referred to the next justice to Northington to examine when Shabeen ought of right to serve in the place of Sanders which if the justice find it of right he ought to serve and refuse to do so, he is desired to bind Shabeen over to the next Quarter Sessions.

676. *Inter Anthony Whatly, inhabitants of Semley.* (Recites **494**)
The court is now informed that the former order took no effect for the provision of Anthony his wife and child. The court therefore refers the same to Mr Walter Southon justice to examine the matter and to do therein according to law and justice.

677. *John Hillgrove to erect a cottage.*
The court is informed by a certificate under the hands of the most substantial inhabitants of the parish of Sedgehill [Sedgehill and Semley] that John Hillgrove of the same place shall erect him a cottage upon the waste ground there near to the church now in the possession of Robert Browne lying in the manor of Mr Thomas Grove lord of the manor of Sedgehill and having got his hand and seal for the erecting the cottage. Ordered that Hillgrove shall erect him a cottage there for his habitation and shall continue the same during his life time without incurring the forfeitures mentioned in the statute.

678. *John Purrier allocated £4 2s for repair of house of correction at Marlborough.*
It appears to the court upon the certificate of William Sadler and Gabriel Marten justices that they have visited the decays of the house of correction near Marlborough and have taken notice of the charge expended on the same for the repair thereof according to an order of Sessions made at Marlborough the first day of October 1650 which charge amounts to the sum of three and twenty pounds nineteen shillings as appears by a bill made thereof and allowed by the justices. Ordered that the Treasurer of the north shall forthwith pay unto Purrier master of the house of correction the sum of four pounds two shillings which he has disbursed towards the reparations of the house of correction.
(See Appendix 2/3 for a detailed account of the expenditure.)

679. *Christopher Blackman to erect a cottage.* (See also **753**)
The court is informed by Christopher Blackman as by a certificate under the hands of most of the substantial inhabitants of the parish of Chicklade that Blackman having erected a cottage upon the waste ground within the manor of John Mervin lord of the manor of Chicklade and having his hand and seal for the continuance of the cottage. Ordered that Blackman shall continue the cottage without incurring the forfeitures mentioned in the statute.

680. *John Knowles allocated £10.*
Whereas Mr John Knowles lieutenant has heretofore had a yearly pension of twenty marks granted him at the Quarter Sessions held at Devizes in the seventh year of the late King's reign [Easter 1631] to be paid him by the Treasurer for the south. Now for that there are so many pensions paid to maimed soldiers within the county by reason of the late wars that the rates of this county will not amount to pay all, which the court taking into consideration does for the reasons aforesaid

revoke the patent so made to Knowles but orders that the Treasurer for the south in lieu thereof and for the present relief of Knowles forthwith pay unto him the sum of ten pounds and that his pension of twenty marks and his patent for pay thereof shall from henceforth cease and be determined.

681.   *Thomas Heyter.*
Thomas Heyter of Wishford yeoman by an order made under the hands of Edward Tooker and Richard Howe justices and by them certified to Marlborough Sessions last was charged to be the reputed father of a base child born on the body of Cutbera Younge of Wishford. And Heyter being bound over to appear at the Sessions to answer the same and entered his appeal from the order whereupon it was then ordered that he should be heard upon his appeal this Sessions. Now upon hearing and examination thereof it appears to the court that Younge delivered of her child within the parish of [Tarrant] Gunville in the county of Dorset and not within this county of Wiltshire so that the justices were not empowered by law to make the order whereupon it was ordered that the order made against Heyter should be null and made void and Heyter to be wholly freed and discharged from the same and that Cutbera forthwith discharged forth of the house of correction. And further that the case concerning the birth of the child should be drawn up and the opinion of the Judges of Assize to be desired therein the next Assizes.

682.   *Potticary and Butcher overseers of the poor of Warminster.* (Recites **533**) Which goods were appraised and sold for the sum of seven pounds and two pence accordingly. And forasmuch as it further appears to the court by the petition of Thomas Potticary and Thomas Butcher that Elye had formerly sold the goods unto Mr Hope who commenced a suit against Potticary and Butcher for the same and recovered by verdict six pounds damages and forty shillings costs so that Potticary and Butcher besides the seven pounds they made of the goods in defending they have disbursed the sum of six pounds eighteen shillings and eight pence. All which the court taking into consideration and conceiving that Potticary and Butcher did do the same on the behalf of the parish in executing of their office as overseers of the poor orders that there shall be an equal and an indifferent rate made upon the whole parish of Warminster for the repaying Potticary and Butcher the sum of six pounds eighteen shillings and eight pence and all other reasonable charges they have been at which rate the court desires the two next justices to confirm.
    (If any refuse to pay, to be bound over.)

General Sessions of the Peace held at Devizes 8 April 1651. Edward Baynton, Francis Swanton, Edward Tooker, William Eyre, Walter South, Thomas Eyre, William Sadler, Gabriel Martin, Richard Green, Edward Stokes, William Shute, John Read.

683. *For viewing the decays of Thomas bridge, Muttons bridge and Harnham bridge.* (See also **704, 731**)
Whereas Thomas bridge, Milford bridge, and Muttons bridge near the city of Salisbury are in great decay for want of reparations and ought to be repaired by the inhabitants of the whole county and forasmuch as the great bridge called Harnham bridge is likewise in great decay for want of reparations and must of necessity be speedily repaired, it not being certainly known who should repair the same. Ordered and desired Edward Tooker, Richard Howe, Giles Eyre, Francis Swanton and Barnaby Coles or any four of them justices to take with them such workmen as they shall think fit and to view the decays of the several bridges and to make an estimate of the charge of the repairing of the bridges and make return thereof under their hands to the next Sessions that a rate may be made for the reparations of the bridges according to the statute in that case made and provided.

684. *Inter inhabitants of Amesbury, Nicholas Harrison.*
The court is informed by Robert Harrison on the behalf of the inhabitants of Amesbury that Nicholas Harrison of the same place has in the time of his constableship received divers sums of money from the parish of Amesbury and has given no account for the same. Ordered Nicholas Harrison shall deliver a true copy of his receipts and disbursements unto the parishioners of Amesbury and attend with his account Mr Tooker, Mr Howe and Mr Swanton or any two of them who are desired to examine the same and to hear what just exceptions the parish can make therein.

685. *Richard Note.*
The court is informed by Richard Note that he was at the last Quarter Sessions chosen constable of the hundred of Alderbury and that he is a very unable man of body to serve in the office being of the age of three score and seventeen years. The court desires the next justice to examine the premises and if it appears unto him to be true then the justice is further desired to send for William Bigges of Porton gent and swear him for the due execution of the office in the place of Note.
    (If he refuses, to be bound over.)

686. *John Whittaker and Phillip Sutton allowed £10 for their loss by fire.* (Refers to **422**. See also **149**, **274**, **396**, **717**)
And whereas at Warminster Sessions there was an order for paying the ten pounds but nothing done concerning the same. The court desires George Ivy to put the same order speedily in execution that Whittaker and Sutton may be paid ten pounds by reason of their great want and necessity.

687. *Abraham Hall.*
Whereas Abraham Hall master of the house of correction at Devizes has disbursed for the repair of the house of correction the sum of twenty two pounds three shillings and eleven pence as by his account thereof appears and has received towards it only the sum of ten pounds. And whereas Mr Thomas Eyre and Mr Sherston justices or one of them were desired to examine Hall's bills of account and to appoint the Treasurer for the north to pay unto him the remainder of his account as by an order in that behalf made at the last Quarter Sessions appears (**668**). And whereas the court is now informed that there is nothing done upon the order and Hall is in great want of his money. The court desires Mr Eyre to take the account of Hall with all convenient speed and examine his bills of account and what moneys he shall find to be due unto him on his account Mr Eyre is desired to appoint the Treasurer for the north forthwith to satisfy the same in regard of his great necessity and the Treasurer is ordered to pay the same accordingly.

688. *Samuel Stile.*
It appears to the court by the complaint of Samuel Stile tithingman of Compton Bassett that he has served the office of tithingmanship by the space of a year and a half and by reason that the leet and lawday there where the tithingman has been usually chosen is not duly kept whereby Stile cannot be discharged from the office and that John Tomkins and Robert Rennolles of Compton Bassett or one of them are fitting men to serve in the office. Ordered that Sir Edward Baynton justice send for Tomkins and Rennolles and swear one of them in the office of tithingman as he shall think fit.
(If they refuse to serve, to be bound over.)

689. *Inter inhabitants of Potterne and Worton and Marston.* (See also **723**)
The court is informed of the multiplicity of poor people in Potterne and of the great charge the inhabitants of that place are at to relieve them and that the inhabitants of the tithings of Worton and Marston within the parish of Potterne refuse to join with the inhabitants of Potterne and other tithings within the same parish for relief of the poor

and prayed the assistance of the court for their order and relief therein. Ordered that the inhabitants of the tithings of Worton and Marston shall forthwith contribute and join in rates with the inhabitants of Potterne and all other tithings within the parish of Potterne and shall likewise join towards the relief of the poor of the parish until they show good cause unto the court to alter the same.

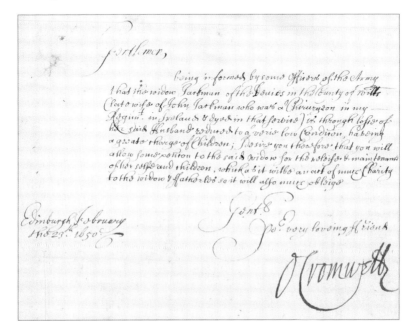

*Cromwell's certificate (WSA, A1/110A/56) referred to in **690**. See also **673**.*

690. *Jane Jackman her pension augmented to £10 per annum.* (Recites **673**)
The court has now received a certificate under the hand of His Excellency the Lord General Cromwell where it appears that John Jackman her late husband was a surgeon in his own regiment in Ireland and died in that service and that Jane through the loss of her husband is reduced into a very low condition having a great charge of children. Ordered that her pension of four pounds per annum shall be augmented and increased to ten pounds per annum to be paid unto her quarterly by the Treasurer for the north, the first payment thereof to begin at midsummer next. And the court further orders that the Treasurer shall forthwith pay unto Jane besides her pension the sum of four pounds upon sight of this order in regard of her present necessity.

691.   *Thomas Merreweather.*
Upon reading a certificate under the hands of the minister churchwardens and overseers of the poor of the parish of Bishops Cannings and divers other inhabitants of the parish that the house wherein Thomas Ruddle lately dwelt in the tithing of Wick in the parish of Bishops Cannings is a very fit tenement to make a common victualling house for the entertainment of travellers. Ordered upon the petition of Thomas Merreweather that he now being to go to live in the house shall keep and is allowed to keep a common victualling house there according to the statute in that case made and provided and to continue the same for one whole year now next ensuing unless the court shall see cause to alter the same.

692.   *Robert Newman.*
Whereas Robert Newman of St Saviours in the borough of Southwark in the county of Surrey shoemaker was bound over to this Quarter Sessions being ordered and adjudged to be the reputed father of a bastard child born of the body of Elianor Lester and being now called has not appeared to answer the same but has made default and forfeited his recognisances and the child remains still chargeable to the parish of Swindon where it was born. The court humbly desires the Right Honourable the Lord Chief Justice of the Upper Bench to be pleased to grant his warrant for the apprehending and taking of Newman and binding of him over with very good sureties to appear at the next Quarter Sessions after his apprehension there to answer the offence and stand to and perform the order of the court in that behalf made.

693.   *40s allocated inhabitants of Mere towards the relieving of Smith.*
(Recites **624**. See also **758, 794, 842**)
The inhabitants finding the sum to be very burdensome to them and are not able to bear the sum any longer without some relief. Ordered that the overseers of the poor of the parish shall be allowed forty shillings towards the relieving of Smith for the time being to be paid by the Treasurer for the south immediately upon receipt hereof.

694.   *Inhabitants of Chiseldon.*
There are some differences between the inhabitants of Chiseldon concerning the reparations of the church and the rates thereof. Ordered that the churchwardens of Chiseldon deliver a copy of their rates unto Mr Calley there and make their account of their disbursements to the parish. And then the court desires the two next justices to grant a warrant to distrain those who shall refuse to make payment of their rates.

(The petition explained that about a year before a public meeting had agreed to repair the church and to move the pulpit to the middle of the church. The repairs went ahead but they deferred moving the pulpit. But Mr Calley and some others refused to pay the rate. A1/110/1651E)

695. *Inter inhabitants of Bapton* [Wylye] *and Codford.* (Refers to **667**) It appears to the court upon reading of an order made at the Quarter Sessions held at Salisbury the fourth day of January last past between the inhabitants of Codford and Bapton concerning the settlement of Elianor Snowe and upon full hearing of counsel learned on both sides at this present Sessions. Ordered that Elianor Snowe shall be forthwith sent to Bapton there to remain and be provided for according to law but with a salvo iure to the parish of Bapton in case they can provide any further testimony on the behalf of the parish for the future.

696. *Inter inhabitants of Latton, Richard Ferribee.* (See also **744**) The court is informed that Richard Ferribee of Latton is now erecting a cottage in Latton not having four acres of land thereunto according to the statute in that case made and provided requires. Ordered that the churchwardens and overseers of the poor of Latton shall forthwith forbid Ferribee to forbear to proceed any further in erecting the cottage until he has got a licence for it under the hand and seal of the lord of the manor and the court has granted him an order for the doing thereof as Ferribee will answer the contrary at his peril.

697. *Thomas Benger.* The court is informed by Thomas Benger of Manningford Bruce [Manningford] that he has served in the office of tithingman at Manningford by the space of eight years there having been no court kept there by reason the lord of the manor is not of age and that by custom there used Frances Webb of the same place ought to serve as tithingman for the tithing in the place of Benger. The court desires Mr William Sadler justice to send for Webb and examine the premises and if he ought to serve in the office then to swear him for the due execution thereof.

698. *John Cole and inhabitants of Bratton.* It appears to the court by the petition of John Cole of Bratton that the inhabitants of Bratton were three several times presented for decay of divers highways within the parish and that Cole his cattle were distrained for the same who has now appeared to the presentments and disbursed for a fine fees and other necessary charges the sum of two pounds nine shillings and a penny in prosecution thereof which charges ought not to be borne wholly by Cole but by the whole parish

of Bratton. Ordered that there shall be an equal and an indifferent rate made upon all the inhabitants of Bratton for the repaying Cole the sum of two pounds nine shillings and a penny.
(If any refuse to pay, to be bound over.)

699. *Inhabitants of Maiden Bradley and Wincanton* [Somerset]. (Refers to **626**)
And for that it now appears that the Judges were not attended the last Assizes but that it was agreed by George Winding one of the parishioners and overseers of the poor of Wincanton on behalf of the parish and Alexander Reddish one of the overseers of the poor of Maiden Bradley on behalf of the parish that both parishes should attend the present Easter Sessions with their witnesses that a final order be made therein and that in the meantime Toogood to continue at Wincanton according to the order made at the Midsummer Sessions last. And now for that the parishioners of Maiden Bradley with their witnesses attended at the present Sessions and that none appeared on the behalf of the parish of Wincanton. Ordered that Toogood and her children shall remain at Wincanton according to the former order and further ordered that if the parish of Maiden Bradley shall be any more troubled by the parish of Wincanton about the settlement of Toogood that the parish of Wincanton shall pay to the parish of Maiden Bradley the sum of three pounds six shillings and eight pence towards their expenses before they be further heard therein.

700. At this present Sessions are appointed and chosen to be Treasurer for the relief of maimed soldiers and mariners within this county for the year following: For the north Henry Blake of Pinnells [Calne Without], for the south Roger Langly of Harnham gent.

701. It is ordered that the rates for the relief of maimed soldiers and mariners in pursuance of several ordinances of Parliament late made for that purpose shall remain in every parish so that there may be levied and paid weekly upon every parish [blank] pence and no more to continue and begin from the time of the present Sessions and shall be collected and paid yearly to the Treasurer appointed for maimed soldiers and mariners according to the statute made 43 Elizabeth.

702. And for the relief of prisoners of the Upper Bench and Marshalsea and of such hospitals and almshouses as are within the county are appointed and chosen to be Treasurers. For the north, Gabriel Goldney of Chippenham gent, [for the south] Randolph Dominick of East Knoyle gent.

703. (See also **424, 537, 576**)
And forasmuch as it now appears unto the court that Richard Rickards of East Knoyle (for whose relief the inhabitants were at first rated to pay towards the relief of the poor of East Knoyle) is lately deceased and thereupon prayed the court that the payment might cease and the inhabitants discharged thereof. Ordered that the payment of the rate of twelve [pence] the week shall cease and be no further paid but to the death of Rickards.

General Sessions of the Peace held at Warminster on Monday 7 July 1651. William Hussey, Richard Grobham Howe, Nicholas Green, Walter South

704. *Mr Edward Tooker and 3 other justices to view Thomas, Milford and Muttons bridges and certify.* (Recites **683**. See also **731, 843**)
The charge thereof will amount unto the sum of two hundred and fifty pounds and that they have taken course for a new building of Muttons bridge (being fallen down) and have disbursed some moneys already therein. Ordered Mr George Ivy to pay unto the Clerk of the Peace the sum of seventy pounds forth of such moneys as are in his hands to be disposed of as the justices shall appoint. And that the same shall be repaid again into the court when the rates are made and collected for the repair of bridges. Also desired the justices to make an equal rate or tax over all the county to raise the sum of two hundred and fifty pounds as to grant forth warrants for the speedy collecting the same according to the statute in that case made and provided which the court will confirm accordingly.

705. *For levying the arrears of maimed soldiers, etc.*
Forasmuch as Mr George Ivy and Mr Swanton were both desired by the court to find out the arrears of maimed soldiers, etc. (to wit Mr Ivy for the north part and Mr Swanton for the south part) who have taken great pains therein and for that it appears that there is still remaining in arrears much moneys within the county. Ordered that Mr William Shute do join in the assisting of Mr Ivy and Mr Edward Tooker do likewise join in the assisting of Mr Swanton who are all desired that they join together in getting in the arrears both in the north and south part of the county with what speed they may and that they may make return thereof to the court that the same may be disposed of for the use of the county. And the court desires all the justices in their several divisions to be aiding and assisting in getting in the arrears.

706. *For repayment of moneys disbursed by the Clerk of the Peace.*
It appears to the court by an order made by the Judges of Assizes that
the Clerk of the Peace was required to sue forth several commissions
for charitable uses within this county and the county of Dorset for
the inquiring forth of lands and other things given for the repair of
Harnham bridge and other bridges and charitable uses in this county
and also for a commission of sewers in this county which several
commissions were to be borne at the charge of the county. And
whereas the Clerk of the Peace was likewise commanded by the court
to prosecute and solicit two several informations in the Crown Office
against the inhabitants of Milford and Salisbury about the reparations
of Muttons and Milford bridges and for the retaining of counsel and
procuring evidence at the trial, the charge whereof comes to twenty
three pounds and ten shillings as appears to the court. Ordered that
the said £23 10s be forthwith paid out of such moneys of the county
as remain in Mr Ivy's hands who is desired to pay the same accordingly.

707. *Little Langford* [Steeple Langford]*and Fisherton Anger.* (Refers
to **472**. See also **765**)
It was formerly ordered by the court that the inhabitants of Little
Langford should pay unto the overseers of the poor of Fisherton Anger
the sum of five shillings a month towards the relief of the poor within
the parish of Fisherton. And forasmuch as Mr Stourton Sadler has
now moved the court for the revoking of the order and has alleged
good reasons for the same. Ordered that the inhabitants of Langford
shall pay all the arrears due upon the order until this Sessions unto the
overseers of the poor of Fisherton and for the future the order shall
be made null and vacated and the inhabitants of Langford discharged
from paying the five shillings a month unless the court shall see cause
to alter the same.

708. The court is informed that Simon Sergent of Ebbesbourne
Wake is a poor aged man and destitute of a house and habitation for
himself and family and having a licence under the hand and seal of
John Boddenham lord of the manor of Ebbesbourne for the erecting
and building of a cottage within the manor and prayed the court for
the confirmation of the same. Ordered that Sergent shall erect and
build him a cottage in some convenient place of the waste of the manor
for the habitation of himself and family during his life time without
incurring the forfeitures mentioned in the statute.

709. *Amesbury hundred.* (Refers to **536**. See also **729, 788**)
The inhabitants of the east part of Amesbury hundred have shown to

the court that they are much burdened and over rated by the western inhabitants of the hundred and have desired to be relieved therein. Ordered that notice be given by the petitioners to the constables of the western part of Amesbury hundred that the inhabitants of the western part or some of them appear at the next Quarters Sessions at Marlborough where the court will hear the differences and settle the same according to equity and justice. And a copy of this order be left with the constable of the western part of the hundred who is to acquaint the inhabitants thereof and that some of the eastern part of the hundred also appear at the Sessions accordingly.

710. *Edington.* (Refers to **620**)
The court is informed that William Tubb did heretofore give to and for the use and benefit of the poor of the parish of Edington the sum of fifty pounds which by order of the court was heretofore invested in the disposal of certain trustees and the greater part of those trustees now disclaim the trust and refuse to intermeddle therein. Ordered that the churchwardens and overseers of the poor of Edington for the time being shall from time to time have the disposal of the fifty pounds and the benefit and profits thereof for the good and benefit of the poor of the parish and make their accounts yearly to the parishioners of Edington for the same.

711. *Inhabitants of Stapleford about Heyter's child.* (See also **741**)
The court is informed by the inhabitants of Stapleford that about a year since John Heyter came with his wife and children into the parish of Stapleford where the rented a house having then a competent estate. But since having idly consumed the same is gone away with his wife and has left three small children upon the charge of the parish who have already relieved them these twelve weeks and that the grandfather and grandmother of the children have a stock of money consisting of eight hundred pounds and upwards and that Mr George Mervin of Pertwood pays an annuity to the grandfather forth of the same. Ordered that Mr Mervin being the great grandfather to the children shall take the children from the parish and keep and relieve them deducting three shillings a week out of the grandfather's annuity which is to be paid to him by Mr Mervin until the court shall see cause to alter the same.

712. *Lucas and Parsons.*
The court is informed by Thomas Lucas of North Bradley that Thomas Parsons the younger of Potterne impleaded him in the county court and caused an action to be entered and a distringas to be returned into the court without giving notice to Lucas or to his attorney Mr

Annyatt and entered a judgment when he was never served with any distringas nor gave any warrant to parsons to cast any essoin into the court for him and that Parsons has levied upon Lucas the sum of nine and forty shillings and three pence besides the chasing of his cattle. The court desires Mr Swanton justice to examine the same and mediate the business between the parties accordingly.

713. *Carroway widow 40s.*
The court is informed by Alice Carroway widow that her husband was hanged at Woodhouse [Horningsham] for his good service to the State. The court (upon her promise she will not trouble the country any more for relief) allows Alice the sum of forty shillings to be paid her by the Treasurer for the north.
(See also **528** and **622**)

714. *Abraham Hall master of the house of correction at Devizes.*
The court is informed by a certificate under the hand of Thomas Eyre justice that there was fourteen pounds seventeen shillings and a penny unto Abraham Hall master of he house of correction at Devizes being the remainder of four and twenty pounds seventeen shillings and a penny by him already laid out towards the repair of the house of correction there. And Mr Eyre by his order of the twelfth day of April 1651 did order and appoint the Treasurer for the north for the year last past to pay the fourteen pounds seventeen shillings and a penny to Hall of which sum Hall has received of him but seven pounds and the residue thereof as yet is not satisfied and paid unto Hall according to the order as Hall informs the court and prayed the assistance of the court that he may be satisfied the same moneys. Ordered the Treasurer to satisfy and pay the remainder of the fourteen pounds seventeen shillings and a penny to Hall forthwith upon sight of this order in regard of his great necessity.

715. *Thomas Parsons bailiff of Potterne and Cannings.*
The court is informed by Thomas Parsons bailiff to Robert Henly lord of the hundred of Potterne and Cannings that about two months since a stranger lodging within the hundred and having a little grey nag was taken upon suspicion of felony and carried before Mr William Eyre and thereupon was committed to the house of correction at Devizes and that Parsons seized upon the nag as felon's good on the behalf of Henly. Ordered that Parsons shall detain and keep the nag in his custody until he shall be otherwise ordered by the court.

716. *John Oakeford.*
The court is informed by John Oakeford of the parish of Heytesbury that the inhabitants there were two several times presented for decay of highways within the parish for which presentments the goods of Oakeford were distrained and has appeared to the same on the behalf of the inhabitants and has disbursed for fees and other charges the sum of seven and twenty shillings and eight pence which charge ought to be borne by the whole inhabitants of Heytesbury. Ordered that there shall be an equal and an indifferent rate made throughout the whole parish of Heytesbury for the collecting and paying Oakeford the sum of seven and twenty shillings and eight pence.
(If any refuse to pay, to be bound over.)

717. *Whittaker and Sutton.* (Refers to **686**. See also **149, 396, 686**)
The court is informed that Mr Ivy by virtue of a former order of the court has paid three pounds unto Mr John Iles mayor of Devizes to the use of John Whittaker and Phillip Sutton two of the inhabitants of Devizes towards the repair of their losses by fire and that he will be ready to pay seven pounds more to Mr Iles being residue of ten pounds formerly allowed to Whittaker and Sutton towards the repair of their losses out of the county's money remaining in his hands. The court desires Mr Ivy to pay the seven pounds unto Iles with all convenient speed that the moneys may be disposed of according to the former orders of the court in that behalf made.

718. *William Game overseer of the highways of Bishops Cannings.*
The court is informed by William Game one of the overseers of the highways of the parish of Bishops Cannings that the inhabitants of Southbroom were presented for decay of a highway within the parish of Bishops Cannings who have now appeared to the same. Ordered that the Clerk of the Peace shall not estreat any more issues returned by the Sheriff against the inhabitants in regard they have appeared to the presentment and made oath that the way is amended. The court is further informed that there is a rate made for the reparations of the highways in regard the statute service will not sufficiently repair the same and that there are some men who have means in the parish that do not pay there. The court desires the two next justices to confirm the rate.
(If any refuse to pay, to be bound over.)

719. *Edward Farleigh for a cottage.*
The court is informed by Edward Farleigh of Heytesbury that he is destitute of a habitation for himself and family and having a licence under the hand and seal of Edward Ash lord of the manor of Heytesbury

for the erecting and building of a cottage in some convenient place within the manor where Mr Thomas Carter the lord's steward shall appoint. Ordered that Farleigh shall erect and build him a cottage in some convenient place within the manor for the habitation of himself and family and the cottage shall continue and be a cottage during his life time without incurring the forfeitures of the statute.

720.   *William Singer.*
The court is informed by Andrew Whatly tithingman of Horningsham in the hundred of Heytesbury that Thomas Stile being elected constable of Horningsham for this year 1651 beginning at Our Lady day last is now deceased. Ordered that William Singer of Horningsham shall be elected constable in the place of Stile. Further ordered that Stile shall within one week next after receipt hereof repair to some justice there to take his oath for the due execution of the office upon pain of ten pounds.
(If he refuses, to be bound over.)

721.   *John Adely and inhabitants of Semley.*
The court is informed by John Adely of Semley that the inhabitants of Semley were two several times presented and once indicted for the decay of divers highways in the parish to which presentments and indictment Adely has appeared on the behalf of the parish and disbursed for fees and other charges the sum of five and forty shillings which charge ought to be borne by the whole parish of Semley. Ordered that there shall be an equal and an indifferent rate made throughout the whole parish of Semley for the repaying Adely the sum of five and forty shillings.
(If any refuse to pay, to be bound over.)

722.   *Anne Willis.*
The court is informed by Anne Willis that about Christmas last she was received as a covenant servant with John Locke of Wylye for one whole year then next following in which service she was begotten with child by Edward Channell for which Locke turned her forth of her service before the year was expired and being now destitute of an habitation and place of abode. Ordered that Anne shall be sent to Locke her master there to remain as a servant until her year shall be expired and the court sees cause otherwise to alter the same.
(A later petition reported that John Locke had refused to obey the order. The inhabitants of Hindon, where Anne then was, wanted the inhabitants of Wylye to be responsible for her as that was where her 'misdemeanour' had been committed. A1/110/1651M/211)

723. *Inhabitants of Potterne and Marston.* (Recites **689**)
Ordered that the tithing of Marston and Worton shall join promiscuously with Potterne and the rest of the tenements there in rates towards the relief of the poor within the parish until the court sees good cause to alter the same.

724. *Henry Keeble for a cottage.*
The court is informed by Henry Keble of Great Durnford labourer that he his wife and children for divers years last past have been inhabitants within the parish of Great Durnford but now are destitute of a house wherein to work and whereby they might be enabled by their honest labour to get their livelihood by reason of the great scarcity of houses in that place for labouring people and whereas Keeble has obtained a licence under the hand and seal of Robert Hide lord of the manor or farm of Great Durnford to erect and build one cottage for his habitation and dwelling in and upon some convenient place of his waste ground called Hutchins Green lying near Pryors Croft belonging to his manor or farm of Great Durnford so as the cottage be allowed by order of the court according to the statute in such case made and provided. Ordered that Keeble shall and may erect and build a cottage on some part of the waste ground for his habitation and dwelling and that the cottage shall remain and be a cottage for his habitation and dwelling for the term of his life and his wife's without incurring the forfeitures mentioned in the statute.

725. *Robert Babb minister of Inglesham.*
At the Quarter Sessions held at Warminster the seventh day of July 1651 it appears to the court as well by the petition and complaint of Robert Babb minister of Inglesham lying part within this county and part within the county of Berkshire as also by an order of Sessions held for the county of Berkshire the 8th day of April last that there are differences and dislikes betwixt Babb and Mary Pound who is bound an apprentice to Babb. And for that it appears by the order made in Berkshire that Babb is discharged of his apprentice now we whose names are hereunder written justices (where one of us is of the quorum) being present at the Sessions for some causes now shown unto us and considering the order do free and discharge Babb from Mary Pound and likewise free and discharge Pound from Babb and from her apprenticeship.

726. *Abraham Hall.* (See also **226**, **592**, **800**, **823**)
Abraham Hall master of the house of correction at Devizes has made his complaint to the court that James Stoakes late one of the overseers

of the poor of Seend detains in his hands the sum of four and twenty shillings which should have been paid to Hall for the keeping and relieving of a bastard child of Elizabeth Somner whilst she was prisoner in the house of correction. The court thinks fit that Stoakes shall forthwith pay him the moneys or show good cause unto the court at the next Quarter Sessions why he does not pay the same.

727.   *Inter Brookeman and Longe.*
Upon examination of the matter in difference between John Brookeman of Warminster and George Longe of the same it appeared unto the court that there is twenty shillings due from Longe to Brookeman which twenty shillings Longe promised to pay in court unto him as follows that is to say ten shillings on the next Saturday and ten shillings on the Saturday following which payment the court orders accordingly. Further ordered that if Longe shall make default of payment thereof then the constables of Warminster are hereby required to apprehend Longe without delay and bring him before the next justice to be bound over to the next Quarter Sessions there to answer his contempt therein.
(The petition explained that about six years ago Long had forcibly evicted Brookeman's wife and pulled the house down. He later agreed to pay compensation of 20s. A1/110/1651T/116)

728.   *John Turner's alehouse suppressed.*
It appears to the court by the presentment of the Grand Inquest of the county and by a certificate under the hands of the minister and chiefest inhabitants of Codford St Peter that John Turner has lately set up an alehouse within the parish where there was never one formerly kept and has no convenient rooms to lodge and entertain travellers and is like to be a nursery for all manner of vice and wickedness and prayed the court that the alehouse might be suppressed. Ordered that the alehouse shall be forthwith suppressed and is by this order to stand suppressed until the court shall otherwise order the same.

General Sessions of the Peace held at Marlborough 7 October 1651. Alexander Staples, William Eyre, William Sadler, Francis Swanton, Gabriel Martin, William Duckett, Edward Stokes, Walter South.

729.   *Inter the east and west part of Amesbury hundred.*   (See also **536**, **709**, **788**)
Ordered that the inhabitants both of the east and west part of the

hundred of Amesbury shall attend at the next Quarter Sessions to be held at Devizes with their several witnesses and that then the court will hear and examine the same and make a final order therein. And in the meantime the rates of the hundred are continued as they now are until it is further heard and settled by the court.

730. *Cricklade inhabitants.*
The court is informed by the inhabitants of the parish of Cricklade St Mary by former orders of the court the farm of Water Eaton was assigned to pay the sum of eight pounds thirteen shillings and four pence yearly towards the relief of the poor of Cricklade St Mary in regard the parish were not able to maintain them in the parish being of so small a value that it amounts not to above £100 per annum since which time the poor have been and are increased to the double for that they have been and are enforced to double their rates but have not power to impose any further rate or tax on the farm and prayed the assistance of the court for their relief therein. Ordered that the farm shall form henceforth pay six shillings by the week for the relief of the poor of Cricklade St Mary the same payment to continue until the court see cause to alter the same.

731. *Bridge money for the north part to be paid to Mr Parker and Dyaper* (Refers to **704**. See also **843**)
Whereas a general rate was made at the last Sessions held at Warminster for the raising of £250 upon the county and that the same should be paid into the Clerk of the Peace. Now for that it will be a great trouble for the constables of the hundreds of the north part of the county to travel to Salisbury to the Clerk of the Peace there. Ordered that all the constables for the north shall pay in their rates imposed on their several hundreds unto Mr Thomas Parker of Leigh and Mr John Dyaper of South Marston who are desired to receive the same any other direction contained in the constables warrant notwithstanding.

732. *Surveyors for Thomas, Milford and Muttons bridges* [Salisbury]. (Recites **704**)
The court appoints George Marshall of Milford, Christopher Batt of Salisbury, William Bragge of Ford and Roger Langly of West Harnham being of the south part of the county and John Merreweather of Market Lavington, John Dyaper of Marston, Thomas Packer of Leigh and William Bayden of Fifield being of the north part of the county or two of them at the least to be surveyors to look to the reparations of the bridges and to give an account thereof unto the court according to the statute in that case made and provided.

733. *Castle Eaton to contribute to the relief of the poor Highworth.*
The court is informed by William Brookeman, Toby Betterton, Richard Corton and other inhabitants of the parish of Highworth that the poor of the parish are very numerous insomuch that the inhabitants are unable to relieve them and that the parish of Castle Eaton in the same hundred and near adjacent to Highworth has but few poor in it that need relief. The court has referred the premises contained in the petition unto Robert Jenner, William Sadler and Gabriel Marten or to any two of them desiring them to call the parties concerned before them who are desired upon hearing thereof to make such order therein as shall be agreeable to law and justice.

734. *Inter Chiseldon inhabitants and Hall.* (See also **945**)
It is ordered that the overseers of the poor of Chiseldon shall pay unto Abraham Hall master of the house of correction at Devizes the sum of fifteen shillings for the keeping and relieving of Roger Ducock a distracted man of that parish formerly committed to his custody for and during the time he remained in the house of correction which was for fifteen weeks as the court is now informed.
(If they refuse to pay, to be bound over.)

735. *Winterbourne to contribute to relief of the poor of Lyneham.*
The court is informed that there are such a multiplicity of poor people in the parish of Lyneham that the inhabitants there are not able to relieve them and prayed the court that the parish of Winterbourne Bassett wherein are very few or no poor people may be joined with them for the relief of the poor of Lyneham. Ordered the inhabitants of the parish of Winterbourne Bassett to pay weekly to the overseers of the poor of Lyneham for the relief of the poor the sum of two shillings and six pence and the same rate is to continue unless the inhabitants of Winterbourne Bassett shall at the next Quarter Sessions show good cause to alter the same and the overseers of the poor of Lyneham are forthwith to acquaint the churchwardens or overseers of the poor of Winterbourne Bassett with this order and leave them a copy thereof.

736. *Richard Durran surveyor of the highways of Brinkworth.*
It appears to the court that Richard Durran one of the surveyors of the highways of the parish of Brinkworth has disbursed and laid forth several sums of money for the repairing of the highways within the parish. It also appears there was a rate made for the reparations thereof (there being no ploughs or materials within the parish but what they provide and buy for money). And that divers of the inhabitants are behind in their rates. The court desires the next justice to bind over

to the next Sessions all such as do or shall refuse to pay their rates allegedly made or which shall hereafter be made for the reparations of the highway within the parish of Brinkworth there to answer their contempt therein.

737. *£10 to Brewer and Hicks for fire.*
The court is informed by William Brewer and Samuel Hicks inhabitants of the parish of Bromham that on the thirteenth day of July last there happened in the house of William Brewer a sudden fire which in short time consumed both their houses and that the value of the loss they sustained thereby amounts to the sum of one hundred pounds or thereabouts to their utter undoing as appears by a certificate under the hands of the chiefest inhabitants of the parish. Ordered that there shall be the sum of ten pounds paid unto them out of the moneys remaining in the hands of Mr George Ivy in regard of their great necessity.

738. *Inhabitants of Hilperton.* (See also **802, 819**)
The court is informed by the inhabitants of Hilperton that Ellis Whatley of the same parish and Anne his wife being fallen into poverty and have relief there and that he has a son named John Whatley living in the same parish being a man of sufficiency and ability to relieve his father and mother according to the statute in that case made and provided. Ordered Mr William Eyre and Mr Nicholas Green justices or one of them to examine the truth of the matter and if they see cause that John Whatley the son be of ability to maintain his father and mother then the justices are desired to ease the parish of Hilperton and to do therein according to law and justice.

739. *John Galloway.* (See also **821**)
The court is informed by William Pullen of Castle Combe that his daughter Sarah is married to Richard Galloway and has a child by him and is since departed from her and that John Galloway of Corsham grandfather to the child is sufficient man to relieve the same. Ordered that John Galloway shall pay unto Sarah his daughter in law the sum of two shillings a week towards the keeping and relieving of her and the child to begin from the present Sessions and to continue till the child be weaned and then John is to take the child and keep if he will or continue the payment of two shillings a week and Sarah shall continue and be settled at Corsham where she now lives unless the court see cause to alter the same.

740. *Inter Butcher and Yewen.*
Complaint has been made to the court by Humfry Butcher of

Tockenham Wick [Tockenham] that William Yewen, Robert Balle, Francis Browne and Gabriel Woolley as the Sheriff's bailiffs have levied the sum of twelve pounds upon the goods of Butcher. Ordered that Yewen and the rest of the bailiffs detain the moneys in their hands until the next Sessions and then to show to the court by what warrant they have for levying the said moneys.

741. *Inter Mervin and the inhabitants of Stapleford.* (Recites **711**)
Now upon hearing Mr Mervin who alleges that he as great grandfather is not chargeable by law to the relief of the children and that he is chargeable to pay the full annuity to the grandfather.   Ordered that the children shall be returned back to Stapleford to be provided for by the churchwardens and overseers of the poor of that parish and that John Heyter the grandfather shall pay unto them three shillings a week towards their maintenance. And that if Heyter the grandfather shall not pay the three shillings a week upon demand that Mr Mervin shall pay the three shillings a week and deduct the same forth of the grandfather's annuity and the grandfather shall make allowance thereof accordingly.

742. *Inter the inhabitants of Calne and Bremhill.* (See also **761**, **767**)
Upon hearing of the matter in difference between the inhabitants of Calne and the inhabitants of Bremhill concerning the settlement of Edith Hazell who as yet remains in the custody of the gaoler of the county she being a distracted woman. Ordered that she shall remain in the gaol where she now is and that the inhabitants of Calne shall pay unto the gaoler the sum of three shillings a week for every week since the last Assizes for her relief and keeping of her and the overseers of the poor of Calne are to give notice to the inhabitants of Bremhill that the matter concerning her settlement shall be heard at the next Sessions that they come provided with their witnesses to prove her settlement at Calne if they can and in case they shall fail therein then they are to pay unto the inhabitants of Calne all such moneys as they shall disburse for the keeping of her till the next Sessions.
    (This entry gives her name as Hoyle but it is clear from **761** that it should be Hazell.)

743. *Castle Combe inhabitants.*
The court is informed by John Morris one of the overseers of the poor of the parish of Castle Combe that Hester the wife of Thomas Humfryes has lately intruded herself into the parish and is likely to come chargeable to them and that Mr Ivy and Mr Shute justices have formerly made their warrant for sending her to Colerne where her

husband then lived who was sent accordingly both she and her husband are both come into the parish of Castle Combe. Ordered that the overseers of the poor of Castle Combe and Colerne shall attend the justices at the next meeting and petty sessions at Chippenham who are desired to examine the truth of the difference and settle Thomas Humfyres and his wife according to law and justice.

744. *Richard Ferribee for a cottage.* (Refers to **696**)
The court is informed by Richard Ferribee of Latton blacksmith that he is a very poor man and destitute of a house and habitation for himself and family and having a licence under the hand and seal of the lord of the manor for the erecting the same upon a certain plot of ground near the Church house. Ordered that Ferribee shall erect and build him a house there for the habitation of himself and family during his life without incurring the forfeitures mentioned in the statute.

(His petition explained that he had kept a workshop in Latton for 16 years but lately the owner of the house in which he lived had sold it to someone else and he had been left homeless. A1/110/1651M/180)

745. *Blackland inhabitants.*
The court is informed by the inhabitants of Blackland that the inhabitants were twice presented for the decay of divers highways there to which presentments John Wheeler has now appeared and disbursed for the inhabitants for fees a fine and other necessary charges the sum of three and fifty shillings which charge ought to be borne by all the inhabitants of Blackland. Ordered that there shall be an equal and an indifferent rate made upon all the inhabitants of Blackland for the repaying Wheeler the sum of three and fifty shillings.
(If any refuse to pay, to be bound over.)

746. *Wroughton tithing.*
It appears to the court that the inhabitants of the tithing of Wroughton were presented for the decay of the stocks within the tithing to which presentment William Sewell [recte Seymour] of the same place has appeared and disbursed for fees a fine and other necessary charges the sum of six and twenty shillings which charge ought to be borne by the whole tithing of Wroughton. Ordered that there shall be an equal and an indifferent rate made upon the whole tithing of Wroughton for the repaying William Seymour the sum of six and twenty shillings. And the court desires William Sadler justice to confirm the rate.
(If any refuse to pay, to be bound over.)
(Sewell is probably a mistake and the correct name is more likely to be

Seymour. There are no wills for this period for anyone called Sewell but there are wills dated 1666 and 1684 for a William Seymour, yeoman)

1652

General Sessions of the Peace held at Salisbury 13 January 1652. Alexander Staples, Edward Tooker, John Dove, Giles Eyre, Barnaby Coles, Walter South, Francis Swanton, Edward Manning.

747. *Martha Birch.*
The court is informed by Martha Birch of the city of Salisbury widow that her late [husband] Daniel Birch served the Parliament in the late wars under the command of Colonel Tomplinson in which service Birch lost his life as by a certificate under the hands of John Dove and Thomas Keynton gent late mayor of the city and divers others appear by reason thereof Martha is fallen into great poverty. Ordered Martha a pension of four pounds and ten shillings a year to be paid unto her quarterly by the Treasurer for the south the first payment to begin at Our Lady day next and to continue until the court shall see cause to alter the same.

748. *Moore discharged of an order for a bastard.*
It appears by an order returned into the court this Sessions under the hands and seals of Edward Tooker and Francis Swanton justices that Gabriel Moore of Wilton is the reputed father of a bastard child born on the body of Joan Babbington who has now appealed from the order according to the statute in that case made and provided. Now the court upon examination of witnesses on both sides adjudge Moore not to be the reputed father of the bastard child and therefore vacate the order and wholly discharge Moore from every clause therein contained and expressed.

749. *Inhabitants of Dinton concerning rates and payments.*
Upon information given to the court that divers sums of money have been heretofore given and bequeathed by several persons for and towards the binding forth apprentices, relief of the poor and other charitable uses within the parish of Dinton which sums remain in the hands of divers inhabitants of the parish without any bond or security given or entered into for the same, whereby the sums are or may be in danger to be lost. And that several sums of money collected and gathered by the several tithingmen of and within the parish from the

inhabitants thereof for contribution and other public payments within these seven years last past, remain in the hands of the late tithingmen being an overplus or surplussage of the rates and payments undisposed and unpaid by the tithingmen to the uses for which the sums were gathered. Ordered that the examination of the premisses be referred unto Robert Hide sergeant at law, John Penruddock, Steven Bowman, Richard South, John Lowe gent and John King yeoman or any three of more of them. And Hide, etc are desired to call the several persons and late tithingmen (in whose hands any of the sums of money remain) before them and to take just and due account from them of the several sums of money remaining in their several hands and to cause them to give very good security unto the parish for the moneys or otherwise forthwith to deliver the several sums of money into the hands of such persons as the referees shall think fit upon such security as they shall allow to be disposed and employed for the uses for which the same were given and other public charges of the parish. And if any of the parties in whose hands any of the sums of money remain shall refuse or neglect to perform and observe such order or rule in or touching the premises as the referees shall make and agree upon then the referees are desired to give notice or information thereof unto some justice who is hereby desired to bind over the party or parties for refusing or neglecting to perform and observe such order or rule unto the next Quarter Sessions.

750. *Mary Olden's pension of 53s 4d.*
The court is informed by Mary Olden of Maiden Bradley widow that Nicholas Olden her late husband served the Parliament as a trooper under the command of Colonel Edmond Ludlow and went with him into Ireland where he lost his life in the service (as by a certificate under the hand of Colonel Ludlow appears) by reason thereof Mary is fallen into great poverty. Ordered and allowed Mary Olden a pension of three and fifty shillings and four pence a year to be paid unto her quarterly by the Treasurer for the south the first payment to begin at Our Lady day next and to continue until the court shall see cause to alter the same.

751 *A bridge called Foot bridge in Lacock in decay.* (See also **905**)
Complaint has been made at this Sessions that a common bridge called Foot bridge in or near Lacock is in great decay for want of reparation and ought to be repaired by the inhabitants of the whole county as it is informed. The court desires that Sir Edward Baynton, William Eyre, George Ivy, Edward Stoakes, William Duckett, Nicholas Green, Edward Michell and William Shute justices or any four of them

whereof one to be of the quorum to call before them such workmen and others as they think fit to view the decays of the bridge and make an estimate of the charge for the repair thereof and also make a rate for the repairing of the same according to the statute in that case made and provided if it cannot be known what particular place or person ought to repair the bridge.

752. The court is informed by Augustine Phelpes of East Harnham [Britford] husbandman that he has served in the office of tithingman for the hamlet of East Harnham by the space of two years which is longer than he ought to serve by the custom there used and that Thomas Giller of the same place is a fitting man to serve in the office for the year ensuing. Ordered that Thomas Giller shall forthwith upon sight hereof repair to the next justice to take his oath for the due execution of the office.

(If he refuses, to be bound over.)

753. *Blackman's order for a cottage.* (Recites **679**)
It also appears by a later order made at Midsummer Sessions last upon pretence that the cottage was and is some nuisance to the highways there and is presented at the leet for the same by reason whereof the former order was then vacated. Now upon reading the certificate of most of the inhabitants of Chicklade it appears that the presentment at the leet was more of malice than matter and that the cottage is no nuisance to the highways there. Ordered that the first order made for the continuance of the cottage shall stand and be of force and the cottage to be an habitation for Blackman without incurring any penalty in the statute notwithstanding any former order to the contrary. And if any person shall be aggrieved for any nuisance that they may prefer their bill of indictment against Blackman for the same.

754. *Aldridge overseer of the poor of West Wellow* [now in Hampshire]. It appears to the court by Mr Staples of counsel on the behalf of Mr Aldridge of West Wellow that he has been lately overseer of the poor there and has disbursed the sum of twelve pounds and ten shillings more that he has received which is consented and agreed unto by the now overseers of the poor there. Ordered that there shall be an equal rate made on all the inhabitants there within one month next for the repaying Aldridge the sum of twelve pounds ten shillings which rate the court desires Edward Tooker and Walter South justices to confirm.

(If any refuse to pay, to be bound over.)

And the court is further informed by the overseers of the poor that Aldridge has five pounds in his hands of the inhabitants and pretends he has disbursed fifty shillings of the same. The court refers the examination of the same unto the justices who are desired to examine the same and to do therein accordingly.

755. *Thomas Carter and inhabitants of Winterslow.* (See also **233**)
Upon reading of a former order of the court concerning some difference between the parishes of Winterslow and Enford about the receiving and maintaining of Jane Carter late of Winterslow single woman and begotten with child by a man of Sussex (not to be heard of) for the settlement whereof the parishioners of Enford petitioned the Lord Chief Justice of the Common Pleas who referred the hearing and determining of the same to the Lord Gorges, William Ashburnham, Sir William Button and Sir John Evelin or any two of them. And Ashburnham and Evelin calling the churchwardens and overseers of the parishes before them in the seventh of March 1637 at which time it was agreed by the consent of the parishes and ordered that the parish of Enford should suffer Jane Carter to remain with her father in law in Enford parish till she was delivered and that the child so born to remain there and that the parish of Winterslow should pay weekly towards the maintenance there of nine pence for the space of seven years from the birth of the child and the parish of Enford should pay weekly six pence during the same term and which moneys was to be paid by the overseers of the poor of the parishes for the time being to the hand of Thomas Carter of Enford father of Jane monthly for the use of the child. And it was further agreed at the end of the term of seven years there should be five pounds especially raised by and between the parishes for binding forth the child apprentice. And that the parish of Winterslow shall be from thenceforth cleared and acquitted from any further charge of the child or mother. And that the payment of nine pence and six pence should begin from the last Sessions before the date of that order being the seventh of March 1637 as by the order then read under the hands of Ashburnham and Evelin appeared. It was then ordered that the fore recited order should stand in force. Now upon complaint made to the court by Thomas Carter that the parish of Winterslow have paid but three years of the seven an are in arrear and behind four years pay and also fifty shillings for binding forth the child apprentice. Ordered the churchwardens and overseers of Winterslow to pay the same upon sight of this order.
(If in default, to be bound over.)

756. *Humfrey Lacye allowed £3.*
The court is given to understand as well by the petition of Humfrey Lacye of Fisherton Anger seavier [sieve maker] as by other credible

testimony that upon Sunday the eleventh of this instant January in the night time Lacye had his dwelling house and all his household stuff and goods and one of his children all consumed and burnt to ashes. And the court commiserating and considering the poverty and miserable condition of Lacye his wife and children being harbourless order and allow Lacye towards his relief the sum of three pounds to be paid unto him by the Treasurer for the south.

757. *Matthew Woodroffe allowed £6 13s 4d.* (See also **787**)
The court is informed by Matthew Woodroffe of Quemerford in the parish of Calne that there happened in his dwelling house a fearful fire insomuch that it burned his house to the ground and consumed the most part of his substance to the value of sixty pounds and upwards to the utter undoing of himself his wife and children. Ordered that Woodroffe shall be allowed the sum of six pounds thirteen shillings and four pence out of the county's stock and to be paid by the Treasurer for the north.

758. *Mere inhabitants allowed 40s.* (Recites **693**. See also **624, 794, 842**)
The inhabitants have received the sum of forty shillings of the Treasurer towards his relief and complained now at this Sessions for some more relief towards the maintenance of Smith. Ordered that the overseers of the poor of the parish of Mere shall be allowed the sum of forty shillings more for the present to be paid by the Treasurer for the south.

759. *Thomas Adlam pension of 53s 4d.* (See also **771, 818**)
The court is informed by a certificate under the hands and public seal of William Greenhall and Richard Hutchington Treasurers for maimed soldiers that Thomas Adlam has served the State as a trooper under the command of Captain Robert Glyn in the regiment of Colonel Tomplinson under the Lord General Cromwell. And that by reason of many wounds he received in the same service he is disabled to follow his calling or perform any further service in the army. Ordered that the Treasurer for the north shall pay unto Adlam the sum of three and fifty shillings and four pence yearly the first payment to begin at the present Sessions and to continue until the court should see cause to alter the same.

760. *Inhabitants of Calne and Heddington.*
Complaint has been made at this Sessions by the chiefest inhabitants of Calne that by reason of multiplicity of poor within the parish of Calne which have weekly relief from the parish and of the inability of the parishioners there to relieve them by means whereof they are

enforced to crave the assistance of some other neighbouring parish. Ordered that the inhabitants of the parish of Heddington having but a small number of poor there do forthwith make a rate within the parish for the raising of ten shillings monthly from this present Sessions to be paid to the overseers and churchwardens of Calne towards the relief of the poor people there according to the statute in that case made and to continue until the court shall otherwise order the same.

761. *Inhabitants of Calne* and *Bremhill about the settlement of Edith Hazell.* (Recites **742**. See also **767**)
Now that the overseers of Calne are for their part ready with their counsel and witnesses but the inhabitants of Bremhill are not ready with their witnesses but allege that John Heath late overseer of the poor of Bremhill being their main witness is so sick that he cannot come to this Sessions. Ordered that the former order of the last Sessions stand in force till the next Sessions and then both parties to be heard without further delay. And if it shall be found that Edith Hazell ought to be settled at Bremhill that then the inhabitants of Bremhill shall reimburse the inhabitants of Calne of all such money and charges as they shall be at.

762. *Thomas Merchant about his apprentice.*
Complaint has been made at this Sessions by Thomas Merchant that there is one Anne Geterell a poor child about the age of nine years placed upon him as an apprentice by the churchwardens and overseers of the poor of Westbury in regard of a roughles [roofless] ground which he rents from the Lady Hungerford wherein he has but a short term to come and in regard he has yielded obedience thereunto and has taken the apprentice. Ordered and desired William Eyre, Nicholas Green justices to call Merchant and the churchwardens and overseers of Westbury before them to examine the grievance and to do therein according to law and equity.

763. *Nicholas Merriefield appeal.*
Whereas by an order returned in Michaelmas Sessions last into this court under the hands of two justices whereby Nicholas Merriefield was charged as the reputed father of a base child begotten on the body of Mary Kirbye whereunto Merriefield entered his appeal according to the statute in that case made and provided and was bound over to present his appeal at this Sessions. Now upon examination of witnesses upon oath and hearing of counsel on both sides, the court vacates and nulls the order and hereby frees, acquits and discharges Merriefield of the same and of every clause contained therein. But

also orders that Merriefield be continued over to appear again the next Sessions and in the meantime that he attend Mr South and Mr Manning being the two next justices who are desired to re-examine the same and to make use of the former examinations or to hear any further testimony therein, it being now deposed in the court by Phillipp [blank] brother to Mary Kirbye that Mary was married about five years since to Anthony Kirbye and that they continue wed together and dwelt at Teffont where they had a child born. And afterwards Kirbye went away from his wife and it was likewise deposed in court by Thomas Hales of Woodlands in the county of Somerset that about August last he writ a letter for Mary to desire a friend of his in Ireland to help Mary to find forth her husband there who is gone accordingly. And that the justices are desired to certify their proceedings and opinion therein to the next Sessions that the court may do therein according to law and justice.
(Upper Teffont (Teffont Magna) in the deposition. A1/110/1652H/219)

764. *Inhabitants of Marston, Worton and Potterne.*
The court is informed by the inhabitants of the tithings of Marston that there is a difference between the inhabitants of Potterne and Worton being all within the parish of Potterne touching the manner of rating to the relief of the poor of that parish for reconciling of which difference the court refers the consideration thereof to Edward Mitchell justice who is desired to send for such parties of all three places as are most interest therein and to reconcile the difference between then if he can but in case he cannot compose the same then he is desired to certify the same at the next Quarter Sessions and then the inhabitants of Worton, Marston and Potterne are hereby required to attend the court that such order may be made therein as shall be agreeable to law and justice.

765. *Inhabitants of Fisherton Anger and* [Little] *Langford.* (Recites **707**. See also **472**)
Now upon the complaint again of the inhabitants of Fisherton Anger of their poverty and of the great burden of poor that lies upon them and also upon hearing of Mr Stourton Sadler one of the inhabitants of Little Langford [Steeple Langford]. Ordered that the monthly rate of five shillings shall be continued and paid monthly to the overseers of the poor of Fisherton from this present Sessions by the two farms there that is to say by the tenants and occupiers of Mr Willoughby's farm three shillings monthly and by the occupiers and tenants of Mr Sadler's farm two shillings monthly and so to continue until the court sees cause to alter the same any former order to the contrary notwithstanding.

(Fisherton Anger said it was a parish of 16 yardlands and had to support 42 poor with another 200 in need of relief. The high number of poor was a result of the earlier visitation of the plague. Little Langford consisted of two great farms worth £300 per annum and the tithing of Avon and Wishford consisted of 15 yardlands but had no poor. A1/110/1652H/177)

766. *Martha Lane widow pension of £3 10s.*
The court is informed by Martha Lane of the city of Salisbury widow that John Lane her late husband served the Parliament as a trooper under the command of Colonel Tomplinson in which service he lost his life as by a certificate under the hand of Colonel Tomplinson appears by reason thereof Martha is fallen into great poverty. Ordered and allowed Martha Lane a pension of three pounds ten shillings to be paid unto her quarterly by the Treasurer for the south the first payment thereof to begin at Our Lady day next and to continue until the court shall see cause to alter the same.

General Sessions of the Peace held at Devizes 27 April 1652. Sir Edward Baynton, Alexander Staples, William Sadler, George Ivy, John Read, Thomas Eyre, Francis Swanton, Giles Tucker, Gabriel Martin, William Shute, Robert Hippisley, Nicholas Green, Edward Mitchell, John Rydout, William Eyre, William Duckett.

767. *Inhabitants of Calne and Langley Burrell.* (Refers to **761**. See also **742**)
Upon hearing of the matter in difference between the inhabitants of Calne and the inhabitants of Bremhill concerning the settlement of Edith Hazell. Ordered that the inhabitants of Bremhill shall be discharged of Edith Hazell and that she shall remain at Calne and be there provided for until the next Quarter Sessions and the same not to be prejudicial unto them in point of settlement. And forasmuch as it now appears upon hearing of the matter that Edward Hazell her husband heretofore upon his disturbance at Calne went from thence to Langley Burrell where he died. It is therefore further ordered that the inhabitants of Langley Burrell shall have timely notice of this order by the inhabitants of Calne that they and the inhabitants of Calne may attend with their witnesses at the next Sessions that the matter may receive a full hearing.

768. *Inter Tibboll and Baskerville.*
Whereas complaint has been made unto the court by Henry Tibboll of

Clyffe Pypard on the behalf of Tobie Tibboll his son that Mr Baskerville of [Winterbourne Bassett] in this county detains and keeps from his son the sum of two pounds four shillings two pence which is due to him for wages. The court desires the two next justices to cause Baskerville to come before them to pay Tibboll his wages.

(If he refuses, to be bound over.)

(Tibboll was to have £3 a year paid quarterly. In addition he was promised each year one of Baskerville's cast off suits and a pair of boots. A1/110/1652E/180)

769.   *Inter Edgar Webb and Amos Hope.*
The court is informed by Edgar Webb one of the constables of the Liberty of Rowde that he has served in the same office by the space of one whole year which is as long as he ought to serve as constable for the Liberty and that there is no court leet kept there nor has been for ten years last past whereby he is like to continue longer in that office than of right he ought unless the court will discharge him hereof. And has nominated Amos Hope of the same place a fit man to serve in the office in that Liberty for the year next ensuing. Ordered that Hope shall serve in that office in the place of Webb and that he shall within one week after the receipt hereof repair to some justice within or near the Liberty there to take his oath for the due execution of the office on pain of twenty pounds.

770.   *John Taylor.*
The court is informed by John Taylor of Atworth that his goods were distrained by Thomas Cooper one of the Sheriff's bailiffs for arrears of Sheriff tourn money being seventeen shillings three pence due from the inhabitants of Atworth and for expenses fees and acquittance thirteen shillings which amounts in the whole to thirty shillings and three pence and the inhabitants of Atworth have not as yet satisfied Taylor for the same. Ordered that there shall be an equal rate made over all the inhabitants of Atworth for the repaying Taylor the said sums besides necessary expenses in prosecuting the same.

(If any refuse to pay, to be bound over.)

771.   *Thomas Adlam his pension of 53s 4d augmented to £4.* (Refers to **759**. See also **818**)
Upon a certificate under the hands and public seal of William Owenhill, Richard Hutchinson, Treasurer, that Thomas Adlam of Melksham has served the State as a trooper under the command of Robert Glynn captain in the regiment of Colonel Tomplinson under the command of the Lord General Cromwell and that by reason of

many wounds he received in the service he is disabled to follow his calling or to perform any other service in the army. Ordered that the Treasurer for the north shall pay unto Adlam a yearly pension of four pounds to be paid quarterly the first payment to begin at the present Sessions and the same to continue until the court shall see cause to alter the same.

772. *John Mannings.* (See also **801, 869**)
John Mannings of Patney was bound over to this Sessions for not entertaining William Nash being placed with him as an apprentice by the overseers of the poor there with the consent of William Sadler and Robert Hippesley justices. Ordered that Mannings shall take his apprentice and attend Mr Staples and Mr Sadler who are desired to examine the premises and to bind the apprentice to some trade if they see cause and to do further therein as shall be agreeable to law and justice.

773. *Daniel Hicks.*
Daniel Hicks has made complaint to the court of divers riots and other misdemeanours committed by William Webb and John Ansty both of Bromham with others. Ordered and desired Thomas Eyre and Edward Mitchell justice to call before them Webb and Ansty and all others therein concerned and to hear and examine the riots and misdemeanours and to bind the offenders over to the next Sessions as they shall see cause to be proceeded against according to law.

774. *Daniel Hicks.*
Daniel Hicks has made complaint to the court of divers riots and other misdemeanours committed by Ferdinand Hughes, William Webb and John Ansty all of Bromham. Ordered and desired Thomas Eyre and Edward Mitchell to call before them Hughes, Webb and Ansty with all such witnesses as may be produced for the proof of the riots and misdemeanours and to hear and examine the riots and misdemeanours and to bind over to the next Sessions as they shall see cause there to be proceeded against according to law.
(This entry appears to be the same as **773** except for the addition of Ferdinand Hughes)

775. *William Flower's order to sell ale.*
Upon reading of a certificate under the hands of the minister and chiefest inhabitants of the town and parish of Melksham that William Flower of the same place barber is a man very fit to sell ale beer and to keep a common victualling house for the entertainment of travellers in

the house where he now dwells. Ordered that William Flower shall and is allowed to keep a common victualling house and to sell ale and beer in the house where he now lives according to the statute in that case made and provided and to continue the same for the space of one whole year unless the court shall see cause to alter the same.

776. *Robert Newman overseer of the poor of Bradford.*
It appears to the court by the petition of Robert Newman of Atworth husbandman that he did in the year 1647 with others serve in the office of overseer of the poor of the parish of Bradford and by the mutual consent of his partner overseers collected and gathered the tithings of Atworth and South Wraxall and paid the poor thereof and at the end of the year yielded up a true and perfect account thereof unto William Eyre and Thomas Eyre justices as well of his receipts as disbursements by which account it appeared that he had disbursed to the poor of Atworth and South Wraxall the sum of one and fifty shillings and nine pence more that he had received of the inhabitants of the said places of which sum or any part thereof he is not as yet satisfied. Ordered that the now overseers for the time being for the parish of Bradford shall make an equal rate throughout the whole parish for the raising of the sum of one and fifty shillings and nine pence with other necessary charges as he has been at concerning the same and to be raised upon the tithings belonging to the parish and pay it over to Newman.
(If any refuse to pay, to be bound over.)

777. *The inhabitants of Hilmarton.*
Whereas there is a difference amongst the inhabitants within the parish of Hilmarton concerning the election and choosing of churchwardens within the parish. The court refers the examination of the premises unto Alexander Staples, William Sadler and Gabriel Martin justices or any two of them to do therein according to law and justice.

778. *William Rutty, Thomas Williams.*
The court is informed by William Rutty and Thomas Williams of Melksham that they on the behalf of the inhabitants of Melksham appeared to a presentment which was preferred against them for not repairing a certain gate within the parish and have disbursed for issues returned into the Exchequer, fees and other necessary charges the sum of three pounds nineteen shillings which ought to be borne by all the inhabitants within the parish. Ordered that there shall be an equal and indifferent rate made on all the inhabitants of Melksham for the repaying Rutty and Williams the sum of three pounds nineteen shillings.
(If any refuse to pay, to be bound over.)

779. *Inhabitants of Trowbridge.* (Recites **635**)
The court is now informed that the justices called before them the parties concerned therein and it was ordered by them with the consent of all parties that there should be a pound rate made upon all the inhabitants within the parish of Trowbridge. Ordered that there be a pound rate made accordingly to be and remain within the parish for future parish rates and the two next justices are desired to confirm the same.

780. *William Stragnell.*
The court is informed by William Stragnell of Laverstock that the inhabitants of Laverstock have been two several times indicted for decay of several highways within the parish to which indictment Stragnell has appeared on the behalf of the inhabitants and has disbursed for fees a fine and other necessary charges the sum of forty seven shillings which charge ought to be borne by the whole parish of Laverstock. Ordered that there shall be an equal and an indifferent rate made on all the inhabitants of Laverstock for the repaying of Stragnell the sum of forty seven shillings.
(If any refuse to pay, to be bound over.)

781. *John Ruffin, Toby Betterton.*
The court is informed by John Ruffin and Toby Betterton of the parish of Highworth that they have been distrained for a sum of money forfeited by the inhabitants of Highworth and Westrop for keeping unlawful measures. Ordered that Ruffin and Betterton together with other of the inhabitants make an equal rate for the charges they have been put into on the inhabitants to be signed by the next justice.
(If any refuse to pay, to be bound over.)

782. *Thomas Palmer.*
The court is informed by Thomas Palmer of Christian Malford they have appeared on the behalf of the inhabitants of Christian Malford and have disbursed for fees a fine and other necessary charges the sum of forty shillings which charge ought to be borne by the whole parish. Ordered that there shall be an equal rate made on all the inhabitants of Christian Malford.
(If any refuse to pay, to be bound over.)

783. *A commission for charitable uses for Harnham bridge.*
Forasmuch as the great bridge called Harnham Bridge lying in or near the city of Salisbury is a bridge of great travel and the roadway from the city of London into all the west parts of this nation and is fallen into

great decay for want of reparations. And for that it is conceived that
the same ought not to be repaired at the charge of the county but by
private and particular persons. And that there is certain lands lying as
well in the county of Dorset as in the county of Wiltshire which were
heretofore given for the repair of the same and are now concealed. And
that there has been heretofore several commissions sued forth to inquire
and find forth what particular persons ought to repair the bridge and
what lands were given for the repair thereof but by reason the former
commissions stood in force but for one year and the lands inquired
after lie in the several counties the commission could not be executed
by reason of the short time of the return thereof whereby there was
no benefit made of the commissions wherefore the justices present at
this Sessions taking the premisses into consideration and considering
the great necessity of the speedy repair of the bridge. Ordered that the
Clerk of the Peace shall on the behalf of the inhabitants of the county,
petition the Lords Commissioners of the Great Seal to desire their
lordships to be pleased to give a warrant for two several commissions
of charitable uses into the several counties of Wiltshire and Dorset
and that they may be made to stand in force for three years together
whereby some benefit may be made thereby. And also that the Clerk
of the Peace procure the like warrant for renewing the Commission of
Sewers whereby more commissioners' names may be added and inserted
therein. And the Clerk of the Peace searches and finds out all books,
evidences, proofs and other things touching the repair of the bridge
which were heretofore either in the custody of the bishop or dean of
the cathedral church of Salisbury and now in the custody of the late
Commissions for Sequestrations of this county or their officers or any
of them who are desired by the justices to deliver the same. And that
the Clerk of the Peace shall from time to time on the behalf of the
county follow and prosecute the execution of the commissions and
disburse and lay forth all moneys concerning the same to be repaid
again from the county out of the county's stock from time to time as
the same shall be disbursed.

784. *Kellaways bridge in decay.*
The court is informed by William Sellman and Peter Gale of Avon
[Bremhill] on the behalf of themselves and divers of the inhabitants
there that there is a bridge called Kellaways bridge anciently built on
the river on Avon over which bridge is a great roadway much used
for all manner of carriages and passings both of horse and foot from
divers parts of the country to London which was broken down by
the command of the Parliament forces for the stopping of the late
King's forces from coming into that country and has been since laid

over with planks but is now grown so founderous that passengers are not able to ravel that way and that it cannot be known or proved what persons lands or tenements or bodies politic ought to repair the bridge which in the judgment of skilful workmen will amount to three score pounds at the least. Ordered and desired Sir Edward Baynton, William Eyre, George Ivy, Edward Stokes, William Shute and William Duckett justices or any four of them whereof one to be of the quorum with all convenient speed to meet together and view the decays of the bridge and inquire who or what lands are chargeable with the repair thereof and what it will amount unto to repair the same and certify their doings therein at the next Quarter Sessions that such speedy course may be taken for the repair thereof as the statute in that case made and provided requires.

785. *John Martin discharged from constable.*
It appears to the court that at the last Quarter Sessions at Salisbury the thirteenth day of January 1652 Mr John Martin of West Ashton was elected and chosen one of the constables of the hundred of Whorwellsdown in the place of William Rawlins and forasmuch as it is now made appear to the court upon the motion of Mr Staples of counsel with Martin that he is a man not fit to execute that office. Ordered that Martin shall be discharged of the office and is not to be chosen any more for the future.

786. *William Stanter.*
The court is informed by William Stanter of Westbury gent that on the twenty sixth day of March last past his goods were distrained by the Sheriff's bailiffs for forty shillings formerly amerced on the inhabitants of Westbury in the charge of Lawrence Washington late Sheriff of this county which forty shillings he paid to Mr Anthony Bird late Undersheriff and for their fees and expenses and an acquittance the sum of eighteen shillings four pence more amounting in the whole to the sum of fifty eight shillings and four pence. Ordered that there shall be an equal rate made over the inhabitants of Westbury for the repayment of the sum of fifty eight shillings four pence to William Stanter.
(If any refuse to pay, to be bound over.)

787. *A certificate for Woodroffe.* (Recites **757**)
Which petition we the justices whose names are subscribed present at the said Sessions do humbly certify to your honours together with the petition and certificate hereunto annexed. And humbly desire the petitioner's relief by way of a collection and brief which we leave to

your honours grace, judgment and directions therein and do humbly take our leave at Devizes the eighth day of April 1651.

788.   *The inhabitants of East and West Amesbury.* (Refers to **729**. See also **536, 709**)
Whereas there have been divers differences betwixt the inhabitants of the east part of the hundred of Amesbury and the inhabitants of the west part of the hundred concerning the rates of the hundred. Now upon hearing of counsel and examination of witnesses on both sides concerning the ancient rates of the hundred. Ordered that the inhabitants of the east part of the hundred shall from time to time hereafter pay the tenth part to all rates, taxes and hundred payments and no more until the court shall see good cause to alter the same.

General Sessions of the Peace held at Warminster 15 July 1652. Alexander Staples, John Ash, John Rydout, Edward Mitchell, Francis Swanton and Walter Ernely.

789.   *John Deackon.*
Whereas john Deackon of Westbury has on the behalf of the inhabitants of Westbury appeared to a presentment and has disbursed for fees, a fine and other necessary charges the sum of five and twenty shillings which charge ought to be borne by all the inhabitants of Westbury. Ordered that there shall be an equal and an indifferent rate made on all the inhabitants of Westbury for repaying Deackon the sum of five and twenty shillings.
(If any refuse to pay, to be bound over.)

790.   *Julian Cockle's child to be sent from Kingston Deverill to Charlton in Somerset.*
It appeared by the examination and confession of Julian Cockle that she being about four years since begotten with child by John Streete and was delivered of the child being a maid child named Elinor within the parish of Charlton Horethorne in the county of Somerset which child was afterwards illegally brought by some of the parishioners of Charlton to Kingston Deverill and there left and is now chargeable to the parish there. Ordered that Elinor be forthwith returned and carried to Charlton there to be delivered to the churchwardens and overseers of the parish to be provide for according to law. And that John Streete be bound to appear at the next Sessions of the Peace to be held for the county of Somerset to perform such order as the justices for the said county make for discharge of the parish of Charlton.

791. *William Butcher for a cottage.*
The court is informed by William Butcher of Bratton labourer that he having a wife and five small children and being destitute of a habitation to dwell in has obtained a licence under the hand of the lord of the manor of Bratton and also a certificate under the hands of the chiefest inhabitants of the parish of Bratton. Ordered that Butcher shall be allowed to erect and build a cottage and the same shall continue during the term of his life and the life of his wife and no longer without incurring the forfeitures mentioned in the statutes.

792. *White Rose for a cottage.*
The court is informed by White Rose of Monkton Farleigh that he having a wife and seven small children and being a very poor man destitute of a house and habitation for himself and family and having a licence under the hand and seal of William Watton lord of the manor of Monkton Farleigh for the continuing of a cottage already built upon ten lug [a plot of about a quarter of an acre] of waste ground within the manor. Ordered that Rose shall continue the cottage for himself and family during his own life and his wife's life and the cottage shall be and continue a cottage without incurring the forfeitures mentioned in the statute.

793. *Fowle.* (See also **832**)
Forasmuch as it appears that Marie Brown late servant of William Fowle of All Cannings is begotten with child by Fowle her master who has surrendered his living to William Fowle his son and absents himself whereby the charge of the child lies upon the parish of All Cannings. The court desires that the two next justices to call all parties interested therein before them together with William Fowle the son and to take order for the discharge of the parish of All Cannings and to charge the son of eighteen pence a week to be paid from this present Sessions forth of the late tenement of William Fowle the elder by his son William Fowle the younger towards the relief of the bastard.

(If he refuses to pay, to be bound over.)

(This entry gives the name as Vowles but in **832** it is Fowle which has been adopted as a known name in All Cannings in the 17th century.)

794. *Inhabitants of Mere 20s.* (Recites **693** and **758**. See also **624, 842**)
And whereas the inhabitants complained now at this Sessions for some more relief for Smith. Ordered that the overseers of the poor of the parish of Mere shall be allowed the sum of twenty shillings for this time only to be paid by the Treasurer for the south immediately upon receipt hereof.

795. *Inhabitants of North Newton concerning the settlement of Wright.*
The court is informed by Mr Staples of counsel on the behalf of the
inhabitants of North Newton that Christopher Wright was last settled
at Wilsford. Ordered that Wright his wife and child shall be sent to
Wilsford there to be provided for by the overseers of the poor there
according to law without prejudice to the parish of Wilsford. And
if the parish of Wilsford shall find themselves aggrieved therein then
they are to give notice thereof to the inhabitants of North Newton
to attend at the next Sessions at Marlborough where there shall be a
final order made therein.
(If the overseers refuse to accept Wright, to be bound over.)

796. *Inhabitants of Lyneham and overseers there.* (See also **810**, **913**)
Whereas William Pinneger, Thomas Luton and Giles Browne late
overseers of the poor of the parish of Lyneham were bound over to this
Sessions for not giving up a perfect account to the parish and for that
none of the parish appeared to make their objections therein. Ordered
that the inhabitants of Lyneham shall deliver unto the overseers a true
copy of their account and all parties interested therein are (together
with the overseers) to attend the justices at the next Quarter Sessions
there to make their objections against the account.

797. *Inhabitants of Imber and Orcheston St Mary.*
The court is informed by the churchwardens and overseers of the
poor of the parish of Imber that Jane Butler an infant daughter of
John Butler of Orcheston St Mary labourer and the infant was of late
brought from Orcheston where she was born to Imber to Katherine
Butler her grandmother who is an inmate and lives in a cottage with
Margaret Peirce of Imber widow her mother which Margaret Peirce
is a very aged woman and has been relieved by the parish for divers
years last past. Ordered that Jane Butler shall be sent to her father and
mother to Orcheston St Mary there to be provided for by the parents
and if in case her parents be not of ability to provide for her then to
be provided for by the overseers of the poor as one of the poor of that
parish of Orcheston.
(If the overseers refuse to accept her, to be bound over.)

798. *Mr Tipper.*
Whereas Mr Tipper of Coulston [East Coulston] was demanded for
find a plough to help repair the highways there he having two yardlands
within the parish. And for that it now appears to the court it is not a
plough land and that there is no arable land belonging to his tenement
neither did hear keep any plough upon the same. Ordered that Tipper

(instead of providing of a plough) shall provide two sufficient labourers to help amend the highways within the parish at such times as he shall be thereunto required.

799. *Jeffery Tipper and Thomas Salter.*
Whereas the inhabitants of Coulston [East Coulston]were presented at Warminster Sessions in the four and twentieth year of the reign of the late King Charles for digging a pit in a highway there and for not appearing to the same presentment there was forty shillings issues estreated into the Exhequer which sum was levied upon Jeffery Tipper and Thomas Salter two of the inhabitants of West Coulston [in Edington]. The court is now informed that the offence was committed within the parish of East Coulston. Ordered that the tithingman of East Coulston together with some other of the parish shall make an equal and an indifferent rate upon all the inhabitants for the repaying of Tipper and Salter as well the sum of forty shillings as all other charges they have been at concerning the business.
    (If any refuse to pay, to be bond over.)

800. *Inhabitants of Seend about Brewer's children.* (See also **226**, **592**, **726**, **823**)
The court is informed by the Inhabitants of Seend that the late wife of Benjamin Somner of Seend deceased is now married to John Brewer an inhabitant of Devizes and is gone thither with her husband and has left behind her three small children to the great prejudice and burden of the inhabitants of Seend. Ordered the overseers of the poor of Seend to carry the three children to Devizes and deliver them to the overseers of the poor of the parish of St John's in Devizes in which parish John Brewer and his wife now live there to be kept and relieved according to law.

801. *John Mannings and his apprentice.* (Refers to **772**. See also **869**)
Whereas William Nash a poor boy was heretofore put an apprentice by the churchwardens and overseers of Patney unto John Mannings and Mannings having yielded obedience and taken the apprentice as he was directed by the court. And for that it now appears that the apprentice is more fitted for a trade than for husbandry and that he has a stock of twenty pounds given him by Margaret Wake deceased which money remains in the hands of Thomas Stretch late overseer for the poor of Patney. Ordered that John Manning is and shall be discharged of his apprentice and shall join with the churchwardens and overseers of Patney to procure Nash to be placed with some fitting handicraft trade and that Stretch shall pay forth of the portion of twenty pounds

so much money as shall place Nash to such a master so as it does not exceed one half of the portion which Stretch is required to do or to be bound to the next Quarter Sessions for his contempt.

802. *John Whatley to pay 2s a week for the relief of his father.* (Refers to **738**. See also **819**)
It appears unto the court upon the oaths of William Stevens and John Hellier that John Whatley son of Ellis Whatley of Hilperton is worth eight score or nine score pounds. The court adjudges him fit to relieve his father and mother now relieved by the parish of Hilperton. Ordered that John Whatley shall pay weekly to the overseers of the poor of Hilperton two shillings a week for the relief of his father and mother to commence from this Sessions and the same payment to continue until he shall show good cause to the court to alter the same.

803. *Edward Gamlyn for taking Nicholas Petty an inmate.* (See also **845**)
The court is informed that Edward Gamlyn of Shrewton has entertained in his house as an inmate Nicholas Petty and his wife who are likely to be chargeable to the parish of Shrewton. The court refers the examination of the premises to the two next justices who are desired to do therein as they shall think fit.

804. *Inhabitants of Upton Scudamore to pay to the overseers of Warminster 5s a week.* (See also **809**)
The court is informed by the overseers of the poor of Warminster that the place is much overburdened with poor people living in that place and prayed the court that Upton Scudamore a place of very great worth having few poor may contribute towards the relief of the poor of Warminster. Ordered that the inhabitants of Upton Scudamore shall pay weekly to the overseers of the poor of Warminster five shillings a week from this Sessions towards the relief of the poor of Warminster and that payment to continue until the inhabitants of Upton Scudamore shall show good cause unto the court to alter the same.

805. *Nicholas Amylls.*
The court is informed by Nicholas Amylls heretofore one of the overseers of the poor of Westbury that upon his account to the parish he was out of purse four pounds sixteen shillings. Ordered and desired that the next justice will examine the truth thereof and make such order for the relief of Nicholas as shall be agreeable to law and justice in case the information prove true.

806. *John Burbadge.*
Whereas John Burbadge of East Knoyle, Anthony Burbadge of the same, Henry Ricketts of the same and Robert Browne of Sedgehill were all severally bound by recognisances at the last Sessions to prosecute their several traverses upon their several indictments this Sessions with effect. And whereas Thomas Bennett and Anthony Burbadge were both likewise bound over to this Sessions by recognisances certified by John Rydout justice to answer unto such things as should be objected against them who have all in contempt of the court refused to do the same and thereby have forfeited their several recognisances. Ordered that the Clerk of the Peace shall estreat their recognisances as forfeited and certify them into the public Exchequer accordingly.

General Sessions of the Peace held at Marlborough 5 October 1652. Alexander Staples, William Eyre, William Sadler, Thomas Escourt, Gabriel Martin, Robert Hippesley, George Ivy, Thomas Eyre, Edward Stokes, John Read.

807. *Mary Burden widow.* (See also **861**)
Whereas the poor estate and condition of Mary Burden of Corsham widow and her children are recommended to the charity of the justices by the Lord General Cromwell whose husband William Burden being a trooper in Colonel Pretty's regiment in the Parliament service in Ireland where he died and left Mary and her children in great want and necessity which the court taking into consideration and in regard of the Lord General's request. Ordered that Mary may be paid towards her present relief for the next year ten pounds forthwith upon sight hereof by the Treasurer of the north forth of such moneys which remains in the hands of Mr Francis Swanton.

808. *The inhabitants of Sherston Pinkney* [Sherston].
It appears to the court that it is agreed the eighth day of October 1647 by the major part of the inhabitants of Sherston Pinkney that a tithingman should be constantly hired every year to execute the office for that tithing and be paid his wages quarterly by all there who usually contribute and pay towards other parcels and tithing payments by an equal rate every one to pay in proportion according to their yearly values there as they pay in other parish and tithing payments. And that Maurice Weekes the then tithingman shall be paid his wages for this year for the time past and to come the sum of thirty shillings to be paid as aforesaid. And that the succeeding tithingman shall be named and appointed yearly and every year upon every Easter Monday

between the hours of nine and eleven of the clock in the forenoon at a meeting for that purpose upon the little green known by the name of the Little Green within Brookeyate by all the contributors or by as many of them as will be at the meeting. And that such of the contributors as shall be then present or the major part of them shall have power to nominate hire and appoint the tithingman and to set and appoint his wages which are agreed to be paid rateably by all the contributors quarterly. And it is also agreed that the tithingman for the time being shall be one of the overseers of the poor if the justice shall think fit so to be as by the agreement whereunto if relation be had more fully may appear. The court confirms the agreement and orders that if any of the inhabitants concerned in the agreement shall refuse to pay, contemn or disobey the same (then to be bound over).

809. *The inhabitants of Upton Scudamore.* (Recites **804**)
And forasmuch as the court is now informed by Mr Staples of counsel with the inhabitants of Upton Scudamore that the inhabitants of Warminster are very able to maintain their own poor themselves without assistance and upon the oath of Thomas Seaman gent that he gave notice to the overseers of the poor of Warminster that the inhabitants of Upton would attend this court to show cause for the vacuating the order and forasmuch as none appeared on the behalf of the inhabitants of Warminster. Ordered that the order of the last Sessions shall be made null and vacuated and the inhabitants of Upton Scudamore freed and discharged from payment of the sum of five shillings a week unless the court shall see cause hereafter to alter the same.

810. *William Pinniger, Thomas Luton and Giles Browne.* (See also **796**, **913**)
The court is informed by William Pinniger, Thomas Luton and Giles Browne late overseers of the poor of Lyneham that they having lately passed their account before Mr Sadler, Mr Hippesley and Mr Marten justices, the justices disallowed eleven pounds nine shillings on their account and ordered them to pay it to Thomas Burchall and Edmond Burchall the now overseers of the poor of that place. And whereas Pinniger etc in obedience to that order have now paid in court to Burchall the sum of eleven pounds nine shillings and have complained that they continue themselves to be much grieved by reason of those disallowances in their account and prayed the court that the account may be examined and some other justices may be added to Mr Sadler, Mr Hippesley and Mr Marten to re-examine the same. The court desires Mr Sadler, Mr Hippesley and Mr Marten and also desires Mr

William Eyre, Mr Ivy, Mr Escourt and Mr Shute justices or any two of them to join with Sadler etc and with all convenient speed to meet together and re-examine the account and allow or disallow therein what they shall think fit and make such order therein as to law and justice shall appertain and if Sadler etc shall not join with Eyre etc for the doing thereof then they or any two of them are desired to proceed in the speedy examination of this order and call all parties interested before them and re-examine the account and allow or disallow what they shall think fit and make such order therein as to law and justice shall appertain.

811. *Cowbridge.*
Upon the presentment of the Grand Jury at this Sessions that the south end of a certain bridge called Cow Bridge in the parish of Preshute as also that the way by the bridge in the river within the parish is in decay and ought to be amended by the parishioners and whereas it is now also alleged by the inhabitants of Preshute that the bridge and way ought to be repaired by the inhabitants of the borough of Marlborough forasmuch as it is of necessity that the decays be forthwith amended and will not admit of any delay. Desired that the inhabitants of Marlborough repair it for the present and the court declares that if the right of repairing thereof upon due proof and trial shall hereafter be found to belong to the parish of Preshute then the inhabitants of Marlborough shall be reimbursed by the parishioners of Preshute all such charges and expenses as they shall defray in such reparation which being so done of necessity shall not be any wise prejudicial to the inhabitants of Marlborough in time to come.

812. *William Liddyard.*
The court is informed by William Liddyard of Poulton within the parish of Mildenhall that he has appeared on the behalf of the inhabitants of Poulton to a presentment against them for decay of a highway within the parish of Mildenhall and has disbursed for fees a fine and other necessary charges in prosecuting the same the sum of three pounds which charge ought to be borne by all the inhabitants of the parish of Mildenhall. Ordered that there shall be an equal and an indifferent rate made on all the inhabitants of the parish of Mildenhall for the repaying Liddyard the sum of three pounds.
   (If any refuse to pay, to be bound over.)

813. *Thomas Weekes for fire.*
The court is informed by Thomas Weekes of Poole [Poole Keynes now in Gloucestershire] blacksmith as also by a certificate under the

hands of most of the substantial inhabitants of Poole that Weekes is a very poor man and his wife sick in the falling sickness and has eight small children to maintain and that about the ninth day of August last past as he was working at his trade being a blacksmith by reason of a sudden whirlwind which broke into his house and blew the fire into the thatch his house was burned down and his goods and household stuff spoiled amounting in the whole to the sum of fifty pounds and upwards as by the certificate more plainly may appear. Ordered and allowed the Treasurer for the north upon sight hereof to pay unto Weekes the sum of six pounds in regard of his great necessity.

814. *Henry Moores.*
Whereas Henry Moores an aged and impotent poor man of Westbury has complained that he is destitute of a house for his succour and habitation and that the overseers of the poor of that place allow him such small relief that he is like to perish and is enforced to seek his relief abroad. Desired Mr Green justice to send for the overseers of the poor of Westbury and examine the truth of the complaint and cause them to allow him such relief and succour as his age and impotency shall deserve.
    (If they refuse, to be bound over.)

815. *Thomas Snowswell and his apprentice.*
The court is informed that the churchwardens and overseers of the poor of Ogbourne St George with the consent of the justices have heretofore bound William Pontinge an apprentice in husbandry with Thomas Snowswell and upon examination of the matter it appears to the court upon oath that the apprentice is infirm and broke bellied whereby he is unfit for his service. Ordered that Snowswell shall be discharged of his apprentice.

816. *Dorothy Garrad and Thomas Loveday for a bastard.*
Upon the humble petition of the overseers of the poor of the parish of Little Hinton [Bishopstone N Wilts] showing that Dorothy Garrad of the said parish being gotten with child and imprisoned for the same whilst she was in that condition so as afterwards the child was born dead and is by that means become impotent and chargeable to the parish and that it was apparent as well by the charge and occasion of Dorothy in her travail as by other circumstance that she was so gotten with child by Thomas Loveday her master whilst she was in his service as also that Loveday being an inhabitant of the parish is well able to relieve her. Desired Mr Sadler and Mr Martin to take the premisses into consideration and to make such order for relief

of Dorothy by Loveday in discharge of the parish as to them shall seem meet and reasonable.

817. *John Webb his apprentice to be placed with Thomas Potter.*
Whereas John Webb of Badbury [Chiseldon] was bound over to this Sessions for refusing to take an apprentice Martha Pontinge placed with him by the churchwardens and overseers of the poor of Ogbourne St George for and in respect of his lands there and whereas Webb has now informed the court that he has had an apprentice from that parish for his lands there and there are divers of that parish that have had no apprentices as namely Thomas Potter and others. Ordered that Webb shall be discharged of his apprentice and that she shall be placed with Potter who is to receive her accordingly.

818. *Thomas Adlam his pension of £5 yearly.* (Recites **771**; see also **759**)
And now upon further consideration of his great want and necessity ordered that he shall be allowed a yearly pension of five pounds to be paid to him the first payment to be made at this present Session and so to continue until the court shall see cause to alter the same.

819. *John Whatley to pay 12d weekly to Ellis Whatley his father.* (Recites **802**. See also **738**)
Which (pension) he refused to pay and was bound over to this Sessions for disobeying the order and forasmuch as he has paid in open court all the moneys in arrear to Edward Graunt one of the overseers of the parish. Ordered that Whatley shall weekly from this Sessions pay the sum of twelve pence and the overseers of the poor there twelve pence more towards the relief of Ellis Whatley and his wife. And the court desires the two next justices to examine and consider of John Whatley's worth and ability and to certify the same to the next Quarter Sessions and then the court (if they see cause) will make some further order therein.

820. *Robert King.*
The court is informed by Robert King of Bremhill that he has appeared to an indictment against the inhabitants of Bremhill for the decay of a bridge within the parish and has disbursed for fees and other necessary charges in prosecuting the same the sum of thirty six shillings four pence which charge ought to be borne by the inhabitants of Bremhill. Ordered that there shall be an equal and an indifferent rate made on all the inhabitants of Bremhill for the repaying King the sum of thirty six shillings four pence.
    (If any refuse to pay, to be bound over.)

821. *John Gallway, Sarah Gallway.* (Recites **739**)
And whereas it now appears to the court that John Gallway the grandfather having paid the sum of two shillings weekly almost one whole year last past and is not of ability to pay the same any longer. Ordered that the child shall remain with her mother at Corsham and the grandfather to pay only but six pence a week until the court shall see cause to alter the same.

822. *Overseers of Alderton* [Luckington] *to pay Joan Russell 45s.*
The court is informed by Joan Russell who was delivered of a bastard child begotten on her body by Anthony Woodward otherwise Woodard and that there was an order made by Mr Green and Mr Ivy justices that Woodard should pay into the hands of the overseers of the poor of Alderton for the time being the sum of eighteen pence every week to be paid monthly every year towards the relief and maintenance of the child until the child come to the age of eight years which child is now dead there being in arrear the sum of forty five shillings unpaid to her the overseers having taken bond from Woodard with sufficient sureties for the payment of the money and for saving the parish harmless. Ordered that the now overseers shall pay unto Joan the sum of forty five shillings which if they shall refuse the justices are desired to bind them over to the next Sessions and the old overseers to whom the bond was made are to make over the bond to the now overseers that they may be enabled to put in suit for their reimbursement.

823. *The inhabitants of St John's Devizes and inhabitants of Seend concerning the settlement of Benjamin Somner's wife and children.* (See also **226**, **592**, **726**, **800**)
Upon reading of an order made at the last Assizes between the inhabitants of St John's in Devizes and the inhabitants of Seend concerning the settlement of three children of the late wife of Benjamin Somner's of Seend and upon full hearing of counsel learned on both sides. Ordered that the two eldest children shall be sent back by the overseers of the poor of St John's to the overseers of the poor of Seend there to be maintained and provided for by the parish and that the inhabitants of St John's shall be discharged of the children for the future and be reimbursed the sum of thirty shillings towards the charges they have been at by the overseers of the poor of Seend and for the other child it is to remain with the mother until it shall be fit to be sent to Seend and then to be there provided for as the other two children are.

824. *Robert Rutt for the making of a rate on the inhabitants of Rushall.*
The court is informed by Robert Rutt one of the inhabitants of
the parish of Rushall that he was distrained for the said inhabitants
upon estreats issuing forth of the court leet kept for the hundred of
Swanborough concerning the decays of two highways being in default
belonging to the inhabitants and has disbursed for the same the sum
of ten shillings and for expenses and other charges in prosecuting
the business for getting the sum of ten shillings the sum of fourteen
shillings more which amounts in the whole to four and twenty shillings.
Ordered that there shall be an equal and indifferent rate made on the
inhabitants of Rushall for the reimbursing unto Rutt the sum of four
and twenty shillings.
(If any refuse to pay, to be bound over.)

825. *Overseers of the poor of Chilton Foliat to pay weekly unto Robert Beale
and Thomas Reeves 2s.*
The court is informed by James Beale and Robert Reeves that Robert
Beale and Thomas Reeves two poor children within the parish of
Chilton Foliat were place as apprentices with Mr Hussey and Mr
Hanslowe of the same parish but by reason their indentures were not
sealed Hussey and Hanslowe refuse to take them by means whereof
the children are like to perish. Ordered that the overseers of the poor
within the parish shall take care for the relieving of the children and
shall allow them weekly twelve pence a piece until the court shall see
cause to alter the same.

826. *William Bishop and William Elliott order for 42s 10d.*
The court is informed by William Bishop and William Elliott the
younger of Trowle [Trowbridge] that they have been at a great charge
for discharging a presentment upon the inhabitants of Trowle presented
at Midsummer Sessions last upon the view of Mr John Ash justice and
have disbursed for fees and other necessary charges in prosecuting the
same the sum of forty two shillings and ten pence. Ordered that there
shall be an equal and indifferent rate made on all the inhabitants of
Trowle for the repaying the sum of forty two shillings and ten pence
unto Bishop and Elliott.
(If any refuse to pay, to be bound over.)

827. *Thomas Allen's order for erecting a cottage.*
The court is informed by Thomas Allen of Chiseldon that he being a
very poor man and destitute of a house to live in to maintain himself
his wife and ten small children having also procured a certificate
under the hand and seal of Mr William Cawley lord of the manor for

erecting of a cottage. Ordered that Allen shall erect and build him a cottage for a habitation during his life without incurring the forfeitures mentioned in the statute.

828. *Richard Humfry and Thomas Lewen for 35s from the inhabitants of West Hatch* [West Tisbury].
The court is informed by Richard Humfry and Thomas Lewen of the tithing of West Hatch that they have appeared to a presentment against the inhabitants of West Hatch for decay of a highway there and have disbursed for fees, a fine and other necessary charges the sum of thirty five shillings which charge ought to be borne by all the inhabitants of West Hatch. Ordered that there shall be an equal and an indifferent rate made on all the inhabitants of West Hatch for the repaying Humfry and Lewen the sum of thirty five shillings.
(If any refuse to pay, to be bound over.)

829. *William Stevens.*
The court is informed by the inhabitants of Rowde that there is a bastard child begotten by William Stevens the younger of Bishops Cannings on the body of Bridgett Slade which bastard child is likely to be chargeable to the parish of Rowde and that William Stevens has secretly conveyed his son away so that there cannot be any legal course taken against William Stevens the younger for the keeping the bastard child. The court therefore refers the examination of the premises to the two next justices who are desired (if they see cause) to bind William Stevens the elder to the next Quarter Sessions to be held at Devizes there to answer the same.

830. *Ralph Freake, William Freake.*
The court is informed by Ralph Freake and William Freake lords of the manor of Hannington that it was formerly ordered and agreed at a court leet there held for the manor aforesaid to enjoin every inhabitant within the parish for every five acres of lands they occupy and enjoy there should carry abroad and place one load of stones and gravel every year to repair the highways within the parish. And forasmuch as many of the inhabitants of late have refused to yield obedience to the order and agreement by means whereof the highways within the parish of Hannington are likely to fall into decay. The court confirms the order and agreement.
(If any refuse to do their service, to be bound over.)

831. To the supreme authority of this nation the Parliament of the Commonwealth of England.

The humble petition of the Justices of the Peace of the county of Wiltshire at the General Quarter Sessions held at Marlborough the fifth day of October 1652.

Showeth, That your petitioners being deeply sensible of the sad deplorable condition of the multitude of poor in this county that depend wholly upon the trade of clothing being minded thereof by the petition annexed and being assured that many (through the decay of that trade) are already without work and those that have any are neither fully employed nor certain of any continuance of that they have, being sensible also that they are not able to subsist one month without their employments. And that the particular parishes in which they live nor the county in general are any ways able to relieve their necessities by reason whereof we fear and have experimentally found in times past and on less occasion they will take such indirect courses to supply themselves which may be of evil consequence to the county in which they live and also to the whole Commonwealth and considering that it is not the condition of this county alone but of all others where the poor do depend on the same trade which renders the inconveniences that may follow (though we do and shall use the uttermost of our endeavours for the preventing of them for the future) to be more general we have therefore thought it our duty to present their condition to you honours.

And do humbly pray that a speedy consideration be had thereof and such an effectual course taken for the speedy prevention of the evils that may ensue as your wisdoms shall seem most meet and convenient. And we shall pray etc.

To the worships the Justices of the Peace of the county of Wiltshire assembled at the General Quarter Sessions of the Peace held at Marlborough the 5th day of October 1652.

The humble petition of the Grand Inquest for the county.

Showeth, That your petitioners are made sadly sensible as well by their own daily view as by the many grievous and lamentable complaints and outcries of divers honest though miserably poor and distressed people of this county who have formerly lived in good fashion and maintained themselves and their families by weaving woollen cloth and by spinning and doing other honest works incident to the trade of clothing who are now in a most sad and famishing condition by reason of their want of work by means of the decay of the trade of clothing occasioned through the general decay of trade in this nation the present sense of all which beforementioned miseries and the fear of the sad and inevitable evils that are likely to ensue such a sea of necessity and misery that is likely to overwhelm the generality of our country wherein many thousand of souls are only sustained by the trade of clothing which is so visibly decayed that not ten in the hundred of looms usually heretofore employed are not now at present employed has induced us to represent the sad estate of our countrymen to your worships.

Wherefore we most humbly beseech your worships to take the said estate and condition of our country into your pious and most serious consideration. And that you would be pleased to use all such possible means as in your wisdoms shall seem meet for the redress and prevention of such present and future calamities as our country is and may be brought into by occasion of the premises. And your petitioners shall daily pray, etc.

John Diaper	John Hopkins	John Yorke
Gabriel Church	John Ayres	John Merreweather
George Mortimer	Ambrose Sanders	William Smith
William Guddings	Leonard Bishop	Thomas Parker
John Durnford	John Seymour	William Morse
John Raffe	Francis Fillips	Christopher Clark
William Shergell		

832. *William Fowle for a bastard on Mary Browne.* (Recites **793**)
And forasmuch as William Fowle has absented himself from the parish of All Cannings and has not disbursed unto Mary Browne the sum of eighteen pence by the week whereby she and her child are like to perish for want of relief. Ordered that the overseers of the poor of the parish of All Cannings shall pay weekly towards the maintenance of her and her child the sum of eighteen pence by the week immediately after this present Sessions and to continue until the court shall see cause to alter the same and the same to be reimbursed to the parish whensoever William Fowle shall be apprehended.

(If the overseers refuse to pay, to be bound over.)

1653

General Sessions of the Peace held at Salisbury 11 January 1653. Alexander Staples, Edward Tooker, John Dove, Francis Swanton, Giles Tucker, Nicholas Green, John Read, Barnaby Coles, Walter South.

833. *Simon Lane.* (See also **273**)
The court is informed by the petition of Simon Lane of Pewsey here read and shown proffered lately to the honourable Mr Justice Attkins

one of the Justices of the Assize for the last Western circuit. Whereas it is set forth that Lane has for the space of about twenty years past kept a licensed alehouse in Pewsey and whereas it also appeared by several certificates subscribed by most of the ablest and best inhabitants of the parish of Pewsey and produced likewise in court that the town and parish of Pewsey is a convenient and fit place for the permitting of one alehouse there and that Lane is a fit person for the keeping thereof for certain reasons contained in the certificate yet upon some information given to Mr Justice Attkins at the last Assizes against Lane it was by order of Assizes suppressed Lane not anywise knowing of any complaint made against him was not present to make his defence. All which being since made appear to Mr Justice Attkins as also that the main grounds whereupon the alehouse was then suppressed was upon a certificate then showed to his Lordship which was made in the two and twentieth year of the late King Charles. And Lane licensed by several justices yearly afterwards until this very time. Upon all which Mr Justice Attkins was pleased to refer the consideration of the whole matter to the justices at this present Sessions whether it should be by them thought fit to continue Lane's alehouse or to suppress it (as by the petition certificates and reference more at large may appear). Ordered that Lane produces a new certificate from the most ablest and sufficient inhabitants of the parish of Pewsey of the conveniency and fitness of the place for an alehouse there and of their accounting and estimating Lane to be an honest civil and fit person to keep the same. The court also desires the justices of that division or any two or more of them to look into the certificate and accordingly to license Lane or otherwise to take care for the suppressing of him as they in their discretion shall think fit.

834. *John Goodwin for £3 from the Treasurer of the north.*
The court is informed by John Goodwin that he has lived in the county of Wiltshire from whence he went forth into the Parliament service and there he lost part of both his feet and besides he received divers other wounds to the great impoverishment of Goodwin and being now recommended to the justices under the hands of the Lord General Cromwell, Lt General Fleetwood, Colonel Dove and Sir John Danvers to be provided for, he having a wife and small children and not able to relieve himself and family without some relief. Ordered that the Treasurer for the north shall pay unto Goodwin towards his present relief the sum of three pounds and that Goodwin satisfies the justices at the next Sessions at what particular place and parish he was resident when he took up arms that a pension may be allowed unto him for the future.
     (George Ivy reported that the inhabitants of Charlton were suspicious of

him and advised that 'You may be more cautious how you give him any further allowance until he makes good proof he took up arms.' A1/110/1653H/168)

835. *Edward Carpenter and Anne Stapleham.*
Upon hearing of the difference between Edward Carpenter and Anne Stapleham of [blank] concerning such moneys as she alleges to be due unto her from Carpenter. Ordered by the consent of both parties that Mr Staples and Mr Sadler justices call the parties before them and to examine the difference and to relieve Stapleham according to law and justice.

836. *William Whittaker concerning the proportioning of his several lands.*
The court is informed by William Whittaker of Bratton that he has divers parcels of lands within the tithings and parishes of Bratton, Westbury, Steeple Ashton, West Ashton, Edington and Hinton which several lands are pasture and meadow and keeps one plough land in Bratton where he does his full service towards the repair of the highways within the parish of Bratton.   And prays the court that his several lands within the   several tithings and parishes may be proportioned according to their several values. The court desires the two next justices to examine the premises and to order what proportion of work he and his tenants ought to bear within the several tithings and parishes for his lands therein according to the statute in that case made and provided.
 (The total value of his lands was £45 a year: Bratton £6, Westbury near £12, Steeple Ashton near £8, West Ashton £8, Edington near £6, Hinton near £8. A1/110/1653H/199)

837. *John Minty and John Hulbert allowed £10 for their loss by fire.*
It appears to the court upon the certificate of the inhabitants of Bromham that upon the six and twentieth day of December last past about one of the clock in the night there happened a sudden and lamentable fire in the house of John Minty in the part whereof lived John Hulbert who lost about one hundred and twenty pounds in goods and household stuff between them whereby Minty and Hulbert together with their families are greatly impoverished. Ordered that the Treasurer for the north shall forthwith upon sight hereof pay Minty and Hulbert or to either of them the sum of ten pounds which is likewise ordered to be divided between them according to the discretion of the two next justices living nearest to Bromham.

838. *Doctor Booreman.*
The court is informed by Doctor Booreman of Stratford [Salisbury]

that the inhabitants of the hundred of Underditch were presented at Christmas Sessions 1649 for decay of St Thomas bridge in the same hundred to which presentment Booreman has appeared on the behalf of the whole hundred and has disbursed for fees and other necessary charges the sum of five and twenty shillings which charge ought to be borne by all the inhabitants of the hundred of Underditch. Ordered that there shall be an equal and an indifferent rate made on all the inhabitants of the hundred for the repaying of Booreman the sum of five and twenty shillings.

(If any refuse to pay, to be bound over.)

839. *Thomas Hanniball, Alexander Stronge and other and the inhabitants of Mere.* (Recites **172**)
And forasmuch as it appears to the court that they are not yet satisfied for the same. Ordered that the overseers of the poor of Mere shall make a rate over all the parish of Mere for the payment of the poor men such moneys as they have disbursed for the inhabitants in erecting the cottage.

(If any refuse to pay, to be bound over.)

840. *George Friend chosen constable of East Harnham.*
The court is informed that Thomas Gillow of East Harnham [Britford] has served in the office of constable there by the space of one whole year last past and that George Friend of the same place ought to serve in the office for this next year. Ordered that Friend shall be constable for the hamlet of East Harnhan for the year ensuing and shall forthwith upon sight hereof repair to the next justice there to take his oath for the execution of the office.

(If he refuses, to be bound over.)

841. *Richard Eggleton.*
Whereas Ricahrd Eggleton of Ogbourne St Andrew being a poor man and not able to pay rent for a house for himself and family and whereas there was a house built by the parish of Ogbourne St Andrew for relief of their poor there which stands upon the common which his brother now lives in and there being one room void in the house. And upon the information of Mr Staples that the house was formerly built by the parish for the relief of their poor and by the consent of Mr Bond lord of he manor there and divers other of the inhabitants. Ordered that Eggleton shall enter into the room and continue the same for the habitation of himself and family without incurring the forfeitures mentioned in the statute.

842. *Andrew Smith and the inhabitants of Mere.* (Recites **624**. See also **693, 758, 794**)
Now upon hearing of the overseers of the poor of Mere. Ordered that the overseers shall pay unto Smith all the arrears due upon the former order being five and twenty shillings and provide for him in some good measure as an impotent of that parish and then the former order of Warminster Sessions to be made null and vacated.

843. *Mr Dyaper and Mr Parker to pay all the bridge money to the Clerk of the Peace.* (Refers to **731**. See also **704**)
Ordered that Mr Dyaper and Mr Parker do forthwith upon sight of this order pay to the Clerk of the Peace such moneys as they have already received and desires Mr Dyaper and Mr Parker forthwith to cause such constables as are behind in payment of the rates of the north part to be bound over to the next Sessions and the like to be done for such constables of the south part as are behind in payment of the rates.

844. *Richard Maurice.*
The court is informed that Richard Maurice of Salisbury shoemaker that he has served the Parliament in the late war in which service he was wounded by means whereof he is not able to get his living and is now fallen into great want and poverty. Ordered that the Treasurer for the south shall pay the sum of forty shillings unto Maurice towards his relief.

845. *Edward Gamlin.* (See also **803**)
The court is informed that Edward Gamlin of Shrewton has entertained Nicholas Petty and his wife as an inmate in his house who are likely to become chargeable to the parish of Shrewton. The court refers the examination of the premisses unto Giles Tooker, Francis Swanton and Edward Mitchell justices or any two of them who are desired to do therein as they shall think fit.

846. *Robert Gumbleton.*
The court is informed by Robert Gumbleton of Britford that he is a very poor man and has sustained a great loss by fire and that his house wherein he now lives is a very fitting house to keep a common alehouse and victualling house as by a certificate under the hands of the minister and most of the substantial inhabitants of Britford more full appears and prays the court to license him accordingly. The court refers the whole examination of the premisses unto the two next justices who are desired to do therein as they shall think fit.

847. *Mr Boddenham and Mr Penny to repair Ebbesborne chancel.*
The court is informed that the chancel in the parish church of
Ebbesborne [Ebbesborne Wake] is in great decay and that Mr John
Boddenham and Mr William Penny ought to repair the same. Ordered
that Mr Boddenham and Mr Penny shall forthwith repair the chancel
or else show good cause to the court the next Sessions why they should
not repair the same.

848. *John Lambe.*
The court is informed by a certificate hereunto annexed under the
hands of most of the inhabitants of Coombe Bissett that there is a
great want of an alehouse there for the entertaining of passengers
and travellers that travel that way it being a common road out of the
western part of the Commonwealth towards London. And that John
Lambe of Coombe Bissett is a very fitting person to keep a common
alehouse and victualling house in the house wherein he now lives and
therefore prayed the court to license Lambe accordingly. The court
refers the examination thereof unto the two next justices who are
desired to examine both the fitness of the person of the said Lambe
and the conveniency of the place to keep an alehouse there and to
license him if they shall think fit.

849. *Mr Aldridge and Mr Bigges.*
The court is informed by Nicholas Aldridge that he was two years
last past constable of the east part of the hundred of Amesbury and
Mr John Bigges of Newton Toney was then constable of the west
part of the hundred and that it was then agreed between them that
Aldridge should send the warrants to Swallowcliffe [recte Swallowfield]
and Wokingham [now in Berkshire] being the remote places in the
hundred and in consideration thereof Bigges was to pay the moiety
of the charge in sending the warrants and that now Bigges denies to
pay the same. The court desires Edward Tooker and Francis Swanton
justices to examine the truth of the premisses and make such order
therein as they shall think fit.

850. *The inhabitants of Tilshead and Edmond Brinsdon.* (See also **881**,
932)
Upon hearing the matter in difference between the inhabitants of
Tilshead and Edmond Brinsdon of the parish of St Edmunds in the
city of Salisbury concerning the settlement of Anne Elliott who was
kept by Brinsdon by the space of three years last past or thereabouts
as he himself confessed in open court and now is sent to the parish
of Tilshead without any lawful order. Ordered that the overseers of

the poor of the parish of Tilshead shall bring and leave Elliott with
Brinsdon to be kept and provided for until the court shall see cause to
alter the same. And that Brinsdon shall likewise pay unto the overseers
of the poor of Tilshead all such reasonable costs and charges as they
have been at in keeping Elliott ever since she was brought by Brinsdon
unto the parish of Tilshead.

(If he refuses to pay, to be bound over.)

851. *Mr John Weekes his order for £25 from the Treasurer for the south.*
Whereas by an order of Christmas Sessions in the four and twentieth
year of the late King [1649] made upon the petition of Mr John Weekes
executor of the last will and testament of Anthony Weekes his brother
deceased showing that Anthony did lend and disburse out of his own
purse the sum of five and twenty pounds towards the repair of Fisherton
and Crane bridges about twelve years then past and paid the moneys
to Mr Andrew Pewde who together with Mr Arthur Poore were by
order of Sessions to take care for the repair of the bridge at the charge
of the county which moneys were neither repaid to Anthony in his
life time nor to John since his brother's death. The court desires Mr
Recorder Stevens, Mr Tooker and Mr Swanton or any two of them
to examine the truth of the petition and make report thereof to the
court as by the order more at large may appear. And whereas Mr
Tooker and Mr Swanton have now certified the court that they have
examined John Weekes and are satisfied that Anthony disbursed the
five and twenty pounds to Pewde and have made the same appear to
the court by a certificate under Pewde's hand that he received the
money and disbursed the same by order of Sessions about the repair
of the bridges and that the money was to be repaid Anthony again
by the county. And whereas further Mr Tooker and Mr Swanton
certify that they cannot anyways find that the five and twenty pounds
was ever repaid to Anthony in his life time or to John his executor
since his death but that Anthony did often times say a little before his
death that the county still owed him the five and twenty pounds as by
the certificate may likewise appear. Ordered that John Weekes shall
upon sight of this order be repaid the five and twenty pounds out of
he Treasury of the south.

852. *Robert Viveash.*
Whereas Robert Viveash of Fittleton is charged to be the reputed
father of a base born child born on the body of Alice Curdy now in
the house of correction at Salisbury. And whereas Alice was brought
to bed and delivered of the child in [blank] in the county of Dorset
and afterwards brought the child from [blank] and left it at Stratford

under the Castle where the child now remains upon the charge of the parish. Ordered by and with the consent of all parties that the two next justices to the parish of Stratford shall call all parties interested before them and examine the business and make such order therein both for the discharge of the parishes and charging the reputed father as the two justices shall see cause and as if the child had been born within this county and the reputed father to have his appeal at the next Sessions in this county if he see cause.

853. *William Bayly for a cottage.*
It appears to the court by the petition of William Bayly of East Harnham [Britford] shoemaker that he is a poor man and destitute of a house for the habitation of himself and family having a wife and four small children and having procured a certificate under the hands and seal of the lord of the manor of East Harnham and also under the hands of some of the substantial inhabitants of the same place wherein they do give their consent to Bayly for the erecting and building him a cottage on some convenient waste place within the manor and therefore prayed the court for the confirmation of the same. Ordered that Bayly shall erect and build him a cottage on some convenient waste place within the manor of East Harnham which shall continue and be a cottage for himself and family during his life time without incurring the forfeitures mentioned in the statute.

General Sessions of the Peace held at Devizes 19 April 1653. William Yorke, William Eyre, Alexander Staples, Thomas Eyre, William Sadler, Edward Mitchell, Walter Ernely, William Shute, Robert Hippisley, Giles Tooker, George Ivy, William Duckett, Edward Stokes, Gabriel Martin, William Blissett and John Read.

854. *An agreement made for the repair of the highways of Chippenham, Langley Burrell and Hardenhuish.*
This agreement tripartite made the fifteenth day of June 1651 between William Lord and William Millsham surveyors of the highways of and within the parish of Chippenham and Richard Scott bailiff of the borough of Chippenham, Anthony Neate gent, Gabriel Goldney senior, Nathaniel Shorly inhabitants of and within the parish on the behalf of themselves and of and with the consent of the rest of the inhabitants of the parish of the first part; Richard Alland and Edmund Hort surveyors of the highways of and within the parish of Langley Burrell and John Alland, Charles Alland, John Alland weaver, William

Hulbert, Thomas Sergent and Robert Jefferyes inhabitants of and within the parish on the behalf of themselves and of and with the consent of the rest of the inhabitants of the parish of Langley Burrell of the second part; and Nicholas Goddin surveyor of the highways of the parish of Hardenhuish, Robert Hawkins clothier and Thomas Brewer inhabitants of and within the parish of Hardenhuish on the behalf of themselves and of and with the consent of the rest of the inhabitants of the parish of the third part.

That where the highways of each parish do lie intermixed the one with the other some nearer unto and some further remote from the parish, for the better supply in amendment of the highways and for the better ease and more conveniency of all the inhabitants for and concerning the amending and repairing the same and for their future peace and quietness. It is considered concluded and agreed unto by and between all the inhabitants in manner following.

And the inhabitants of Chippenham, Langley Burrell and Hardenhuish do for themselves and the rest of their inhabitants now or hereafter being, hereby interchangeably grant, condescend, concede and agree each of them with the other. That the inhabitants of the parish of Chippenham shall and will at their own proper costs and charges from time to time and at all times hereafter so often as shall be needful well and sufficiently repair and amend so much of the highways as do lie in either of the parishes of Langley Burrell or Hardenhuish hereafter mentioned. That is to say from the furthest part of the Grype opposite unto some part of Sambornes farm through Samborne lane or the hollow way commonly called Bristell way opposite unto the higher part next Chippenham of the inclosure of Robert Hawkins. And also from the mill end up the hill to the Crossways in the field and from thence to the highway commonly called Tedbury [Tetbury] or Malmesbury way unto the hither part next Chippenham of Robert Baker's leaze commonly called Butly. And that the inhabitants of Langley Burrell shall and will also from time to time and at all times hereafter so often as shall be needful at their own proper costs and charges well and sufficiently repair and amend so much of the highways as do lie in either of the parishes of Chippenham and Hardenhuish hereafter mentioned. That is to say the ways extending from the Crossways both unto Chippenham field gate and Kellaways bridge. And that the inhabitants of the parish of Hardenhuish shall and will also from time to time and at all times hereafter so often as shall be needful at their own proper costs and charges well and sufficiently repair and amend so much and such parts of the ways as do lie in either of the parishes of Chippenham and Langley Burrell hereafter mentioned. That is to say from the hither part of the inclosure of

Robert Hawkins to the top of Ferword hill and also from the hither part of Robert Baker's leaze commonly called Butts unto Kynton gate in the parish of Kington St Michael.   And that the inhabitants of each parish shall from time to time and at all times hereafter save, defend and keep harmless and indemnified each of them the other of and from all costs charges and damages which shall and may at any time hereafter issue, further be levied upon or against them or any of them respectively out of any court or courts whatsoever of this Commonwealth for or by reason of any fault or insufficiency or any of the highways lying and being in any of the parishes for the which the inhabitants of the several and respective parishes have undertaken and have hereby severally granted and concluded to repair and amend. And it is further concluded and agreed by and between all the inhabitants that this present agreement shall be so speedily and conveniently as may be at the equal and indifferent costs and charges of the inhabitants of each parish and enrolled amongst other the records of the Court of the General Quarter Sessions of the Peace of this county.   To the end that if any of the inhabitants of any of the parishes shall not at any time hereafter observe and keep on their and every parts and behalf severally and respectively this present agreement in repairing and amending the several highways as aforesaid.   The inhabitants of any of the parishes sustaining damage thereby may appeal to be relieved as the court shall order and adjudge against any other of the inhabitants which shall not observe and keep this present agreement.   In witness whereof to one part of this present agreement with the inhabitants of Chippenham, the inhabitants of Langley Burrell and Hardenhuish have set their hands. And to one other part of this agreement remaining with the inhabitants of Langley Burrell the inhabitants of Chippenham and Hardenhuish have set their hands.   And to the other part of this agreement remaining with the inhabitants of Harenhuish the inhabitants of Chippenham and Langley Burrell have set their hands the day and year first above written.

855.   *Thomas Tibboll.*
The court is informed by Thomas Tibboll of Eastmanstreet [Calne] that he has appeared to a presentment against them at Easter Sessions 1650 for decay of a highway within the tithing and have disbursed for fees a fine and other necessary charges the sum of six and twenty shillings six pence which charge ought to be borne by all the inhabitants of the tithing of Eastmanstreet.   Ordered that there shall be an equal and an indifferent rate made upon all the inhabitants of the tithing of Eastmanstreet for the repaying Tibboll the sum of six and twenty shillings six pence.
        (If any refuse to pay, to be bound over.)

856. *Ferdinand Parry.*
There was five pounds heretofore given to the poor of the parish
of Ogbourne St Andrew which came into the hand of Ferdinand
Parry late of Easton Grey deceased and that William Parry his son is
his executor and has refused to pay the five pounds with the interest
thereof unto the now overseers of the poor of Ogbourne St Andrew
for which he was bound over to this Sessions. Ordered (by the consent
of Parry) that he shall pay unto the churchwardens and overseers of
the poor of Ogbourne St Andrew the sum of five pounds together
with all the interest in arrear thereof.

857. *Amos Hope and John Webb constables of Rowde.*
The court is informed by Amos Hope and John Webb constables of
the liberty of Rowde that they have served in that office as constables
there by the space of one whole year last past and that Robert Stevens
and James Stille the elder ought to serve in the office for this next year.
Ordered that Robert Stevens and James Stille shall be constables for the
liberty of Rowde in the places of Amos Hope and John Webb for the
year ensuing and shall forthwith upon sight hereof repair to the next
justice there to take their oaths for the due execution of their office.
(If they refuse, to be bound over.)
(The text gives 'John Stevens' but that is obviously a mistake.)

858. *William Medcalfe for to erect a cottage.*
The court is informed as well by the petition of William Medcalfe of
Kington St Michael as also by a certificate under the hands of most of
the substantial inhabitants within the parish that he is a very poor man
and destitute of an habitation for the succour of himself and family and
having procured a licence under the hand and seal of the lord of the
manor of Kington St Michael for the erecting of a cottage in a certain
place there called Toll hill and therefore prayed the court to confirm
the same. Ordered that Medcalfe shall erect and build him a cottage
in the place aforesaid for the habitation of himself and family which
shall continue to be a cottage during his life time without incurring
the forfeitures mentioned in the statute.
(The plot consisted of five poles lying west of the road from Chippenham.
A1/110/1653E)

859. *Richard Watts for a cottage.*
The court is informed that Richard Watts of Broad Town is a very poor
man and destitute of a house and habitation for himself and family as
by a certificate under the hands of most of the substantial inhabitants
of Broad Town appears and having procured a licence under the hand

and seal of the lord of the manor for the erecting and building him a cottage upon some of the waste ground within the manor of Broad Town prayed the court to confirm the same. Ordered that Watts shall erect and build him a cottage on some of the waste ground within the manor which shall continue and be a cottage for the habitation of himself and family during his life without incurring the penalties mentioned in the statute.

860. *For collecting the arrears of maimed soldiers.*
Forasmuch as Mr George Ivy and Mr Swanton were heretofore both desired by the court to examine and find out the arrears of maimed soldiers and mariners, to wit Mr Ivy for the north part and Mr Swanton for the south part of the county who have taken great pains therein. And for that it appears that there is still remaining arrear much moneys within the county. Now ordered and desired that Mr Edward Stokes and Mr William Shute do join in the assisting of Mr Ivy in the north part and Mr Edward Tooker and Mr John Reade do likewise join in the assisting of Mr Swanton in the south part who are all desired that they join together in getting in the arrears of this county with what speed they may and that they make return thereof to the court that the sums may be disposed of for the use of the county. And the court desires all the justices in their several divisions to be aiding and assisting in getting in the arrears.

861. *Mary Burden £10.* (See also **807**)
It is ordered by the court upon the petition of Mary Burden of Corsham widow late wife of Captain William Burden who died in the service of the Parliament in Ireland that the Treasurer of the north shall pay unto Mary the sum of ten pounds in regard of her present necessity and this order shall be his discharge for the same. But the Treasurer is first to satisfy and pay all former pensioners and orders which are due and payable this present Sessions and not satisfied.
(Burden lost £120 in goods and merchandise which he had taken to Ireland as well as £100 he had spent on horses for his men. A1/110/1653E/244)

862. *Inhabitants of Teffont, inhabitants of Sutton Mandeville concerning settle of Lush.*
Upon hearing the matter in difference between the inhabitants of Teffont and the inhabitants of Sutton Mandeville about the settlement of William Lush. Ordered upon the motion of Mr Swanton of counsel with the inhabitants of Teffont that Lush shall be sent to Sutton Mandeville that being proved to be the last place of his settlement as

a covenant servant with one Sanger there to remain until the court shall see good cause otherwise to order the same.

863. *Robert Hayter chosen constable of Branch and Dole hundred.*
Upon reading the petition of Robert Hayter of Wylye showing that at the last Quarter Sessions he was chosen to be one of the constables of the hundred of Branch and Dole and that in obedience to order of Sessions he took his oath and according to his best ability has executed the office hitherto with an intent to move the court at this Sessions for his discharge by reason of his disability he being not able to travel neither can he write or read and besides a man of mean estate and has been almost ever since the lat Assizes and still is very sick and weak that he cannot attend at this Sessions in person for to be discharged. And for that it is likewise certified to the court by Edward Tooker and Francis Swanton justices that they conceive it fit for Hayter to be discharged of the office by reason of his inability. Ordered that Hayter shall be discharged of the office and that John Fricker of Wylye shall be nominated and chosen to be constable of the hundred in his stead. And it is further ordered that Fricker shall within one week next after notice hereof repair to some justice to take his oath for the due execution of the office upon pain of twenty pounds.
(If he refuse, to be bound over.)

864. *Robert Geerish and Francis Hill.*
The court is informed by Robert Geerish and Francis Hill late churchwardens of Broughton Gifford that they did disburse for the parish in the time they were churchwardens there the sum of six pounds nineteen shillings and eleven pence more than they received of them and prayed the court for their relief therein. The court desires William Eyre and Thomas Eyre justices to call the now churchwardens together with Geerish and Hill before them and examine the premisses and do further therein as they shall think fit.

865. *Inhabitants of Bremhill and Langley Burrell.*
Whereas the inhabitants of Bremhill and Langley Burrell were at Midsummer Sessions last indicted for the decay of Kellaways bridge unto which indictment Robert Kinge on the behalf of the Bremhill inhabitants and John Alland on the behalf of Langley appeared and consented to a trial in Michaelmas Sessions last and then a verdict passed against the inhabitants. Now forasmuch as it appears to the court an the motion of Mr Glanvill of counsel with the inhabitants that they were not privy to the trial. Ordered that a new indictment be preferred against the inhabitants this Sessions and that they appear and

plead thereunto instantly and a trial be had the next Sessions and that William Sellman and Peter Gale give their evidence again at the next Sessions by consent of all parties and the pain of ten pounds imposed for the repair of the bridge at Michaelmas Sessions be respited.

866. *Inhabitants of Bedwyn and John Purrier.*
Whereas there is one [blank] Hussey of Little Bedwyn a dangerous distracted man and very unfit to go abroad in the country for fear of any hurt that he may do to his neighbours who is committed to John Purrier master of the house of correction near Marlborough. Ordered hat there shall be the sum of three shillings six pence a week allowed to Purrier for and towards the maintenance of Hussey from the parish of Little Bedwyn and the overseers of the poor of the parish are to see the same paid accordingly together with what charges he has been at in procuring this order.

867. *Henry Woundye's cottage.*
The court is informed as well by the petition of Henry Woundye of Collingbourne Ducis as also by a certificate under the hands of most of the substantial inhabitants there that he is a very poor man and destitute of a house for the habitation of himself and family and procured a licence under the hand and seal of the Right Honourable the Marquess of Hertford lord of the manor prayed the court to confirm the same. Ordered that Woundye shall erect and build him a cottage upon some waste ground there which shall continue and be a cottage during his life time without incurring the forfeitures mentioned in the statute.

868. *Robert Harris.*
The court is informed by Robert Harris of Etchilhampton that he being tithingman of Etchilhampton did disburse divers sums of money which he is not yet repaid by the inhabitants and that Robert Harding, Roger Poulton the elder, William Dorchester and John Dorchester being tithingmen there for several years last past and have not gave up their accounts to the inhabitants of the tithing neither have delivered such moneys as is conceived remain in their hands. The court desires Walter Ernely justice to examine the accounts both of Harris and Hardinge etc and to make such order for the relief of Harris as to law and justice shall appertain.

869. *John Somers.* (See also **772**, **801**)
It appears to the court that John Somers of Devizes shoemaker had William Naish placed as an apprentice with him by the churchwardens and overseers of the poor of Patney which is very unfit for the trade

and is now at this present Sessions for divers causes here showed in court discharged of the apprentice and that Somers has been at great charges and trouble about the apprentice. Ordered that in regard Naish had a stock given him by his aunt which remains in the hands of Thomas Goddard of Ogbourne, Somers shall be paid the sum of five pounds by Goddard on sight of this order in satisfaction of the trouble and charges he has been at about the apprentice. And Somers is to deliver Naish to the churchwardens and overseers of the poor of Patney and be by them placed forth an apprentice to John Mannings of the same place who is to have forty shillings of the money remaining in Mr Goddard's hands and to receive and keep Naish unless he can show good cause to the contrary the next Quarter Sessions to be held for the county.

870. *Inhabitants of Heddington.*
The court is informed by Robert Child and Humfry Scott surveyors of the highways of Heddington with the great part of the inhabitants that the highways of Heddington consist much of pitched causeways and that it cannot be sufficiently repaired by statute labour by reason there are no materials to be digged within the parish for the amending of the same. Ordered that the highways shall from henceforth be repaired by making an equal pound rate on the inhabitants.
(If any refuse to pay, to be bound over.)

871. *Churchwardens of Sutton Benger and John Peirce and others.*
The court is informed by the churchwardens and overseers of the poor and the rest of the inhabitants of Sutton Benger that Maurice Hartfordsher about three years since having a personal estate of the value of thirteen pounds by the year or thereabouts in Sutton Benger and since deceased having left five grand children very young upon the parish. And whereas John Peirce, Samuel Martyn and others have possessed themselves of the estate of thirteen pounds to their use and cast the children upon the parish. Ordered that it shall be referred to the consideration of Mr Ivy, Mr Shute, Mr Escourt and Mr Stokes justices or any two of them to call the parties before them and to do therein according to law and justice and to certify at the next Sessions what they have done therein.

872. *Abraham Hall and the inhabitants of Calne.*
Whereas Elianor Neate was committed to the house of correction at Devizes for having a bastard being a poor simple woman and not able to work. The court therefore thinks fit an orders that the overseers of the poor of Calne shall pay unto Abraham Hall master of the house of

correction the sum of twelve pence a week towards the maintenance of Elianor together with what he has disbursed for this order.

873. *Abraham Hall.*
The court is informed by Abraham Hall master of the house of correction at Devizes that he has expended and laid out much money about the repairing of the house of correction and has much money due to him for the keeping of several prisoners to him committed by the justices. The court refers the examination thereof to Mr Ivy justice who is desired to call all parties interested therein before him and to take such course for his relief as shall be agreeable to law and justice.

874. *Robert Barnes and Sir William Button about £38 13s 4d for salary.*
In pursuance of an order of the Honourable Court of Chancery made the twelfth of February last between Robert Barnes plaintiff and Sir William Button defendant whereby the salary of eight and thirty pounds thirteen shillings and four pence in the same order mentioned was referred to the three next justices to put an end to it for the plaintiff's satisfaction or in default thereof to the bench of justices their Quarter Sessions to hear and determine the same as to justice appertains. And upon oath made in court that notice of the order was given to Sir William Button by a true copy thereof delivered into his own hands together with a note in writing under the hands of three justices whereby he was summoned to attend at this Quarter Sessions to show cause why he should not make payment of the salary unto Barnes. And upon hearing of several witnesses no procured in open court proving the alary contracted for and the service done. The court being fully satisfied of the justice intended by the Court of Chancery touching the salary orders that Button shall upon notice given him of this order pay unto Barnes the salary of eight and thirty pounds thirteen shillings and four pence.
    (If he refuse to pay, to be bound over.)

875. *Alice Webb to get her service.*
The court is informed that there is one Alice Webb of Poulshot who has had two bastard children but will not confess who is the father of them. Ordered that Webb shall get herself into some service within one month after notice of this order or else be sent to the house of correction at Devizes to be dealt with all according to law.

876. *Thomas Harry chosen constable of the close of Salisbury.*
Forasmuch that at the Quarter Sessions held at Devizes the nineteenth of April 1653 complaint was made to the court that the Close of

Salisbury being heretofore a liberty within itself exempt both from city and county by reason the late Bishop and Dean of Salisbury had a particular charter for keeping of Sessions appointing and making of constables there. But by reason of the late abolishment of the Bishops and Deans there has not been any constable sworn for many years past by means whereof the public peace cannot be so well preserved or the disturbers thereof punished as they ought. The court taking the inconvenience thereof into consideration nominates and appoints Thomas Harry gent being an inhabitant within the Close to be constable of the liberty and thereupon orders that he repair within one week after receipt and notice hereof to the next justice to take his oath for the due execution of the office upon pain of five pounds and that there be for the future a new constable chosen for the liberty at Christmas Sessions yearly.

(Ecclesiastical dignitaries were abolished by a Parliamentary Ordinance of October 1646. They were restored with the return of Charles II in 1660.)

877.   *Clerk of the Peace to cause Harnham bridge to be repaired.*
Upon reading of several orders both of Assizes and Sessions as also of certain letters both from the Lord Chief Baron Wylde (being Judge of Assizes of this county) and others in open court touching the difference depending betwixt this county and the hospital of St Nicholas in repairing of Harnham bridge before the Grand Jury who were desired by the court to take the orders and letters into their consideration and to signify their opinions thereupon in writing unto this court under their hands which being done accordingly. And thereupon it is ordered in pursuance of the Lord Wylde's letter directed to the justices at this Sessions that there be forthwith some stone bought and laid upon the bridge to preserve the ribs and arches thereof from further decay. And the Clerk of the Peace who lives near the bridge is desired to cause the same to be done and to be reimbursed again out of the Treasury of the county and this to be done without prejudice to the county in point of right and the Clerk of the Peace is also desired by the court on the behalf of this county to prosecute the business against the master of the said hospital and to retain counsel therein in this next term and drive the same to a speedy trial and that there be money raised to defray the charge in law if there be none in the Treasurer's hands.

878.   *Nicholas Amylls overseer of Westbury.*
Upon reading of an order of this court made at Midsummer Sessions last and the certificate of Mr Ash and Mr Green justices made thereupon concerning Nicholas Amylls heretofore one of the overseers of the poor of Westbury and upon hearing of the matter it was alleged that

the parties complained against were not heard what they could say for themselves before the certificate was made. Ordered and desired that Mr Ash and Mr Green or any one of them to call all parties interested therein before them together with such testimony as either side can produce concerning the matter complained of and re-examine it again and make such order that the said four pounds sixteen shilling alleged to be due to Amylls be forthwith paid unto him.

(If those adjudges to pay refuse, to be bound over.)

879.   At the Quarter Sessions held at Devizes are appointed and chosen to be Treasurers for the relief of maimed soldiers and mariners for the year following:
> For the north: Richard Diggs of Purton
> For the south: George Duke of Bulford gent.

Ordered that the rates for the relief of maimed soldiers and mariners in pursuance of several ordinances of Parliament late made for that purpose shall remain within every parish of this county so that there may be levied and paid weekly upon every parish throughout the county three pence and no more to commence and begin from the time of this Sessions and shall be collected and paid yearly to the Treasurer appointed for maimed soldiers and mariners according to the statute 43 Elizabeth [1600-01].

880.   And for the relief of prisoners of the Upper Bench and Marshalsea and of such hospitals and almshouses as are within the county are appointed and chosen to be Treasurers:
> For the north: Henry Hawkins of Ashton Keynes gent.
> For the south: Christopher Gray of Wilton, gent.

881.   *Inhabitants of Tilshead and* [Edmond] *Brinsdon.* (Recites **850**. See also **932**)

And Brinsdon refusing to obey the order was again complained of at this Sessions and stood committed until he should pay to the overseers of Tilshead the sum of three pounds seven shillings and six pence which the parishioners of Tilshead disbursed in keeping Elliott which Brinsdon promised in open court he would pay accordingly and desired leave to go and fetch the money. But Brinsdon went away in contempt of the court without paying the £3 7s 6d whereupon the court orders that Brinsdon stand still committed and a warrant of the good behaviour to be issued forth for his apprehension.

General Sessions of the Peace held at Warminster 12 July 1653. William Yorke, John Ash, Edward Mitchell, John Read, Francis Swanton, John Rydout, Walter South and John Eyre.

882. *Robert Lucas.*
It appears to the court by a certificate under the hands of the inhabitants of the parish of Keevil that Robert Lucas being a very poor man and desolate of a house his father being dead who left him a cottage that he built on the waste ground of the parish which is violently kept from him. Ordered that Lucas shall be again placed into the said house.
(If any one molest him, to be bound over.)

883. *Thomas Page.*
The court is informed by the petition of Thomas Page clerk one of the inhabitants of the tithing of Quemerford [Calne] that he was about the second day of May last distrained by two of the Sheriff's bailiffs for issues estreated against the inhabitants for not repairing the highways within the tithing of Quemerford and has paid the bailiff for the issues and their fees the sum of three pounds five shillings and four pence which sum ought not to be borne by one particular person but by the inhabitants of the whole tithing. Ordered that there shall be an equal rate made on the tithing of Quemerford for repayment the sum of three pounds five shillings and four pence to Page and all other his reasonable charges which he has been at in prosecution thereof and in the procuring of this order.
(If any refuse to pay, to be bound over.)

884. *Elizabeth Withy to be sent to Rodden.*
The court is informed that Elizabeth Withy widow who lived in a place called Rodden near Frome Sellwood in the county of Somerset for the space of three years now last past having had four small children with her and that Withy is newly come to Corsley and where she has lately built her a cottage on the waste ground. Ordered upon full hearing of counsel on both sides that Withy shall be forthwith carried back to the overseers of the poor of Rodden that being the place where she and her children last inhabited and were lawfully settled there to be provided for by the overseers as poor of that parish until the court shall see very good cause to alter the same and this to be with saving the right to either parish.

885. *Richard Smart.*
The court is informed that Richard Smart of Kingston Deverill gent

has appeared on the behalf of the inhabitants of Kingston Deverill to an indictment against them for decay of a highway within the parish and has disbursed for fees a fine and other necessary charges the sum of seven and thirty shillings which charge ought to be borne by all the inhabitants of Kingston Deverill. Ordered that there shall be an equal rate made on all the inhabitants of Kingston Deverill for the repayment of Smart the sum of seven and thirty shillings.

(If any refuse to pay, to be bound over.)

Then similar entries:

886. John Sudden of Horningsham for 36s 6d for decay of a highway.

887. Henry Steyner of Lower Dunhead [Donhead St Andrew] 48s for decay of a highway.

888. William Durneford of Longbridge Deverill 34s 8d for decay of a highway.

889. William Whittaker of Bratton 28s 8d for decay of a highway.

890. Robert King of Bremhill 38s 2d for decay of Kellaways bridge.

891. John Alland of Langley Burrell £3 14s 4d for decay of Kellaways bridge.

892. *Richard Jacob a maimed soldier allowed 40s for his present relief.* (See also **936**)
The court is informed that Richard Jacob late of Tytherington [Heytesbury] has served the Parliament in the late wars under the command of Lieutenant General Ludlow in which service he was wounded as by a certificate under the hand of Nicholas Greene and most of the inhabitants of Tytherington appears. The court therefore allows unto Jacob the sum of forty shillings for his relief to be paid him by the Treasurer for the south.

893. *Robert Rimell.*
Whereas Robert Rimell of the parish of Corsley was bound over to this Sessions for refusing to take an apprentice and that it was made appear to the court that the apprentice was bound unto his mother and not to him. Ordered that Rimell shall be discharged of his recognisances and desires Mr Ash, Mr William Eyre and Mr Green justices or any two of them to examine the same and take such course therein as shall

be agreeable to law and justice.

894. *The late overseers of Seend to account or to be committed.*
The court is informed by the now overseers of the poor of Seend that the late overseers of the parish of Seend have not as yet given up an exact account to the parish for the year last past. It is therefore desired by the court that the two next justices near to Seend call the late overseers before them and take their account and to allow the account or disallow it as they find cause and that they pay in the arrears thereof if any be or to be committed to the gaol according to the statute in that case made.

895. *Inhabitants of Beechingstoke and John Hayward and Thomas Hayward.*
Whereas there are differences betwixt the inhabitants of Beechingstoke and John Hayward and Thomas Hayward concerning the house or cottage and goods of Richard Hayward lately deceased. Ordered that the cottage be left to the disposal of the parishioners of Beechingstoke with the consent of the lord of the manor and that the rest of the differences betwixt the parties be referred to the examination of Mr William Yorke, Mr Edward Mitchell and Mr Walter Ernely or any two of them to dispose and order as they shall think fit of the goods of the deceased.

896. *Inhabitants of Codford St Peter and inhabitants of Boyton concerning the settlement of Henry Younge.*
Whereas there is a difference between the inhabitants of Codford St Peter and the inhabitants of Boyton concerning the settlement of Henry Younge about nine years old being the son of Francis now the wife of Ellis Surman of Ashton within the parish of Codford. Ordered that Henry shall remain at Boyton the place of his birth unless the inhabitants of Boyton give good security to the parish of Codford (such as they like of for discharging and saving harmless of the inhabitants of Codford from Henry). And also that Ellis Surman has satisfaction from the inhabitants of Boyton for the keeping Henry before this Sessions. And the court desires John Rydout and Edward Mitchell justices to settle the premisses and to do further therein as they shall see cause.

897. *Mr Seymour and Thomas Streete.*
Whereas Thomas Streete of Bedwyn was bound to the good behaviour to appear at this Sessions for abusing of Mr Seymour overseer of the poor of Bedwyn in the execution of his office. And for that Mr Seymour did not appear to inform the court of the misdemeanours

done unto him. The court desires Mr Alexander Staples, Mr William Blissett, Mr William Sadler and Mr Gabriel Martin or any two of them to call Seymour and Streete before them and to examine the abuse and to do therein as they shall see cause.

898. *Elisha Chandler to continue a cottage.*
Forasmuch as it appears to the court that Elisha Chandler of Bromham being a very poor man has with the consent of William Sherston and the churchwardens and other the parishioners of Bromham erected a cottage upon some of the church land there and further desires the ratifying thereof by the court. Ordered that the house shall continue and remain as a cottage for habitation without incurring the penalty of the statute.

899. *Bartholomew Stevens and John Atwood suppressed from selling of ale without licence.*
The court is informed by the inhabitants of Upavon that Bartholomew Stevens and John Atwood of the same place have been several times suppressed from selling ale in Upavon yet they do still continue selling of ale and beer there contrary to several orders in that behalf made. Ordered that Stevens and Atwood shall be suppressed from selling ale for the future and shall pull down their signs before Bartholomewtide [24 August] next.
      (If the do not do so, to be bound over.)

900. (See also **919**)
Whereas John Taunton was bound over to this Sessions for discharging an order of this court made between Nicholas Amylls and John Taunton concerning the payment of four pounds and sixteen shillings by Taunton to Amylls which money upon hearing of the matter in open court Taunton has now paid and deposited in the hands of Mr William Coles Clerk of the Peace according to the directions of the court and alleges that Thomas Bennet ought to pay the moneys and prayed the court that the matter may be referred to the examination of some of the justices. Ordered that the difference between Taunton and Bennett touching the moneys shall be referred to the hearing and examination of William Eyre, John Ash, Nicholas Green and Edward Mitchell justices or any two of them who are desired with all convenient speed to call the parties before them and their witnesses and examine the differences and order Bennet to repay the four pounds and sixteen shillings to Taunton if they shall find just cause to do the same. And they are desired to certify their doings therein at the next Quarter Sessions.
      (Taunton leased Westbury Parsonage from Bennet A1/110/1653T/143-145)

**General Sessions of the Peace held at Marlborough 4
October 1653. William Yorke, William Eyre, John Ash,
Thomas Eyre, James Ash, Gabriel Martin, William Sadler,
Robert Hippisley, John Read, Edward Stokes, Willam
Blissett, Francis Swanton, William Shute, Edward Mitchell
and William Kinge.**

901. *John Ferris and Francis Baskerville.* (See also **903, 904, 926**)
The court is informed by John Ferris of Richardstone [Winterbourne
Bassett] that he has served Francis Baskerville as a covenant servant
for the space of five years last past and that he was to have yearly of
Baskerville four pounds and a suit of clothes of which he is in arrear
eight pounds and eleven shillings and four suits of clothes and refuses
to pay and satisfy Ferris for the same. The court desires the two next
justices to send for Baskerville before them and examine the truth
of the premises and if they see cause to bind him over to the next
Quarter Sessions there to answer the same.
(In his petition Ferris is described as a coachman. A1/110/1653M/240)

902. *Inhabitants of Broughton Gifford and Monkton.*
The court is informed by the inhabitants of the parish of Broughton
Gifford that there is in the parish two several tithings which are called
by the names of Broughton tithing and Monkton tithing and heretofore
known by the name of Little Broughton tithing, the which tithing has
been time out of mind known to join together in all taxes rates and
payments imposes on and made in the parish. And whereas there has
been laid out by the tithing of Broughton Gifford for conveying of
prisoners to the common gaol of the county the sum of ten pounds
or thereabouts and that the tithing of Monkton would not contribute
thereunto according to their proportion imposed on them by the
tithing of Broughton. Ordered that it shall be referred to Mr John Ash,
Mr William Eyre and Mr William King justices or any two of them
who are desired to call the parties interested therein and to confirm
the rate throughout the whole tithing if they see cause and to make
such order therein as shall be agreeable to law and justice.

903. *John Milles and others and Mr Baskerville about wages.* (See also
901, 904, 926)
The court is informed by John Milles, Joseph Coleman, Henry
Coleman, John Coleman, Daniel White and William Player of Berwick
Bassett labourers that they were employed by Mr Baskerville to reap
his corn within the parish of Winterbourne [Bassett] for which work
Baskerville is indebted unto John Milles etc the sum of twenty pounds

and seventeen shillings and refuses to pay the same unto them. The court desires the two next justices to examine the truth of the premisses and do therein as to law and justice shall appertain.

(The petition states that they were employed on reaping his crop of wheat. A1/110/1653M/25)

904. *John Milles and Mr Baskerville about wages.* (See also **901, 903, 926**) The court is informed by John Milles of Berwick Bassett that he has been employed at several times by Mr Baskerville to do his work at Richardstone [Winterbourne Bassett] for which work Baskerville is indebted unto Milles the sum of three pounds sixteen shillings and six pence and refuses to pay the same unto him. The court desires the two next justices to examine the truth of the premisses and do therein as to law and justice shall appertain.

905. *Foot bridge in the parish of Lacock and Raybridge there.* (See also **751**) Forasmuch as an ancient bridge called Foot bridge lying within the parish of Lacock is in great decay for want of reparations and not certainly known whether the bridge ought to be repaired by the parish of Lacock or the inhabitants of the whole county. And forasmuch as it appears by the certificate of Sir Edward Baynton, William Eyre, William Duckett and Edward Stokes justices that a later built bridge called Raybridge lying over the river of Avon and lying within half a mile of the bridge called Foot bridge is not so useful and convenient for passengers and carriages from London, Bristol, Bath and other places as Foot bridge is, neither can it be made so convenient and with so small charge. And that it is the desire of the inhabitants of Lacock by reason the way leading up and down Nash hill from Raybridge together with the same bridge is in great decay and is very chargeable to the inhabitants of Lacock and much straightened that one carriage cannot pass by another and that Raybridge may be taken down and the materials employed for repair of Foot bridge. Ordered that William Eyre, Thomas Eyre, James Ash, Edward Mitchell, Edward Stokes, William Shute, John Reade, William Sadler, Gabriel Martin, Robert Hippesley and William King or any four of them whereof one to be of the quorum to call before them such workmen and others as they shall think fit and to view the Foot bridge and make an estimate of the charge of repair thereof with materials of Raybridge and make a rate for one moiety of the charge upon the inhabitants of the county for the repair of the same according to the statute in that behalf made in case it cannot be known who should repair the same excluding the inhabitants of Lacock forth of the rate. And it is also agreed by the court in behalf of the county and the inhabitants of Lacock that the inhabitants of Lacock shall bear one moiety of the charge for the repair of Foot bridge and the inhabitants of the county the other moiety and the materials of Raybridge to be allowed thereunto. And that the inhabitants of Lacock (after the same bridge is so repaired and amended) shall from time to time at their own charge repair the bridge and also maintain and continue a footbridge over the river of Avon where Raybridge now stands and the justices are desired by the court to make further treaty with the inhabitants of Lacock and do therein as they shall see cause.

(The issue of Reybridge and Foot bridge caused a long, running dispute. There was a petition supporting the proposal signed by 58 people headed by Charles Talbot and John Talbot. But, later, after the work had started, there were three petitions (with 84, 103 and 66 names respectively) trying to halt the work and restore Reybridge. The work seems to have gone ahead with, later in 1654, an account for £264 15s for work on taking down Reybridge, carriage of the stone and work on Footbridge. A1/110/1654T)

906. *William Cottle.*
Whereas William Cottle of Box was committed at this Sessions to the house of correction at Devizes for selling of ale without licence. Ordered that if Cottle shall enter into recognisance with sufficient sureties (such as William Eyre shall approve of) never to sell ale without licence then he shall be discharged forthwith out of the house of correction for the same.

907. *Inhabitants of Christian Malford and Seagry inhabitants.*
The court is informed by the inhabitants of Christian Malford that they have a great many poor people within the parish so that they are not able to relieve them and that the parish of Seagry has but very few poor. Therefore prayed the court that the inhabitants of Seagry might contribute towards he maintenance of the poor people within the parish of Christian Malford. The court refers the examination thereof unto William Eyre, Edward Stokes and William Sadler justices or any two of them who are desired by the court to examine the truth of the premises and certify their proceedings therein at the next Quarter Sessions that then the court may make a full order therein.

908. *Elianor Chandler to have 18d weekly of Thomas Chandler.*
The court is informed by Elianor Chandler of Swindon that her husband is gone into the service of the State in Ireland and left her five small children who have nothing to keep and relieve them but by her own labour and that Thomas Chandler of Stratton [Stratton St Margaret] grandfather to her children is of ability to relieve them.

Ordered that Thomas Chandler the grandfather shall pay eighteen pence weekly unto Elianor towards the relief of the children. And the court desires the next justice to examine the necessities of Elianor and to do therein for her further relief as they shall think fit.

909. *Mary Stockman.*
Forasmuch as it appears to the court by the petition of Mary Stockman that she was committed to the house of correction at Devizes for absenting herself out of her master's service being one Doctor Burges of Wells in the county of Somerset and that it likewise appears to the court that she is not able any longer to perform such service for her master as she ought in regard that she has the palsy. Ordered that she shall be discharged out of the house of correction and that such clothes as she has left in the house of Doctor Burges shall forthwith on sight hereof be delivered unto her or unto such person as she shall appoint to receive the same.

910. *Robert Perry.* (See also **921**)
The court is informed by Robert Perry of Great Bedwyn that he has been in the State's service and there received certain wounds so that he is disabled to get his maintenance. Ordered that it shall be referred to Mr Martin, Mr Sadler and Mr Blissett justices or to any two of them to certify at the next Quarter Sessions what they have done therein.

911. *Lawrence Ady one of the overseers of Aldbourne.*
Whereas Lawrence Ady one of the overseers of the poor of Aldbourne was bound over from the last Sessions for not passing his account of the moneys he received and disbursed during the time he was in that office and ordered by the court to bring in a certificate thereof to this Quarter Sessions. And whereas he now alleged to the court that he had passed his account accordingly but failed to bring in a certificate thereof. Ordered Ady to make it appear to Mr William Sadler and Mr Blissett justices within two months now next ensuing that he has made a true and just account to the parish of the moneys he received and disbursed during the time he continued in that office.
(If he fails to do so, to be bound over.)

912. *Stephen Webb to entertain Alice Parker his servant.*
Whereas Stephen Webb was bound over to this Quarter Sessions for turning away Alice Parker his covenant servant out of his service before her time was expired. Now upon hearing of the matter in court it appears that there was a quarter of a year to come of the time she was covenanted to serve him when he turned her away and that she

was turned away without the allowance and consent of any justice. Ordered that Webb shall retain Alice into his service again and she is to serve him as long from this time as she was put away before her covenant year was expired.

913.   *Giles Browne, William Pinneger and Thomas Luton.*   (See also **796, 810**)
Forasmuch as it appears to the court by the petition of Giles Browne, Thomas Luton and William Pinneger late overseers of the parish of Lyneham that about Easter last was twelve month they delivered up their accounts both to the parishioners and the justices and that the overseers then chosen with divers others of the parishioners approved thereof until about a month after Sir William Button raising divers exceptions to the account Mr Sadler, Mr Hippesley and Mr Martin justices ordered that they should pay the sum of eleven pounds nine shillings to the new overseers and for their not payment thereof were bound to Warminster Sessions last was twelve month where Browne etc paying the said moneys in court and showing to the court their grievances therein were (according to an order of Sessions) upon re-examining their accounts to Mr Ivy and Mr Shute justices allowed the said eleven pounds nine shillings being now again in the hands of Browne etc shall be by them kept without rendering any further account for the same and likewise orders that they shall have the sum of eight pounds allowed and paid to them by the now overseers of Lyneham in regard of the great charges and expenses they have been at about the same.

> (If the overseers refuse to pay, to be bound over.)
> (The legal charges were detailed:

To Mr Sadler's clerk for 3 recognisances when we were bound over	0	7	6
To Mr Stevens' constable for his fee at Warminster Sessions	0	10	0
To Mr Staples' clerk for a copy of information	0	2	0
To our fees to the Clerk of the Peace	0	14	6
For our expenses and forfeiture	1	13	4
For an order	0	3	0
At Marlborough Sessions to Mr Glanvill for his fee	0	10	0
For a process at that Sessions	0	2	6
For an order there	0	3	0
For our expenses there	1	0	0
For our expenses in going to the justices to meet about Marlborough order	0	10	0
For a copy of that order and for the justices' warrant			

to bring in the Inhabitants of Lyneham	0	2	0
At a meeting at Chippenham for our expenses and 16 witnesses	0	12	0
To Mr Ivy's clerk for writing for us there	0	3	0
Spent at Malmesbury at Petty Sessions	0	3	0
For our expenses at the Devizes Sessions	0	6	0
Spent at Clack	0	9	0
Spent at Marlborough Sessions	0	15	0
	8	4	10

A1/110/1653M)

914. *John Bartlett and Jane Wastefeild.*
The court desires Edward Stokes and Henry Blake justices to send for Mrs Jane Wastefeild, William Silke and John Bartlett to treat with them about the forcible entries now in question and reconcile all the differences between then touching that matter if they can and mediate a friendly end thereof that the public peace of the Commonwealth may be preserved and future differences and suits prevented.

915. *George Sloper to be master of the house of correction at Devizes.*
Whereas it appears to the court that Abraham Hall committed several misdemeanours as he was master of the house of correction at Devizes for which the court thinks fit to discharge him out of the office and put in a more fitting man in the same place. And desires Thomas Eyre, Edward Mitchell, Edward Peirce and Thomas Payne justices or any two of them (whereof Mr Eyre and Mr Mitchell to be one) to take the account of Hall of all such stock and goods of the county's as were delivered unto him when he first entered on the office and likewise allow unto Hall such reasonable disbursements as he has justly laid out and expended about the house of correction for which he has had no former satisfaction or allowance. Further ordered and appointed that George Sloper worsted comber shall be master of the house of correction in the place of Hall and shall correct all such prisoners as shall be sent thither and set them to work and shall receive the stock of the county which remains in the possession or custody of Hall and the justices are likewise desired to take a true and just inventory of the same and deliver a copy thereof to the Clerk of the Peace. And Sloper shall enter into a bond with good and sufficient sureties unto the Clerk of the Peace in such a time as the justices shall think fit as well for the due and faithful execution of his office as also for the redelivery of all such stock goods and implements of the county's as shall come into his hands and be inventoried as aforesaid.

916.   *Richard Amor, John Monday, John Ashton and Thomas Poulton.*
Forasmuch as complaint has been made to the court by Richard Amor,
John Monday and John Ashton all of Pewsey that Thomas Poulton
of Pewsey has commenced several actions in the county court against
Amor etc for several sums of money amounting in the whole to
fourteen pounds for a supposed contribution due from the inhabitants
of Pewsey to the late garrison of Faringdon and made over to Poulton
by the Lord Grandison sometime governor of the garrison. Ordered
and desired (by the consent of all the parties) that John Ash, Edward
Mitchell, James Ash and William Blissett justices or any two of them to
call all the parties before them and hear and examine the premises and
make some end and order therein or otherwise to bind over Poulton
to the next Sessions and certify their proceedings therein.

917.   *Nathaniel Thorely, John Ely to have £8 13s 8d from the inhabitants
of Chippenham.*
Forasmuch as Nathaniel Thorely and John Ely of Chippenham have
appeared to an indictment against the inhabitants of Chippenham for
decay of a certain bridge within the parish and have disbursed in charges
the sum of three and thirty shillings and eight pence. And likewise
paid for issues to the Sheriff both out of the Exchequer and Crown
Office the sum of seven pounds amounting in the whole to the sum
of eight pounds thirteen shillings and eight pence which charge ought
to be borne by all the inhabitants of Chippenham. Ordered that there
shall be an equal rate made on all the inhabitants of Chippenham for
the repayment of the sum of eight pounds thirteen shillings and eight
pence.
     (If any refuse to pay, to be bound over.)

918.   *The hospital at Salisbury.*
The court is informed that there is a hospital or almshouse at East
Harnham [Salisbury] towards the maintenance whereof there is paid
yearly from the Treasurer the sum of ten pounds. And forasmuch as
the power and placing of people there is challenged by some private
persons. The court desires that Edward Tooker, Francis Swanton,
John Reade and Bennett Swayn justices or any two of them to call
before them all persons claiming any such power or interest therein
ad to examine the first foundation of the almshouse and what lands
or other things belong or were given for the maintenance thereof and
in whose occupation the same is and what persons or persons are in
the same house and by whom they were there placed and to make a
certificate thereof to the next Quarter Sessions.

919. *John Taunton and Thomas Bennett.* (Refers to **900**)
Upon hearing the matter in difference between John Taunton and
Thomas Bennett concerning the payment of four pounds sixteen
shillings in question in the presence of counsel learned on both sides
and upon reading the certificate of John Ash and William Eyre justices
made by virtue of an order of reference from the last Quarter Sessions.
It appeared that they calling the parties before them and hearing and
debating the matters in difference and proving a decree then showed
unto them that for the year 1643 being the year in question the rate
for the poor of the parsonage was six pounds and sixteen shillings and
that Taunton enjoyed the parsonage only three months of the year
and paid towards the rate of the poor the sum of forty shillings being
a month more than was due and was then put out and intermeddled
no more therein that year in his own right but the residue of the tithes
and profits of that year was received some by Doctor Henchman,
some by the late King's forces and some by Mr Bennett and some
remained in the hands of the parishioners which by the decree Bennett
was to receive and Taunton discharged therefrom as by the certificate
remaining of record in this court more fully appears. The court now
confirms the certificate and orders that the now overseers of Westbury
do forthwith charge the sum of four pounds sixteen shillings so in
arrear upon the year's rate of the parsonage of Westbury and get the
same confirmed by two justices according to the statute in such case
made and provided and then take a distress for the same upon the
parsonage and therewithal reimburse Nicholas Amylls heretofore one
of the overseers of the poor of Westbury the four pounds sixteen
shillings that he may have no further cause to complaint.

1654

**General Sessions of the Peace held at Salisbury 10 January
1654. William Yorke, Edward Tooker, Giles Eyre,
Alexander Thistlethwaite, John Dove, Francis Swanton,
Edward Mitchell, Robert Hippisley.**

920. *Inhabitants of Highworth for a rate for repair of ways.*
Whereas the highways in the parish of Highworth were presented to be
in decay and that there has been a distress taken on Thomas Edwards
of Hampton in the parish of Highworth for the same. Ordered that
there shall be an equal rate made over the whole parish of Highworth
for the repayment of such charges Edwards has been at therein.
       (If any refuse to pay, to be bound over.)

921. *A pension of 40s to Robert Perry.* (Refers to **910**)
The court is informed by Robert Perry of Great Bedwyn labourer that
he was a soldier in the late wars in the service of the State and that he
took up arms in the service first at Charnhamstreet [Hungerford] and
was afterwards wounded in the service as by the certificate under the
hand of Colonel Bingham showed in court at the last Quarter Sessions
it did appear. It now appears to the court by a certificate under the
hands of Mr William Sadler and Mr Martin that upon examination
of the matter by virtue of an order of Sessions it appeared to them
that Perry took up arms at Charnhamstreet under the command of
Captain Judeley. Ordered in regard Perry is become impotent by reason
of his wounds that he shall be allowed a pension of forty shillings a
year towards his maintenance and shall be paid him quarterly by the
Treasurer for the north.
(The certificate records that he fought at the battle of Edgehill.
A1/110/1654H/143)

922. *Susan Studly, the inhabitants of Downton.*
The court is informed by Susan Studly of East Downton widow that
the inhabitants of East Downton were presented for not repairing a pair
of stocks within the parish and that a certain time and pain was then
set and appointed by the court for repairing and amending the same
which through neglect of the tithingmen was not done accordingly
but continued a long time without any repairing or amending for the
default whereof there were certain estreats issued forth against the
inhabitants of East Downton the discharge whereof amounting in the
whole to the sum of 18s 10d which Studly has disbursed and laid out.
Ordered that there shall be an equal rate made on the inhabitants of
the tithing of East Downton for the repayment of Studly the sum of
18s 10d.
(If any refuse to pay, to be bound over.)

923. *Desborough, Appleton and Chequer 3 persons in gaol to have some
allowance out of their goods seized.*
The court is informed that Mathew Desborough, Isaac Appleton and
Stephen Chequer now prisoners in the gaol of Fisherton Anger and
committed thither by Edward Tooker for a supposed robbery were
apprehended at Keevil where the bailiffs or officers belonging to the
lords of the manor there seized upon such moneys, horses and goods
as were found upon them as felons' goods and detained the same in
their hands refusing to allow to the prisoners out of the same what is
reasonable and fitting towards the maintaining of them in prison. The
court desires Nicholas Green justice to send for the bailiffs or officers

or any other person or persons in whose hands or custody the money or goods are and take course that there be an allowance out of the same towards the maintaining of the prisoners.

(If any of them refuse to allow the same, to be bound over.)

924. *Henry Richman.*
Whereas Henry Richman of Christian Malford was bound over to this Sessions by William Shute justice at the prosecution of Jane Coller a covenant servant for one whole year for detaining her wages being the sum of seven and fifty shillings. Ordered that the sum of fifty seven shillings be paid into the hands of Mr Shute on Friday next and that Mr Shute is desired to examine the same whether Jane has not served out her year and to allow Richman for the time of her absence if he see cause.

(If he neglects to pay, to be bound over.)

925. *Thomas Batt.*
Whereas Thomas Batt of the parish of Great Bedwyn is a very poor aged man and very destitute of a house and habitation for himself and family. Ordered that the overseers of the poor of Great Bedwyn shall pay unto Batt 12d weekly unless they shall provide a house for him or show good cause to the next justice why they should not do the same.

(The detailed petition explains that his parents had lived in a house which was falling down so he built a cottage for them on the waste in which he also lived for 22 years. But when his parents died, Lord Seymour evicted him and leased the cottage to someone else. A1/110/1654H/139)

926. *Mr Baskerville to pay wages.* (See also **901**, **903** and **904**)
Whereas it appears to the court upon oath that there are several sums of money due to John Milles, Thomas Smyth and Andrew Venn of Berwick [Berwick Bassett] from Francis Baskerville that is to say to Milles four pounds sixteen shillings, to Smyth three pounds and to Venn three pounds four shillings and ten pence and that there have been former orders made therein which have taken no effect and that Milles etc have been put to great charges and have suffered great damages in the prosecution thereof. Ordered that Baskerville shall pay unto Milles etc their several wages within one week after notice of this order or leaving a copy thereof at his dwelling house together with such damages as Milles etc have sustained in the prosecution hereof and shall be allowed to them by Mr Sadler, Mr Blissett and Mr Hippisley justices or any two of them. And if he shall refuse to pay the same then Mr Sadler etc or any two of them are desired by the court to grant their warrant to the Sheriff and all other officers for the

apprehending and carrying of Baskerville to the common gaol of the county there to remain until he shall pay the wages and such charges as shall be adjudged him to pay.

927. *Mary Prewet of Clarendon.*
It appears by the petition of Mary Prewet widow that Ambrose Prewet her late husband and she lived about twenty years in Clarendon Park next Winchester gate in a little house there which house about Lent last was burnt and that since that time she and her children have continued in the house called Tibbols Lodge in the parish of Laverstock where she still continues. Ordered that Mary Prewet and her children shall be and continue in the lodge where they now are until the inhabitants of the parish of Laverstock shall show good cause to the court to the contrary. And the court likewise refers the examination of the premisses to Edward Tooker, John Dove and Francis Swanton or any two of them to do therein as they shall see cause according to law and justice and to make certificate thereof to the next Sessions.

928. *Mr Francis Bennett to pass his account.*
It is ordered by the court that Mr Francis Bennett shall with all convenient speed pass his account before Mr [Edward] Tooker and Mr [Francis] Swanton justices of the moneys he has formerly received concerning the relief of maimed soldiers and mariners and the relief of the poor prisoners and about the commission for charitable uses before the late troubles. And the justices are herby authorised to appoint Bennett to pay the moneys remaining on his account to such persons for the service of the county as they shall think fit.

929. *Inhabitants of Barford and Baverstock.*
Complaint has been made to this Court of Sessions by the inhabitants of Barford [Barford St Martin] that they being over pressed and burdened with multiplicity of poor people within the parish so that they are not able to relieve them theirselves but desire the help and assistance of the inhabitants of the parish of Baverstock [Dinton] being the next parish thereunto adjoining and of the same hundred who have very few or no poor at all within their parish. The court desires Edward Tooker, John Dove and Francis Swanton or any two of them to call before them the overseers of the poor of each parish and if they find cause, to consider what weekly or monthly sum the inhabitants of Baverstock shall allow or pay towards the relief of the poor people of Barford and to make certificate thereof to the next Quarter Sessions that the court may proceed accordingly.

930. *For getting one measure throughout the county.*
Forasmuch as there are divers laws and statutes heretofore made for the making and using of one measure according to the standard in the Exchequer to be used within this Commonwealth. And whereas by a late statute made in the seventeenth year of the late King Charles [1641-2] entitled an Act for the regulating the office of Clerk of the Market, the reformation of false weights and measures, it was enacted that from thenceforth there should be but one weight, one measure and one yard according to the standard of the Exchequer to be used through the realm as well in places privileged as without (any usage or custom to the contrary notwithstanding). And that whosoever should sell, buy or keep any other weight, measure or yard then as aforesaid whereby any corn, grain or other thing is bought or sold should forfeit for every such offence five shillings (being thereof lawfully convicted by the oath of one sufficient witness before any justice of the peace, mayor or other head officer of the county, city or town corporate respectively) which sum or forfeiture of five shillings shall be levied by the churchwardens or overseers of the poor of the parish where such offence should be committed to the use of the poor of the parish of the goods and chattels of such offenders by way of distress and sale of the offender's goods rendering the overplus to the party offending and in default of such distress to be committed to prison there to remain without bail or mainprise until he should pay the same as by the statute more fully appears. Now forasmuch as the justices at this present Sessions assembled taking into consideration the great abuses daily committed within this county by means of the inequality of weights and measures therein used to the great deceit of many people of this county and especially of the poorer sort do hereby order and require all persons whatsoever within this county to reform their weights and measures according to the standard of the Exchequer and that they neither sell, buy or keep any other measure but according to the standard on pain of such forfeitures and penalties as expressed in the recited statute. And the court also requires the churchwardens and overseers of the poor in every respective parish to cause the forfeitures and penalties to be levied accordingly. And the court likewise requires the Sheriff of this county to cause this order to be forthwith published in all market towns within the county and post up copies thereof.

931. *Inhabitants of Stapleford and John Gilbert.*
Upon hearing the matter in difference betwixt the inhabitants of Stapleford and John Gilbert concerning the rating and taxing of Gilbert proportionably according to his plot of ground lying within the parish

of Stapleford. Ordered by and with the consent of both parties that Gilbert shall pay and contribute towards the relief of the poor of the parish of Stapleford such rates and taxes as are or shall be proportionable to his allotment imposed on him by the overseers of the poor and this payment is to begin at this present Sessions and so to continue until the court shall see good cause to alter the same.

932. *Inhabitants of Tilshead and Edmond Brinsdon.* (Recites **850** and **881**) And Brinsdon refusing to obey the orders was again complained of at this Sessions and the court taking the contempt of Brinsdon into consideration orders that a warrant of good behaviour be again issued forth against Brinsdon and that he stand still committed until he pay the three pounds seven shillings and six pence together with all such charges and expenses as the inhabitants of Tilshead have or shall be at in prosecution of the business and to be afterwards continued over to the good behaviour unto the next Sessions there to answer his contempt of the several orders of Sessions.

933. *The tithing of Milford and Pitton.*
It appears to the court upon the complaint made by the tithingmen of the several tithings of Milford [Laverstock] and Pitton concerning the carrying and conveying of hue and cry and cripples from Milford to Pitton and so likewise from Pitton to Milford which is so tedious and troublesome unto them by reason there is no common horseway leading towards Pitton and that they are so far distant the one from the other that it cannot be done without great trouble and charge and that the tithingman of Laverstock refuses to receive such hue and cry from Milford as he and his predecessors have done time out of mind. The court desires Edward Tooker, Francis Swanton, John Dove and John Reade justices or any two of them to call the parties interested before them and examine the same and make such order and settlement therein as they shall think fitting.

934. *The Clerk of the Peace to pass his account.*
The Clerk of the Peace has by several orders and directions of the court laid forth and disbursed for the inhabitants of the county several sums of money both for the repair of Harnham bridge [Salisbury] and for suing forth the several commissions of charitable uses for the finding out of certain lands heretofore given for the repair of the bridge and likewise for prosecuting a bill of indictment against the master of St Nicholas hospital and bringing the same to a speedy trial. Ordered and desired that Mr Edward Tooker, Mr Giles Eyre, Mr Francis Swanton, Mr John Reade and Mr William Coles justices or any two of them

to take the account of the Clerk of the Peace of all such moneys of the county as remain in his hands and of all his disbursements as well about the repair of the bridge as the prosecution of the commissions and indictment as is already disbursed and laid forth and give a speedy order and directions for the reimbursing the same again forth of such moneys of the county as remain either in the Treasurer's hands or any other whatsoever.

935. *Soloman Hillman.* (Refers to **571**. See also **958**)
It appears to the court by the petition of Soloman Hillman of Warminster that he was a soldier in the Parliament service about eight years and in that service he received many wounds whereby he is utterly disabled to do anything towards the getting of his living and that about four years last past he was allowed a pension of four marks a year which has not been sufficient to maintain himself his sickly wife and one child. The court desires Mr Green and Mr Mitchell justices to examine the truth of the petition and certify at the next Quarter Sessions whether they think fit that his pension shall be augmented or not.

936. *Richard Jacob a pension of £2 13s 4d.* (See also **892**)
It appears to the court by the petition and a certificate under the hand of William Ludlow that Richard Jacob served in the Parliament service under the command of Colonel Ludlow in which service he was dangerously wounded by means whereof he is disabled to do any further service. Ordered and allowed Jacob a yearly pension of two pounds thirteen shillings and four pence to be paid him quarterly by the Treasurer for the south until the court shall see cause to alter the same. And the court further orders and allows unto Jacob the sum of thirteen shillings and four pence for his present relief to be paid him by the Treasurer.
    (The certificate records that 'he behaved himself honestly, faithfully and stoutly'. A1/110/1654H/132)

General Sessions of the Peace held at Devizes 4 April 1654. William Yorke, William Sadler, Edward Mitchell, William Shute, John Read, William Blissett, Edward Stokes, Gabriel Martin, Thomas Grove, William Eyre and Robert Hippisley.

937. *Thomas Browne for begetting Joan Stratton with child.*
Thomas Browne of Overton [West Overton] was bound over to this Quarter Sessions for begetting Joan Stratton with child by means whereof she is grown lame and impotent and likely to become

chargeable to the parish of Overton. Ordered and desired William Sadler and William Blissett justices to examine the truth of the premisses and to make such order therein as shall be agreeable to law and justice and certify their doing therein to the next Quarter Sessions.

938.   *The parish of Westport united to Malmesbury.*
Whereas William Yorke, William Sadler, Gabriel Martin justices and other their fellow justices at the Quarter Sessions have been informed that the parish of Westport is a very small place and the church thereof demolished and lies very convenient to be united unto Malmesbury whereunto it lies adjacent. Ordered that the parish of Westport shall be united to the parish of Malmesbury and one register is to serve for both the places according to an Act of Parliament in that case lately made and provided.

(The petition explained that the inhabitants of Westport had no 'exercise' on the Lord's Day in the morning and that they got christened and buried at Malmesbury church. A1/110/1654E/177)

939.   *Nicholas Toogood constable of the hundred of Alderbury.*
The court is informed by Giles Gantlett one of the constables of the hundred of Alderbury that he is a man very unfit for the office in regard he is sixty eight years of age and very infirm in body and can neither write or read and therefore prayed the court for his relief therein. Ordered that Nicholas Toogood of Alderbury shall be constable of the hundred for this next year in the place of the said Giles Gumbleton and shall within one week next after notice of this order repair to the next justice there to take his oath for the due execution of the office upon pain of twenty pounds.

(If he refuses, to be bound over.)
(The clerk has obviously made a mistake. It is clear from the petition that it should be Gantlett, not Gumbleton. A1/110/1654E/129)

940.   *The inhabitants of Atworth for repair of their highways.*
The court is informed by the inhabitants of Atworth that they have heretofore repaired their highways within the parish by labourers and ploughs according to every man's proportion but by reason there are several causeways that cannot be repaired by such labourers and therefore prayed the court that there might be a rate made throughout the parish of Atworth for the levying of such moneys as are needful for the repair of the highways for the present and so to continue for the future. The court confirms the same accordingly and orders that there shall be an equal rate made on all the inhabitants of Atworth for

the repair of the highways within the parish so to continue for the future unless the court shall see cause to alter the same.

941.   *Roger Ward for continuing a cottage.*
The court is informed by a certificate under the hands of most of the substantial inhabitants within the parish of Ashton Keynes that Roger Ward of Ashton Keynes is a very poor man and has formerly erected a cottage for the habitation of himself and family and has since procured licence from the lord of the manor for the continuing of the cottage and therefore prayed the court to confirm the same. Ordered that the cottage so erected shall continue and be a cottage during his life time and no longer without incurring the forfeitures mentioned in the statute.

942.   *Richard Gay for erect a cottage.*
It appears to the court that there is one Richard Gay the younger of Kington St Michael labourer that has licence under the hands and seals of the lords and ladies of the manor of Kington and a certificate from the inhabitants of the parish for erecting of a cottage on a small plot of the waste ground belonging to the manor lying near to the common pound and adjoining the wall of Elizabeth Bowne spinster containing about four luggs. Ordered that Gay shall erect him a cottage on the plot of ground for the succour of himself and family for and during his life and no longer without further order and without incurring the forfeitures in the Act of Parliament.
　　(The certificate said that Gay 'is for his behaviour quiet and sober and willing to betake himself to any labour that his lameness will suffer him to undergo'. A1/110/1654E/169)

943.   *Inhabitants of Chippenham, inhabitants of Stanley.*
Upon hearing of the matter in difference between the inhabitants of Chippenham and Stanley [Bremhill] concerning the repair of the highways within the parish of Chippenham. Ordered and desired William Eyre, Edward Stokes, Nicholas Green and William Shute justices or any two of them to examine the premises and make such order for the repair of the highways as they shall think fit agreeable to law and justice.

944.   *Edward Martyn for wages due to Richard Clarke his servant.*
Whereas Edward Martyn of Studley in the parish of Trowbridge was bound over to this Sessions for detaining the wages of Richard Clarke his servant from him and forasmuch as it appears to the court upon hearing of the matter that there is six pounds sixteen shillings confessed

in court by Martyn to be due to Clarke for his wages and promised in court forthwith to give him security for the payment thereof and is now gone away without performing the same in contempt of the court. Ordered that Martyn shall stand committed until he shall pay the same and the next justice is desired to grant his warrant against Martyn and send him to the common gaol there to remain until he shall pay unto Clarke the sum of six pounds sixteen shillings.

945. *The master of the house of correction of Marlborough and the parish of Chiseldon about Roger Ducocke.* (See also **734**)
The court is informed by the master of the house of correction near Marlborough that for above a whole year's space last past he has had in his custody Roger Ducocke of Chiseldon committed to him by Mr Martin justice for divers misdemeanours being a lunatic man and is allowed but six pence a week towards his maintenance. All which the court taking into consideration and conceiving it to be too little to maintain him orders that the parish of Chiseldon shall pay unto the master of the house of correction the sum of two shillings weekly from henceforth during the time of continuance there towards his maintenance and in default thereof the master is to carry back Ducocke to the parish of Chiseldon and deliver him to the overseers of the poor there to be provided for by them according to law.

946. *The master of the house of correction of Devizes for repair of the house.*
The court is informed by the master of the house of correction at Devizes that the house is in great decay and that the reparations thereof will amount unto above twenty pounds or upwards upon the view of several workmen. The court desires William Yorke, Thomas Eyre and Edward Mitchell justices or any two of them to call some workmen of skill unto them and view the decays of the house of correction and to take such course therein as in their discretions they shall think fit and certify their proceedings therein at the next Quarter Sessions.
(See Appendix 2/4 for a full account of the expenditure.)

947. *Margery Bayly for an allowance from Margery Mayo.*
It appears to the court by the petition of Margery Bayly of Chippenham widow that her late husband William Bayly being deceased her whole estate is determined and that it likewise appears to the court by the oath of Theophilus Comely that her mother Margery Mayo has an estate worth sixty pounds by the year. The court desires William Eyre, Edward Stokes and William Shute justices or any two of them to call the parties before them and examine the same and if they shall upon examination of the business find Margery Mayo to have a competent

and sufficient estate then to allow Margery Bayly four shillings a week to be paid to her by Margery or more if they shall so think fit and the first payment thereof to commence from this present Sessions.

(The petition explained that Margery Bayliff's husband had died much in debt. Her mother's estate was being managed by John Mayo her grandson. A1/110/1654E/177)

948. *Walter Woodman to pay £3 for placing his bastard an apprentice.* Upon hearing the matter in difference between Walter Woodman and Thomas Wayte one of the overseers of the poor of Westport [Malmesbury] concerning a bastard child which Woodman was heretofore adjudged to be the reputed father. Ordered by and with the consent of both parties that Woodman shall pay the sum of three pounds before Michaelmas next to the churchwardens and overseers of the parish of Westport towards the placing the bastard child an apprentice according to an order made by Mr Jenner and Mr Ivy justices.

(If he defaults, to be bound over.)

949. *John Grante.*
It appears to the court by the petition of John Grante that on the five and twentieth day of March last at the court leet held for the hundred of Bradford by Daniel Wylcarly gent steward did upon the presentment of the jury there appoint Robert Harris and John Dick to be constables of the hundred but afterwards imposed the office on John Grante. The court therefore refers the examination of the truth of the petition to William Eyre and James Ash justices who are desired to consider thereof and to do therein what shall be agreeable to law and justice and certify the court thereof at the next Quarter Sessions.

950. *Daniel Drake for keeping two bastard children.*
Whereas it appears to the court by the petition of Daniel Drake keeper of the gaol of Fisherton Anger that Margery Kenger late of Chalfield [Atworth] widow and Joan Burt of Manton in the parish of Preshute singlewoman were both of them committed to the gaol for that they were both with child and have since their commitment been delivered of two several children in the gaol and having both of them received their trial at the last Assizes held for the county, Kenger was sentenced by the law to suffer death and was executed accordingly and since her death Drake has disbursed towards the keeping of the child the sum of 20s. And Burt having likewise received her trial at the Assizes was thereupon acquitted, Drake has likewise laid forth towards the keeping of her child the sum of 30s and therefore prayed the court that there might be some speedy course taken both for the

repayment of the several sums above mentioned as also the disposing and keeping of the children for the future. The court desires Edward Tooker, Francis Swanton and John Reade justices or any two of them to consider the premisses and to make such order for keeping of the children and reimbursing of Drake as they shall think fit and agreeable to law and justice.

(If any refuse to obey the orders made, to be bound over.)

(The costs were: Margery Kendger's child, for putting it to nurse for 5 weeks at 3s a week and for linen and woollen 5s. Jane Burt's child, keeping for 15 weeks at 2s a week. A1/110/1654E/174)

951. At the present Quarter Sessions are appointed and chosen to be Treasurers for the relief of maimed soldiers and mariners within this county for the year following: for the north, John Jacob of Norton, gent; for the south, John Mompesson of Tidworth, gent.

952. Ordered by the justices at this present Sessions assembled that the rates for the relief of maimed soldiers and mariners in pursuance of several ordinances of Parliament late made for that purpose shall remain within every parish of this county so that there may be laid and paid weekly upon every parish throughout the county (blank) pence and no more to commence and begin from the time of this Sessions and shall be collected and paid weekly to the Treasurers appointed.

953. And for the relief of prisoners of the Upper Bench and Marshalsea and of such hospitals and almshouses as are within the county are appointed and chosen to be Treasurers: for the north, William Gale of Corston, gent; for the south, Richard Fitz of Chilmark, gent.

954. *Robert Wallis discharged of his apprenticeship.*
Be it remembered that at the Quarter Sessions held at Devizes for the fourth day of April in the year of Our Lord God 1654 upon the oath of Elizabeth Wallis and Robert Weston of Ramsbury that John Rogers having one Richard Wallis bound to him as an apprentice Weston his master is run out of the county. Ordered that the apprentice should be discharged from his master for the future. In witness whereof we the justices (whereof one of us is of the quorum) whose names are subscribed being present at the said Sessions have hereunto set our hands and seals the day and year first above written.

955. *Edith Garrett wife of Robert Garrett and her child to be sent from Kingston Deverill to Corton to her husband.*
The court is informed by Mr Hyde of counsel with the inhabitants

of Kingston Deverill that Robert Garrett having heretofore married with Edith Phillips of Kingston Deverill and is now become a covenant servant with Mr Mompesson of Corton [Boyton] and his wife with one child remains at Kingston Deverill and she will not live with her husband whereby she and her child are likely to be chargeable to the parish and prayed the court that the wife of Garrett with her child may be sent to her husband at Corton by him to be kept and provided for. Ordered that the overseers of the poor of Kingston Deverill shall take Garrett's wife and child and carry them to Corton and leave them with Garrett her husband there to remain and by him to be provided for according to law.

956. *Concerning the settlement of Anne Pryor's bastard child.*
Forasmuch as it appears to the court upon the oath of Anne Pryor that her bastard child whereof Stephen Whitter is the reputed father and now in the keeping of Mathewe Sheeringe of Trowbridge and is so hardly kept for want of food and clothes that it is like to perish. Ordered that the matter shall be referred to the consideration of William Eyre, John Ash, Nicholas Green and James Ash justices or any two of them who are desired to examine the truth of the information and if it appears to be true then the justices are desired to appoint the child to be taken away from Sheeringe and place him with Mary Pryor mother of Anne. And Richard Whitter father of Stephen is ordered to pay eighteen pence weekly to Mary Pryor for the keeping thereof and to give the child clothes fitting for it in regard of its great necessity and to continue the payment thereof until he shall bring forth his son to answer his offences.

957. *Edward Coombes to keep 2 of his grandchildren or to keep one and pay 5s a month to the overseers of Kingston Deverill towards the keeping of the other.*
Forasmuch as the court is informed by Mr Hyde of counsel with the inhabitants of Kingston Deverill that John Romsey and his wife of that place are both dead and left behind them four children on the charge of the parish. And that Edward Coombes grandfather to the children has taken one of them from the charge of the parish and kept him ever since. And forasmuch as it now appears to the court upon the oaths of Andrew Leversedge and Peter Hurle that Edward Coombes has an estate worth threescore pounds a year and is of ability to keep another child of the said four children. Ordered that Coombes shall take and breed up one child more of the four children and the overseers of the poor of Kingston Deverill are to carry the child to his grandfather who is hereby ordered to receive it and breed it up. And in case the grandfather shall refuse to receive it and breed it up then

he is hereby ordered to pay five shillings by the month to the overseers of the poor of Kingston Deverill for the keeping thereof and to keep the first child besides.

(If he refuses to obey this order, to be bound over.)

958.   *Soloman Hillman his pension of 4 marks increased to £4 by the year.* (Refers to **935**; see also **571**)

And whereas at this Sessions the justices have certified the court that they have inquired into and examined the condition of Soloman Hillman and are thoroughly satisfied by credible persons as well of his faithful service in the time of the wars as of his impotent condition by reason thereof and do think fit that his pension of four marks be increased to four pounds by the year as by the certificate appears. Ordered that the pension be increased to four pounds a year and likewise orders and appoints the Treasurer for the south to pay unto Hillman the sum of four pounds by the year to be paid him quarterly towards his relief and maintenance in regard of his great necessity and the many wounds he has received in the Parliament service, the first payment thereof to begin at Midsummer day next and to continue until further order.

APPENDIX 1

NAMES OF JUSTICES ATTENDING QUARTER SESSIONS COURTS

Number of Courts Attended

	1642	1643	1644	1645	1646	1647	1648	1649	1650	1651	1652	1653	1654
Robert Hyde	I	I	I										
William Button	2	2											
John Penruddock	3	I											
Francis Swanton	2	2	2		I	I	2	4	4	3	3	4	I
Edward Hungerford		2											
Theobald Gorges	2												
Thomas Hall	2		I										
Robert Drew		3	I										
Charles Gore	I												
Robert Eyre	I		I										
John Farewell	I												
John Glanville		I	I										
John Danvers	I												
James Long	I												
Edward Ernle		I	I	I									
William Wallis		I		I									
Richard Goddard			I			I	I						
Thomas Bennett			I		2		3						
John Topp			I										
William Hussey					2	2	I	I	2	2			
William Eyre					2	3	2	I	3	2	2	2	I
Edward Tooker					2	3	I	2	3	2	I	I	I
George Ivy					2		3	2			2	I	
Anthony Ashley Cooper						I				2			
George Howe						I	I						
Robert Nicholas						2	2		I				
John Norden						I	3						

Number of Courts Attended

	1642	1643	1644	1645	1646	1647	1648	1649	1650	1651	1652	1653	1654
William Sadler						I	2	I	2	3	2	2	I
Robert Hippisley						I	I	I	I		2	2	2
William Stephens							I	2					
Giles Eyre							I		I	I	I		I
Richard Aubrey							I						
William Yorke						4	I					3	2
Barnaby Coles							I	I	I	I	I	I	
Richard Grobham Howe							I	2	2	2			
Edmund Ludlow							I						
John Dove							I						I
John Long							I	2	I				
Robert Jenner							I						
William Littleton							I	4	2				
Thomas Eyre								2	3	2	I	2	
Nicholas Green								2	2	I	I	I	
Edward Stokes								I	2	2	I	2	I
Walter South								I	3	4	I	2	
Henry Martin								I					
John Read								I	4	2	2	4	I
William Shute								I	3	I	I	2	I
Richard Green									2	2			
Gabriel Martin									3	2	2	2	I
Edward Baynton									I	I	I		
Alexander Staples									I	2	4	2	
John Dove										I	I	I	
Edward Manning										I	I		
William Duckett										I	I	I	
Giles Tucker										I	I		
Edward Mitchell											2	3	2
John Rydout											I	I	
John Ash											I	2	
Walter Ernely											I	I	
Thomas Escourt											I		
Giles Tooker												I	
William Blissett												2	I
John Eyre												I	
James Ash												I	
William Kinge												I	
Alexander Thistlethwaite													I
Thomas Grove													I

APPENDIX 2

REPAIRS TO HOUSES OF CORRECTION

1.   A note of the charge of the house of correction near Marlborough wanting repair 1650. (A1/110/1650E/146)

For timber boards and iron and workmanship	7	0	0
For glassing the house	0	10	0
There is for 8 and twenty hundred of tile(?) work	2	12	0
For 10 quarters of lime	3	0	0
For a load of gravel	0	7	0
For 8 hundred of last	0	10	0
For a load of flat	1	0	0
One dozen of crease	0	3	0
2 bushels of tile pins	0	6	0
8 thousand of 3 penny nails	0	18	0
3 thousand of 4 penny nails	0	9	0
2 thousand of 6 penny nails	0	10	0
2 hundred of brick	0	6	0
2 load of earth	0	4	0
Laid out by the keeper already			
For repairing of the wall of the house	0	10	0
For glassing the windows	0	10	0
For making two houses of office in the house	0	10	0
For the order and fetching of him	0	2	0
The sum of £22	12	8	

2. A true account of Abraham Hall, master of the house of correction within the borough of Devizes of his disbursements in and about the repairing and amending of the house beginning from Midsummer Sessions 1650. (A1/110/1651H/163)

For a load of stones and a load of white earth and a man's labour to amend the chimneys and fireplaces	0	9	0
Pd to Cornelius Wyatt carpenter for his labour and his timber which was used before	0	12	0
Pd to William Phippe tyler for his work done about the house	3	8	8
Pd for the lattice windows for the kitchen and for the women's prison and making the floors	0	12	0
Pd to John Hedges blacksmith for bars, cramps and nails and for amending the locks and for two new keys	1	16	2
Itm for a new brass for the mill and for work done about the mill	0	9	0

Itm for timber that amended the stock loft and the new bench in the porch	0	5	0
Itm to John Weekes for new glass and for amending all the windows about the house	3	0	0
Itm for lime and hair and new crests for the house	1	2	8
Itm for repairing the well	0	4	0
Itm paid to the minister for his dues	0	5	8
Itm paid to the Chamberlain's chief rent	0	2	0
Itm paid for the two orders at Sessions	0	8	0
Itm to Cornelius Wyatt for timber boards and work as appears by his note	9	8	3
Itm to a clerk for writing my accounts	0	1	6
	22	3	11

And for my own pains what your worships please to allow me.

3. A note of the charge that was bestowed in repairing the house of correction near Marlborough. (A1/110/1651H/170)

Paid to John Burgis the slater for a parcel of slates	0	10	0
Itm for a load of slates from the quarry	1	0	0
Itm paid to him for 2 bushels of tile pins	0	6	0
Itm paid to him for laying 28 hundred of slater's work at 4s the hundred	5	12	0
Itm paid to him for plastering the walls, making a halfpace and a back in the hall chimney and putting a window at the stairs head and plastering the stairs	0	10	0
Itm paid to William Wilkins for 10 quarters of lime	3	0	0
Itm paid to William Pike joiner for boards wainscot timber and workmanship by his bill appears	5	0	0
Itm paid for 2 loads of sand 8s and 2 loads of white earth 5s	0	13	0
Itm paid for 6 hundred of laths	0	8	0
Itm paid to the glazier as by his bill appears	0	17	0
Itm paid for 5 bushels of seeling hair	0	3	4
Itm paid for a rudder to sift the lime withal	0	0	6
Itm paid to Robert Hobbes the smith for locks, nails, 18 pair of gimbals to hang the window lids and other iron work as by his bill appears	2	6	8
Itm paid for 2 hundred of bricks	0	6	0
Itm paid for 14 creases	0	3	6
Itm laid out by John Purryer keeper of the Bridewell for repairing the house in the times of the troubles	2	3	0
Itm allowed to him for his travel in providing materials for the workmen (if the court approves)	1	0	0
	23	19	0

4. The total bill for the repair of the house of correction at Devizes in 1654 amounted to £7 12s 1d (A1/110/1654T/147)

John Yeustace of Devizes for ridding the well 18d and for drawing it up 12d	o	2	6
John Wyatt for a welldrock 12s, for a weather board to the well 1s, for 3 days work about the mill and the well 4s 6d	o	17	6
John Wyatt for two posts for a penthouse and other things 3s and for his man's work 2s 6d	o	5	6
Abram Hall for lattice in the buttery	o	1	o
Mr Bennett's clerk for an order to desire the justices to view the house of correction	o	3	o
William Harris of Potterne for repairing the malt mill	o	1	o
Samuel Taylor of Devizes for mending the bucket	o	o	6
Cornelius Kingston for mending the brick wall of the house for labour	1	10	o
Mr White for eleven hundred of bricks at 3s the hundred	1	13	o
For twenty sacks of lime at 2s per sack	2	o	o
John May of Devizes for a lock and staple 3s, for a lock and staple 3s 6d, for a lock and staple 1s 4d	o	7	10
For a lock 1s 4d, for two half hundreds of nails 11d, for nails 1d	o	2	4
For a lock 4s, for four staples 4d, for cramps and sprigs 1s 8d	o	6	o
For nails 5d, for half hundred of nails 10d, for two shoulder sterts 3d	o	1	6
For one shoulder stert 2d, for nails 1d, for a plate 2d	o	o	5

INDEX OF PERSONS AND PLACES

Unless prefixed by p. (e.g. p.321) the index refers to entry numbers, not page numbers. Roman numerals (e.g. xvii) refer to pages of the introduction. The names of justices sitting at each sessions are included in Appendix 1 showing their records of attendance. Surnames prefaced by Mr, are not associated with justices unless there is a clear link.

INDEX OF SUBJECTS

A selective index: Cross references to some examples are given in the introduction.

WILTSHIRE RECORD SOCIETY
(AS AT AUGUST 2014)

President: Dr Negley Harte
Honorary Treasurer: Ivor M. Slocombe
Honorary Secretary: Miss Helen Taylor
General Editor: Dr V. Bainbridge
Assistant Joint Editor: S.D. Hobbs

Committee:
D. Chalmers
Dr A. Craven
Dr D.A. Crowley
Mrs S. Thomson
K.H. Rogers

Honorary Independent Examiner: C.C. Dale
Correspondent for the U.S.A.: Senior Judge R.W. Ogburn

PRIVATE MEMBERS

Adams, Ms S, 23 Rockcliffe Avenue, Bathwick, Bath BA2 6QP

Anderson, Mr D M, 6 Keepers Mews, Munster Road, Teddington, Middlesex TW11 9NB

Badeni, Countess June, Garden Cottage, Norton, Malmesbury SN16 0JX

Bainbridge, Dr V, 60 Gloucester Road, Lower Swainswick, Bath BA1 7BN

Banks, Mr B H, 16 Velley Hill, Gastard, Corsham, SN13 9PU

Barnett, Mr B A, 3 The Orangery, Academy Drive, Corsham, SN13 0SF

Bathe, Mr G, Byeley in Densome, Woodgreen, Fordingbridge, Hants SP6 2QU

Bayliffe, Mr B G, 3 Green Street, Brockworth, Gloucester GL3 4LT

Bennett, Dr N, Hawthorn House, Main Street, Nocton, Lincoln LN4 2BH

Berrett, Mr A M, 10 Primrose Hill Road, London NW3 3AD

Berry, Mr C, 17 Fore Street, Hayle, Cornwall TR27 4DX

Blake, Mr P A, 18 Rosevine Road, London SW20 8RB

Box, Mr S D, 73 Silverdale Road, Earley, Reading RG6 2NF

Brand, Dr P A, 155 Kennington Road, London SE11 6SF

Brown, Mr D A, 36 Empire Road, Salisbury SP2 9DF

Brown, Mr G R, 6 Canbury Close, Amesbury, Salisbury SP4 7QF

Browning, Mr E, 58 Stratton Road, Swindon SN1 2PR

Bryson, Dr A, Humanities Research Institute, 34 Gell Street, Sheffield S3 7QW

Carrier, Mr S, 9 Highfield Road, Bradford on Avon BA15 1AS

Carter, Mr D, Docton Court, 2 Myrtle Street, Appledore, Bideford EX39 1PH

Cawthorne, Mrs N, 45 London Road, Camberley, Surrey GU15 3UG

Chalmers, Mr D, Bay House West, Bay Hill, Ilminster, Somerset TA19 0AT

Chandler, Dr J H, 8 Lock Warehouse, Severn Road, Gloucester GL1 2GA

Church, Mr T S, 12 Cathedral View,

Winchester SO23 0PR

CLARK, Mr G A, Highlands, 51a Brook
Drive, Corsham SN13 9AX

CLARK, Mrs V, 29 The Green,
Marlborough SN8 1AW

COLCOMB, Mr D M, 38 Roundway
Park, Devizes SN10 2EO

COLES, Mr H, Ebony House, 23 Lords
Hill, Coleford, Glos GL16 8BG

COLLINS, Mr A, 22 Innox Mill Close,
Trowbridge BA14 9BA

COLLINS, Mr A T, 36 Wasdale Close,
Horndean, Waterlooville PO8
0DU

COLMAN, Mrs P, 37a Bath Road,
Atworth, Melksham SN12 8JW

CONGLETON, LORD, West End Lodge,
Ebbesbourne Wake, Salisbury SP5
5JW

COOMBES-LEWIS, Mr R J, 45 Oakwood
Park Road, Southgate, London
N14 6QP

COOPER, Mr S, 12 Victory Row, Royal
Wootton Bassett, Swindon SN4
7BE

COWAN, Mrs E, 24 Lower Street,
Harnham, Salisbury SP2 8EY

CRAVEN, Dr A, 17 Steamship House,
Gasferry Road, Bristol BS1 1GL

CROOK, Mr P H, Bradavon, 45 The
Dales, Cottingham, E Yorks HU16
5JS

CROUCH, Mr J W, 25 Biddesden Lane,
Ludgershall, Andover SP11 5PJ

CROWLEY, Dr D A, 7 Eversley Court,
Wymering Road, Southwold IP18
6BF

CUNNINGTON, Ms J, 2766 Folkway
Drive, Unit 40, Mississauga, Ont.
L5L 3M3, Canada

DAKERS, PROF C, Ferneley Cottage,
Water Street, Berwick St John,
Shaftesbury SP7 0HS

D'ARCY, Mr J N, The Old Vicarage,
Edington, Westbury BA13 4QF

DAVIES, Mrs A M, Barnside, Squires
Lane, Old Clipstone, Mansfield
NG21 9BP

DUNFORD, Mrs J, 2 Greenditch House,
Parsonage Lane, Chilcompton,
Radstock Som BA3 4JU

DYSON, Mrs L, 1 Dauntsey Ct, Duck
St, West Lavington, Devizes SN10
4LR

EDE, Dr M E, 12 Springfield Place,

Lansdown, Bath BA1 5RA

EDWARDS, Mr P C, 33 Longcroft Road,
Devizes SN10 3AT

FIRMAGER, Mrs G M, 72b High Street,
Semington, Trowbridge BA14 6JR

FOSTER, Mr R E, Cothelstone, 24
Francis Way, Salisbury, SP2 8EF

FOWLER, Mrs C, 10 Ullswater Road,
Wimborne, Dorset, BH21 1QT

FOY, Mr J D, 28 Penn Lea Road, Bath
BA1 3RA

FROST, Mr B C, Red Tiles,
Cadley, Collingbourne Ducis,
Marlborough SN8 3EA

GAISFORD, Mr J, 8 Dudley Road,
London NW6 6JX

GALE, Mrs J, PO Box 1015, Spit
Junction, NSW 2088, Australia

GHEY, Mr J G, Little Shute, Walditch,
Bridport DT6 4LQ

GODDARD, Mr R G H, Sinton
Meadow, Stokes Lane, Leigh
Sinton, Malvern, Worcs WR13
5DY

GOSLING, REV DR J, 1 Wiley Terrace,
Wilton, Salisbury SP2 0HN

GOUGH, MISS P M, 39 Whitford Road,
Bromsgrove, Worcs B61 7ED

GRIFFIN, D, C J, School of Geography,
Queen's University, Belfast BT7
1NW

GRIST, Mr M, 38 Springfield, Bradford
on Avon BA15 1BB

HARDEN, Mrs J O, The Croft, Tisbury
Road, Fovant, Salisbury SP3 5JU

HARE, Dr J N, 7 Owens Road,
Winchester, Hants SO22 6RU

HARTE, Dr N, St Aldhelm's Cottage,
5 Stokes Road, Corsham SN13
9AA

HEATON, Mr R J, 60 Roberts Ride,
Hazlemere, High Wycombe HP15
7AF

HELMHOLZ, PROF R W, Law School,
1111 East 60th Street, Chicago,
Illinois 60637 USA

HENLY, Mr C R G, 27 Harden's Close,
Chippenham SN15 3AA

HERRON, Mrs Pamela M, 25 Anvil
Crescent, Broadstone, Dorset
BH18 9DY

HICKMAN, Mr M R, 184 Surrenden
Road, Brighton BN1 6NN

HICKS, Mr I, 153 Cornbrash Rise,
Trowbridge BA14 7TU

HICKS, PROF M A, Department of History, University of Winchester SO22 4NR

HILLMAN, MR R B, 20 West Ashton Road, Trowbridge BA14 7BQ

HOBBS, MR S, 63 West End, Westbury BA13 3JQ

HORNBY, MISS E, 70 Archers Court, Castle Street, Salisbury SP1 3WE

HOWELLS, DR Jane, 7 St Mark's Rd, Salisbury SP1 3AY

HUMPHRIES, MR A G, Rustics, Blacksmith's Lane, Harmston, Lincoln LN5 9SW

INGRAM, DR M J, Brasenose College, Oxford OX1 4AJ

JAMES, MR & MRS C, 20 The Willows, Yate, Bristol, BS37 5XL

JEACOCK, MR D, 16 Church Street, Wootton Bassett, Swindon SN4 7BQ

JOHNSTON, MRS J M, Greystone House, 3 Trowbridge Road, Bradford on Avon BA15 1EE

KEEN, MR A.G. 38 Rawson Street, Bilton, Harrogate HG1 4NU

KENT, MR T A, Rose Cottage, Isington, Alton, Hants GU34 4PN

KITE, MR P J, 13 Chestnut Avenue, Farnham GU9 8UL

KNEEBONE, MR W J R, 12 Hollis Way, Southwick, Trowbridge BA14 9PH

KNOWLES, MRS V A, New Woodland Cottage, Stanton St Bernard, Marlborough SN8 4LP

LANSDOWNE, MARQUIS OF, Bowood House, Calne SN11 0LZ

LAURENCE, MISS A, 1a Morreys Avenue, Oxford OX1 4ST

LAWES, MRS G, 48 Windsor Avenue, Leighton Buzzard LU7 1AP

LEE, DR J, 66 Kingshill Road, Bristol, BS4 2SN

LUSH, DR G J, 5 Braeside Road, West Moors, Ferndown, Dorset BH22 0JS

MARSH, REV R, 67 Hythe Crescent, Seaford, East Sussex BN25 3TZ

MARSHMAN, MR M J, 13 Regents Place, Bradford on Avon BA15 1ED

MARTIN, MS J, 21 Ashfield Road, Chippenham SN15 1QQ

MASLEN, MR A, 27 Fell Road, Westbury BA13 2GG

MATHEWS, MR R, 57, Anthony Road, Denistone, NSW 2114, Australia

MOLES, MRS M I, 40 Wyke Road, Trowbridge BA14 7NP

MONTAGUE, MR M D, 115 Stuarts Road, Katoomba, NSW 2780, Australia

MOODY, MR R F, Fair Orchard, South Widcombe, East Harptree, Bristol BS40 6BL

MORIOKA, PROF K, 3-12, 4-chome, Sanno, Ota-ku, Tokyo, Japan

MORLAND, MRS N, 33 Shaftesbury Road, Wilton, Salisbury SP2 0DU

NAPPER, MR L R, 9 The Railway Terrace, Kemble, Cirencester GL7 6AU

NEWBURY, MR C COLES, 6 Leighton Green, Westbury BA13 3PN

NEWMAN, MRS R, Tanglewood, Laverstock Park, Salisbury SP1 1QJ

NICOLSON, MR A, Sissinghurst Castle, Cranbrook, Kent TN17 2AB

NOKES, MR P M A, 14 Staverton Road, Oxford OX2 6XJ

OGBOURNE, MR J M V, 4 Aster Drive, Stafford ST16 1FH

OGBURN, MR D A, 110 Libby Lane, Galena, Missouri 65656, USA

OGBURN, SENIOR JUDGE R W, 303 West Hahn's Peak Avenue, Pueblo West, Colorado, 81007, USA

PARKER, DR P F, 45 Chitterne Road, Codford St Mary, Warminster BA12 0PG

PATIENCE, MR D C, 29 Priory Gardens, Stamford, Lincs PE9 2EG

PERRY, MR W A, 11 Buttercup Close, Salisbury SP2 8FA

POWELL, MRS N, 4 Verwood Drive, Bitton, Bristol BS15 6JP

PRICE, MR A J R, Littleton Mill, Littleton Pannell, Devizes SN10 4EP

PRIDGEON, DR E, 85 Kings Chase, Brentwood, Essex CM14 4LD

RAYBOULD, MISS F, 20 Radnor Road, Salisbury SP1 3PL

RAYMOND, MR S, 38 Princess Gardens, Trowbridge BA14 7PT

ROBERTS, MS M, 45 Spratts Barn, Royal Wootton Bassett, Swindon SN4 7JR

ROGERS, MR K H, Silverthorne

House, East Town, West Ashton, Trowbridge BA14 6BE

ROLFE, MR R C, 4 The Slade, Newton Longville, Milton Keynes MK17 0DR

SAUNT, MRS B A, The Retreat, Corton, Warminster, BA12 0SL

SHARMAN-CRAWFORD, MR T, One Mapledurham View, Tilehurst, Reading RG31 6LF

SHELDRAKE, MR B, The Coach House, 4 Palmer Row, Weston super Mare, BS23 1RY

SHEWRING, MR P, 73 Woodland Road, Beddau, Pontypridd, Mid-Glamorgan CF38 2SE

SINGER, MR J, 49 Bradwall Road, Sandbach, Cheshire CW11 1GH

SLOCOMBE, MR I, 11 Belcombe Place, Bradford on Avon BA15 1NA

SMITH, MR P J, 6 Nuthatch, Longfield, Kent DA3 7NS

SNEYD, MR R H, Court Farm House, 22 Court Lane, Bratton, Westbury BA13 4RR

SPAETH, DR D A, School of History and Archaeology, 1 University Gardens, University of Glasgow G12 8QQ

STONE, MR M J, 26 Awdry Close, Chippenham SN14 0TQ

SUTER, MRS C, 16 Swindon Road, Highworth, Swindon, SN6 7SL

SUTTON, MR A E, 22 Gravel Hill, Wimborne BH21 1RR

TATTON-BROWN, MR T, Fisherton Mill House, Mill Road, Salisbury, SP2 7RZ

TAYLOR, MR C C, 11 High Street, Pampisford, Cambridge CB2 4ES

TAYLOR, MISS H, 14 Pampas Court, Warminster BA12 8RS

THOMPSON, MR & MRS J B, 1 Bedwyn Common, Great Bedwyn, Marlborough SN8 3HZ

THOMSON, MRS S M, Home Close, High St, Codford, Warminster BA12 0NB

VINE, MR R E, 11 Brocks Mount, Stoke sub Hamdon, Somerset, TA14 6PJ

WAITE, MR R E, 18a Lower Road, Chinnor, Oxford OX9 4DT

WARREN, MR P, 6 The Meadows, Milford Mill Road, Salisbury SP1 2SS

WILLIAMSON, B, 40 Florence Park, Bristol BS6 7LR

WILTSHIRE, MR J, Cold Kitchen Cottage, Kingston Deverill, Warminster BA12 7HE

WILTSHIRE, MRS P E, 23 Little Parks, Holt, Trowbridge BA14 6QR

WOODWARD, A S, 35 West Ridge Drive, Stittsville, Ontario K2S 1S4, Canada

WRIGHT, MR D P, Gerrans, Coast Road, Cley-next-the-Sea, Holt NR25 7RZ

YOUNGER, MR C, The Old Chapel, Burbage, Marlborough SN8 3AA

UNITED KINGDOM INSTITUTIONS

Aberystwyth
  National Library of Wales
  University College of Wales
Bath. Reference Library
Birmingham. University Library
Bristol
  University of Bristol Library
  University of the West of England
Cambridge. University Library
Cheltenham. Bristol and
    Gloucestershire Archaeological
    Society
Chippenham
  Museum & Heritage Centre
  Wiltshire and Swindon History
  Centre

Coventry. University of Warwick
  Library
Devizes
  Wiltshire Archaeological & Natural
  History Society
  Wiltshire Family History Society
Durham. University Library
Edinburgh
  National Library of Scotland
  University Library
Exeter. University Library
Glasgow. University Library
Leeds. University Library
Leicester. University Library
Liverpool. University Library

London
  British Library
  College of Arms
  Guildhall Library
  Inner Temple Library
  Institute of Historical Research
  London Library
  The National Archives
  Royal Historical Society
  Society of Antiquaries
  Society of Genealogists
Manchester. John Rylands Library
Marlborough
  Memorial Library, Marlborough
    College
  Merchant's House Trust
  Savernake Estate Office
Norwich. University of East Anglia
  Library
Nottingham. University Library
Oxford

Bodleian Library
  Exeter College Library
Reading. University Library
St Andrews. University Library
Salisbury
  Bemerton Local History Society
  Bourne Valley Historical Society
  Cathedral Library
  Salisbury and South Wilts Museum
Southampton. University Library
Swansea. University College Library
Swindon
  English Heritage
  Swindon Borough Council
Taunton. Somerset Archaeological and
  Natural History Society
Wetherby. British Library Document
  Supply Centre
York. University Library

INSTITUTIONS OVERSEAS

AUSTRALIA
Adelaide. University Library
Crawley. Reid Library, University of
  Western Australia
Melbourne. Victoria State Library

CANADA
Halifax. Killam Library, Dalhousie
  University
Ottawa, Ont. Carleton University
  Library
Toronto, Ont
  Pontifical Inst of Medieval Studies
  University of Toronto Library
Victoria, B.C. McPherson Library,
  University of Victoria

EIRE
Dublin. Trinity College Library

GERMANY
Gottingen. University Library

JAPAN
Sendai. Institute of Economic History,
  Tohoku University
Tokyo. Waseda University Library

NEW ZEALAND
Wellington. National Library of New
  Zealand

UNITED STATES OF AMERICA
Ann Arbor, Mich. Hatcher Library,
  University of Michigan
Athens, Ga. University of Georgia
  Libraries
Atlanta, Ga. The Robert W Woodruff
  Library, Emory University
Bloomington, Ind. Indiana University
  Library
Boston, Mass. New England Historic
  and Genealogical Society
Boulder, Colo. University of Colorado
  Library
Cambridge, Mass.
  Harvard College Library
  Harvard Law School Library
Charlottesville, Va. Alderman Library,
  University of Virginia
Chicago
  Newberry Library
  University of Chicago Library
Dallas, Texas. Public Library
Davis, Calif. University Library
East Lansing, Mich. Michigan State
  University Library

Evanston, Ill. United Libraries,
    Garrett/Evangelical, Seabury
Fort Wayne, Ind. Allen County Public
    Library
Houston, Texas. M.D. Anderson
    Library, University of Houston
Iowa City, Iowa. University of Iowa
    Libraries
Ithaca, NY. Cornell University Library
Los Angeles
    Public Library
    Young Research Library, University
    of California
Minneapolis, Minn. Wilson Library,
    University of Minnesota
New York
    Columbia University of the City of
    New York
Piscataway, N.J. Rutgers University

    Libraries
Princeton, N.J. Princeton University
    Libraries
Salt Lake City, Utah. Family History
    Library
San Marino, Calif. Henry E.
    Huntington Library
Santa Barbara, Calif. University of
    California Library
South Hadley, Mass. Williston
    Memorial Library, Mount Holyoke
    College
Urbana, Ill. University of Illinois Library
Washington. The Folger Shakespeare
    Library
Winston-Salem, N.C. Z.Smith
    Reynolds Library, Wake Forest
    University

LIST OF PUBLICATIONS

The Wiltshire Record Society was founded in 1937, as the Records Branch of the Wiltshire Archaeological and Natural History Society, to promote the publication of the documentary sources for the history of Wiltshire. The annual subscription is £15 for private and institutional members. In return, a member receives a volume each year. Prospective members should apply to the Hon. Secretary, c/o Wiltshire and Swindon History Centre, Cocklebury Road, Chippenham SN15 3QN. Many more members are needed.

The following volumes have been published. Price to members £15, and to non-members £20, postage extra. Most volumes up to 51 are still available from the Wiltshire and Swindon History Centre, Cocklebury Road, Chippenham SN15 3QN. Volumes 52–66 are available from Hobnob Press, c/o 8 Lock Warehouse, Severn Road, Gloucester GL1 2GA

1. *Abstracts of feet of fines relating to Wiltshire for the reigns of Edward I and Edward II,* ed. R.B. Pugh, 1939
2. *Accounts of the parliamentary garrisons of Great Chalfield and Malmesbury, 1645–1646,* ed. J.H.P. Pafford, 1940
3. *Calendar of Antrobus deeds before 1625,* ed. R.B. Pugh, 1947
4. *Wiltshire county records: minutes of proceedings in sessions, 1563 and 1574 to 1592,* ed. H.C. Johnson, 1949
5. *List of Wiltshire boroughs records earlier in date than 1836,* ed. M.G. Rathbone, 1951
6. *The Trowbridge woollen industry as illustrated by the stock books of John and Thomas Clark, 1804–1824,* ed. R.P. Beckinsale, 1951
7. *Guild stewards' book of the borough of Calne, 1561–1688,* ed. A.W. Mabbs, 1953
8. *Andrews' and Dury's map of Wiltshire, 1773: a reduced facsimile,* ed. Elizabeth Crittall, 1952
9. *Surveys of the manors of Philip, earl of Pembroke and Montgomery, 1631–2,* ed. E. Kerridge, 1953
10. *Two sixteenth century taxations lists, 1545 and 1576,* ed. G.D. Ramsay, 1954
11. *Wiltshire quarter sessions and assizes, 1736,* ed. J.P.M. Fowle, 1955
12. *Collectanea,* ed. N.J. Williams, 1956
13. *Progress notes of Warden Woodward for the Wiltshire estates of New College, Oxford, 1659–1675,* ed. R.L. Rickard, 1957
14. *Accounts and surveys of the Wiltshire lands of Adam de Stratton,* ed. M.W. Farr, 1959
15. *Tradesmen in early-Stuart Wiltshire: a miscellany,* ed. N.J. Williams, 1960
16. *Crown pleas of the Wiltshire eyre, 1249,* ed. C.A.F. Meekings, 1961
17. *Wiltshire apprentices and their masters, 1710–1760,* ed. Christabel Dale, 1961
18. *Hemingby's register,* ed. Helena M. Chew, 1963
19. *Documents illustrating the Wiltshire textile trades in the eighteenth century,* ed. Julia de L. Mann, 1964
20. *The diary of Thomas Naish,* ed. Doreen Slatter, 1965
21–2. *The rolls of Highworth hundred, 1275–1287,* 2 parts, ed. Brenda Farr, 1966, 1968
23. *The earl of Hertford's lieutenancy papers, 1603–1612,* ed. W.P.D. Murphy, 1969
24. *Court rolls of the Wiltshire manors of Adam de Stratton,* ed. R.B. Pugh, 1970
25. *Abstracts of Wiltshire inclosure awards and agreements,* ed. R.E. Sandell, 1971
26. *Civil pleas of the Wiltshire eyre, 1249,* ed. M.T. Clanchy, 1971
27. *Wiltshire returns to the bishop's visitation queries, 1783,* ed. Mary Ransome, 1972
28. *Wiltshire extents for debts, Edward I – Elizabeth I,* ed. Angela Conyers, 1973
29. *Abstracts of feet of fines relating to Wiltshire for the reign of Edward III,* ed. C.R. Elrington, 1974
30. *Abstracts of Wiltshire tithe apportionments,* ed. R.E. Sandell, 1975

31. *Poverty in early-Stuart Salisbury*, ed. Paul Slack, 1975
32. *The subscription book of Bishops Tounson and Davenant, 1620–40*, ed. B. Williams, 1977
33. *Wiltshire gaol delivery and trailbaston trials, 1275–1306*, ed. R.B. Pugh, 1978
34. *Lacock abbey charters*, ed. K.H. Rogers, 1979
35. *The cartulary of Bradenstoke priory*, ed. Vera C.M. London, 1979
36. *Wiltshire coroners' bills, 1752–1796*, ed. R.F. Hunnisett, 1981
37. *The justicing notebook of William Hunt, 1744–1749*, ed. Elizabeth Crittall, 1982
38. *Two Elizabethan women: correspondence of Joan and Maria Thynne, 1575–1611*, ed. Alison D. Wall, 1983
39. *The register of John Chandler, dean of Salisbury, 1404–17*, ed. T.C.B. Timmins, 1984
40. *Wiltshire dissenters' meeting house certificates and registrations, 1689–1852*, ed. J.H. Chandler, 1985
41. *Abstracts of feet of fines relating to Wiltshire, 1377–1509*, ed. J.L. Kirby, 1986
42. *The Edington cartulary*, ed. Janet H. Stevenson, 1987
43. *The commonplace book of Sir Edward Bayntun of Bromham*, ed. Jane Freeman, 1988
44. *The diaries of Jeffery Whitaker, schoolmaster of Bratton, 1739–1741*, ed. Marjorie Reeves and Jean Morrison, 1989
45. *The Wiltshire tax list of 1332*, ed. D.A. Crowley, 1989
46. *Calendar of Bradford-on-Avon settlement examinations and removal orders, 1725–98*, ed. Phyllis Hembry, 1990
47. *Early trade directories of Wiltshire*, ed. K.H. Rogers and indexed by J.H. Chandler, 1992
48. *Star chamber suits of John and Thomas Warneford*, ed. F.E. Warneford, 1993
49. *The Hungerford Cartulary: a calendar of the earl of Radnor's cartulary of the Hungerford family*, ed. J.L. Kirby, 1994
50. *The Letters of John Peniston, Salisbury architect, Catholic, and Yeomanry Officer, 1823–1830*, ed. M. Cowan, 1996
51. *The Apprentice Registers of the Wiltshire Society, 1817–1922*, ed. H. R. Henly, 1997
52. *Printed Maps of Wiltshire 1787–1844: a selection of topographical, road and canal maps in facsimile*, ed. John Chandler, 1998
53. *Monumental Inscriptions of Wiltshire: an edition, in facsimile, of Monumental Inscriptions in the County of Wilton, by Sir Thomas Phillipps*, ed. Peter Sherlock, 2000
54. *The First General Entry Book of the City of Salisbury, 1387–1452*, ed. David R. Carr, 2001
55. *Devizes Division income tax assessments, 1842–1860*, ed. Robert Colley, 2002
56. *Wiltshire Glebe Terriers, 1588–1827*, ed. Steven Hobbs, 2003
57. *Wiltshire Farming in the Seventeenth Century*, ed. Joseph Bettey, 2005
58. *Early Motor Vehicle Registration in Wiltshire, 1903–1914*, ed. Ian Hicks, 2006
59. *Marlborough Probate Inventories, 1591–1775*, ed. Lorelei Williams and Sally Thomson, 2007
60. *The Hungerford Cartulary, part 2: a calendar of the Hobhouse cartulary of the Hungerford family*, ed. J.L. Kirby, 2007
61. *The Court Records of Brinkworth and Charlton*, ed. Douglas Crowley, 2009
62. *The Diary of William Henry Tucker, 1825–1850*, ed. Helen Rogers, 2009
63. *Gleanings from Wiltshire Parish Registers*, ed. Steven Hobbs, 2010
64. *William Small's Cherished Memories and Associations*, ed. Jane Howells and Ruth Newman, 2011
65. *Crown Pleas of the Wiltshire Eyre, 1268*, ed. Brenda Farr and Christopher Elrington, rev. Henry Summerson, 2012
66. *The Minute Books of Froxfield Almshouse, 1714–1866*, ed. Douglas Crowley, 2013

VOLUMES IN PREPARATION

The Register of John Blyth, Bishop of Salisbury, 1493–1499, edited by David Wright; *Wiltshire papist returns and estate enrolments, 1705–87*, edited by J.A. Williams; *The parish registers of Thomas Crockford, 1613–29*, edited by C.C. Newbury; *Wiltshire rural industry organiser surveys and reports, c. 1938–c.1957*, edited by Ian Hicks; *Public health in 19th-century Wiltshire*, edited by Negley Harte; *The Churchwardens' accounts of St. Mary's, Devizes, 1600–1700*, edited by Alex Craven. The volumes will not necessarily appear in this order.

A leaflet giving full details may be obtained from the Hon. Secretary, c/o Wiltshire and Swindon History Centre, Cocklebury Road, Chippenham, Wilts. SN15 3QN.